Date Due			
DEC 3 0			
JAN 2 4			
FEB 8			
OCT 9			
OCT 27			
NOV 1 0			

THE BIBLE, WORD OF GOD
IN WORDS OF MEN

THE BIBLE, WORD OF GOD
IN WORDS OF MEN

by

JEAN LEVIE, S.J.

P. J. KENEDY & SONS

NEW YORK

This book is a translation of *La Bible, Parole Humaine et Message de Dieu*, published by Desclée de Brouwer, Paris-Louvain, in 1958. The English version is by S. H. Treman.

Nihil obstat: Hubertus Richards S.T.L., L.S.S., *Censor deputatus*
Imprimatur: E. Morrogh Bernard, *Vic. Gen.*
Westmonasterii, die 14a Julii, 1961
The Nihil obstat and Imprimatur are a declaration that a book or pamphlet is considered to be free from doctrinal or moral error. It is not implied that those who have granted the Nihil obstat and Imprimatur agree with the contents, opinions or statements expressed.

Library of Congress Catalogue Card No.: 61-14295

MADE AND PRINTED IN GREAT BRITAIN

59127

CONTENTS

ABBREVIATIONS

DZ   Denziger-Bannwart, *Enchiridion Symbolorum*
EB   *Enchiridion Biblicum*
NRT *Nouvelle Revue Théologique*
RB   *Revue Biblique*
RSR *Recherches de sciences religieuses*

FOREWORD

Two CONSIDERABLE tasks confront the Christian exegete. His first task is concretely and objectively to situate the inspired authors in history, and the civilization of their own milieu and period. He must understand them as they were understood by their contemporaries, as they understood themselves and would have explained themselves in accordance with the ideas of their times. He must at the same time always be making an implicit comparison between our modern mentality and that of men of the past. Now the last hundred years have shown this task to be far more complex than it was formerly thought to be, whether we are concerned with the mentality of Orientals belonging to the nineteen centuries before Christ, or of Palestinians who were the contemporaries of Jesus. History, archæo-logy, philology and literary psychology have made very great advances, and these have led to certain inevitable results in the interpretation of Scripture.

Consequently, the second task of the Christian exegete becomes plain, and it, too, is increasingly complex. *It is through men that God speaks to us.* Quite recently Pius XII in his Encyclical *Divino afflante Spiritu* reminded us that we must begin by understanding the man, the inspired author, in order to arrive at the word of God. Any progress in the historical appreciation of the man has its repercussion on the appreciation of God's message. Thus the second task of the Christian exegete, in union with the Church and helped by all the enlightment his faith supplies, is to rise from the human word to the divine message. This is, perhaps, accomplished today with a better and clearer understanding than it was at the end of the nineteenth century. In the last sixty years the lessons of history, the results of controversy, the progress of the biblical movement and the successive statements of the Magisterium have all deepened the understanding of the interpretation of Scripture among Catholics.

These two tasks of Christian exegesis are closely bound up together. Theological interpretation runs the risk of being artificial when it is not based on a proper understanding of history. But for us Christians historical exegesis of the Bible is devoid of interest when it does not terminate in theology or religious ideas.

This book takes its stand at the meeting place of these two exegetical tasks. How are we to proceed from the human word, understood objectively, to the understanding of the divine message? The Church alone is wholly competent to undertake such a task but, as Christians, all of us live in the Church and think with her and in her. Hence we must endeavour to understand this immense task that she has undertaken down the centuries and to associate ourselves with it by our own moral and intellectual effort; we must be alive to everything that is implied by the Catholic interpretation of holy Scripture. This book will have achieved its purpose if it has helped its readers to a fuller realization of what is meant by the Christian's personal contact with the inspired word of God.

This is not a technical work intended to supply specialists in Scripture with new and erudite material; it is addressed to all Christians who are interested in the modern biblical movement. Its purpose is to emphasize an essential aspect of the Christian understanding of Scripture, namely the problem which arises when we undertake to interpret it beginning with the inspired author understood at the human level and progressing from there to an understanding of God's message, together with the conditions, divine laws and human rules of this undertaking. I have endeavoured to study this problem from two points of view.

First, in Part I, *Progress in History and Biblical Exegesis* (1850-1960), I have considered the remarkable advance in oriental archæology and knowledge of ancient history, the variety of critical views held during the period, the controversies between exegetes and theologians, the biblical movement which at one point degenerated into the Modernist heresy, the work of the Magisterium: all these helped to formulate the problem with increasing clarity and contributed to its gradual solution. I have purposely kept the text within the limits required by a book intended to popularize the subject; but to help those who may desire to pursue their researches further I have provided in support of my descriptions and judgements a certain number of bibliographical references chosen from among those which seemed to be more easily accessible to the greatest number of readers. These more technical additions have been added in smaller type so as not to hinder the continuous reading of the text.

Then, in Part II, using the conclusions from this history of exegesis and taking my stand on the fundamental elements of the problem—the word of God, the word of man, better understood and clarified by the teaching of the Magisterium—I have endeavoured to emphasize certain more pressing aspects of the question which seem likely to promote a more accurate understanding of the interpretation of Scripture. This second, more doctrinal part remains independent of the first; although it is shorter it seems to me more important than the first part and emphasizes aspects of Catholic exegesis that I believe to be essential. It can, without disadvantage, be studied first, but the two parts support each other and by two different ways lead to the same conclusions.

During the 1939-45 war appeared the Encyclical *Divino afflante Spiritu* (1943), which marks a date of fundamental importance in the history of Catholic exegesis. It confirmed, developed and broadened several of the guiding rules laid down by Leo XIII in the Encyclical *Providentissimus Deus* (1893). Moreover, it was the first of a series of interventions by the Magisterium, all contributing to the progress of exegesis. In Part I, I have provided a detailed commentary on these documents with the intention of being of some service in this way to theologians and exegetes.

One of the fundamental conditions for progress in exegesis is the mutual effort for comprehension and sympathy between the Scripture scholars who do the work and the Christian public which reads the results of their labours. This book has been written for the purpose of making such beneficial and fruitful contact easier. One of its aims is to make known beyond the restricted circle of experts the most interesting discoveries of modern biblical archæology, and the most significant advances in philology, literary and historical criticism, as far as these fall within my main purpose, which is to show the effect of these advances on the interpretation of the Bible. But it has also been my intention to keep clearly in view the fundamental desire of Christians for the religious and theological interpretation of the Bible. Catholic exegesis must aim at linking up with dogma while, of course, preserving complete objectivity by respecting and clearly defining the proper limits of each discipline, the historical and the theological, but always progressing towards that religious synthesis which is the climax of our attempt to understand the word of God.

In the survey devoted to the history of exegesis I have obviously been obliged to adopt a definite position; I have endeavoured to do so with the utmost objectivity and honesty. I have made no secret of my admiration for and gratitude towards those masters who, at a difficult period and with foresight and determination, paved the way for the advance of Catholic exegesis. Nor have I hidden how much I regret that well-meaning but narrow conservatism which lasted too long and on occasion showed itself suspicious and aggressive. I have duly acknowledged the technical, historical and philological contribution to the interpretation of the Bible made by Protestant scholars of the nineteenth and twentieth centuries, but at the same time I have tried to show clearly the immense harm done to Christian understanding of the scriptures by the liberal Protestantism which was predominant in Germany until 1914. I have candidly noted the steady advance in religious and theological interpretation achieved in many centres of Protestant exegesis since 1918. Gratifying efforts at collaboration have taken place between Catholic and Protestant exegetes, with the concern on both sides to emphasize the Christian message of the Bible. The great danger, nowadays as formerly, as many are aware, is religious liberalism which gradually erodes the lofty principles of Christianity. Throughout this book I have never concealed, but have reasserted again and again, my profound conviction of the *fundamental* rôle of the Church in the interpretation of the Word of God. The reasons for this are stated and elaborated under various aspects in several sections of the book.

I must express my gratitude to Mgr Coppens, Professor of Old Testament Exegesis at the University of Louvain, and to Fr Charles Matagne, my colleague in teaching holy Scripture; both have read my manuscript and offered valuable suggestions. I am grateful also to M. Roger Demortier, Secretary of the Museum Lessianum, who gave me constant help in the preparation of the manuscript.

PART I

Progress in History and Biblical Exegesis

1850-1960, a century of research and discovery.

INTRODUCTION

OLDER PEOPLE, both priests and laity, are sometimes surprised at the far-reaching and rapid development that is nowadays to be seen in the sphere of biblical knowledge and interpretation. How far we have travelled from what was commonly accepted in Catholic circles fifty years ago! These people are well aware of course that in their lifetime they have witnessed the birth of wireless telegraphy, aviation, the cinema and more recently the atomic bomb. But, they argue, is not the Bible the word of God, unchangeable as God himself? Undoubtedly the *divine message* of the Scriptures remains today, exactly the same as it was one hundred or nineteen hundred years ago. But Scripture is the word of God in the words of men; it is expressed in human language, and among the discoveries and progress made in the last century a deeper and more detailed knowledge of men of ancient times, including the way they thought and expressed themselves, forms one of the more useful results of historical research. Naturally this was bound to have repercussions on the whole field of Christian biblical scholarship which took account of the new knowledge acquired.

In this first part my intention is to show by means of certain characteristics chosen from among many how, since the middle of the nineteenth century, history studied objectively has raised biblical problems in an entirely new way. I would like to indicate in broad outline certain stages in the exegetical, archæological and historical research of the last century in an attempt to bring out certain definite lessons for our interpretation of Scripture, and thus to demonstrate to non-specialists why in the course of this last hundred years the biblical problem arose, and was bound to arise, in a guise far different from any it had previously assumed. In this way I hope to show them how the *human* aspect of Scripture appears

3

today. The period 1850-1960 is from this point of view one of the most fruitful and enlightening; this is clearly to be seen in the Church's biblical pronouncements. It is highly significant to find in the second edition of the *Enchiridion biblicum* (2nd edn, 1954)[1] that of the 260 pages devoted to ecclesiastical documents on biblical topics, only thirty have a bearing on the period prior to 1890, whilst there are 230 for the period since 1890, i.e. from the time when the results of long research began to emerge as relevant to biblical exegesis.

It is true that a hundred years ago Catholic histories of the Old Testament were influenced by the correct point of view for Christian interpretation of revelation, namely that the Old Testament has religious significance, truly and fully, only when contemplated in the light of Christ. But how vague and indefinite was the picture of Israel's history then current; the figures of Jewish history were invested with the feelings, attitudes and actions of Catholic confessors, martyrs and virgins. 'Holy King David' was transformed as far as possible into the likenesses of the most modern saints of the west, canonized by the Church. The blunt, uncouth voices of the Hebrew prophets often took on the smooth accents of medieval or Renaissance spiritual authors. There was scarcely a trace of the Semitic, eastern setting. The cardinal mistake made by this approach was that it lacked all feeling for historical evolution; in fact it gave not the least hint of the radical changes that had occurred during the twenty centuries of Jewish history. And though theology asserted that Old Testament revelation was a very partial and gradual affair, only too often Bible history ranked all periods on the same level of religious truth, and at the same stage of moral perfection, and tended to equate them all with Christian truth and perfection. More than once the Old Testament, which was only a preparation and a heralding of the New, was put forward unwittingly as though it were the complete light and final norm.

That, helped by the uncertain date of many of the books of the Bible, explains many historical anachronisms. To take a concrete case, the messianic expectation was presented right from the beginning (or at least from David's time), complete with its essential

[1]*ENCHIRIDION BIBLICUM.* Documenta ecclesiastica Sacram Scripturam spectantia. Auctoritate Pontificiae Commissionis de re biblica edita. 2a editio aucta et recognita. Rome-Naples 1954. 3a editio 1956.

characteristics, as unchanging throughout its history. The contemporary of King Solomon is pictured awaiting his Messiah-Saviour in exactly the same way as John's disciples when they asked Jesus, 'Are you the one who is to come, or must we await another?'. Thus, the messianic argument, classical since the beginnings of Christianity, was never constructed from an historical standpoint, but always propounded as a dogmatic thesis. There was no attempt to describe the awakening, the growth, the various changes in the great expectation of the kingdom of God down the centuries; instead the scattered elements belonging to vastly different periods were collected together in one logical scheme without regard to their literary or historical context.

There was a comparable lack of appreciation of the progress of the Jewish revelation in the study of other religious ideas—those of God, sin, and prophecy, for example. Here again the synthesis of Old Testament religion was not constructed in and through the study of history, but on a logical plan where all its stages and moments of progress were identified. The method was historically incomplete; it was pedantic, rather than human, leaving in the minds of its hearers a false notion of Israel's development. It can be understood then that a more accurate knowledge of the people of ancient times has profoundly altered the presentation of this history of God's people before Christ's coming.

The New Testament, appearing in the context of Greco-Roman civilization, did not to the same degree stand to benefit from the revival of interest in the eastern background of Scripture. Nevertheless, much progress has resulted from a better appreciation of the Jewish mentality in Christ's lifetime, a more thorough knowledge of Hellenistic culture in New Testament times, a new critical approach to the problems of authenticity and historicity, that has been increasingly more discerning and exact, and a keen study of the oral tradition of the Gospels. Moreover, critical investigation of the New Testament, by reason of its very development in the course of a single century, by its gradual shift from a subjective hypercriticism to a better appreciation of the data of tradition, can be for us extremely instructive and enlightening. At the same time, deeper understanding of the spiritual and theological aspects of the Christian message by a large number of critics emerges as an encouraging feature of exegesis in recent years (since 1945).

There can be no question of setting out here a systematic and technical scheme of exegetical progress in the last hundred years. Another volume would be required for this. My purpose is merely to note in chronological order certain characteristic features of the biblical movement of this period, and particularly those which bring out more clearly the part played by man, by the inspired author as a man, in the presentation of God's message.

My plan is very simple. The history of this century is quite naturally divided into two parts by the historic date of 4 August 1914; the 1914-18 war marks in exegesis, as in many other human undertakings, a real break in continuity, a dividing line between two epochs, two intellectual and religious climates. In each of these two periods three aspects of the exegete's work will be noticed. Firstly, in both, though with differing implications, there were certain remarkable discoveries of archæology, history and philology which focused new, unexpected and, on occasion, disconcerting light on the historical bases of the interpretation of the Bible. Then there were the profound effects, both scientific and religious, of these technical advances on the two principal schools of exegesis which were and still are to be found in the universities and seminaries of Europe and America—Protestant exegesis with its many doctrinal and sectarian differences, and Catholic exegesis with its dogmatic unity and its control by the hierarchy. This part of the book is therefore concerned with the atmosphere and tendencies prevailing among both Catholic and Protestants together with the general conclusions reached by them firstly before 1914 and then after the end of the 1914-18 war. Obviously, in the history of Catholic exegesis an important place will be given to the study and interpretation of the decisions and directives of the supreme ecclesiastical authority.

Chapter I

THE FIRST GREAT EXCAVATIONS OF BIBLICAL AND MIDDLE EASTERN ARCHÆOLOGY: 1850-1914

THE PRIMARY acquisition of the past century has been the discovery of the ancient East, the ordinary human setting of the history and thought of Israel[1]. The language and civilization of Egypt, Accad, Sumer, Assyria, Babylon and the Hittites, Phoenician culture, the archæology of the Middle East and of Palestine, all of them factors in the life of Israel and largely unknown at the beginning of the nineteenth century, have been studied with undeniable success during the last hundred years. We begin by tracing the first stage down to 1914.

The deciphering of the Egyptian hieroglyphs and the discovery of ancient Egyptian civilization

From the middle of the nineteenth century the results gradually obtained in Egyptology began to shed light on biblical studies. The ancient Egyptian yielded his first secrets as early as 1822 to Champollion, a Frenchman; two important scientific expeditions (a French one in 1798, a Prussian in 1842) had gathered a vast harvest of texts and monuments; the methodical exploration and excavations

[1]From the outset books were published giving the results of excavations in the East for the use of historians and exegetes. The volumes by H. Gressmann, *Altorienalische Texte und Bilder zum Alten Testament*, 2 volumes, Tübingen, 1st edn 1909 and by A. Jeremias, *Das Alte Testament im Lichte des Alten Orients*, 1st edn 1904, several later edns of both, have long been regarded as classics. The two recent works by J. B. Pritchard, *Ancient Near Eastern Texts relating to the Old Testament*, Princeton, 1950, 2nd edn 1955, and *The Ancient Near East in Pictures relating to the Old Testament*, Princeton, 1954 provide much up-to-date information. See also J. Finegan, *Light from the Ancient Past, The Archaeological Background of the Hebrew-Christian Religion*, Princeton, 2nd edn, 1959. G. Contenau, *Manuel d'archéologie orientale*, 4 volumes, Paris, 1927-47 and A. G. Barrois, *Manuel d'archéologie biblique*, 2 volumes, Paris, 1939-53 are valuable but of a more technical nature. A useful work is the small book by K. Galling, *Textbuch zur Geschichte Israels*, Tübingen, 1950; also, M. Burrows, *What Mean These Stones?* New Haven, 1941, American Schools of Oriental Research.

2

begun in 1850 by Mariette, which continued on and off until 1914 yielded, or were instrumental in the first interpretation of, a remarkable and varied series of documents. Expert archæologists, beginning with Rougé and Chabas (France), Lepsius and Brugsch (Germany), Birch (England) and continuing with G. Maspéro, Flinders Petrie, A. Erman, J. H. Breasted, etc., ensured the continued and successful progress in Egyptology.

The dynastic history of Egypt, reconstructed from the lists found at Abydos, Saqqarah and Karnak, and especially from the royal papyrus discovered by Diovetti and preserved at Turin, threw considerable light on a number of events in the history of Israel, fixing their date and place but also raising certain problems. The following are some examples taken from among many. The period of the Hyskos invasion suggests a possible setting and an approximate date for the preponderant rôle of a Semite, Joseph, in the administration of the country and the establishment of his kinsmen in Goshen, but no trace of these events recorded in Genesis has to date been found in Egyptian historical documents. However the 'Egyptian colouring' of many details in this part of Genesis and the beginning of Exodus appears very distinctly. The date of the Exodus is still the subject of discussion, with dates between the fifteenth century (eighteenth dynasty) and the thirteenth century (nineteenth dynasty) finding support, but the majority of historians are at present inclined to favour the latter date. The Egyptian list of Palestinian cities subject to Sheshonk I (first Pharaoh of the twenty-second dynasty) throws light on the references in 3 Kings 14. 25 and following verses (Sesac in the Vulgate). And so on throughout Old Testament history.[2]

Literary evidence also is particularly informative; we can confine ourselves here to two well-known documents which provide considerable information about the land of Canaan before the arrival

---

[2]The history of Egypt, of its civilization and the archæological excavations that have been carried out there, has given rise to a great number of works. In French there are the very full and carefully documented works by E. Drioton and J. Vandier in the Clio series, Paris, 1st edn 1938 (republished, 1946) and by E. Drioton, *L'Egypt pharaonique*, Paris, 1959, or the older works by G. Jequier, *Histoire de la civilisation égyptienne* (1st edn, Paris, 1913; 4th edn, 1930) and by G. Maspéro, *Egypte* in the series 'Histoire générale de l'art', Paris, 1st edn, 1911 (reprinted). Cf. also the many useful works by J. Capart (Brussels). On the history of the excavations: J. Baikie, *A Century of Excavation in the Land of the Pharaohs*, London, 1929 and Flinders Petrie, *Seventy Years in Archæology*, London, 1932.

of the Hebrews; one is the story of Sinuhe, one of the classics of ancient Egyptian literature (twelfth dynasty) telling the romantic story of Sinuhe, an exile from Egypt in the asiatic East, and giving his impressions of the journey; the other is the Letters of Tell el-Amarna (discovered in Egypt in 1887), in Accadian with a number of Canaanite idioms and written in cuneiform script, being the correspondence of the vassal Canaanite sovereigns with their Egyptian overlords, Amenophis (Amen-hotep) III and his successor, Amenophis IV (fifteenth-fourteenth centuries).

The Egyptian Wisdom and moral literature has many similarities in thought and structure with the Wisdom literature of Israel and there is possibly some connection, direct or indirect, between the moral sentences of Amenenope and the Hebrew book of Proverbs, 22.17—24.22. In any case, Egyptian sapiential writings were always highly esteemed in Israel; it was from the Egyptians that the author of Kings (3 Kings 4. 30 Vulgate; 5. 10 Hebrew) sought a comparison in order to praise the wisdom of Solomon, and St Luke (Acts 7. 22) tells us that Moses was trained in all the learning of the Egyptians.[3]

On many points (archæology of the temples, liturgical vestments and customs, religious hymnology) biblical study derives great benefit from Egyptology;[4] even the contrasts (for example with Egyptian faith in the next world and life after death) are enlightening and instructive. These few features, taken at random from among very many, prompt the reflection that there will be profound differences between the way in which Bossuet, for example, envisaged the history of Israel in his *Discours sur l'histoire universelle* and that of a modern biblical scholar.

[3]Two useful works may be mentioned on this subject without necessarily accepting all their conclusions: E. Peet, *Egypt and the Old Testament*, London, 1922 and P. Humbert, *Recherches sur les sources égyptiennes de la littérature sapientiale d'Israel*, Neuchâtel, 1929. See also the present author's article 'L'Egypte et Israel. A propos d'un texte égyptien récemment découvert' in *NRT*, 1924, pp. 558-63.

[4]There may also be mentioned during this period the discoveries of S. Schechter in the Cairo Geniza, end of 1896-beginning 1897: MSS fragments in Hebrew (copied between the ninth and twelfth centuries) of the book of Ecclesiasticus, hitherto only known through the Greek text; two MSS of an unknown text that was called the 'Document of Damas' which was to assume great importance since the discoveries at Qumrân in 1947. Cf. on these discoveries, P. E. Kahle, *The Cairo Geniza*, London, 1947.

The deciphering of cuneiform script and the discovery of Assyrian, Babylonian and Accadian civilizations

Of greater importance for the Old Testament was the deciphering of the cuneiform scripts and through them the access obtained to Assyrian, Babylonian, Accadian and Sumerian civilizations. In this case the influences are direct and profound; Accadian, Assyrian and Hebrew are semitic languages; Ur in south Chaldea was in Hebrew tradition the place whence Abraham came and contact between the two cultures was continual.

In 1802 Grotefend, a classical philologist and a master at the Göttingen gymnasium, though completely ignorant of oriental languages, was the first to succeed in deciphering the cuneiform script of the first group of trilingual inscriptions at Persepolis, a discovery which was to lead in three successive stages to unexpected results. The first stage was the deciphering of the old Persian cuneiform alphabet, the simplest cuneiform writing, which enabled all the others to be interpreted. This stage was begun by the work of the Danish scholar Niebuhr (1765) and the German Tychsen (1798), definite progress was made by Grotefend in 1802 and a successful conclusion was reached in 1836 (after the philological studies by Burnouf on the Avesta). The second stage then began; it was the deciphering of the Assyro-Babylonian and Accadian cuneiform characters and the recovery of a literature and of a semitic civilization closely allied to that of Israel. This huge task is still going on at the present time, but it gave definite evidence of maturity in 1857 when the London Asiatic Society obtained from an expedition to Assyria the transcript of a newly discovered inscription, dating from the time of Tiglath Pileser I (twelfth century B.C.); it was decided that a competition should be arranged for its interpretation; the four leading Assyriologists—Oppert (France), Hincks (Ireland), Talbot and Rawlinson (England)—agreed to the test; a month later they sent in their translations, carried out independently; with certain slight differences of detail they showed remarkable agreement in all important respects. The test was decisive; after 1857 Assyriology was regarded as established. Of course, it was only at its beginning and was to be perfected, to achieve greater precision and scientific order in the intervening years down to our own day. But the tool for the work was ready and the heavy labour of deciphering the thousands of tablets accumulated at the British Museum could be profitably undertaken. The third stage, which began in 1857, but was more and more in evidence after 1880, was the recovery of another literature, non-Semitic and older still than that of the Accadian Semites, which had exercised a profound influence on the latter; this was the Sumerian literature which takes us back to the fourth millenary B.C.[5]

Side by side with the stages of the deciphering of the languages occurred the first and strikingly fruitful archæological excavations.[6] The Frenchman Botta, beginning in 1842 and later Place, excavated Khorsabad near Mosul and discovered the summer palace built by Sargon II (722-705) at Dur Sharrukin, the Versailles of the Assyrian kings, together with many cuneiform tablets. The most important Assyrian cities were then excavated—Niniveh and its surroundings by the Frenchmen Botta and Place, by the English explorers Layard, Loftus and Rassam; then Nimrud, the former Kalah, the second capital of Assyria, was excavated by the English, and so on. One after the other the palaces of the greater Assyrian kings so closely involved in the history of Israel were discovered: at Nimrud, the ninth-century palace of Salmanasar II who exacted tribute from Jehu, king of Israel; at Kuyunjik the seventh-century

[5]In connection with the decipherment of cuneiform script a fourth stage could be added, initiated by the excavations by Winckler at Boghaz-keui (Asia Minor) in 1906 and clarified since 1918 as a result of the work by Hrozny, Friedrich, Götze, Delaporte etc.: it is the decipherment of a new language, Indo-European this time, the Hittite language, i.e. of the 'Sons of Heth' ('Hethei' of the Vulgate) frequently mentioned in Genesis and other books of the Old Testament. It amounts to a recovery of the Hittite literature of Asia Minor. But this concerns Scripture only secondarily, in matters of detail. A summary bibliography on the Hittites will be found below, p. 88, n. 24.

[6]The most recent books on Mesopotamian archæology are: A. Parrot, *Archéologie mésopotamienne*, Paris, 2 volumes, 1946, 1953; *Découverte des mondes ensevelis*, Paris-Neuchâtel, 1952 and the *Cahiers d'archéologie biblique*, published periodically since 1952; R. T. O'Callaghan, S.J., *Aram Naharaïm. A Contribution to the History of Upper Mesopotamia in the second Millennium B.C.*, Rome, 1948; P. Jouguet, J. Vandier, etc. *Les premières civilisations* in the series 'Peuples et civilisations', new edn, Paris, 1950 (1st edn, 1926). Earlier but still useful are the books by L. Delaporte, *La Mésopotamie* in the series 'Bibliothèque de synthèse historique', Paris, 1923 and *Le Proche Orient asiatique* in the 'Clio' series, Paris, 1938; by C. F. Jean, *Le milieu biblique avant Jésus-Christ*, 3 volumes, Paris, 1922-36 and *La Littérature des Babyloniens et des Assyriens*, Paris, 1924; by G. Contenau, *La civilisation d'Assur et de Babylone*, Paris, 1937 and, more recently, *La vie quotidienne à Babylone et en Assyrie*, Paris, 1950. To the series of texts referred to above by Pritchard, Gressmann etc. must be added for Mesopotamia: P. Dhorme, *Choix de textes religieux assyro-babyloniens*, Paris, 1907 and R. W. Rogers, *Cuneiform Parallels to the Old Testament*, London, 1912. Of course the classic works by B. Meissner, *Babylonien und Assyria*, 2 volumes, Heidelberg, 1920-5 and the histories of Assyria by Sidney Smith, London, 1928 and of Babylon by L. W. King still remain useful. Below are listed the numerous works by Sir L. Woolley in connection with his excavations.

palaces of Sennacherib who fought against Ezechias of Judah, of Asarhaddon and of Assurbanipal. The walls of these huge buildings, blackened by fire, often stood head high and were still covered with bas reliefs all round the banqueting hall, depicting hunting or battle scenes; they now adorn the walls of the Louvre or the British Museum.

Then in 1847, in excavating Assurbanipal's palace, north of Kuyunjik hill near Niniveh, Layard discovered two rooms whose floors were littered with the remains of cuneiform tablets to a depth of some eighteen inches. It was the remains of a library. Assurbanipal (668-626) had been anxious to collect in his palace the works of the writers of Assur, Babylon, Sumer and Accad. Carefully transcribed on clay by many scribes, meticulously arranged, catalogued and numbered with a precision worthy of the best of librarians, they formed the royal library 'beyond all the dreams of my predecessors', as the king himself says. This library was recovered for us, damaged of course, partially destroyed or reduced to dust, but remaining nevertheless of incalculable value. Upwards of 20,000 tablets or fragments found their way to the British Museum.

Assyriologists, achieving increasing mastery of the language, after 1857 set about interpreting the many documents already accumulated in London and Paris together with those, still more numerous, brought to light by successive excavations. The whole history of the ancient East was about to be transformed, to be known more clearly and widened in scope; facts briefly mentioned in the Bible are described in the royal annals at length, by witnesses; vague Assyrian figures appearing in the book of Kings became living and active characters; the imprecise and vague chronology of the Old Testament became linked with precise dates, determined by astronomy. One day Hincks discovered among the Kuynjik tablets long lists of Assyrian officials (Limmu) dating from the reign of Bin Nirari II (tenth century) to that of Assurbanipal (seventh century); he realized that these officials, like the eponymous Archontai of Athens, gave their name to the year, so that these lists enabled the exact years of many events of sacred history between 911 and 650 to be fixed: thus the battle of Qarqar (855-854) when Achab and Hazael fought against Salmanasar III; Jehu's tribute to Salmanasar III in 842 (according to the obelisk in the British Museum on which king Jehu is shown paying his tribute); the taking of Samaria

(722-721); the siege of Jerusalem by Sennacherib in 701, etc.

In this short account only a few examples of the discoveries affecting the Old Testament can be chosen. We confine ourselves to three which caused a sensation at the time.

In 1872 the press of all countries was full of news about a cuneiform tablet that had just been published and translated by George Smith. It was the Assyrian story of a flood, of the building of a vessel by a favourite of the gods and the coming to rest of the vessel upon a high mountain, Mount Nishir:

> To the land of Nishir the ship took its course.
> The mountain of the land of Nishir held fast the ship and allowed it not to stir . . .
> When the seventh day came,
> I (Uta Napishtim) sent forth a dove and let her go,
> The dove went and returned,
> But there was no resting place and she returned . . .
> Then I sent forth a raven and let her go.
> The raven flew away, and she beheld the easing of the waters.
> And she ate, wading and croaking, but did not return.[7]

Uta Napishtim then leaves the ark to offer a sacrifice to the gods:
> The gods tasted the odour,
> The gods tasted the sweet smell,
> The gods descended upon the offerer like a cluster of flies.

Compare the well-known account in Genesis 8. 6-12 and its conclusion, 8. 20-21: 'And Noe built an altar unto the Lord: and taking of all cattle and fowls that were clean, offered holocausts upon the altar. And the Lord smelled a sweet savour, and said: I will no more curse the earth for the sake of man.'

To the Assyro-Babylonian epic of the flood there were added later the epic of creation, the poem of the suffering righteous man, psalms (especially psalms of repentance) and hymns analogous with those of Israel. It soon became apparent that such creation and flood narratives did not originate primarily at the Assyrian period but went back into the past of these Semitic and Sumerian literatures, to periods anterior to the time when they appeared in the Hebrew

[7]Translation from *Sacred Books of the World* by A. C. Bouquet, Penguin 1955, p. 51.

Genesis; what was immediately striking was the religious superiority of the Hebrew narratives; their monotheism is in marked contrast to the polytheism of Accad and Sumer. These coincidences and differences nonetheless raised problems of an entirely new kind in the interpretation of Scripture.

Our second example is the recovery at Tell el-Amarna in Upper Egypt—referred to above—of the archives of Amenophis IV (1375-1358); among other things of value they contained the correspondence, written in Assyro-Babylonian and in cuneiform script, that in the fifteenth and fourteenth centuries B.C. passed between the petty kings of Canaan, among them the king of Urusalim (Jerusalem), and their Egyptian overlord; so at that time the diplomatic language, used even by the Egyptian Pharaoh, was the language of Mesopotamia and it was known also to the petty local rulers whose usual language was the 'Canaanite tongue' (that is, Hebrew), spoken in Palestine long before the Israelites arrived there. Josue had not yet led the Hebrew people into Canaan and already the letters of the Canaanites, whom he was about to conquer, were being read (they are still legible today), letters of the kings of Urusalim long before David seized Jerusalem as his capital.

A third example. In 1897 in the mountains of Elam at Susa the extent of Mesopotamian civilization was again demonstrated; the French expedition (under de Morgan and Fr Scheil, O.P.) in 1901 dug up the well-known Code of Hammurabi (eighteenth century B.C.?); its close similarity with certain laws of the Pentateuch is well known (Exodus 20. 22-23).

In 1914, when the First World War began (it caused the suspension of all work for a time) the archæological advance in Accadian speaking countries (ancient Accadian, Babylonian, Assyrian) was in full swing and making constant progress; the German architect, R. Koldewey, had been excavating in Babylon since 1899 in order to reconstruct the topography and history of the city;[8] Andrae and his

---

[8]The excavations went on until 1917. Two fundamental books record and explain the results of this work: R. Koldewey, *Das wiedererstehende Babylon*, 4th edn, Leipzig, 1925 and E. Unger, *Die heilige Stadt nach der Beschreibung der Babylonier*, Leipzig, 1931. The excavations concentrated especially on architecture; the city as it was in the time of Nabuchodonosor, the savage conqueror and destroyer of the kingdom of Juda and of Jerusalem (586). Interesting accounts in J. Plessis, *Babylone et la Bible* in the *Dict. de la Bible*, suppl. I, 1928 and A. Parrot, *Babylone et l'Ancien Testament* (Cahiers d'archéologie biblique, no. 8) Paris-Neuchâtel, 1956.

colleagues had been at work at Assur since 1903;[9] in Persia the French expedition, under de Morgan's direction, continued its excavations and discoveries.[10] In the Hittite country the excavation which began with the remarkable discovery of the royal archives in the Hittite capital of Boghaz-Keui by Winckler in 1906-7 (see above, p.11 n. 5), continued with the excavations of Hogarth, Lawrence and Woolley at Karkemish on the Euphrates after 1912. And there were still others at work, all making ready for the great archæological advance of 1918-39.

It would be naïve to suppose that these explorations and discoveries always resulted in showing that the Bible 'tells the truth' in every detail (scientific, historical and chronological details and so on). They do indeed provide interesting and suggestive confirmation at more than one point, but also they gradually compelled acceptance of a wider, more human understanding of the real meaning of the principle of biblical inerrancy and led to a clearer discrimination, stimulating us, in the words used by Pius XII in 1943, 'to make proper use of the aids afforded by history, archæology, ethnology and other sciences, in order to discover *what literary forms* the writers of that early age intended to use, and did in fact employ'.

The deciphering of Sumerian and the discovery of Sumerian civilization

We can now turn our attention to the third stage in the deciphering of cuneiform script; it takes us to Southern Mesopotamia and leads us by way of many documents with biblical reference to a period twenty centuries before Abraham.

By beginning exploration in this region de Sarzec, a Frenchman, opened up to archæology great and wonderful prospects for the future. As vice-consul at Basra he undertook four successive excavating expeditions at Tello (the ancient Lagash) between 1877 and 1901, the year of his death; his example was followed by English and American archæologists; from 1878 to 1882 Rassam excavated Sippar, the ancient city of the Sun; in 1889, the Americans, under Hil-

---

[9]Cf. W. Andrae, *Das wiedererstandene Assur*, Leipzig, 1938; summary treatment in A. Parrot, *Archéologie mésopotamienne*, I, pp. 214-34.

[10]Excavations began in 1897 and after the interruption of 1914-18 continued until 1939. They were extremely fruitful not only in indigenous texts and monuments but in those seized by the kings of Elam and carried off to their capital, e.g. the code of Hammurabi. Twenty-nine large volumes contain the records of the expedition and the objects discovered during these excavations form a large proportion of the valuable collection in the Louvre.

precht's direction, began to excavate the site of a third ancient city, Nippur (now Nuffar); the first excavations which continued until 1900 brought to light records of immense value—tens of thousands of tablets, of extraordinary interest. After 1900 archæologists were at work on many sites in the south of Mesopotamia—Cros at Lagash (1903-9), de Genouillac at Kish, German archæologists after 1913 at Warka, ancient Uruk (the Arach or Erech of Gen. 10. 10).

These expeditions revealed the existence in Mesopotamia during the third and fourth millenniums of a highly civilized society: small kingdoms, living side by side—Kish, Kutha, Agade, Eridu, Ur, Larsa, Lagash, Uruk, Nippur, etc.[11] These were the Sumerian Kingdoms.

Take as an example the kingdom of Lagash between 3500 and 3000 under the kings Ur Nina, Eannatum and Entemene: 'Under their prosperous guidance in this fertile plain flourished a population of shepherds, farmers and craftsmen: carpenters, joiners, blacksmiths, goldsmiths, makers of statuary, blenders of perfume, builders and caulkers of boats, leather workers who made use of the skins of animals slain in sacrifice. Their wages were in proportion to the utility of the work done; the wives, in addition to their personal share, received an allowance fixed according to the number of their children' (family allowances, therefore, in 3000 B.C.).[12]

Sumerian art was highly developed at an early date. Assyrian art between 800 and 600 B.C. thus appears as no more than one single period of an immense artistic evolution of which the superb statuary of Gudea (2500-2000 B.C.; now in the Louvre) marked its highest point. The scribes of the third millennium had already engraved on their clay tablets many epic narratives and prayers which in the seventh century were added to his collection by Assurbanipal's officials.

---

[11]The Sumerian discoveries, e.g. those at Ur, are mentioned below. It will be enough here to list some recent works of a general nature which form a good introduction to the subject: L. Woolley, *The Sumerians*, 1st edn, 1928 (many reprints); H. O. Schmökel, *Das Land Sumer. Die Wiederentdeckung der ersten Hochkultur der Menschheit*, Stuttgart, 1955, and *Ur, Assur und Babylon*, Stuttgart, 1955; S. N. Kramer, *History Began at Sumer*, Chicago, 1956. On the excavations: H. Frankfort, *The Birth of the Civilization of the Near East*, New York, 1956; S. Lloyd, *Foundations in the Dust. The Story of Exploration in Mesopotamia and the great Archæological Discoveries made there*, Pelican, 1955. Lastly, on the language (grammars, dictionaries, literature) and religion the works of A. Deimel, S.J., C. J. Gadd, M. Witzel, O.F.M., C. F. Jean and, especially, A. Poebel.

[12]Charles F. Jean, *Le milieu biblique avant Jésus-Christ*, I, pp. 9-10, Paris, 1922.

But what about the language? The first excavations at Kuyunjik had uncovered side by side with Assyro-Babylonian writings a large number of cuneiform tablets written in another language which was neither Semitic nor Indo-European and which was preserved in the second and first millenniums before Christ as a sacred language, a liturgical language, serving much the same function as Latin among Catholics of the West. At that time it was no longer spoken anywhere but was very carefully taught in the priestly schools; several manuals, drawn up at that time for the theological student—spelling books, dictionaries, grammars—enabled scholars in the twentieth century gradually to master the structure of this complex, agglutinative language. At this point the excavations in southern Mesopotamia at Tello, Sippar and Nippur revealed vast numbers of documents in this language—contracts, legal texts and literary matter of the third and fourth millennium before Christ. However far we go back in the history of southern Mesopotamia we find two languages, Accadian, a Semitic language and Sumerian, an agglutinative language, and also two nations living side by side, the people of Accad in the North and that of Sumer in the South.

With increasing clarity it appeared that cuneiform script had not originated with the Semites; it had been borrowed by them from their neighbours of Sumer, a people of different stock. Moreover, the originality of Sumer is not confined to the invention of cuneiform script. Although it is not always easy to determine the language in which this or that epic, hymn or legend now preserved for us either in two forms, Semitic and Sumerian, or else only Semitic, was first written, the hypothesis which looks to Sumer for the first written expression of the creation and flood narratives has consistently gained ground. The Hebrew religious vocabulary contains certain words that appear to be derived from Sumerian (by way of Accadian)— Hekal (temple) for example, Paroket (the temple veil) etc. Like Egypt, Sumer possessed collections of proverbs as early as the third millennium and this, together with other arguments pointing in the same direction, has led biblical critics to date parts of the book of Proverbs before the exile of 586 whereas at first they were thought to be post-exile.

For the religious teaching of the Bible to exert its influence upon us it is certainly not necessary for us to unravel the mystery of all these contributory factors; but study of this kind helps us to plumb the depths and complexity of the divine plan of revelation; the part played by human action and psychology in the expression of God's message is shown to be one of hitherto unsuspected richness and scope. Increasingly Scripture appears as the word of God in human language. When the first inspired authors in Israel desired to describe for us the origins of man and of their own people it could hardly be expected that they could be totally independent of the traditions and ideas of those powerful races who preceded them in history by many centuries and exerted a very considerable influence on the Near East. All this necessarily raised biblical problems in a light far different from that envisaged by scholars of the Middle Ages and of the Renaissance.

Palestinian and Syrian Archæology

Palestinian archæology, which later was to produce such amazing results, began in 1890. In 1865 the Palestine Exploration Fund had been started in London; it set on foot the systematic, organized study of the country. Before sinking trenches or excavating, it was first necessary to explore and to establish as far as possible the topographical and geographical map of the region. This was the work of the Survey of Western Palestine carried out between 1871 and 1877 which resulted in six large quarto volumes published under this title in 1881 and following years and also in the large map of western Palestine (1880). In 1881 began the *Survey of Eastern Palestine*; in 1890, under the direction of Flinders Petrie, Bliss and Macalister, the excavations in Palestine started (Tell el Hesy, Jerusalem, Tell Zakaryeh, Tell Sandahannah, Tell el Djezer = Gezer, etc.). The *Palestine Exploration Fund's Quarterly Statements* began publication in 1866. In 1877 was founded the *Deutscher Verein zur Erforschung Palästinas* with its official publication, beginning in 1878, *Zeitschrift des deutschen Palästina Vereins*. In 1890 the French Dominicans opened their biblical school (Ecole pratique d'études bibliques) at Jerusalem which later became the official French archæological school in Palestine. Other archæological institutions were successively founded, for example, the Deutsche Orientsgesellschaft in 1898, the American School of Oriental Research at Jerusalem in 1900 etc., and Palestinian archæology made increasingly marked progress. Many sites were excavated between 1900 and 1914 (in addition to those of the Palestine Exploration Fund) such as the

excavations at Taanach (E. Sellin, 1901-4), Megiddo (G. Schumacher, 1903-5), Jericho (Schumacher and Watzinger, 1907-9),
Beth Sames (Mackenzie, 1910-12) and Samaria (G. A. Reisner and
C. S. Fisher, who began here in 1908-10) to mention only the chief
locations; exploration and excavation, halted during the First
World War, increased in number and yielded especially rich results
from 1918 onwards.[13]

In Transjordan in 1869 the French archæologist Clermont
Ganneau identified the Stele of Mesa, king of Moab (ninth century,
B.C.) which at that time was the oldest known specimen of Semitic
alphabetic script. He took an impression of it, thus enabling it to
be pieced together again after the Arabs had smashed it because they
thought that it contained some treasure.

Phoenician and Syrian archæology dates from 1856 with the
chance discovery of the sarcophagus of Eshmunazar to the South
of Saida (the ancient Sidon); it bore an inscription of twenty-two
lines in Phoenician. In 1860 there followed Ernest Renan's expedition to Phoenicia with the first sites excavated in the country and the
discoveries which went to enrich the Louvre. In 1887 came the discovery of the necropolis of Saida (Hamdy Bey) with its seventeen
sarcophagi now in the Constantinople Museum. The *Corpus In-
scriptionum semiticarum* was begun in Paris in 1881.

Mention must also be made on account of their connection with
Palestinian and Syrian archæology of the researches into Aegean
civilization which yielded especially valuable results; Troy, Mycenae
and Tyrinth were first excavated by Schliemann and then by
Dörpfeld in the nineteenth century; Crete was excavated by Evans
in 1900 and the following years.

Finally we must recall the many studies in ethnography and
folklore which, even before 1914, were devoted to modern nomadic

[13]We shall have to return to the important excavations after 1918 but may
mention here certain useful works of recent date that are easily available. In the
first place, the remarkable list (down to 1938) provided with very full references,
by L. Hennequin, *Fouilles et champs de fouilles en Palestine et en Phénicie* in the *Supplément
du Dictionnaire de la Bible*, III, col. 318-524; then W. F. Albright, *The Archæology of
Palestine*, Penguin, 1949; *Recent Discoveries in Bible Lands*, New York, 1955; *The
Archæology of Palestine and the Bible*, New York, 1st edn, 1932; G. E. Wright, *Biblical
Archæology*, Philadelphia, 1957; M. F. Unger, *Archæology and the Old Testament*,
Grand Rapids, 1954. Among earlier works: F. Kenyon, *The Bible and Archæology*,
London, 1940; J. Simons, *Opgravingen in Palestina tot aan de Ballingschap*, Ruremonde-
Maaseik, 1935; C. Watzinger, *Denkmäler Palästinas, Eine Einführung in die Archäologie
des heiligen Landes*, 2 volumes, Leipzig, 1933-5; R. A. S. Macalister, *A Century of
Excavation in Palestine*, London, 1925.

Semites, the Bedouin of our own day, studies which effectively contributed to a better understanding of the character, traditions and customs of the first ancestors of Israel.[14]

---

[14]For example the books by P. A. Jaussen, O.P.: *Coutumes des Arabes au pays de Moab*, Paris, 1908; *Coutumes palestiniennes, I Naplouse et son district*, Paris, 1927. Also the series of volumes by G. Dalman, *Arbeit und Sitte in Palästina*, Gütersloh, 1928-41.

CHAPTER II

TRENDS IN BIBLICAL CRITICISM IN THE LIBERAL PROTESTANT MOVEMENT
1870-1914[1]

IT WAS round about 1870 that, first in Germany and then in other countries, the great collective inter-university effort at interpretation of the Scriptures first began to take shape; it has come to be one of the principal characteristics of modern study of the Bible. A very great number of analytical and synthetical studies were devoted to the history of Israel and to biblical exegesis. Important series of commentaries were published in Germany, England and France enlisting the aid of the best scholars so that by the individual contributions the whole field of the Old and New Testaments should be covered. This movement was in agreement with the Protestant idea of revelation according to which sacred Scripture is the only certain expression of the word of God; unfortunately, in the second half of the nineteenth century, the main current was often liberal and purely historical rather than religiously orthodox and theologically

[1] This account of the evolution of Protestant criticism both in this chapter (1870-1914) and in Chapter VI below (1918 to the present day) has been written from the point of view that is fundamental to this volume—a better understanding through the history of exegesis since 1850 of man's part as the inspired interpreter of God's message, the divine method of giving us his message through the agency of men. There is no intention of giving here in these few pages a complete history of Protestant exegesis, nor indeed of Catholic exegesis. Several Protestant historians of recent years have endeavoured to recount the various phases of the history of Protestant exegesis, either since the Reformation or at the present day. We have observed with interest that in some of them are to be found the same underlying ideas as those which guided us in the writing of this book, despite divergences of conclusion and judgement. The following are some of the works in question: E. C. Kraeling, *The Old Testament since the Reformation*, London, 1955; J. K. S. Reid, *The Authority of Scripture*: *A Study of the Reformation and Post Reformation Understanding of the Bible*, London, 1957; H. F. Hahn, *The Old Testament in Modern Research*, London, 1956; H. J. Kraus, *Geschichte der historisch-kritischen Erforschung des Alten Testaments von der Reformation bis zur Gegenwart*, Neukirchen, 1956; E. C. Blackman, *Biblical Interpretation: the Old Difficulties and New Opportunities*, London, 1957; A. G. Hebert, *Fundamentalism and the Church of God*, London, 1957 and a recent article by E. Käsemann, 'Neutestamentliche Fragen von heute' in *Zeits. f. Theol. u. Kirche*, 1957, pp. 1-21.

21

constructive. It was the history, rather than the religious under-standing of the doctrine and of Jewish and Christian thought, which preoccupied many of these university professors. A great number of these Protestant commentaries of the pre-1914 period were imbued with an atmosphere of philosophical and theological scepticism, especially in Germany, though less in England, combined very often with remarkable technical, philological, exegetical and historical skill.

Causes of the development of liberal exegesis during this period

Several causes combined to promote the expansion of this exegetical movement and its undeniable progress.

The first, as we have just seen, especially for the Old Testament, was the recovery of its oriental background that was effected during the nineteenth century. It was from within an historical and literary context increasingly better understood in respect of language, events, ideas, methods of exposition and of style, that the history of Israel and the religious and literary evolution of the Old Testament needed to be rethought. This was a new undertaking in the history of biblical exegesis and it was to be expected that results also would be new and not wholly in accordance with the time-honoured explanations of the older biblical textbooks.

A further cause was the progress achieved in historical method and study by the wonderful development of classical philology at the end of the nineteenth and the beginning of the twentieth century. F. A. Wolf's *Vorlesungen* (1785) is usually regarded as the foundation of classical philology. At the beginning of the nineteenth century the latter made remarkable progress with men like Niebuhr (d. 1831), Humboldt (d. 1835), Otf. Muller (d. 1840) and G. Herrmann (d. 1840). And there were others. Greek and Roman antiquity came to be understood with increasing insight not only in regard to the evolution of ideas, to philosophy and religion but also to their various social, economic, artistic and literary characteristics. Inevitably this technical approach and historical method together with the more advanced philological exegesis were applied to the Bible, both to the Old Testament and, particularly, to Christian origins.

A third cause was the clearer understanding of Semitic biblical languages as a result of the philological and exegetical progress of the nineteenth century. In the light of the comparative grammar, vocabulary and stylistics of the other Semitic languages (especially

Accadian, the various Aramean and Syriac dialects, as well as Arabic) the Hebrew text was often more perfectly rendered than it had been before and a closer comprehension and insight into biblical Aramaic and the Aramaic spoken by Jesus could be obtained. Of course, in this connection the proficiency attained in previous centuries was already considerable; Hebrew exegesis had for long profited from the Aramaic Targums, from the work of the Massoretes at the beginning, as also from the labours of Jewish grammarians from the tenth century onwards and the various Christian scholars since Reuchlin (1455-1522). And St Jerome's contribution to the linguistic interpretation of the Old Testament is well known. In the nineteenth century W. Gesenius (d. 1842) by his Hebrew grammar and his *Thesaurus linguae hebraicae* (1829-58) was the pioneer in grammatical and linguistic work which continued during the ensuing hundred years with vitality and with fruitful results in many general works or detailed studies, thus making a major contribution to the elucidation of many passages of the Old Testament.

We must also go back to the past, to the end of the eighteenth and the beginning of the nineteenth centuries to discover the historical reasons for the liberal character of German critical exegesis in the second half of the nineteenth and the beginning of the twentieth centuries. It is common knowledge that in the eighteenth century the intellectual movement in France was influenced by Voltaire and in Germany was dominated by the *Aufklärung*. German literature of the eighteenth century with Lessing, Goethe and even Schiller, was more pagan than Christian; the great German philosophers of the end of the eighteenth and beginning of the nineteenth centuries did not think, nor construct their systems on a Christian basis; Schleiermacher's theology, for example, was a religious philosophy sharply divorced from the fundamental tenets of Christian Christology. Strauss's *Leben Jesu*, which appeared in 1835 and exerted profound influence in intellectual circles, was devoid of authentic Christian faith. With its constant Positivist emphasis in historical or scientific research and its growing suspicion of all metaphysics, the Christianity of the German universities between 1870 and 1914 clearly showed its liberal character. In 1870-4, in the well-known book by A. Ritschl (*Die christliche Lehre von der Rechtfertigung und Versöhnung*), expression was given to a saving formula apparently reconciling a Protestant idea of the Christian religion (though one singularly remote from Luther's) with the radically liberal tendency of biblical exegesis. Later in this book it will be necessary to note the various trends and differences of emphasis in this summary presentation of the movement, but it seemed important at the outset to show how the scholar, like every human being, is dependent on his milieu and the past, sometimes on a past that is already remote in history.

Certain features of the collective inter-university character of scriptural research since 1870

This is not a history of exegesis with a complete list of names and works. Nevertheless, to indicate clearly the collective inter-university character assumed by exegetical research at this period certain significant examples (with their date) are here given. As the century progressed so the number of series of publications increased.

As early as 1832 H. A. W. Meyer had founded at Göttingen the *Kritisch-exegetischer Kommentar über das Neue Testament* which up to the present day has managed to maintain its critical value by constant revision with the aid of well-chosen collaborators of technical ability. From the outset the tendency was towards as thoroughgoing a grammatical, stylistic and historical exegesis as possible; this trait has been maintained in the successive volumes of the series and accounts for the fundamental value of many of them. Nevertheless, towards the end of the nineteenth and the beginning of the twentieth century, a certain number of them, contrary to the theological and religious principles of the founder of the series, took their inspiration from the liberal Protestantism then prevalent in Germany.

Between 1890 and 1914, especially, there was a great proliferation of important series of works on Scripture, many of which reflected the liberal Protestant spirit of the period: thus for the Old Testament may be mentioned *Handkommentar zum Alten Testament* edited by Nowack which began in 1892; the *Kurzer Handkommentar zum Alten Testament* by Marti (1898); *Die Schriften des Alten Testaments in Auswahl neu übersetzt und für die Gegenwart erklärt* (Gressmann, Gunkel, etc.) began in 1909; in comparison with this latter series the *Kommentar zum Alten Testament* (by Sellin; 1913-) gives evidence of a more religious, conservative Protestant tendency. For the New Testament: *Handkommentar zum Neuen Testament* (H. J. Holtzmann, Lipsius, Schmiedel, etc.) began in 1890; the *Handbuch zum Neuen Testament* by Lietzmann in 1906; the *Schriften des Neuen Testaments neu übersetzt und für die Gegenwart erklärt* (by Johannes Weiss) also in 1906. The list could be prolonged by the enumeration of encyclopaedias like the *Realenzyklopädie für protestantische Theologie* of Herzog Hauck (of more moderate tendency, begun in 1896) or *Die Religion in Geschichte und Gegenwart* of Schiele, Gunkel, etc. (more radical tendency, begun in 1909).[2]

[2]This list does not include works of popularization like *Religionsgeschichtliche Volksbücher* (a series edited by M. Schiele) intended to spread the spirit of liberal Protestantism among the people.

At the same period the great series of English Protestant commentaries began to be published: the *International Critical Commentary* in 1895 (Old and New Testaments, religious in tone and containing some remarkable works like the commentary on the Epistle to the Romans by Sanday and Headlam); the *Westminster Commentaries* (theological) begun in 1904. There were also the important encyclopaedias: the *Dictionary of the Bible* (Hastings) was issued between 1898 and 1904 (moderate and religious in tone); the *Encyclopaedia biblica* by Cheyne (more radical) between 1899 and 1903. The first volume of Hastings's *Encyclopaedia of Religion and Ethics* appeared in 1908.

This dry catalogue of Protestant commentaries on the Old and New Testament has been given here in order to bring out clearly how hard, uncompromising and complex was the task confronting the Catholic exegetes who began their scientific careers about 1880. If they were historically minded they could not fail to observe the technical worth of this liberal Protestant exegesis; consequently, by careful study they had to adopt these conclusions which were well founded and lasting and, with historical and theological insight often difficult to attain, leave aside what was of uncertain historial foundation or what was seemingly or actually irreconcilable with Catholic dogma or theology. It may be questioned whether they were always prepared by their past, their seminary training and Catholic exegesis of previous periods, to make this discrimination calling for a combination of history and theology. Those who, at a difficult period, were equal to the task, deserve the special recognition of modern Catholic workers in this field. We shall examine in the next chapter this Catholic movement for the renewal and advance of biblical studies.

Principal tendencies of Protestant literary and historical criticism between
   1870 and 1914

What were the tendencies of this immense collective inter-university effort in biblical studies between 1870 and 1914 as it found expression in the commentaries listed above? There can be no thought here of giving even an outline of the many and complex aspects of this movement. As was mentioned above, it was principally historical rather than theological, although it entailed serious theological consequences. Certain German Protestant exegetes, like Edward König (1846-1933; his important works date from 1881), Auguste Dillmann (1823-94; his biblical works were published between 1864 and 1894; his biblical theology, posthumously, in

1895), Theodor Zahn (1838-1933, principal works after 1881), Adolphus Schlatter (of Swiss origin, 1852-1938, whose main work was on the New Testament and Judaism at the time of Christ) always endeavoured conscientiously to combine biblical criticism and the religious idea of the Bible in their studies. But German Protestant exegesis of this period for the most part evinced a liberal tendency while acutely raising new problems that demanded a solution.

As often happens in all human controversies, the first objection to a traditional view is absolute, ruthless, going straight to the precise contrary; the conservative reaction is sweeping, aggressive, equally obstinate on secondary points as on the fundamental assertion. Time is required to see matters in perspective together with the intervention on both sides of keen perspicacious minds capable of freeing themselves both from the restrictions of their background and habits of thought and from the attraction of novelty and scientific allurements, so that light may be produced by the conflict of ideas. It is worth pointing out that biblical criticism has often begun with critical excess and then, from a more objective study of detail, a closer attention to the complexity of reality has led to self-criticism and to a gradual modification, mitigation and, sometimes, to a fundamental revision of the original assertions. On the other hand, Catholic exegesis, with increasing awareness of the deep complexity of God's action on the minds of the inspired authors has understood the human mediation of God's message, has learned to distinguish the various literary forms in history and not to confuse literary authenticity and inspiration. It has come to understand that rather than make God conform to our methods of teaching Christianity we must adapt our teaching methods to God's plan.

From the literary and historical criticism of the second half of the nineteenth century we can choose, merely as examples to be dealt with briefly, four aspects from among many which show clearly the profound changes in the biblical problem as it is envisaged by recent generations and which could never have been foreseen by the theologians and preachers of the seventeenth century.

1.   *The authenticity of the books of the Old Testament*
In the forefront was the literary criticism of the Pentateuch and its literary composition.

After about the beginning of the third century B.C. (at least ten centuries, therefore, after Moses) it is clear from Israel's literature that the Jews regarded Moses as author of the 'Law', of the 'book of the Law' (2 Paralip. 23. 18; 25. 4; 30. 16; 33. 8; Ecclus 24. 22); at the time of our Lord Jewish opinion was unanimous (Philo, Josephus, 4 Esdras, contemporary rabbis in the Talmud) in attributing to Moses the five books of the Pentateuch. Our Lord and the apostles in quoting texts from the Pentateuch preface them with the current formula, 'as Moses said,' or 'as it is written in the book of Moses', though of course the mere use of this formula is no ground for the inference that this literary tradition is thereby confirmed by divine authority. Moses' authorship of the Pentateuch (except for the final account of the death of Moses) remained the traditional opinion until the end of the seventeenth century, nor was it seriously challenged until the second half of the nineteenth century. Obviously such a tradition possessed great apologetic value; if Moses wrote the Pentateuch, it is not only an eye-witness, but also the leading actor in the events, who records the miracles worked by God on behalf of his people at the time of the Exodus; it is the great leader of Israel, well informed about the history of his nation, who relates for us the history of the patriarchs (Gen. 11 *et seq.*).

Modern critical discussion about the origin of the Pentateuch, initiated by the Oratorian Richard Simon in 1678 (Bossuet was in violent opposition to his views) and continued by the Catholic doctor Jean Astruc in 1753, was developed on a scientific basis in the second half of the nineteenth century (Vatke, Ewald, Kuenen, Reuss, Graf) and found its principal exponent in J. Wellhausen (more especially after 1878).

At this distance in time it is possible nowadays to distinguish more clearly two closely connected and interdependent essential features in Wellhausen's work; on the one hand there is the painstaking and detailed literary criticism emphasizing the composite character of the five books of the Pentateuch, and showing them to be the combination of documents of very different dates (J, E, D, P), a threefold legislative code belonging to three great eras JE, D and P) finally brought together in a single code and bringing the final composition of the five books (though on the basis of earlier documents) down to a date in the fifth century B.C. On the other hand, there is a religious criticism representing the evolution of the religion of

Yahweh in Israel, according to a naturalist point of view, deleting any authentic divine intervention in favour of the Chosen People and making Israel pass from 'monolatry' at the time of Moses to monotheism under the influence of the prophets after the eighth century—an immanent religious evolution quite independent of any revelation.

Thus put forward, Wellhausen's system appeared to Catholics and to orthodox Protestants as a complete denial of their religious view of the Old Testament. The ensuing controversy was long and animated on historical and philological matters as well as religious. This is not the place to summarize it; a fully documented account will be found in the book by J. Coppens, *Histoire critique des livres de l'Ancien Testament*, 3rd edn, Tournai, 1942. J. Wellhausen's historical hypercriticism of the Pentateuch, as well as of the other books of the Old Testament, was refuted on many points of detail by a more discriminating and less inflexible literary criticism; his religious criticism was corrected by scholars with greater knowledge of Christian theology.

Nevertheless, at the conclusion of this extensive investigation certain details of the method gained acceptance, at least as the best working hypotheses in the present state of knowledge. The composite character of the Pentateuch is recognized by the majority of exegetes and the four fundamental documents, or in any case three of them (J, D, P) seem sufficiently established to form a solid basis for interpretation. The fundamental legislative codes, collected together in the Pentateuch, do represent three different periods in the history of Israel. No one any longer regards Moses as the final author of the five books of the Pentateuch; his influence and activity are sought rather at the origins of the legislation and the narrative.

What happened with the Pentateuch occurred also with the other books of the Old Testament. To begin with, there was an extreme critical approach to the date and authors of the Psalms, many scholars assigning them to as late a period as that of the Machabees, then there was a gradual return to more moderate positions but not to the extent of regular acceptance of the conclusions held as definitely established a century previously, nor of the date or authors implied by the titles of the Psalms. Of course, the Old Testament still bristles with problems and uncertainties. But for example those

Catholic exegetes who still feel that they can attribute to the eighth century and to the prophet Isaias chapters 40-66 of the book bearing his name are increasingly rare. Nor does the new date in any way diminish the religious and prophetical value of these remarkable chapters. Dated during the exile of the sixth century (or, partially, immediately afterwards) they stand out the more boldly and with increased meaning in the religious evolution of Israel. Since the middle of the nineteenth century a critical reappraisal of biblical authenticity has been at work. During the first decades it was frequently radical and daring, later modifying its conclusions (putting back, for example, to before the exile, writings that had been dated to the fifth century) but arriving at solid results through this collective inter-university endeavour and at likely dates that could not have been imagined in former times.

Catholics, for their part, learnt by their personal investigations to make a distinction between criticism bearing on authenticity and literary criticism on the one hand and inspiration on the other. The first question is open and concerns philology and history, the second is a matter of faith, as defined by the Councils of Trent and of the Vatican. And it would be profoundly regrettable if there should continue among us a literary indolence of the kind that in 1946 could reproduce a passage, written in good faith by its author in 1887 in these terms:[3] 'The books of the Old Testament are thus divided according to their subject matter: 1. books of the Law: the Pentateuch, comprising Genesis, Exodus, Leviticus, Numbers and Deuteronomy of which Moses is the author except for the last chapter which is attributed to Josue. 2. Historical books, namely, the book of Josue, of which Josue himself is probably the author, Judges and Ruth, apparently written by Samuel; the four books of Kings, Samuel being probably the author of the first save for the last seven chapters; the second was written by the seers Nathan and Gad while the third and fourth can probably be attributed to Jeremias or Esdras; the two books of Chronicles (Paralipomena) probably written by Esdras . . . the book of Tobias, of which the two Tobias are the authors; the book of Judith, written probably by the high priest Joachim and that of Esther attributed to Mardochaeus; the book of Job whose author is probably Job himself,

---

[3] J. Berthier, M.S., *Abrégé de théologie dogmatique et morale*, 6th French edn, revised and corrected by a group of priests, Lyons, 1946, pp. 28-9.

though some say that it was written by Moses. 3. The moral books which comprise, in the first place, the Psalms certainly composed for the most part by David and of which some, as their titles show, are to be attributed to Moses, Solomon, Asaph, Iduthun (Ethan) and Jeremias; the books of Proverbs, Ecclesiastes, the Song of Songs were by Solomon, the book of Wisdom by one of the seventy interpreters.'

These conclusions were singularly out of date when they were put together with confidence in 1887 by a dogmatic and moral theologian who was ill-informed on historical matters; nevertheless, they are characteristic of the position adopted by certain Catholic popular works of the beginning of the nineteenth century and show clearly the long way that Catholic scholars had to travel before reaching, either in 1900 or 1960, the established conclusions of biblical criticism concerning the authenticity of the Old Testament. By adopting these conclusions Catholic thought loses nothing of the eternal religious value of the divine message. Rather is it in a better position to understand this message as it has evolved and developed in time. Yet what a large measure of conflict and acrimonious discussion was needed before it could make up its mind to accept this great benefit.

2. *Historical narratives of the Bible and scriptural inerrancy*
More difficult, because it involved theological conclusions generally admitted in traditional thought, was the question of the *historical form* of many narratives in the Old Testament. Modern critical study of the historical books of the Old Testament very soon perceived problems that hitherto had not been raised. We can begin with simpler ones before going on to the more difficult.

Comparison of biblical data with the Assyro-Babylonian evidence, known at the time, had already raised new problems concerning the chronology and synchronization of the kings of Judah and Israel. Were all the dates and figures, often difficult enough to reconcile with each other and with contemporary history, necessarily guaranteed by scriptural inerrancy or could they be regarded as ancient documents quoted by the inspired author (implicit quotation)? Taking into account the topography of Palestine and Egypt how could the accuracy be allowed of such figures as 600,000 men fit for military service, since this implied between two and a half and three million Israelites living within the boundaries of the land of Goshen and making their way along the recorded route across the Sinai peninsula? For long, exegesis was satisfied by explaining these figures as mistakes in transcription due to the errors of the copyists and not to the inspired authors; it soon became clear that this explanation was artificial and out-of-date and that a solution must be sought in the nature of ancient history itself.

Other more difficult and complex questions soon arose. For comparison with the ancestral genealogies (Genesis 5. 3-32) with lives of astonishing length there was discovered in Accadian and Sumerian literature a list of ten early Mesopotamian kings before the Flood of incredible longevity, far more so indeed than that attributed to the ancestors of Israel. Certain similarities of names in the two lists also aroused attention. On the other hand, study of the sources of the Pentateuch revealed that this extreme longevity of ancestors is only mentioned in this Chapter 5 (the priestly narrative) of the Pentateuch, seems unknown to J and E and is hardly in agreement with the number of the living harboured in Noah's ark to escape the Flood. In addition in Genesis 10 (also belonging to P for the most part) the history of the peoples is recorded in terms of family groups; for example, the sons of Cham (Chus, Mesraim, Phuth and Canaan) are names of countries as are also those of their children. Is all this to be taken literally or does it reveal a primitive method of writing history to which we must adapt ourselves if we are to understand it and not approach it with the *a priori* requirement that it should be in accordance with that of modern civilization?

Many other features of ancient historical method are revealed by careful study and with the aid of folklore, primitive ethnography and comparison with the literatures contemporary with Israel. Such are, for example, the combination of two accounts in a single narrative in the Pentateuch (two successive accounts of the creation: J and P: Genesis 1-2.4 and 2.5-25); two accounts of the Flood mixed up together (J and P) in spite of contradictory statements (Genesis 6-8) and so on; possibly two acounts, also intermixed, of Joseph sold by his brothers (J and E: Genesis 37. 12-36). Then there are popular accounts, with the character of ancient traditions, handed down for long by word of mouth, gradually embellished, continually being made more concrete and lively, legend being naturally mixed with history. In short, it was observed to what a large extent these narra-

tives, contrary to the *a priori* assumptions of former times, in recounting the dealings of God with men appeared to be put together
in accordance with a very free, popular and primitive historical
form. Christian exegetes gradually came to see that for the purposes
of their theological assumptions it was unreasonable to postulate
that God should have miraculously withdrawn the human trans-
mitters of his message from their milieu and period to endow them,
thirty centuries in advance, with the critical mentality of a modern
historian. Fr M. J. Lagrange was the first among Catholics to lay
down these principles clearly in his well-known lectures at the
Institut Catholique at Toulouse in November, 1902, under the
general title 'La méthode historique surtout à propos de l'Ancien
Testament'. This was the preliminary sketch of the notion of
'literary forms' in history as it was later sanctioned by Pius XII in
1943.

Historical criticism, however, went much further; here as elsewhere the tendency at the outset was far more audacious and pro-
vocative. It was the very content of biblical history, upholding the
whole religious edifice, which was undermined all along the line
by a determined hypercriticism.[4] A stroke of the pen abolished the
whole of the history of the patriarchs who were regarded as 'lunar
myths' (E. Stucken, 1896-1907) or Canaanite gods (E. Meyer, 1906)
or Canaanite heroes adopted by the Israelites into their own history
(H. Weill, 1923).[5] The hypotheses of Edward Meyer (*Geschichte des
Altertums*, 5 volumes, 1884-1902 and various writings on biblical
history) denied entirely the sojourn in Egypt and turned the story
of Moses and the origins of the religion of Yahweh upside down.

Gradually, however, biblical criticism, better informed as a result,
to some extent, of the findings of archæology, itself corrected its
former assertions, and a dialogue between Catholic exegesis and
critical exegesis once more became progressively possible, since the
positions adopted on both sides were no longer those of the initial
controversies. Nowadays we can understand better the real worth
and the effective rôle of those exegetes, both Catholic and Protestant,

---

[4]From this can be understood the radical refusal by conservative exegetes to
allow the slightest concession. The refusal of any concession seemed to them the
only way of not being involved in a situation with pernicious and fatal consequences.
[5]On these points see the articles by Fr de Vaux, O.P. in the *Revue biblique*,
July, 1946, pp. 321-368; 1948, pp. 321-347; 1949, pp. 5-36: 'Les patriarches hébreux
et les découvertes modernes.'

religiously devoted to the Bible, whose important work was done between 1880 and 1914.

3. *Criticism of the authenticity and dates of the Gospels*

It was here particularly that liberal exegesis turned at the outset to radical hypercriticism. It was the more keenly felt by its opponents since it affected the very source of their Christian belief. The positions adopted after 1845 by Baur and what has been called the school of Tübingen are well known since they have been popularized in many manuals of apologetics. They asserted that the first Gospel is a revision (belonging to the first half of the second century) in the direction of the universalist teaching of Paul of a first-century document upholding the narrow point of view of primitive Judaeo-Christianity. The second Gospel was written about 150; the third was an orthodox adaptation, made after 150, of the gospel of Marcion the heretic, written about 140; the fourth Gospel belonged to the second half of the second century. Thus, none of the four was written by the author to whom tradition assigned it or possessed any guarantee as valid evidence. During the second half of the nineteenth century these extreme positions were progressively given up in favour of others nearer to the assertions of tradition. At the end of the period that we are now considering, that is, in 1914, liberal criticism, generally speaking, admitted that the first Greek Gospel was composed between A.D. 70 and 90, it acknowledged as justified the attribution to Mark of the second Gospel and placed the date of its composition a little before, or a little after, A.D. 70; in about 1906 the third Gospel was unhesitatingly attributed to Luke by Harnack and, since then, by an increasing number of critics; the fourth Gospel was not recognized as the work of the Apostle John but at least the date assigned by a great number was the end of the first century, the traditional date. This critical evolution appeared therefore to be, as Harnack termed it, a return to tradition, *zurück zur Tradition*. Of course, that does not mean that the recognition of the historical value of our Gospels underwent a similar evolution during those sixty years; new problems mentioned below emerged in the meantime. Yet it is interesting to notice that Ernest Renan, when his faith was shaken and he left the seminary of Saint-Sulpice in 1845, did not do so in the same critical climate as Alfred Loisy when he broke definitively with the Church at the beginning of the twentieth century. It is by no means easy for the independent scholar, however intelligent, to transcend the intellectual climate of his own period to rediscover beyond it the Christian balance of his thought.

4. *The problem of the origin of Christianity and of the Church*

The fundamental problem which was central to all the study, research and controversy of the second half of the nineteenth and the beginning of the twentieth centuries was the problem of Jesus: Jesus in history, the 'Christ of history' as distinct from 'the Christ of faith'. This problem was in the forefront of the Modernist controversy. The decree *Lamentabili* of 3 July 1907 is devoted almost entirely to these errors about Christ, his life, divinity, his work of revelation and of founding the Church. It is true, of course, that rationalism which denies the divinity of Christ and the supernatural character of his mission and work does not date from the nineteenth century; at all periods, from the very beginning, it has existed side by side with Christianity. It showed strongly aggressive tendencies in the eighteenth century under the influence of Voltaire and the French encyclopaedists, of Frederick II and the *Aufklärung* in Germany. But it is in the nineteenth century, especially after the life of Jesus in German published by Strauss in 1835, that the problem of Jesus was examined and discussed *on historical grounds*. For Strauss interpreted the evangelical narratives, particularly the accounts of miracles, as the result of a long evolution of legends. In France, too, Ernest Renan's *Vie de Jésus* (1863) appeared at the beginning of the movement of negative historical criticism of Christian origins.[6] This work, literary and romantic rather than strictly scientific, by the pervasive subtlety of its style exerted a pernicious influence in French-speaking countries. Nevertheless, it provoked a useful reaction; it showed Catholics the need for a more thorough study of Christianity in history, and to some extent contributed to the revival of French Catholic Exegesis. In England, the Anglican J. R. Seeley's *Ecce Homo* (1866) stirred up heated controversy; it extolled Jesus the man in an extremely attractive manner at the expense of his divine transcendence.

[6]We attempted to depict certain features of Renan's religious character in *Sous les yeux de l'incroyant*, 2nd edn, pp. 58-65. Numerous unpublished documents on Renan's youth have been collected together by J. Pommier in various works and articles appearing since 1923. The most recent, and most significant, study is by J. Chaix-Ruy, *Ernest Renan*, Lyons, 1956.

The liberal German notion of historical Christianity had its theological justification, as we have seen, in the well-known work by A. Ritschl, *Die christliche Lehre von der Rechtfertigung und Versöhnung* (1870-4). The principal exegetes and historians of liberal Protestantism interpreted Christian origins in accordance with the spirit of Ritschl's book—this was true of the many contributors to the *Handkommentar zum Neuen Testament* (beginning in 1890, published at Tübingen by Mohr), of the *Grundriss der theologischen Wissenschaften* (same date and place) and of Adolph von Harnack, the great Protestant historian of dogma, in his lectures (1900) on the essence of Christianity (*Das Wesen des Christentums*).

The understanding of Jesus, the interpretation of his work and thought raised at the outset an extremely serious problem of method. Whoever the historian, however conscientious and objective he strives always to remain, he is obliged to approach texts and facts with the assumptions acquired by his experiences in investigation and with a philosophy of life and of the world. If his is a materialist conception of human life his view and synthesis of the facts of history will be made on the basis of the economic laws of existence; and as these laws are always in operation he will be able perhaps to discern them the more clearly, but at the same time his mind will be closed to other aspects of real life and powerless to grasp the religious phenomenon in the profundity of its truth. It was with a narrow and purely extrinsic understanding of the religious phenomenon that, in the second half of the nineteenth century, research into the history of religions began, and it was already dominated by these superficial notions of ancient religions that many came to the study of the fact of Christianity. In 1910, in Paris, Catholics in the audience of a famous Egyptologist experienced a certain uneasiness, as may well be imagined, at hearing him use in his explanation of Egyptian religion the recognized terms for Christian realities (salvation, incarnation, redemption, etc.), which were all for him religious terms that, wherever they occurred, belonged to the same level of childish belief. In accordance with proper historical method, religious thought, the religious phenomenon, can only be rightly-understood if the investigator already possesses or at least adopts as a working hypothesis (if he possibly can) a religious conception of life and of God's direct and personal call to the human soul; otherwise, the essential nature of the whole phenomenon will remain incomprehensible to him. And this is still truer if an attempt is made to understand the thought of Jesus, the mind of Jesus, who, according to the Christian view, is both really human—and therefore subject to historical appreciation—and at the same time superhuman, transcending his age and background and thereby remaining mysterious for all.

There can be no thought of listing here, even summarily, the various researches and evaluations that took place in the second half of the nineteenth century and the beginning of the twentieth on the subject of Christian origins, the exegesis of fundamental points in the Gospels, Ritschl's liberal conception (Harnack) or the eschatological conception (J. Weiss, Schweitzer) of the message of Jesus, the various reconstructions of the teaching of the apostles and of the theology of the primitive Church.

In this immense task of research which found expression in a great number of commentaries, theologies of the New Testament, specialized studies on the origin of essential points of the Christian faith, there is often much to admire in the perfection of the technique of exegesis, the discerning essays in synthesis and the valuable comparisons of texts and facts, but there are also serious and striking deficiencies which vitiated the whole progress of research.

The first and most important deficiency, to be encountered in many of the exegetes of the period, is the entire absence of Christian understanding of the Christian *fact*. It is impossible to grasp the inner meaning of Christ and his work without examining it, at least hypothetically, from the only point of view that enables him to be understood. To act otherwise is to be like blind men holding forth about colours. Of course, since Jesus appeared in history as a perfectly human being, the historian is obliged to study him in history and by means of history, he must interpret his utterances with the help of the vocabulary of those times, seek to understand his thought on the basis of the contemporary intellectual climate. The historian must guard against the 'extrinsicism', too long prevalent in theology, which examined the text in the light of our dogmatically developed Christian thought and claimed to read in them the clear statements that had only been gradually established in the course of centuries. But he must also be careful not to attribute to Jesus, on principle and *a priori*, a thought limited to the ideas and tendencies of his times and must beware of interpreting spontaneously as a gloss, an embellishment added by the early Church, everything in the Gospel texts that betrays a deeper preoccupation with the future. Although Jesus desired to belong to his own milieu and period, essentially he transcends them both and in the Christian view his thought is coherent, free from contradiction, only if it is interpreted as both belonging to his times and transcending them. The historian who approaches Jesus with an historical method built up on past experience as an historian, and who reduces the person and message of Jesus to the proportions of persons and teaching that he has learned to know in his human experience as an historian, has from the outset no hope of understanding what he is studying. On the other hand, he will understand it better the more closely and profoundly, as an historian, he is open to comprehension of the Christian solution of life.

Another defect of the liberal interpretation of Christian origins in the second half of the nineteenth century was a constant tendency to what has been called 'historicism'; this is a subtle error difficult to define and best seen by some examples. In this category may be included the identification of those texts trying to express a thought or movement of thought with the totality of this thought and its deepest implications; the denial, practically speaking, that the reality can be richer in content than the witnesses were able formally and explicitly to express it; an insufficient awareness of the history of words, of their progressive enrichment in a thought—did words like 'Son of God', 'Messiah', 'justice of God' have exactly the same meaning, the same content, in the thought of the apostles when they encountered the Master for the first time as when they had been for two years and three months in his company? Does the Jewish meaning of a term, before Christ, express accurately the Christian meaning of this term in the primitive Church? Again, it is 'historicism' to be unable to discern, beneath the texts, the continuity of a movement of thought—by what right can it be postulated *a priori* (save through rationalist prejudice) that there is a break in continuity between Christ's thought about his own person and work and that of the apostles and of the primitive Church about Christ and that the most explicit Gospel passages *must be* the creation of early Christian theology? The 'historicism' of 1850-1914, a reaction against the 'extrinsicism' of the theologians of former times, went to the opposite extreme and lost sight of the fact that a document is an indication of the realities of the past but is not necessarily its complete and definitive expression.

Finally, as the third deficiency in the history of Christian origins during these years of predominant liberal Protestantism (without claiming that these three tendencies are an exhaustive list of those prevailing at the period) we may note an excessive mistrust of writings of the evangelists and apostles and an instinctive propensity to scepticism. While literary criticism of the authenticity (of the Gospels, etc.) between 1850 and 1914 showed a marked return to the traditional positions, that was certainly not true of historical criticism of the content of the Gospels.

The fundamental error of Ritschl's system, however, remains the basic weakness of his religious philosophy—the unconscious but arbitrary choice made from the teaching of Christ of those values which happened to correspond most suitably with the religious state of the German university mentality of the second half of the nineteenth century, but which on a last analysis were derived neither from an integral dogmatic synthesis of Christ nor from a coherent and total historical synthesis. During the last phase of its existence, at the beginning of the twentieth century (1900-14), the supremacy of liberal Protestantism founded on Ritschl's system was under heavy attack in Germany university circles. Three such attacks may be mentioned.

The eschatological school, with Baldensperger, J. Weiss, A. Schweitzer, A. Loisy, showed clearly the dogmatic, *a priori* nature of liberal Protestantism but in its one-sided interpretation of the Gospels and the primitive Church, went to extremes and thereby falsified the (undeniable) eschatological standpoint of the Gospels; like the school of Ritschl it remained fundamentally rationalist and naturalist.

The history of religions (Reitzenstein, Lidzbarski, *Religionsgeschichtliche Versuche und Vorarbeiten*, founded in 1903 by A. Dieterich and R. Wunsch, etc.) emphasized the limitations and narrowness of liberal Protestantism and regarded itself as applying the principles of this naturalist liberalism more logically by studying primitive Christianity in comparison with the other religions of antiquity, as a mere result of previous religious movements, whether Jewish or pagan. For example, it placed Christianity side by side with Hellenism and its cult 'mysteries', with Hermetic religion, with

Mandaeism (Lidzbarski), with the religious folklore of various peoples (e.g. James Frazer in England, Saintyves in France). All this was no doubt an a-christian notion of religion but it showed clearly the artificial character of Ritschl's liberal Protestant synthesis as a durable Christian synthesis.

Finally, the controversy about the existence of Jesus (J. M. Robertson, 1900; P. Jensen, 1906; W. B. Smith, 1906; A. Drews, 1909) claimed to push to its logical conclusion the scepticism of liberal Protestantism and ended by doubting the very existence of Jesus; but in this case critical reaction was clear and immediate and very soon no more was heard of this odd conclusion.

After 1918 Protestant exegesis progressed beyond, and partially corrected in certain matters, the deficiencies of the nineteenth-century liberal Protestant movement; we return to this below.

CHAPTER III

TRENDS IN CATHOLIC EXEGESIS: 1880-1914

WHAT WAS the reaction of Catholic exegesis to the scientific progress of the nineteenth century and the steady development of liberal criticism? It was under the pontificate of Leo XIII, especially after 1890, that Catholic exegesis and theology seemed to feel clearly the first impact of these new aspects of biblical studies and of the powerful influence of the naturalist interpretation of the times.

The breadth of vision with which the Archbishop of Perugia, who became pope at the age of sixty-eight under the name of Leo XIII, envisaged the Church's mission in contemporary society is well known. He set himself the task of 'leading back to the Church the modern world which was growing away from her; far from isolating herself from the world the Church must enter it in a spirit of conquest . . . Especially, and right from the beginning of his pontificate, of set purpose he proposed to re-establish the influence of the Church in the intellectual life of the contemporary world . . . , to promote among the clergy an ideal of true culture and to restore a high level of ecclesiastical studies.'[1]

Undoubtedly Leo XIII's understanding attitude did much to establish among the Catholic clergy a spirit of intellectual work, of optimistic and enthusiastic research, which came to the fore particularly in the sphere of positive theology—exegesis, patrology, history of dogma and history of the Church.

[1] E. Hocedez, S.J., *Histoire de la théologie au XIXe siècle*, volume III, *Le règne de Léon XIII*, Brussels, Édition Universelle, 1947. Significant of this intention of the pope's was the fact that shortly after his accession he took two pastoral letters on modern civilization that he had written while archbishop of Perugia and published them, adding a third on the same subject. All his first acts as pope bore evidence of the same trend: in 1883 he opened the Vatican Library to all research workers, whether Catholic or not; he emphatically encouraged the foundation of Catholic Universities, of Catholic faculties of theology; in addition his later acts, dealing with the social question and the renewal of Thomistic philosophy, should be remembered.

Circumstances were favourable. In Germany the faculties of Catholic theology, which belonged to the official universities, already possessed a long tradition of scientific work. For example, the Catholic faculty of theology at Tübingen in the nineteenth century produced men like Möhler (author of *Symbolik*), Kuhn (*Lehrbuch der Dogmatik*, 3 volumes, 1846-68) and Hefele (*Conciliengeschichte*, 7 volumes, 1855-74); that of Munich could claim theologians like Deutinger (1815-64), Klee (1800-40), and J. G. Görres, the historian of mysticism (1776-1848); great hopes had been placed on the brilliant qualities of Döllinger, the historian of theology (1799-1890) who unfortunately left the Church after the definition of papal infallibility. Other theological centres like the seminary of Mainz, with J. B. Heinrich, the theological faculty of Wurzburg (with Denzinger, Hettinger and Hergenröther) were well prepared to undertake historical and exegetical work. In Belgium the Catholic University of Louvain, re-established in 1835, already possessed by 1878 a well-founded tradition in patrology, oriental languages and exegesis (Beelen, de Harlez etc). At the time of Leo XIII's accession, France, taking advantage of the law on the freedom of higher education (1875), demanded for so long before that date, had just set up its Catholic Universities (or Instituts Catholiques)—Paris, Lille and Lyons in 1876, Angers in 1877 and Toulouse in 1879. They were to play a predominant part in the exegetic work of this period. In the United States the Catholic University at Washington was founded in 1887. And the list could be continued of the Catholic faculties of theology with Rome and its Universities or Pontifical Institutes, Austria, Syria (University of St Joseph, founded in 1881) together with the theological colleges of the principal religious Orders. What is important here is to note at the outset the predominant rôle of the Catholic faculties of theology in Catholic exegesis under the pontificates of Leo XIII and Pius X.

Until about 1890 Catholic exegesis continued for the most part in the severely traditional, not to say classic, climate of preceding periods. In France Renan's *Vie de Jésus*, by its pernicious influence, had already shown clearly the need for the renewal of Catholic biblical studies; the counter effort was evidenced between 1879 and 1892 by the publication of Catholic lives of Jesus which enjoyed a large circulation and were known for long as classics among French-speaking Catholics. Such were, for example, *Jésus*, volume II of

Bougaud's *Le Christianisme et les temps présents* (1872-4); the lives of Jesus by Fouard (1st edn, 1890), Le Camus (1st edn, 1883), Fr Didon, O. P. (1st edn, 1890) and Lesêtre (1st edn, 1892). The series of books of the Old and New Testaments which in 1880 was the most popular in clerical circles was *La Sainte Bible*; it had the Vulgate text with French translation on the opposite page together with a commentary (Paris, Lethielleux). The enterprise was due to the initiative of Drach, a converted Jew; it included a great number of volumes (edited by Drach, Bayle, Clair, Crelier, Fillion, Lesêtre and Trochon) and was to continue until after 1900. It was intended for the largest possible public and its principal aims were edification and apologetics. The *Manuel biblique* (1st edn, 1878, four successive volumes) published by Abbés Vigouroux and Bacuez rapidly became the usual textbook in French seminaries and went through several editions. In 1907, Abbé Brassac undertook the task of revising and rewriting it in the light of modern exegetical progress (12th and following edns); these editions were placed on the index on 12 December 1923; this is referred to below.

In 1886 there began to be published in Paris (Lethielleux) a new Latin commentary on the whole Bible; this was the *Cursus Scripturae Sacrae*, published under the direction of three German Jesuits, professors of Holy Scripture at the scholasticate of their Order, Frs Cornely, Knabenbauer and von Hummelauer. Each undertook a considerable share of the work involved. The volumes came out in rapid succession. In general their tendency was conservative. However, Fr von Hummelauer, who was responsible for the Old Testament, on account of the very questions with which he had to deal, was gradually led to abandon some of the older positions which he rightly judged to be no longer tenable. Fr Cornely also published (1885-7) a *Historica et critica Introductio in utriusque Testamenti libros*, a work of great learning which went through more than twelve editions (revised successively by Frs Hagen and Merk).

The transitional character of the period 1878-90 can be seen also in the Catholic exegesis of other countries—Germany, Austria, Belgium and Rome. But it is not the purpose of this book to provide a history of modern Catholic exegesis; here it is intended only to point out certain characteristic features.

Between 1890 and 1914 two features of Catholic exegesis are

immediately obvious to any observer. On the one hand there was the great effort of Catholic scientific work provoked by direct contact with—and the impact of—the recent archæological and historical discoveries, and with the undoubted advances and unjustifiable deviations of nineteenth-century liberal exegesis. On the other hand, there was, for the same reasons, the division of Catholic scripture scholars into three fairly clearly divided and often hostile groups; between them the struggle was on occasion extremely bitter and painful.

What were these three groups? Firstly, there were the conservatives who considered traditional solutions to biblical problems perfectly satisfactory and up to date in face of critical exegesis, which they repudiated as a whole, regarding it as rationalist and fundamentally opposed to the supernatural. Then there were the informed progressives who, remaining closely attached to the Church and the established conclusions of Catholic theology, distinguished in contemporary criticism between the literary and historical results that were acceptable or capable of discussion and the naturalist conception with which independent research was too often imbued; this they entirely rejected. Lastly, the other progressives, led astray and beguiled by the prevailing critical trends, as they saw them, ill-served by their insufficient theological background and by their somewhat perfunctory Christianity, soured on occasion by certain excessive attacks or unjustified suspicion, gradually broke away from the Church and abandoned their faith.

What made this period of the history of the Church especially distressing was, on the one hand the incapacity of the conservative group, at least of the majority of them, to distinguish between the sound and necessary progress attempted by the second group and the imprudent daring of the third; to the conservative section both were equally worthy of condemnation, both seemed to them alien to the authentic current of faith. On the other hand, among the third group no less blameworthy were their deceitful methods of dissimulation, anonymous articles, and their external attitude of fidelity to the Church while estrangement from the faith had for long past existed in their heart: behaviour of this kind naturally created an atmosphere of suspicion and distrust among the general body of the faithful as well among the ecclesiastical authorities.

There is no need to deal here with the bitter controversies between individuals; they have been exhaustively dealt with elsewhere.[2] We confine ourselves to the two trends mentioned above and only in so far as they concern the exegetical movement. In the first place, we shall examine the intensity of the Catholic scientific effort at this period by giving some indication of the work accomplished; then, to make intelligible the struggle between the three groups of exegetes, we show in order some of the ecclesiastical and conservative objections—whether doctrinal or historical and positive—which occasioned the controversy among Catholics during these troubled years.

The intensity of the Catholic exegetical effort, 1890-1914

The beginning of this period is marked by three developments, inspired by three personalities who were especially representative of the three groups that have just been mentioned.

The first and most important Catholic development at this period was the foundation in 1890 by Fr M. J. Lagrange, O.P.[3] of the Ecole pratique d'études bibliques, a centre for higher studies in Scripture situated in Jerusalem at the very heart of the country of the Bible. In 1892 the School established and took charge of the *Revue biblique* which rapidly became a lively centre of Catholic exegesis throughout the whole period 1890-1914. From the beginning the review's policy was both progressive and attentive to the data of theology. It tackled unhesitatingly many difficult problems—the nature of inspiration, the first chapters of Genesis, the sources of the Gospels, the doctrine of immortality in the Old Testament and so on. Being on the spot it was able to follow closely the progress of Palestinian archæology and in this field it was to play a leading part. Its evaluation of scientific works published by critics belonging to the Protestant school were always distinguished by calm objectivity and competent discussion. Among the collaborators of the early years were included the leading Scripture scholars whatever their tendencies: 'Sulpicians like M. Vigouroux and his friend M. Le

[2]For example: E. Hocedez, *Histoire de la théologie au XIXe siècle*, volume III, *Le règne de Léon XIII*, Brussels, 1947; E. Lecanuet, *La vie de l'Église sous Léon XIII*, Paris 1930; J. Rivière, *Le modernisme dans l'Église*, Paris, 1929; also from the modernist side, A Houtin, *La question biblique chez les catholiques de France au XIXe siecle*, 2nd edn, Paris, 1902.

[3]On Fr Lagrange, see F. M. Braun, O.P., *L'oeuvre du P. Lagrange, Étude et bibliographie*, Fribourg, 1943; *L'oeuvre exégétique et historique de R. P. Lagrange*, in *Cahiers de la Nouvelle Journée*, fasc. 28, Paris, 1935; cf. also the article by Fr. H. Vincent, O.P., in the *RB*, 1938, pp. 321-54; also article by the present writer in *NRT*, 1938, pp. 466-72.

Camus; Jesuits like Frs Cornely (German), Corluy (Belgian), Knabenbauer (German), van Kasteren (Dutch); Dominicans like Frs Didon, Faucher, Lacôme, Ollivier, Scheil; secular priests like Abbés Batiffol, Hyvernat, Thomas and Jacquier.'[4] Finally, in 1900, Fr Lagrange was in a position to announce the project of a complete commentary of a scientific nature on Holy Scripture. In 1902 the first volume of the series appeared, the *Livre des Juges* by Fr Lagrange. The immense services rendered to Catholic exegesis by the weighty volumes of *Études bibliques*, which have come out regularly down to the present day, being continually republished and highly esteemed by Scripture scholars everywhere, is well known.

Another development, for which Abbé Vigouroux, the principal representative of the conservative school, was responsible, was the foundation in 1891 of the *Dictionnaire de la Bible;* the last part of which was published in 1912. In spite of its deficiencies, the excessively and scrupulously conservative nature of its articles, the too restricted attention paid to certain fields like biblical theology—the article on 'faith' (*foi*) runs to only a page, the same length as that on 'liver' (*foie*) immediately following—the *Dictionnaire* rendered real services to Catholic exegesis. M. Vigouroux's principal fault was to keep his extensive erudition on oriental matters and his biblical exegesis in watertight compartments, without attempting to use the former to renew and deepen the latter. M. Vigouroux became in 1903 the secretary of the Biblical Commission and, in collaboration with Dom Laurent Janssens, signed its decrees until 1912 (he died in 1915).

A third development, already an indication of the thought of its originator, was the publication in 1892 by Alfred Loisy, who had been teaching Scripture at the Institut Catholique since 1884, of a review popularizing for a wider public the main points of his exegetical teaching. This was *L'Enseignement biblique*. Alfred Loisy was remarkably gifted as a philologist and exegete, possessed a shrewd and penetrating mind but evinced also a marked tendency on the one hand to a hypercritical scepticism and on the other to an ingenuous trust in his own conjectures. His methods of research were very personal and he might indeed have done much to promote the advance of exegesis provided he had kept under control certain tendencies of his intellectual temperament and had been sustained

[4]F. M. Braun, O.P., *L'oeuvre du P. Lagrange*, 1943, p. 31.

in his scientific endeavour by a more extensive and profounder theology. From the first his teaching at the Institut Catholique was outstanding. In 1890 he published his thesis for the doctorate, *Histoire du canon de l'ancien Testament;* in 1891 came *Histoire du canon du Nouveau Testament.* In 1892 and 1893 he published, as was mentioned, *L'Enseignement biblique.* Very soon his teaching and writings became the subject of bitter controversy and it was to defend this professor of the Institut that Mgr d'Hulst, its rector, published in *Le Correspondant* (25 January 1893) the article on the biblical question which provoked the Encyclical *Providentissimus.* Alfred Loisy's later works, together with his entire intellectual attitude, did immense harm to the progress of Catholic exegesis; mistrust was engendered in many minds and among certain ecclesiastical authorities against progressive tendencies in exegesis considered to lead inevitably to deviations of the same kind.[5]

Works of Catholic research and developments of all kinds continued indefatigably during this fruitful period. There can be no question of listing here the many individual works of value which were published at this time, but it will certainly be of interest to chronicle according to the year of their commencement the various collective undertakings—series of works, encyclopaedias, reviews, which first saw light between 1890 and 1914 together with the names of their originators or principal collaborators; they form a striking proof of the hard work which characterized this period.

At the head of the list must be placed certain reviews then already in existence for some time which played a part in exegetical research or in the controversies of the period with which we are concerned.

The *Theologische Quartalschrift* was founded at Tübingen in 1819 as the organ of the faculty of Catholic theology at the University, a faculty which, throughout its long history, gave to Catholic scholarship many theologians and Scripture scholars of great value (cf. above p. 41 and below, p. 129); on the editorial committee, between 1890 and 1914 figured P. Schanz, Scripture scholar, theologian and writer in apologetics (d. 1906), F. X. Funk, well known for his work in patrology (d. 1908) and J. Belser, New Testament scholar (d. 1916).

[5]The present writer attempted a short appraisal of Loisy's work and methods in a chapter of *Sous les yeux de l'incroyant,* 2nd edn, pp. 191-214: 'La défection d'Alfred Loisy'. On the same subject the following provide useful information: M. J. Lagrange, *M. Loisy et le modernisme,* Paris, 1932 and the pages devoted to Loisy in J. Rivière, *Le modernisme dans l'Eglise,* Paris, 1929. The two following works were written in defence of Loisy's memory: M. D. Petre, *Alfred Loisy. His religious Significance,* Cambridge, 1944; Fr. Heiler, *Der Vater des katholischen Modernismus Alfred Loisy* (1857-1940), Munich, 1947.

The French Jesuits' review, founded in 1856, which in 1862 adopted the title *Études religieuses, historiques et littéraires par les Pères de la Compagnie de Jésus*, was to play a by no means negligible rôle in the exegetical controversies of 1890-1914, at first with a conservative tendency with Frs L. Méchineau and J. Brucker, and then gradually adopting a cautiously progressive line under Frs F. Prat, A. Durand and (after 1900), J. Lebreton and L. de Grandmaison, who became editor in 1908.[6]

The *Zeitschrift für katholische Theologie* (Innsbruck Jesuits) was founded in 1877; among its collaborators in New Testament exegesis between 1899 and 1907 was Fr L. Fonck, S.J., who in 1909 was entrusted with the organization and direction of the Pontifical Biblical Institute.

The *Bulletin critique de littérature, d'histoire et de théologie*, founded in 1881 by Abbé Trochon, was edited for a great part of this period by E. Beurlier, L. Duchesne, L. Lescoeur, H. Thedenat, A. Baudrillart whose reviews and critical notices at that time exercised a powerful influence in Catholic circles.

1892. *Revue biblique* of the Dominican Fathers in Jerusalem. Its great value and the important part it has played in Catholic biblical work, some of its principal collaborators and articles of moment from the time of its establishment were mentioned above.

1895. *Biblische Studien*, published at Freiburg by Herder. An exegetical journal founded by Otto Bardenhewer and at first edited by him and then by J. Göttsberger and J. Sickenberger. In it appeared many contributions of value to Catholic exegesis: among its collaborators may be mentioned, P. Schanz, J. Belser, B. Bartmann, A. Bludau, Fr von Hummelauer, N. Peters, M. Faulhaber, J. Nikel, H. Herkenne, M. Meinertz, F. Maier, F. Tillmann, A. Schulz, H. J. Vogels, S. Landersdorfer and H. Höpfl.

1895. *Revue du clergé français*, edited after 1898 by Abbé Bricout (Paris, Letouzey). It is mentioned here because it contained many exegetical articles and was actively concerned in the evolution of ideas and the controversies of the period. It ceased to appear in 1921.

1896. *Bibliothèque de l'enseignement de l'histoire ecclésiastique* (Paris, Gabalda). Among the first volumes published were: Pierre Batiffol, *Littérature grecque chrétienne*; Paul Allard, *Le Christianisme dans l'Empire Romain*; R. Duval, *La Littérature syriaque*; J. Tixeront, *Histoire des dogmes* (several volumes).

1896. *Revue d'histoire et de littérature religieuses*, founded at the instance of Abbé Loisy with Paul Lejay as secretary. It was to take an active part in the modernist movement, publishing several articles that were rightly condemned by ecclesiastical authority and was obliged to suspend publication in 1907. A. Loisy, having left the Church, revived it in 1910 and edited it until 1923.

1899. *Dictionnaire de théologie catholique* (Paris, Letouzey) edited by Abbés Vacant and Mangenot. It was conceived on a more extensive scale and with wider scope than the *Dictionnaire de la Bible* of Vigouroux, and was destined to render great

[6]The *Nouvelle Revue Théologique*, founded in 1869, during this period was a review devoted to moral theology and canon law; its only intervention in the controversies of this period was by the publication in extenso of the acts of the Holy See—Leo XIII's Encyclical *Providentissimus Deus* in 1893, the Encyclical *Pascendi* and the decree *Lamentabili* (Latin text and French translation) in 1907 etc. It was only in 1926, under the direction of the Jesuit theological college at Louvain, that it widened its scope to all branches of ecclesiastical science.

services in the scriptural field as in the other sacred sciences. Its publication was to continue for more than fifty years and it is a lasting monument to Catholic scholarship.

1900. *Revue d'histoire ecclésiastique* founded at the University of Louvain by Professors Cauchie (Church history) and Ladeuze (patrology and New Testament exegesis). Its calm objectivity and broadness of views, both in conception and realization, quickly obtained for it respect and trust in all scholarly circles; among its exegetical collaborators at this time were A. Camerlynck, H. Coppieters, F. X. Funk, P. Ladeuze, E. Tobac, A. van Hoonacker.

1901. *Studi religiosi*, an Italian progressive review, founded by Minocchi, Semeria and Buonaccorsi; unfortunately, it developed an increasingly modernist tendency.

1902. *Études bibliques* (large octavo volumes). The series opened with Fr Lagrange's *Livre des Juges* (1902) and *Isaie* (1905) by Fr Condamin, S.J., *Choix de textes assyro-babyloniens* by P. Dhorme (1907), *Les douze petits prophètes* by A. van Hoonacker (1910), *Les livres de Samuel* (1910) by P. Dhorme, *Saint Marc* (1911) by Fr Lagrange, O.P., *L'Ecclésiaste* (1912) by E. Podechard (1914), *Canaan d'après l'exploration récente* (1914) by H. Vincent, O.P. In 1957 the series comprised upwards of forty volumes in large octavo.

1902. *Theologische Revue* (Münster, Aschendorff), founded by Professor Diekamp with the collaboration of other professors of the theological faculty at Münster. Its principal aim was the review and critical appraisal of theological works, including those on exegesis.

1902. *Theologische Studien der Leogesellschaft* under the editorship of the professors of the theological faculty of the University of Vienna, Ehrhard and Schindler; among the collaborators in exegesis between 1902 and 1914 may be mentioned M. Faulhaber and J. Döller.

1903. *Biblische Zeitschrift* founded by J. Göttsberger (professor of Old Testament exegesis) and J. Sickenberger (professor of New Testament exegesis). Its policy from the first was one of avowed progress in exegesis allied with an informed theological viewpoint.

1904. *Bibliothèque de théologie historique* of the Institut Catholique in Paris. In this series appeared *Théologie de saint Paul* by F. Prat, S.J. (1st edn, 1908) and *Origines du dogme de la Trinité* by J. Lebreton, S.J. (1st volume; principally exegetical, 1909).

1906. *Revue pratique d'apologétique* (Paris, Beauchesne) under the direction of Baudrillart, Guibert, Lesêtre, etc. Although it was only occasionally concerned with the Bible it must nevertheless be mentioned here on account of several articles of importance by Frs de Grandmaison, S.J. (on the development of dogma), Lebreton, S.J. (on the study of Christian origins, modernism and the origin of apologetics), the famous controversy between Frs Tyrrell and Lebreton and scriptural articles by Touzard, Lesêtre, Lepin, Rivière, Bardy, etc.

1907. *The Catholic Encyclopaedia.* Begun in 1907, this encyclopaedia, published in New York, for exegesis and theology included several contributors from Europe. It comprised fifteen volumes and two volumes of indexes and supplements.

1907. *Revue des Sciences philosophiques et théologiques* (founded and edited by the Dominican Fathers of Le Saulchoir). Its high philosophical and theological standard is well known. Its notes on biblical theology were written by Fr A.

Lemonnyer (1907-14); among the Scripture scholars collaborating during these first years may be mentioned Frs B. Allo, P. Dhorme, P. Synave (Dominicans); P. Ladeuze, Frey, C. F. Jean, F. Buzy.

1908. *Biblische Zeitfragen*. This series was founded and edited by J. Nikel (Old Testament) and I. Rohr (New Testament). Less technical than the *Biblische Studien* and intended for a wider public, it is often very useful on account of its synthetical approach and the high standard of its popularization. In it will be found, for example, general studies on the period of the letters of Tell el Amarna (K. Miketta), on the excavations in Palestine (P. Karge), the excavations of Mesopotamia (T. Witzel, O.F.M.), on Hellenism and Judaism in the last century before Christ (P. Heinisch) and many works of biblical theology, adapted especially to the teaching needs of the seminaries of this period, by J. Nikel, F. Tillmann, Fr Maier, J. Döller, etc.

1909. *Dictionnaire apologétique de la foi catholique*, founded by Fr A. d'Alès, S.J. Conceived and carried out with a keen sense of the apologetic needs of the times and a happy choice of informed collaborators, it contained many articles of value on exegesis and biblical theology (among others, those by d'Alès, Condamin, Coppieters, Durand, de Grandmaison, Höpfl, de La Brière, Lebreton, Lemonnyer, Lepin, Mangenot, Prat, Tobac, Touzard, Vaccari, etc.).

1909. *Theologie und Glaube*, the organ of the faculties of philosophy and theology of the seminary at Paderborn: between 1909 and 1914 it contained exegetical studies by N. Peters, F. Feldmann, A. van Hoonacker, K. Pieper, A. Schultz, F. Tillmann, I. Benz, P. Dausch, A. Eberharter, M. Meinertz, K. Holzhey, J. Göttsberger.

1910. *Alttestamentliche* and *Neutestamentliche Abhandlungen*. These two series, the first under the editorship of J. Nikel, the second of M. Meinertz (both published, up to the present day, by Aschendorff at Münster) were destined to render great service to Catholic exegesis. In both series four volumes appeared before 1914 with works on the Old Testament by P. Heinisch, P. Karge, J. Feldmann, etc. and on the New Testament by M. Meinertz, A. Steinmann, K. Pieper, H. Bertrams etc.

1910. *Recherches de Science Religieuse*, founded by Frs de Grandmaison, S.J., and J. Lebreton, S.J., has throughout its history and right up to the present day preserved the openness of mind and the high standard of its two founders. During the short period 1910-1914 studies and notes on progress in New Testament exegesis appeared by J. Lebreton, various biblical articles by Frs J. Calès, A. Durand, F. Bouvier, A. Condamin, J. Huby, F. Prat.

1910. *Freiburger Theologische Studien*, the organ of the theological faculty of Freiburg, was founded by G. Hoberg and G. Pfeilschifter and is still appearing. From the beginning it contained exegetical work by A. Allgeier, H. Schumacher, E. Kalt, L. Gaugusch.

1912. *Die heilige Schrift des Neuen Testaments*, founded and edited by F. Tillmann, soon came to be known as the Bonn Bible (Hanstein). Its intention was to provide a wide public (priests and educated layfolk) with a commentary of high standard on the New Testament, written by specialists and, on this account, of use to Scripture scholars also. At the outset occurred an episode which is a good indication of the difficulties of exegetical work at this period, menaced by fear of the errors of modernism. F. Maier had undertaken the commentary on the first three

Gospels; his explanations, which today would no longer give rise to any criticism, at that time appeared to be rash, especially on account of his solution of the synoptic problem. The bishop demanded the suspension of the publication after the appearance of the first fascicules; the editor of the dictionary was obliged to entrust another scholar, P. Dausch, with the interpretation of the three synoptic Gospels. The whole of the New Testament Commentary was completed between 1912 and 1919 in ten stout volumes. In 1923 was added a similar series for the Old Testament: *Die Heilige Schrift des Alten Testaments*; these volumes have been republished, revised and brought up to date on many occasions up to the present day. They have proved very useful.[7].

The *Pontifical Biblical Institute*, founded in 1909, could only begin the publication of its reviews and series after the 1914-18 war; but it is necessary to point out here its important contribution to biblical studies. In order of date may be mentioned: the quarterly review *Biblica*, specially devoted to exegesis and the history of the Old and New Testaments, begun in 1920, the series *Orientalia* (*Commentarii de rebus Assyro-Babylonicis, Arabicis, Aegyptiacis, etc.*) 1920; the bimonthly review, in Latin, intended for the clergy, *Verbum Domini*, also in 1920; the review *Orientalia*, published three times a year since 1932.[8]

The only reason for furnishing this long list has been to show clearly the Catholic effort at collective work under the pontificates of Leo XIII and Pius X, since it is the fruits of this effort that contemporary exegesis is now reaping. Both the daring endeavours of some, and the excessive timidity of others are nowadays enlightening for us; men must feel their way, sometimes make mistakes, hesitate on occasion before seeing their way clear. This anxious quest, carried on in the thick of a sometimes bitter conflict of ideas and tendencies merits closer examination.

And this brings us to the second part of our study dealing with the conservative and ecclesiastical objections, of a doctrinal or historical and positive nature, which at that time were raised against the application by Catholics of the new critical methods. We shall examine these objections to see how far they were right, farseeing and

[7]In *NRT* after 1926 will be found reviews of most of the volumes of both these series.

[8]Exegetical progress and production between 1890 and 1914 makes this period in the history of Catholic theology one of the most interesting and fruitful periods of the scientific revival. To show clearly the manifold aspects of literary production and printed exegetical work during the period would have meant exceeding the limits of a book of this sort, and that is why attention has been confined to the publication of the many collective works of Catholic exegesis as a sign of the work accomplished. But the printed literary work was only a part of the exegetical work of this period. It would also have been significant to study the effort for a scientific revival in oral biblical teaching in universities, seminaries and theological colleges. In this sphere also in many places there was carried out work that was solid, done in obscurity, often under difficulties but often, too, remarkably fruitful for the training of exegetes of the future.

lasting and also how far some of them were only a traditional opinion, passively received and conscientiously defended, but which discussion and the progress of ideas would serve to correct and illuminate. It is by the wholesome clash of human ideas that in every field progress is achieved, for it leads to results most rapidly and effectively, to the extent that men's minds are more open, more understanding of the ideas of others and free from violent partisanship and narrow zeal. Such, unfortunately, was not always the state of affairs in the exegetical conflict during these critical years. The Church included at that time men of deep faith and keen critical sense who certainly at the outset encountered opposition and were tried sometimes by distressing ecclesiastical measures, but in whom the Church, both hierarchy and faithful, gradually came to recognize the true interpreters of her teaching and in whom she placed increasing confidence. The greatest of these at this period from the exegetical point of view was, I think, Fr M. J. Lagrange, O.P.[9]

Conservative and ecclesiastical objections and the Catholic effort at a solution

To begin with, we consider the objection which was the most fundamental and the most frequently repeated but which unfortunately is also the vaguest and as a result the least adapted to concrete instances and profound tendencies: 'Your critical methods spell rationalism.' Of course, it is undeniable that the basis of liberal Protestant criticism was often a radical rejection of the supernatural, an exclusively rational conception of the history of Israel and of the origin of Christianity. But it is also undeniable that to seek to understand the work of God here below in its historical contingencies, to follow it in its human evolution and causalities, to discover the dates, the characteristics, the ancient form of the inspired writings by means of tried critical methods, to estimate the historical form and the moral and religious ideas of these books in the light of the milieu and period and of the whole body of

[9]On Fr Lagrange see the bibliographical details in note 3. Biographies of other scripture scholars or theologians of this period can be read with profit, for example, J. Lebreton, S.J., *Le Père Léonce de Grandmaison*, Paris, 1932; J. Calès, S.J., *Un maître de l'exégèse contemporaine, le Père Ferdinand Prat*, S.J., Paris, 1942; J. Coppens, *Le Chanoine Albin van Hoonacker*, Bruges, 1935; J. Coppens, *Paulin Ladeuze, exegeet en oriëntalist*, Brussels, 1940; J. Colsen, *Poels*, Ruremonde, 1955. Also worth consulting: J. Guitton, *Portrait de M. Pouget*, Paris, 1941 and many portions and notes in the two volumes: *Correspondance: Maurice Blondel-Auguste Valensin*, 1899-1912, Paris, 1957.

semitic literature, to seek the sources of these books and the critical value of these sources, it is undeniable that all this is a sound interpretation of the human element in God's plan, of the sort that God requires of our intelligence created by him and called to go to him by way of everything that we are.

Another criticism often—and rightly—urged against certain Catholic exegetes at this period, especially against those who were later to leave the Church, was their failure to appreciate the theological implications of the problems raised. The separation of exegesis and theology was often made into a principle by several Catholic critics of this period. 'We endeavour to establish the facts by the ordinary methods of history; we leave it to the theologians to adapt their principles and their requirements to these established historical facts.' This was to lose sight of the considerable part played by religious or irreligious assumptions in historical convictions; anyone who examines facts spontaneously includes them in his personal experience of facts of this kind, and this experience is conditioned by what he has been and what he is. The materialist economist will see the living reality of history differently from one who is not a materialist; the same facts will appear in a different light to these two judges. And the divergences will become acute when it is a question of religious facts, and still more acute when these are supernatural facts which are only to be understood historically in the light of the supernatural viewpoint. Of course, this supernatural viewpoint can never hide from us the reality and complexity of natural causality; it is not enough to be a strictly speculative theologian, it is also necessary to be a clearsighted historian, a complete man. But no one is a clearsighted historian of religious matters if he is incapable of seeing them in their essential aspect, the religious aspect made clear by their doctrinal content, whether dogmatic or theologically interpretative. This lack of theological and philosophical training was one of the causes of the eventual modernism of several Catholic scripture scholars of that time. And it has been one of the clear gains of religious history and exegesis, both Catholic and Protestant since 1918, that Christian theology has once more found its way into the interpretation of Christian events.

Another and equally frequent objection took a shrewder form: 'Your exegesis deviates from the living interpretations of the Church as it has been handed down during the centuries; it disagrees with

the interpretation of the Fathers of the early centuries.' This objection lasted for some time because it contained considerable truth as
well as a profound misunderstanding. It was based on a fundamental confusion between the general spirit of ecclesiastical and
patristic interpretation and the technical details of a particular
exegesis. Thus it is certain that the traditional notion of the choosing
of the people of Israel, of the divine revelations (whatever precise
form they took) which enlightened and guided them, and of God's
plan leading up to Christ, the Son of God, must remain the Christian
exegete's unchanging basic rule. And it is certain that understanding
of Christ, as Saviour and Son of God, and a grasp of the teaching
of Paul and John, reached in patristic literature a loftiness and depth
that can never be set aside. But it is no less certain that the knowledge of ancient history and geography, biblical ethnography and
ancient methods of historical narration, possessed by the Fathers
and older interpreters of Scripture, could no longer be considered
on the same level with the new knowledge at the service of critical
exegesis. Modifications due to more recent knowledge of this sort did
not imply a modification in the Christian view of history as it is
shown to us by the Fathers and doctors of the Church but an
adaptation of its spirit within a new setting. In the light of these
former controversies there emerges the full significance of Pius XII's
statement that few texts of Scripture have been defined by the
Church and that those passages in which the unanimous interpretations of the Fathers imposes a definitive interpretation on modern
exegesis are rare.

A further serious objection untiringly raised against every Catholic
critical endeavour appears to be more intricate: 'You are under-
mining the fundamental principle of the inerrancy of Scripture.'
This objection was raised at every stage and the effort to answer it
contributed not a little in clearing the way for legitimate progress.

In the first part of the nineteenth century the objection was
couched in the scientific context, from the point of view of the
agreement between faith and the natural sciences. It was urged that
geology, in the order and length of the stages of evolution of the
universe and of the earth that it shows us, contradicts the first
chapter of Genesis, the work of the six days of creation. And so were
worked out the system of days being equal to eras and the many
attempts at 'concordism'; in this view, the Bible far from being

contradicted had been in advance of modern scientific discoveries. This was a naïve speculation which could not be upheld for long. The making of man's body by God from the slime of the earth (in Genesis 2) was thought to exclude for ever every evolutionary theory applied to the human body. In reading page after page of many theologians of repute, repeating these ideas in every possible form, one is painfully struck by the great gulf between them and fourth-century theology, by the breadth of view and openness of mind of St Augustine in comparision with modern timidity. And the impression becomes more painful still in reading the nineteenth-century theologico-scientific passages on the possibility of Jonas remaining three days in the whale's belly, on the geographical or ethnographical universality of the flood. The repulses suffered in these fields had, like the unfortunate condemnation of Galileo, a fortunate result: Catholics began to understand that the Bible had not been written to anticipate the progress of science but to lead man to eternal salvation. And Leo XIII, in the Encyclical *Providentissimus*, laid down clearly that the Bible did not claim to give expression to a scientific explanation of the universe but to a judgement based on the appearances as they are manifested to our human senses.

The objection based on the inerrancy of Scripture in the realm of science was not very formidable and fairly quickly disposed of; it caused more difficulty and was overcome more slowly in the realm of ancient history. Religious respect for the Bible had habituated many minds readily enough to attribute a more definite, more certain historical value to the data provided by it than to the records of history or of archæology. Traditional biblical chronology, fixing creation in 4004 B.C., was still regarded by many as beyond doubt, when Accadian and Sumerian history disclosed civilizations at an advanced stage and giving evidence of a lengthy past in the fourth millennium B.C., or when, still more clearly, prehistory was able to put back the existence of man to dates far earlier, dates which have continued to recede as a result of further research. At the beginning of the twentieth century textbooks of oriental history were still being given to Catholic students which began the history of Egypt with the arrival of Mizraim (Mesraim), son of Ham, and endeavoured to connect this initial event with the most ancient evidence then known of the history of Egypt.

It is easy enough to understand, then, the astonishment and the scandal caused to many when the ancient narratives of Genesis—history of origins, history of the patriarchs—or the other books of the Pentateuch, Josue or Judges, began to be studied by contemporary criticism in regard both to their literary and historical forms, according to the same methods and with the same criteria that had been employed for the other works of ancient literature. It is true that Catholic exegetes observed and rightly pointed out the religious superiority of the Israelite history of origins over similar Accadian or Sumerian accounts; they discreetly emphasized the transcendence in Israel of the ideal of God, of the idea of the covenant of love between Yahweh and his people, in comparison with contemporary Semitic thought. But how could they honestly, and in accordance with their conscience as sincere historians, solve the strictly historical problem confronting them of the character of these ancient narratives and their popular, discursive, legendary manner of narrating the past of a nation? For several of these scholars, who keenly realized the difficulty, the temptation was strong to have immediate recourse to the easiest solution of limiting scriptural inspiration, or at least biblical inerrancy, solely to religious or moral truths. But the tradition of the Church on this point was too constant, unanimous and clear to countenance such a limitation. Moreover, religious authority, after the Encyclical *Providentissimus Deus* of Leo XIII (1893) energetically forbade it. Gradually, then, under the combined pressure of Christian tradition on the one hand and historical objectivity on the other, there emerged from the efforts of the most conscientious and competent exegetes the first explanations which, after the setbacks and progress usual in the movement of ideas, were to find approval in the Church. For example, in about 1900 was formulated the system of 'implicit quotation' which openly raised the problem of 'sources', of the investigation and critical study of sources for inspired history as for all history written by man; gradually also there emerged the system of 'literary forms' in history which was progressively tried after the end of the nineteenth century and systematically formulated by Fr Lagrange in his Toulouse lectures (November, 1902). The Encyclical *Divino afflante Spiritu* explicitly sanctioned this principle of literary forms in history.

Nevertheless, with the emergence of these two systems, the complexity of the problem of inerrancy in historical matter was far from being fully solved. But they did form at that time a first intuition of a wider, more fundamental truth: sacred Scripture, God's message, was written by men, in human language, at specific periods and in particular surroundings, both periods and surroundings being freely chosen by God. Once more in Christian theology we are brought face to face with its central mystery which governs its whole internal structure, the dogma of the Incarnation, the dogma of God made man, of the Word made Flesh. It has never been easy for man perfectly to reconcile these two aspects of Christian reality; the heresies of the first Christian centuries, from Docetism which did away with the human reality of Christ and Ebionism which diminished his divinity, down to the great Christological heresies of the fourth and fifth centuries, were erroneous reconciliations of these two aspects. Scriptural progress in the twentieth century consisted in a better understanding of the part played by the man, the actual man, in his milieu and period, in the expression of God's message, without sacrificing any of the divine value of this message. In the course of this volume this point recurs frequently.

Such were the principal doctrinal objections raised between 1880 and 1914 against the biblical criticism of Catholic scholars. This account was not intended to be complete but only to indicate by means of a few examples the general tendency of the conservative opposition, to show what was of value in it to ensure safe progress and what was gradually superseded and finally left behind as outmoded.

Before going on to consider some of the positive objections pertaining to literary and historical fact it seems important to point out that any advance in exegetical work in the Catholic Church must be made in close solidarity with the faithful. The Church progresses slowly because she constitutes a whole people going forward. The fastest must match their pace with the ability of the body of Christian people to follow, and the hierarchy has always aimed at maintaining the balance of religious thought throughout the various groups entrusted to it. One of the weaknesses of nineteenth-century German Protestantism was the gulf between the liberal tendencies of most of the universities where the pastors were trained and the unimpaired traditional faith of the parishes entrusted to these pastors. On account of its organization such a situation could not arise in the Catholic Church; intellectuals on occasion have to suffer by it, but such trials bear fruit for the following generation.

The literary and historical factual objections were many and varied. Some of them are mentioned here in their logical order, but there is no intention of giving a chronological list of the various controversies.

In the first place must be considered the questions concerning the literary authenticity and date of the inspired writings. The controversies on these matters are reflected in the first replies of the Biblical Commission: June, 1906, on the Mosaic authorship of the Pentateuch; May, 1907, on the Johannine authorship of the fourth Gospel; June, 1908, on the authenticity of the second part of Isaias (Chapters 40-66); May, 1910, on the Davidic authorship of a certain number of Psalms and on the dates and nature of the Psalms in general; June, 1911 and June, 1912, on the authenticity and mutual relations of the synoptic Gospels; June, 1913, on the authenticity of the Acts of the Apostles and the pastoral Epistles; June, 1914, on the Epistle to the Hebrews. All these replies were intended for the guidance of Catholic teaching in seminaries and universities, the purpose for which the Commission was instituted. They took in general a negative form, laying down that the critical objections against the literary authenticity of the writings in question were, according to the case, incapable of invalidating this authenticity or insufficiently established to compel the abandonment of this authenticity; thus with slight differences of degree they cautioned Catholic teachers against pure and simple acceptance of the arguments of biblical criticism on the subjects studied.

On many points the future was to show the way more clearly. After the 1914-18 war criticism itself returned to more conservative positions concerning the date of many of the sapiential writings and of various Psalms; the authenticity of the Acts of the Apostles as the work of Luke was admitted by an increasing number of critics. On the other points, like the composite authorship of the Pentateuch, Catholic exegesis was constrained to accept the arguments of the critics and to adopt a wider interpretation of the Commission's replies (2-4) on the Pentateuch (DZ 1998-2000). The reply on the second part of Isaias was substantially the most reserved of the Commission's decisions (DZ 2115-9); it consisted in saying that the critical arguments did not compel (*cogere*, DZ 2118) the traditional position to be given up, that they did not definitely solve the problem (*evincere*, DZ 2119). Fifty years later Catholic exegesis is tending increasingly to the date of the exile (586-538) or immediately afterwards as the period when Isaias 40-66 was written.

There can be no question here of tracing the history of the discussions between Catholics on the problem of the author and date of the Pentateuch, the Psalms and the second part of Isaias. Here the questions were of a purely literary nature requiring solution by historical, philological and literary methods; they did not directly concern doctrine. The divine message of Isaias 40-66 remained untouched whether these chapters were written in the eighth century by the prophet Isaias or in the sixth century by other inspired prophets. What was at stake was the tradition concerning the authors and dates of these books; but this tradition was not a dogmatic tradition handing down a dogma of faith from one century to another. It was in this direction that, in 1955, on the publication of the second edition of the *Enchiridion Biblicum*, the present secretary and under-secretary of the Biblical Commission were to guide the interpretation of the decrees of the period 1906-14. The matter is referred to again below.

One of the useful results of these controversies was the establishment of a clearer distinction between dogmatic tradition and mere literary tradition. Yet it is a pity that so much time was required for this distinction to prevail everywhere in all minds.

More serious were the problems raised on the content of the sacred books.

Concerning history and the various popular forms of ancient history something has been said above in dealing with inerrancy. Throughout this period, and almost to the time of *Divino afflante Spiritu* Catholic exegesis did not dare to attempt a synthesis in this field. There were of course monographs on matters of detail, assessments of the histories of Israel written by Protestants, essays on the oriental milieu and the setting of the history of Israel, but there was no scientific history of Israel written by a Catholic. It was impossible

for one to be written as long as the suppositions on the character of
the oldest biblical historical books had not been clarified.

We come now to doctrine, the theological problems raised by the
Old Testament. Three of these may be mentioned here from among
many which formed the subject of many critical studies during these
years and on which Catholic biblical scholars were obliged to adopt
a definite position either in books and articles, if they considered the
ground sufficiently clear for them to proceed or, in any case, in their
university and seminary teaching. The first problem was that of the
monotheism of Israel. The classical critical view was that the
religion of Israel at the time of Moses was only monolatry, that
Yahweh was the God of Israel as Kamosh was of Moab, and Baal
of Canaan. From monolatry Israel only went over to monotheism
(Yahweh the only God of the universe) gradually under the influence
of the prophets after the eighth century. The second problem was
that of the evolution of the priesthood and centralization of worship
in the temple at Jerusalem. By the distinction of sources in the
Pentateuch with, consequently, the different dates distributed over
the centuries for the legisation therein contained, independent
criticism was led to fix successive stages in the historical development
of the priesthood and formal worship in Israel. What was thought
to have been established as the law of God at the time of Moses,
in this view had only been attained in part at the time of Josias,
in the second half of the seventh century and only completely at the
time of Esdras (458-432). The task of Catholic exegesis in the face
of this new problem was exceedingly complex. The third problem
concerns the history of the expectation of better times in the future,
of messianic hope in Israel. Catholic apologetics had grown accustomed to group together in a logical rather than a chronological
synthesis those texts of the Old Testament traditionally regarded
as foretelling Christ, the Messias. This expressive arrangement of
texts, widely known through textbooks and preaching, had assumed
in traditional thought a sacred, inviolable character. Put back into
their immediate historical context all were not quite so obvious as
they had appeared. Some of them showed evidence of misinterpreta-
tion, others were no longer valid save in the spiritual, typical sense.
Of course, substantially the hope of better times, the messianic
expectation, remained one of the characteristic features of the
religion of Israel in the last centuries before Christ, but in its new

form this outline was obviously different from that formerly put forward; and certain texts became the subject of heated argument as if the whole of Christianity was at stake in each one of them. Here again the task confronting Catholic exegesis was by no means easy.

But the most anxious and difficult task confronting Catholic exegesis was to show in the face of increasing denial the supernatural character of the work of Christ and of the origin of Christianity. It is enough to read the decree *Lamentabili* of the Holy Office (3 July 1907) to observe that the sixty-five errors of modernism there enumerated were almost all concerned with the person and work of Christ and that almost all implied in their authors a radical and definitive opposition between the Christ of history and the Christ of faith. This went to the very heart of Christianity and every really Christian exegete, closely attached to his faith with all his intelligence, whether his tendencies were conservative or progressive, perceived at once that the modernist error was the very denial of Christianity. The principal representative of French modernism in exegesis was, as is well known, Alfred Loisy; the propositions condemned in the decree *Lamentabili* for the most part are taken from his books and articles. The tendencies of his thought and his earlier works were mentioned above. At this point we can confine ourselves to a general estimation of his method and that of the modernist commentators on the New Testament. It was always too narrow, seeking unconsciously, under the pressure of doubt or unbelief, to reduce the thought and action of Christ to the human level of our personal experience of men and things. By an erroneous scruple of critical objectivity it declined in any historical judgement about Christ candidly to consider the supernatural explanation required by faith of a consciousness which is both in time and transcends time. For we must honestly and boldly accept in our historical studies the explanation which faith offers us concerning Christ, if we are to be able to see that it alone provides the supreme vindication and the most perfect synthesis of the historical data, and if we are also to see that the Christ of faith corresponds perfectly with the Christ of history.

Chapter IV

RELIGIOUS AUTHORITY AND THE BIBLICAL MOVEMENT: 1890-1914

AT THE beginning of this study it was stated that the ecclesiastical documents concerning the Bible collected together in the *Enchiridion Biblicum* (2nd edn) occupy thirty pages relating to the period before 1890 and 230 from 1890 to 1953. This fact alone is clear evidence of the very great importance of this period in the history of Catholic exegesis and the gravity of the problems raised. Between 1890 and 1914 three major interventions of ecclesiastical authority require close study for a better understanding of the biblical movement in the Church and of the Church's reaction to this movement.

The first intervention was by Leo XIII in the Encyclical *Providentissimus* in 1893 right at the beginning of the Catholic effort at a more advanced exegesis; the setting up of the Biblical Commission in 1902 was its complement. The second intervention, in its essential form, occurred in 1907 with Pius X's Encyclical *Pascendi* against modernism and the decree *Lamentabili*, condemning sixty-five propositions tainted with modernism or reformism; it was completed by other measures, for example, the project of a critical revision and new edition of the Latin Vulgate (1907) and the foundation of the Pontifical Biblical Institute (1909). As the third intervention are grouped together here the various replies of the Biblical Commission between 1905 and 1914.

The Encyclical Providentissimus (1893)

The Encyclical *Providentissimus* (18 November 1893) although occasioned by certain keen controversy in France as a result of an article by Mgr d'Hulst (see above, p. 46) was meant principally, according to Leo XIII's intention, as an exhortation and a positive direction for a more intensive, efficacious and up-to-date study of Scripture among the Catholic clergy. ('For a long time we have

cherished the desire to give an impulse to the noble science of holy
Scripture and to impart to Scripture study a direction suitable to the
needs of the present day. The solicitude of the apostolic office
naturally urges and even compels us to desire that this ground
source of Catholic revelation should be made safely and abundantly
accessible to the flock of Jesus Christ.') The Encyclical was also
intended as an authoritative reminder of the Catholic principles of
biblical exegesis; yet this reminder was in no wise couched as a
reproval or condemnation; it was quietly inserted into the introductory remarks as required by the nature of the subject under
discussion.

The Encyclical may be divided and summarized as follows:

After showing the excellence of Scripture (*EB*, 2nd edn, nos. 81-7)
and recalling what the Church through the Fathers, the medieval
theologians and the popes has done to promote Scripture studies
(88-99), Leo XIII states his desire to ' impart (to the bishops) such
counsels as seem best suited for carrying on successfully the study of
biblical science' (100). For this purpose he draws attention to the
opponents, whom he calls the 'rationalists', all of whom are assumed
to be outside the Catholic Church, and to their assertions, to the
harm they cause to souls (Nos. 100-01); hence the need to oppose
this false science with 'the ancient and true science, which the
Church through the apostles has received from Christ' (102).

At this point begin the directives given by Leo XIII.

First directive. Teaching of holy Scripture in seminaries and universities must be in accordance with the importance of this science and
the needs of the present time. Hence, (a) professors of Scripture must
be well chosen and adequately trained (103); care must be given to
(b) the method of giving the introductory course on Scripture (104)
and (c) the choice of the portions of Scripture to be explained, so as to
avoid the two extremes of error ('the mistake of giving a mere taste
of every book, and of dwelling at too great length on a part of one
book'); passages to be chosen and explained with a suitable fullness so
that students 'may learn from the sample put before them to love and
use the remainder of the sacred books during the whole of the rest of
their lives' (105); (d) teaching must be based on the Latin Vulgate.
'At the same time other versions, which Christian antiquity has approved, should not be neglected, more especially the original texts.'
(e) rules of scriptural interpretations: in addition to the rules for

the interpretation of any ancient text (107) attention must be paid to what is peculiar to Scripture as the work of the Holy Spirit, to the divine mysteries contained in Scripture, and to the other meanings underlying the literal sense ('moreover the literal sense frequently admits other senses'). Then there is the religious obscurity in which the sacred books are wrapped; hence no one can begin their study without a guide; God has entrusted the Scriptures to the Church so that in the interpretation of his words she may be our guide and teacher. Hence the Vatican Council renewed the decree of the Council of Trent (DZ 786) 'declaring its "mind" to be this—that in matters of faith and morals, pertaining to the building up of Christian doctrine, that is to be considered the true sense of holy Scripture which has been held and is held by our holy Mother the Church, whose place it is to judge of the true sense and interpretation of the Scriptures; and therefore none should interpret holy Scripture in any other way or contrary to the unanimous opinion of the Fathers.' Leo XIII continues: 'This most wise decree . . . by no means prevents or restrains the pursuit of biblical science, but rather protects it from error, and greatly assists its real progress.' It is the exegete's duty to conform to this rule. Other points of doctrine, for which there is no authentic interpretation, will be explained in accordance with the analogy of faith; Catholic doctrine, as authoritatively proposed by the Church, should be held as the supreme law (Nos. 108-9).

In addition, the professor of Scripture 'must be well acquainted with the whole of theology and deeply read in the commentaries of the holy Fathers and Doctors, and other interpreters of mark'. There must be respect for the exegesis of the Fathers, though this does not prevent the commentator, for reasonable motives, pushing his inquiry and exposition beyond the exegesis of the Fathers. Nor must the allegorical sense given by the Fathers to certain texts be neglected, especially when this interpretation arises naturally from the literal sense and rests on a great number of authorities. No doubt the authority of other Catholic commentators is less, but given the continual progress of biblical studies in the Church their commentaries must be given that honour which is their due.

It is not fitting that in ignorance or contempt of the remarkable works which Catholics have left in abundance the exegete should prefer to them the books of non-Catholics. 'Although the studies of non-Catholics used with prudence may sometimes be of use to the Catholic scholar, he should nevertheless bear well in mind that the sense of holy Scriptures can nowhere be found incorrupt outside the Church and cannot be expected to be found in writers who being without the true faith, only know the bark of sacred Scripture and never reach its pith' (110-3).

Second directive. 'The whole teaching of theology should be pervaded and animated by the divine Word of God.' The reasons adduced for this directive are the example of the Fathers and the greatest theologians, the nature of Catholic dogma and theology which are essentially derived from the sources of revelation, the apologetical value of Scripture, as evidence, in the proof of the mission and divinity of Christ, of the constitution of the Church and the primacy of Peter (114-6).

Third directive, motivated principally by present-day rationalism; the Church must be provided with defenders specially trained to wield the critical weapons used by her opponents. For this purpose:

(a) In the first place these defenders need to make a profound study of oriental languages, especially of Semitic languages—hence the obligation in universities of setting up special chairs for the study of these languages—and a solid initiation theoretical and practical in the art of criticism. At this point Leo XIII protests against the excesses of 'higher criticism' which in discussions on the origin, integrity and historical value of the sacred books relies on the intrinsic character of the work and pays no attention to historical evidence although this 'witness of history is of primary importance'; insistence on the internal evidence alone leads inevitably to disagreement and dissension and the reflection of the bias and the prejudice of the critics (117-9).

(b) Next, there is the need to contend against the abusive use made of the natural sciences to attack the inerrancy of the Scriptures. Leo XIII, after pointing out that there can be no real discrepancy between the theologian and the scientist as long as each confines himself to his own province, quotes the passage from St Augustine[1] stating that the inspired writers, or more accurately, 'the Holy Ghost who spoke by them did not intend to teach men these things, that is to say the essential nature of the things of the visible universe, things in no way profitable for salvation'. Leo XIII continues:

[1] *De Genesi ad litteram*, II, 9, 20.

'Hence (these writers) did not seek to penetrate the secrets of nature, but rather described and dealt with things in more or less figurative language or in terms which were commonly used at the time, and which in many instances are in daily use at this day, even by the most eminent men of science.' Just as in ordinary speech words are used to describe what comes under the senses, so the sacred writer 'went by what sensibly appeared'.[2] In matters of this kind the commentator is not bound by the interpretations of the Fathers who expressed the ideas of their own times, though in their interpretations we must carefully note what they laid down as of faith or as intimately connected with faith and in what they are unanimous. For in those things which are not *de necessitate fidei* the saints could hold divergent opinions just as we can (120-2).

(c) Leo XIII then goes on to consider history, using to link the two paragraphs the well-known phrase which has caused much discussion: *Haec ipsa deinde ad cognatas disciplinas, ad historiam praesertim, iuvabit transferri* ('These [principles] here laid down, it will be useful to transfer to cognate sciences, and especially to history'— 123).

This section of the Encyclical *Providentissimus* is possibly the one which was most considerably completed and added to by the Encyclical *Divino afflante Spiritu*. In 1893 Catholic exegesis still lacked valid solutions to the historical problems and objections raised by contemporary criticism; many of those who were most keenly aware of the real difficulties, in contradiction with traditional principles of interpretation, had endeavoured to find solutions either by proposing the limitation of inspiration or the limitation of inerrancy merely to the truths concerning faith or morals. Leo XIII at this point protested against these unjustifiable attempts. In addition, in 1893 the Thomist notion of inspiration, which safeguarded far better the real, complete causality of the human author, as the free instrumental cause, under the action of God, the principle cause, had not yet found full acceptance in all the theological schools; 'dictation' of the Scriptures by God was commonly spoken of, an expression that is nowadays carefully avoided. On these two points theological progress, from the Encyclical of 1893 to that of 1943, seems undeniable. Consequently, Leo XIII's underlying intention of applying in the historical field solutions in line with those he had proposed in

---

[2] St Thomas Aquinas, *Summa Theol.*, para. I, qu. LXX, art. 1 ad 3.

the field of physical science could only be fully realized by his successor in 1943.

We can now continue our summary of the Encyclical.

Leo XIII protests against the biased tendency he frequently finds in rationalist criticism which unhesitatingly trusts ancient books and books and documents of profane history but evinces instinctive distrust towards Scripture. He then draws attention to the two primary tasks to be performed by any critic who encounters historical difficulties: he must make certain of the accuracy of his text so as to remove the possibility of error by copyists; he must also make certain of the real meaning of the text thus freeing it from more or less traditional but inaccurate interpretations. But it is forbidden to resort to the limitation of inspiration to certain parts of Scripture or to admit that the sacred author himself was mistaken: 'It is absolutely wrong and forbidden either to narrow inspiration to certain parts only of Holy Scripture or to admit that the sacred writer has erred. For the system of those who, in order to rid themselves of those difficulties, do not hesitate to concede that divine inspiration regards the things of faith and morals, and nothing beyond, because (as they wrongly think) in a question of the truth or falsehood of a passage we should consider not so much what God has said as the reason and purpose which he had in mind when saying it—this system cannot be tolerated. For all the books which the Church receives as sacred and canonical are written wholly and entirely, with all their parts, at the dictation of the Holy Ghost; and so far is it from being possible that any error can co-exist with inspiration, that inspiration is not only essentially incompatible with error, but excludes and rejects it as absolutely and necessarily as it is impossible that God himself, the supreme truth, can utter that which is not true.'

This is the faith of the Church, defined at the Councils of Florence and Trent and repeated and formulated again at the Council of the Vatican whose definition is quoted at length in the Encyclical (*DZ* 1787).

Leo XIII continues: 'Hence because the Holy Spirit employed men as his instruments, we cannot therefore say that it was these inspired instruments who perchance have fallen into error and not the primary author. For by supernatural power he so moved and impelled them to write—he was so present to them—that the things which he ordered, and those only, they first rightly understood then willed faithfully to write down, and finally expressed in apt words and with infallible truth. Otherwise it could not be said that he was the Author of the entire Scripture.' This teaching is then confirmed by quotations from St Augustine and St Gregory and by the method, which is given as an example, in which the Fathers formerly endeavoured to solve the difficulties of Scripture (123-7).

(d) The many and extensive branches of history and science, which in fact are needed for an adequate technical defence of Scripture, exceed the powers of one man, theologian or exegete. Therefore Leo XIII calls on the specialists in these sciences so that on occasion they may lend their aid to the Church in the defence of Scripture. He also praises the steps taken to provide funds for the training of Catholic specialists in these various branches. He exhorts the Catholic defenders of Scripture to be firmly convinced that God, the creator of nature and the inspirer of the Scriptures, cannot contradict himself; an apparent contradiction between a scriptural statement and a scientific or historical statement cannot be absolute and definitive, since truth cannot contradict truth; there may be error in our interpretation of the scriptural statement or error in the scientific or historical assertion that contradicts it; many of the objections to the Scriptures in the past have now disappeared since they were worthless; in the same way a certain number of explanations formerly put forward of scriptural texts which did not concern faith or morals have been corrected by a more careful study of the true sense of the texts (128-32).

The Encyclical concludes with an exhortation to the bishops to apply these directives; they must seek to promote scriptural studies everywhere; all priests are exhorted to apply themselves to the reading and understanding of the Bible with reverence and devotion.

'Given at Rome at St Peter's on 18 November, 1893, in the sixteenth year of our pontificate.'

The Encyclical *Providentissimus* appeared at a time when Catholic exegesis was still painfully feeling its way in the face of the serious problems raised by independent criticism. The Encyclical, intended essentially as an urgent call to thorough study of the Bible, far from slowing down or impeding exegetical work, on the contrary strengthened and encouraged what was already being done and provoked new developments. This emerges very clearly from the intensity of the Catholic biblical movement during the last ten years of Leo XIII's pontificate. The two fundamental principles recalled by Leo XIII (the inspiration of the whole of Scripture in all its parts and inerrancy extending to the whole of Scripture and not merely to the statements concerning faith and morals) were repeated by Pius XII with the same clarity in 1943 as in 1893. The emphasis laid on these two principles in 1893 was a great advantage for the future; it laid down clearly the limits within which Catholic scholarship was to seek the solution to the historical problems raised. On the other hand, by offering in the light of a quotation from St Thomas a possible solution to the difficulties drawn from physical science founded on 'the terms commonly used at that time' and by adding to this solution a passage from St Augustine pointing out that the teaching on the essential nature of the things of the visible universe was 'in no way profitable to salvation', Leo XIII guided Catholic biblical studies towards the solution of historical literary forms in conformity with the usual mentality of the period. This solution was gradually developed by the leading Catholic scholars and sanctioned by Pius XII in 1943.

In its concrete application of the facts of revelation to the new aspects of human culture, which is one of the duties of the Church, a pontifical Encyclical is necessarily bound up with the intellectual climate of its milieu and period, a milieu and period which it must guide along the way leading to God. It recalls the eternal principles of Christian truth according to the stage of progress of Christian thought reached at that moment of history and with the purpose of preparing more effectively for the morrow the further progress of the world in Christ *usque ad plenitudinem aetatis Christi*, which is the purpose of the Redemption. It is in the context of this efficacious development and progressive enlightenment that the beneficial character of the authority of the Church is best understood. And it appears clearly from a comparison of the two Encyclicals *Providentissimus Deus* and *Divino afflante Spiritu*, the second completing the first and only being possible as a result of it. *Providentissimus* was more dogmatic than exegetical, thus reflecting the tendency of contemporary Catholic exegesis which as a whole remained more dogmatic and theological than critically historical. *Divino afflante Spiritu* was clearly more exegetical and historical and was written in the light of the critical advances of Catholic exegesis of the preceding fifty years.

It is no part of our task to study here the reaction of critical or Catholic opinion to the papal Encyclical of 1893; to understand what it meant for biblical scholarship of the period compare Alfred Loisy's judgement on it[3] in his *Mémoires*, 1930, volume I, Chapter XI, 'L'encyclique Providentissimus' (pp. 302-9, judgement of the Encyclical; pp. 311-5, his letter of submission and memorandum justifying his position; pp. 317-8, Rome's reply; Chapter XII, pp. 331-40, 347-8; 351-8, reactions in England: articles in the *Contemporary Review*) with the article by Fr M. J. Lagrange, O.P., 'A propos de l'encyclique Providentissimus' in the *Revue biblique*, January, 1895, pp. 48-64. Fr Lagrange there reviews recent Catholic studies of the Encyclical—those of Fr Brucker, S.J. in *Études*, Abbé C. Robert and Canon Didiot of Lille (he also quotes an article from the *Gazette de France*). The particular interest of Fr Lagrange's study lies in two points; firstly, the attempts of the writers he studies to proceed from Leo XIII's remarks about natural science to reasoning of the same kind about history; secondly, the fundamental conclusions that Fr Lagrange personally draws from the Encyclical of the need for the extension and intensification of biblical studies in all seminaries and Catholic universities.

The establishment of the Biblical Commission (1902)

Leo XIII in setting up the Biblical Commission (Apostolic Letter, *Vigilantiae*, 30 October 1902) had primarily and especially in mind the advance of biblical studies. All that is known of the influences which led him to establish it, the choice of Fr David Fleming, O.F.M., as Secretary, the names of the forty-one consultors chosen for the greater part from among progressive scholars,[4] the initial project of choosing the Jerusalem Dominican Fathers' *Revue biblique*

---

[3]A. Loisy, who in this passage waxes ironical at some length about the Encyclical and rejects it 'as an unacceptable programme for men of learning' (p. 308) adds at once, however, that Leo XIII in writing it 'believed that he had done an enlightened and praiseworthy work'; 'thought that he had made provision for later scriptural studies in the Church'. We need not dwell on Loisy's ironical remarks, but he was not mistaken about the constructive intentions on the part of Leo XIII; it is certain that the Encyclical *Providentissimus* in no wise slowed down the progress of Catholic exegesis; the fifteen following years were, as we have shown, a period of remarkable output in Catholic biblical studies.

[4]Cf. *Annuaire pontifical catholique*, by A. Battandier, VII, 1904, pp. 572-4.

as the Commission's official organ, the rules laid down for the Commission—all this shows the clear intention of this step which was meant to be constructive rather than repressive. Nevertheless, the pope intended the Commission to exercise a certain supervision and, in controversy between Catholic biblical scholars, to exercise a decisive rôle. The serious character of the modernist crisis under the pontificate of Pius X was the cause of several important changes in the tendencies and activities of the Biblical Commission.

The Encyclical Pascendi and the decree Lamentabili (1907)

At the end of the pontificate of Leo XIII and the beginning of that of Pius X, the Gospel exegesis of several progressive Catholic critics, especially of Alfred Loisy, assumed tendencies increasingly independent of traditional principles and conclusions. It was not only disagreement with certain classical interpretations of the Gospels, but Catholic dogmas that were discussed from the historical point of view and the very fact of inspiration and inerrancy was called in question. At the same time there appeared in the writings of Alfred Loisy signs of a disagreement with the Christian faith far deeper than mere divergences from classical exegesis, a disagreement his *Mémoires* later revealed to have been consummated before his clash with ecclesiastical authority.[5] The consequences arising from this state of affairs were exceedingly unfortunate for the legitimate progress of Catholic exegesis. In conservative circles all progressive exegesis was compromised by the excesses of a noisy minority which attracted all the attention; after 1900 especially, the best among the orthodox scripture scholars were brought to a standstill by the suspicion surrounding them and a decline set in among certain sectors of Catholic exegesis, becoming more marked as time went on down to the 1914 war.

The history of modernism and the various currents of thought—religious philosophy, theology, criticism and exegesis, institutional reform—which came together in this movement of ideas, are outside the scope of this book. It is well known that the Encyclical *Pascendi Dominici Gregis* intended to present a synthesis and to gather together in a logically constructed system the various tendencies, often

[5]In addition to many other signs his correspondence with Maurice Blondel (February-March, 1903) whose Christian faith was shocked by the book *L'Évangile et l'Église*, is sadly significant in this respect, while the depth of Blondel's faith emerges as strong as it is enlightened.

obscure and subconscious, on occasion experienced rather than thought out, by which certain minds were then obsessed. By taking these ideas to their logical conclusion the Encyclical showed their pernicious character which was irreconcilable with Catholic dogma.[6] But it did not thereby assert that the synthesis thus constructed was deliberately and consciously held by each of those who were then called modernist and in fact fully deserved this name.

In critical exegesis, the only subject which interests us here, Alfred Loisy's is the name legitimately regarded as the principal representative of Catholic modernism. He always denied that he was led to his critical opinions by means of a definite religious philosophy, but, like many other modernist exegetes of that time, he never realized that his method of approach to the text of the Gospels contained from the outset an implicit denial of any trans-cendence in Christ's intelligence; explicitly and immediately, by means of the texts, Loisy sought to find in every doctrinal statement of Christ's the way in which a consciousness that, in his view, was only human and limited would state the doctrine then under con-sideration. This doctrine he rethought within the limited setting of the contemporary milieu, the needs of its immediate hearers and of the circumstances of the time; whatever seemed to go beyond these requirements of the Palestinian historical context of that particular period were regarded as a projection into the text of the Gospel of the faith of the primitive Church; the 'natural man' in himself was unconsciously the basis of his historical judgement on Christ. As the Encyclical *Pascendi* rightly points out, the modernists' method 'is to put themselves into the position and person of Christ, and then to attribute to him what they would have done under like

[6]For a long time it was not known who could have been the writer so well informed about contemporary movements of ideas in France, England and Italy and about the many books in various languages giving expression to them, combining this knowledge with such a shrewdness and firmness of personal thought, as to have been the author of such a synthesis. From whom did Pius X request this work which he afterwards revised, approved and confirmed by his supreme authority? It appears, according to a well documented study by Canon Rivière in the *Bulletin de littérature ecclésiastique* of Toulouse (April-September, 1946) 'Qui rédigea l'encyclique Pascendi?' that its principal author was Fr Joseph Lemius, O.M.I., a Frenchman, born in 1860, D.D. and Ph.D., Procurator General of his Congregation in Rome, a consultor of several Roman Congregations and, after 1917, Qualificator of the Holy Office; he died in 1923. In the article quoted and in the correction of certain details (*ibid*. Oct.-Dec. 1946) will be found concrete par-ticulars about the circumstances of the writing of the Encyclical (the article is summarized in *L'Ami du Clergé*, 5 December 1946 and 17 April 1947).

circumstances'. In Gospel exegesis, however, historical objectivity demands that we should openly take into account the explanation of faith, with all its implications, if we desire to understand the reality which is the goal of our investigation, namely, the consciousness of the Man-God.

In the modernist exegetical movement, as it was represented by Alfred Loisy and a few others, two aspects require to be distinguished carefully and treated differently.

In the first place, there is that sort of 'panic'[7] which at that time seized a small number of the French and Italian clergy; the historical Christ, studied by means of a method that was unconsciously or wilfully naturalist, seemed to them irreconcilable with the Christ of faith; this Christ of faith, without the help in their thought and lives of a sufficiently extensive and profound theology and of an intense personal religious life, became progressively diminished in their religious consciousness; the dogmas about Christ and his work became blurred in their eyes and mere methods of thought, symbols, and soon for several of them formulas pure and simple. The modernists sought every means, either under their own name or various pseudonyms, to spread these destructive views, and they reached, upset and alienated from the Church young priests and seminarists. Loisy's *Mémoires*, the writings of Albert Houtin, the recently published posthumous diary (*De la foi à la raison*) by Prosper Alfaric are evidence enough of the pernicious influence of the first modernists' books and articles. Liberal Protestant and anticlerical newspapers and reviews encouraged the movement with their news items and sympathetic reports. As it developed after 1900 Modernism constituted for the Church a very great danger which could only be warded off by radical action, generally and speedily applied. The decree *Lamentabili sane exitu* and the Encyclical *Pascendi Dominici gregis* were necessary and eminently salutary measures which cut down the evil at its roots. That certain special steps taken during what was in a sense a state of siege unfortunately affected some leading personalities who were above

---

[7]This was the term used very rightly in 1908 by Fr Lebreton in a discerning article in *Revue pratique d'apologétique*, VI, p. 466, on the modernist movement: 'Certain writers willingly claim it as a conquering invasion; in reality it is a panic; it does not originate in a deeper understanding of Christianity but in a more acutely felt impression of critical objections; one after the other metaphors are used to express the panic provoked by these attacks . . .'

all suspicion cannot be denied, nor that a narrow and short-sighted society, organized by narrow-minded reactionaries for the purpose of delation to the Holy Office was at work for some years.[8] Benedict XV's formal censure in his encyclical *Ad beatissimi Apostolorum Principis* (1 November 1914) revealed its existence and brought it to an end. But it remains true that the speed and firmness of the repression of modernism by Pius X saved the Church and, as even the leading modernists realized, entirely arrested the movement within the Church.

The second aspect to be mentioned, distinct from the first, is the nature of particular propositions contained in the decree *Lamentabili*. Most of them were directly due to Alfred Loisy or were framed according to the tenor of his statements. The majority refer to Christian origins and raise the important question of the way in which the message of Jesus was given in history, was received and understood by the primitive Church and is in agreement with what the Church believes and understands today. From the historical point of view it is a fundamental problem of Christian

[8]An incident of the 1914-18 war brought by chance to the knowledge of historians a significant part of the secret documents belonging to this undertaking. A search carried out in 1915 for political reasons at the house of a lawyer at Ghent, by the German government then occupying Belgium disclosed a whole secret correspondence, of pre-1914 years, between the head of the undertaking, Mgr Benigni, and his informer at Ghent. The letters which passed between these correspondents made constant use of pseudonyms: thus the pope was called *Maman, Michel* etc.; Cardinal Merry del Val, *George :* the bishops, *tantes* (aunts), priests, *neveux* (nephews); Benigni signed himself as *Arles* and called his informer *mon cher Junius* (my dear Junius) ; and so on. The organization was called *La Sapinière* (fir plantation). It was painfully obvious that the organization avidly sought every possible indication (actions, private conversation etc.) which could be denounced by various means to the Roman authorities and thus cast suspicion on certain persons in high places or those engaged in various work who were regarded as insufficiently conservative or tainted with modernism. In Belgium leading personalities like Cardinal Mercier, Mgr Ladeuze, Rector of the University of Louvain, Fr Rutten, O.P., were attacked; abroad Cardinal Amette, archbishop of Paris, Mgr Faulhaber, the Dominican theological faculty at Fribourg (called 'a broth of modernistic tendencies'), the Jesuits of the *Civiltà Cattolica* ('mealy mouthed ferrets') etc. The later history of these documents does not concern us here, nor how they came to the knowledge of historians like Abbé Mourret in France, how a considerable part of the photographs ended up in the episcopal archives of Ruremonde. The clear declaration repudiating all such manœuvres by Benedict XV at his accession brought such odious campaigns to a close; but they reveal the painful atmosphere that narrow-minded Integrists endeavoured to foment in ecclesiastical circles. Cf. on this organization, L. J. Rogier and N. de Rooy, *In Vrijheid herboren. Katholiek Nederland 1853-1953*, The Hague, 1953, pp. 523-33; cf. also certain complementary details in J. Colsen, C.M., *Poels*, Ruremonde, 1955, pp. 531-4 and certain documents and information in the polemical pamphlet by N. Fontaine, *Saint-Siège, 'Action Française' et 'Catholiques intégraux'* p. 57, note 4, and pp. 138-53.

exegesis, apologetics and theology; at the end of the nineteenth century and in the twentieth this problem was raised in a form far more acute than ever before. Its solution with real historical objectivity and exact dogmatic and theological understanding is just as much our duty now as it was in 1907. After upwards of half a century Loisy's narrowness and deficiencies of method can be seen more clearly, as too can be seen certain deficiencies and gaps in the methods of the period previous to his and against which he reacted by going to the opposite extreme. In the Church a condemnation by the very fact of its being the rejection of an error is the indication of a problem that has been raised and at the same time guidance towards its true solution.

The replies of the Biblical Commission

The Biblical Commission, as was pointed out above, was regarded by Leo XIII as an instrument of progress in biblical exegesis intended to provide secure and effective guidance to the Catholic teaching of holy Scripture. The two secretaries named in 1903 (January) were M. Fulcran Vigouroux, a French Sulpician and Fr David Fleming, O.F.M., an Irishman; the former was of conservative tendency, the latter more progressive. The Cardinals composing the Commission were in 1903 Rampolla, Satolli, Segna and Vivès y Tuto; Cardinal Merry del Val, chosen by Pius X as Secretary of State, was soon added to their number. After the death of Cardinals Satolli (d. 1910), Segna (d. 1911), Vivès y Tuto (d. September, 1913), and Rampolla (d. 1913), at the end of 1914 the Cardinals of the Biblical Commission were Van Rossum, Merry del Val, Lorenzelli, Serafini and Gasquet. The forty-one consultors chosen in 1903 represented several countries and various shades of opinion in the Catholic exegetical movement. Other consultors were appointed during the years following.

The two first replies of the Biblical Commission (13 February 1905 on implicit quotations and 23 June 1905 on narratives only apparently historical—*narrationes specietenus tantum historicae*—in the historical books of the Old Testament, were signed by Fr Fleming and dealt temperately with two problems which in scriptural research were to assume increasing importance; the point is dealt with again in this book.

In September 1905, under the pontificate of Pius X, Fr Fleming was replaced as secretary of the Biblical Commission by Fr Laurent Janssens, O.S.B., a Belgian theologian. After this date all the decrees of the Commission until 1914 (and beyond) appeared under the signatures of Fulcran Vigouroux, P.S.S. and Laurent Janssens, O.S.B.

Obviously this is not the place to study and interpret the many replies of the Biblical Commission between 1906 and 1914; they concerned almost all the literary problems of authorship, date and integrity of the inspired writings; they were all drawn up in the especially difficult atmosphere of the modernist crisis; later in this book we note the discreetly qualified interpretation semi-officially given in 1955.[9] At this point mention is confined to a simple list of the replies with a short indication of their subject-matter; a footnote indicates the pages of this book where the problem dealt with by the Commission is mentioned.

Old Testament. On the Mosaic authenticity of the Pentateuch (27 June 1906; Moses the author of the Pentateuch essentially speaking, either directly or by means of writers approved by him: *EB*, 2nd edn, 181-4; *DZ* 1997-2000).[10] On the authenticity of chapters 40-66 of Isaias (29 June 1908: 'no decisive argument for the attribution to another than Isaias'; *EB*, 2nd edn, 291-5; *DZ*

[9]After the progress in research and the advance in ideas achieved between 1900 and 1943 this interpretation became necessary. Non-Catholic Scripture scholars have pointed out and emphasized the different spirit of the outlook and phraseology of *Divino afflante Spiritu* and the outlook and phraseology of the Biblical Commission in its replies. During the months preceding his death (October 1945) the Protestant Scripture scholar Hans von Soden wrote his impression of the Encyclical *Divino afflante Spiritu*, intending them probably for publication (it took place after his death in the second volume of *Urchristentum und Geschichte*, pp. 177-94 with the title 'Papst Pius XII über die zeitgemasse Förderung der Biblischen Studien'); he summarized the Encyclical objectively and at length, being fully aware of and pointing out its qualities of intellectual comprehensiveness and desire for scientific progress, but then compared these directives with the replies of the Biblical Commission: of 1906 on the Mosaic authenticity of the Pentateuch, of 1908 on Isaias's authorship of Chapters 40-66 of the book which bears his name, of 1909 on the historical character of the first three chapters of Genesis, of 1910 on the Davidic authorship of the greater number of Psalms. He showed clearly the logical assumptions of the Encyclical in comparison with the logical assumptions of some of these replies. We do not believe that the opposition between the two can today be denied; if Pius XII's directives had already been in existence and could have been experienced by the ecclesiastical mentality prevailing between 1906 and 1914 more than one of the Commission's answers would have been couched in different terms. In the Church, as in every human society, the legitimate progress of ideas must be allowed the time to form and bear fruit gradually. What is essential is to be aware of the fundamental advance ensured by divine guarantee despite human imperfections that are inevitable.

[10]See above, pp. 26-8, 57-8; below, pp. 116, 124, 127, 181-4, 185-6.

2115-9).[11] On the historical character of the first three chapters of Genesis (30 June 1909: the substantial historical truth of these events of the origin of human history but (*DZ* 2123) maintaining the literal historicity of certain features as *formatio primae mulieris ex primo homine* . . .; *divini praecepti, diabolo sub serpentis specie suasore, transgressio: EB*, 336-43; *DZ*, 2121-8).[12] On the Davidic authenticity of the greater number of the Psalms (1 May 1906: *praecipuum Psalterii carminum David esse auctorem: EB* 344-51; *DZ* 2129-36).[13]

New Testament. On the Johannine authenticity and historical truth of the Fourth Gospel (29 March 1907: *EB* 187-9; *DZ* 2110-2). On the author, date and historical truth of the Gospel according to St Matthew (19 June 1911; *EB* 388-94; *DZ* 2148-54. On the authors, dates and historical truth of the Gospels according to St Mark and St Luke (26 June 1912; *EB* 395-403; *DZ* 2155-63). On the synoptic problem (26 June 1912: *EB* 404-5; *DZ* 2164-5). On the author, date and historical truth of the Acts of the Apostles (12 June 1913: *EB* 406-11; *DZ* 2166-71). On the author, integrity and date of the pastoral Epistles of St Paul (12 June 1913: *EB* 412-5, *DZ* 2172-5). On the author and manner of composition of the Epistle to the Hebrews (4 June 1914: *EB* 416-8; *DZ* 2176-8). On the Parousia or second coming of our Our Jesus Christ in the Epistles of St Paul (18 June 1915; *EB* 419-21; *DZ* 2179-81).

[11]See above, pp. 29, 57-8.
[12]See below, pp. 181-4, 185-6.
[13]See above, p. 57; below, pp. 116-17.

CHAPTER V

THE DEVELOPMENT OF ARCHÆOLOGY AND THE AUXILIARY BIBLICAL SCIENCES FROM 1918 TO THE PRESENT DAY

THERE HAS been a notable progress in the extent and depth of the auxiliary biblical sciences since the end of the 1914-8 war. The following aspects of them deserve notice.

Since 1918 archæological excavations have developed in a way surpassing all previous calculations, and both the older and more recent results have been increasingly significant in the collective labour of deciphering and interpreting the many written documents brought to light, especially the discoveries at Qumrân since 1947. Egyptian papyri, numerous and in good condition thanks to the dryness of the soil, have helped Christian literature and the Bible, as well as secular literature, both Greek and Egyptian. The textual criticism of the Old and New Testaments has not only perfected its methods since the end of the nineteenth century, but has been enriched by fresh manuscripts of the Bible from Egypt and, since 1947, from Palestine itself. Patristic exegesis has profited from fortunate discoveries of lost works, and in certain aspects has been studied more thoroughly, in particular with regard to the evolution of the New Testament text. And to conclude this summary I must draw attention to the most striking and rewarding outcome of scientific Biblical study in the twentieth century: exegetes have come to know better the men of former ages, with their particular way of speaking, narrating and writing.[1] This is essential if we are to understand correctly the inspired interpreter in human terms of the divine message.

[1]We have based the arrangement of this chapter on the six trends in scriptural studies in the twentieth century, which Pius XII listed in a key passage of his encyclical *Divino Afflante Spiritu* (1943), which is quoted in full in chapter VII below. It was Pius XII himself who drew the attention of Catholics to the progress of scientific research in the twentieth century; and he emphasized as a chief result of this progress the improved knowledge of the human discourse of men of former times.

1. *The remarkable development of archæological excavation since* 1918.[2]

After the 1914–18 war the Arab countries of the Middle East were freed from Turkish domination; Lebanon and Syria were established as autonomous states under the French mandate, in the name of the League of Nations; Iraq and Palestine came under the British mandate; and this state of things lasted until the Second World War. It was a very favourable situation from an archæological point of view; a number of excavations were begun and developed with unparalleled intensity; archæological institutes and schools of various countries (France, Great Britain, the United States, and in time the indigenous national societies), often helped financially by the mandatory states or by the funds of societies for scientific research, competed in enthusiasm and competence and were enabled to bring their discoveries to the notice of historians and archæologists in detailed publications more rapidly than had hitherto been possible.

It is not my purpose to give here a general picture of these researches and their results; as in the preceding chapters, I shall simply try to show by means of some sufficiently characteristic examples, what great influence archæology exercised on biblical exegesis during those years. And, once more, it is not a question of proving by parallelisms and over-simplified interpretation of documents, that 'the Bible was right'. The aim is, in the light of these discoveries, to get to know and to give definition to the concrete modalities of the truth of the message of Scripture, in its environment

[2]Short general bibliography. In addition to the works quoted above (p. 7), for Egypt (p. 8), for Mesopotamia (p. 11), especially for the Sumerian countries (p. 16) and Palestine (p. 19), the following general works on the archæological excavations and their results, begining with 1915, should be added: C. M. Watson, *Fifty Year's Work in the Holy Land*, London, Palestine Exploration Fund, 1915; G. A. Barton, *Archeology and the Bible*, Philadelphia, 1916; C. M. Cobern, *The New Archæological Discoveries and their Bearing upon the New Testament*, 1st edn, 1918, 9th revised edn, 1930; J. Garrow Duncan, *Digging up Biblical History. Recent Archæology in Palestine and its bearing on the Old Testament*, 2 volumes, London, 1931; H. V. Morton, *Through the Lands of the Bible*, London, 1938; A. Parrot, *Découverte des mondes ensevelis*, Paris-Neuchâtel, 1952,; *Cahiers d'Archéologie biblique* (nine numbers to date), Paris-Neuchâtel, 1952, and other works which will be quoted below; L. Woolley, several works quoted below; W. Keller, *The Bible as History*, London, 1958; cf. also: *L'Ancien Testament et l'Orient. Études présentées aux VIes Journées bibliques de Louvain* (September, 1954) in *Orientalia et Biblica Lovaniensia* I, Louvain, 1957. In the *National Geographic Magazine*, December 1956, supplement, there is a map of the ancient East showing sites of excavations. Relevant bibliographical details for each excavation are given in the course of this chapter.

and epoch, so as to understand better the human presentation of the message of God.

Egypt

In 1922 Howard Carter discovered the famous tomb of Tutan-khamen, a pharaoh of the eighteenth dynasty. With a wealth of detail—clothing, furniture, artistic achievement, religious painting—it displayed the court life of an Egyptian monarch of the fourteenth century before the Christian era, at the time when Jacob's descendants were living in the Egyptian land of Goshen.[3]

During twelve years of excavation at Tanis (the residence of the twenty-first dynasty) Pierre Montet[4] discovered and identified several royal tombs of the twenty-first and twenty-second dynasties, in particular that of Psusennes (eleventh dynasty: contemporary with Saul and David) whose mummy was enclosed in three sarco-phagi, one within the other, of silver, black granite and rose-coloured granite. Montet, with much probability, identified Tanis with Avaris the fortified capital of the Hykos kings; he thought that Tanis was also Pi-Ramses, the royal residence of Ramses II (probably the Pharaoh of the Exodus: nineteenth dynasty), a town which, according to Exodus I. 11, the Israelites were compelled to assist in building. (Others identify Pi-Ramses with Quantir).[5]

The proto-Sinaitic inscriptions discovered in the Sinai peninsula, the first of them by Flinders Petrie, the rest (in 1930) by the American expedition of Sarabit-el-Khadim, inscriptions which seem to date from the reign of Amenemhat III (end of the nineteenth and beginning of the eighteenth centuries) do not directly concern Biblical studies, but they have a vivid bearing on the history of the alphabet. Various attempts have been made to interpret them—among others, by H. Grimme since 1923. To obtain an initial idea of them it will be sufficient here to refer to the articles in RB, 1933,

[3]H. Carter and A. Mace, *The Tomb of Tut-ankh-amon*, London, 1923.
[4]Pierre Montet, *Tanis. Douze années de fouilles dans une capitale oubliée du Delta égyptien.* Coll. Bibliothèque Historique, Paris, 1942.
[5]The excavations at Saqqarah, a cemetery fifteen miles south of Cairo (1923-8) under the direction of Cecil Firth, do not directly concern the Bible; but the discovery of a temple of Zozer, the first king of the third dynasty, of his tomb as well as that of the last king of the second dynasty, show once again the high perfection of ancient Egyptian art in these first centuries of the third millennium before Christ.

p. 303 and in the *Museon* (G. Ryckmans) 1932, p. 157 ff; and for more complete study to the *Harvard Theological Review*, 1932, pp. 95-203; to the work of the explorers of 1930: Starr and Butin: *Excavations and Proto-Sinaitic Inscriptions at Sarabit-el-Khadim* in 1936 and to the various works of H. Grimme in 1923, 1927, 1934 as well as to the reviews of these works in the technical journals.

Egyptian investigations bear more significantly on the Bible through the manuscripts and papyri that have been discovered. I will return to these later.

Southern Mesopotamia

Investigations in the regions of Sumer and Accad with the aim of a better understanding of the evolution and mutual relations of these two advanced civilizations, have increasingly extended the history of the Middle East through the third and fourth millennia B.C. as far as the most ancient proto-historic periods. Before the stages of Mesopotamian civilization characterized by cuneiform writing (hence bringing the investigation on to the plane of history in the strict sense, from +3000 B.C.), archæological excavations have brought to light earlier proto-historic stages in these regions.[6] These have been designated by the names of the towns where they were first encountered: first, the most ancient, the Obeid period (Tell-el-Obeid near Ur; Hall's excavations in 1919 and Woolley's in 1924); then the Uruk period (Warka: German excavations in 1912-3 and 1928-39); then the period of Jemdet-Nasr (near Kish; excavations by M. E. Mackay and S. Langdon: 1925-6); lastly, the dynastic-archaic period which corresponds to the (more or less mythical) dynasties of Ur previous to the Royal Tombs and the first dynasty of Ur.[7]

---

[6]Cf. G. Contenau, *Manuel d'archéologie orientale*, volume IV, *Les découvertes archéologiques de* 1930-39, Paris 1947, pp. 1938-2040.

[7]These proto-historic periods are of great interest for the history of the progress of human civilization in these regions. In the book by G. Contenau, quoted above, there is a singularly thought-provoking comparison (pp. 2060-84). The ancient eastern world of the fourth millennium and the beginning of the third: it is between these proto-historic periods in Mesopotamia and the contemporary periods in Egypt (the end of the predynastic period and the Thinite period in Egypt correspond to the Uruk and Jemdet-Nasr periods), in Crete and in the Aegean islands, in the civilization of the Indus, in Iran etc. It is particularly instructive to follow, in these far distant times, the progressive formation of writing, from the hieroglyphics of Uruk, Jemdet-Nasr and archaic Ur, to the later cuneiform writing. (cf. the table in Contenau *loc cit* p. 1825).

After the Second World War, four even more ancient periods were unearthed (especially in the most northern part of Mesopotamia) and this brings us to the fifth millennium and the very threshold of pre-history. These also were designated by the sites which provided the best information about them: Hassuna, Samarra, Halaf and Eridu.[8] They present problems of much interest concerning the mingling and succession of races in these regions and the influence of near-by countries such as Iran and India upon the civilization of Mesopotamia. But these problems are more relevant to the history of mankind than to that of the people of Israel, since the latter only began about 1850 (or even later?) when Abraham left Haran for Canaan at Yahweh's command.

Among the tells of Southern Mesopotamia which were studied and excavated after 1918, that which acquired the widest celebrity was certainly Tell-el-Mugheyir, the site of the ancient town of Ur, according to the Bible Abraham's original home. Already in 1854, the British consul of Bassora, J. E. Taylor, had suspected the importance of this imposing edifice, a great mound of bricks, easy to climb. Excavations began in this place in 1922. They were directed by Sir Leonard Woolley, an archæologist who had previously directed excavations in Egypt, and at Karkemish on the Upper-Euphrates. They were to last until 1933 and had remarkable results. Sir L. Woolley, an excellent writer, has given an account of them and indicated their results in a number of stimulating popular works. At the same time the official reports have been issued in large volumes with a wealth of illustration.[9]

The excavations at Ur, concurrently with those of Obeid and other towns in southern Mesopotamia and with the help of the famous Oxford prism W.B.444, completed by W.B.62, have enabled the origins of history in the lands of Sumer and Accad

[8]Cf. A. Parrot, *Découverte des mondes ensevelis*, Paris, 1952, p. 73.

[9]C. L. Woolley, *Abraham. Recent Discoveries and Hebrew Origins*, London 1936; *Ur of the Chaldees*, London, 1929 (1st edn); *The Sumerians*, Oxford, 1928 (1st edn); *The Excavations of Ur and the Hebrew Records*, London, 1929 (1st edn); *Ur Excavations: Publications of the Joint Expedition of the British Museum and of the University of Pennsylvania*. I. *Al Obeid*. II. *Royal Cemetery*, 1927 and 1934; IV, *The Archaic Periods*, 1936; V. *Ziggurat and its surroundings*, 1939. *Ur Excavation Texts*. I. *Royal Inscriptions* by C. J. Gadd, Léon Legrain, Sydney Smith, E. K. Burrows, London and Philadelphia, British Museum and the University of Pennsylvania, 1928; idem, *Plates*, Album comprising photographic reproductions (plates A-W) and copies of texts (plates I-LIX).

to be fixed with increasing precision.[10] After the first 'post diluvian' dynasties of Kish and Erech, with their legendary chronology, the first dynasty of Ur (which, according to Woolley, begins in 3100 B.C.) brings us right into history proper: its first King Mes-an-ni-Pad-da is now attested by a contemporary document.

Later on the excavations disclosed and evaluated the vast and rich constructions of the third dynasty of Ur (2278-2170, according to Woolley; 2050-1940, according to S. N. Kramer and R. de Vaux O.P.)[11], in particular the work of Ur-Nammu (Ur-Engur) its first king. They disclosed the sacred enclosure (437 yds long by 260 yds wide) for the worship of the moon-god Nannar (Sin among the Semites) and his goddess consort Nin-gal ('the great lady'), and, inside this enclosure, the remains of five temples of different periods, and the imposing staged tower, the Ziggurat (begun at the time of the first dynasty) the base of which forms a block 65 yds long, 48 yds wide and 21 yds high. It is completed by three further stages of smaller dimensions, and was rebuilt several times in the course of history. Many other religious and artistic treasures were discovered in this enclosure, showing the advanced civilization of Ur at this remote period.

The excavations outside the enclosure brought to light very fine living quarters, far superior to those discovered by the German archæologists in Babylon for the period of Nabuchodonosor. They were, said Woolley, 'two storied houses with thirteen or fourteen rooms, round a central court which provided air and light for the dwellings'.[12]

The seasons 1927-8 and 1928-9 were devoted to the excavation of the oldest cemetery within the enclosure. Woolley, basing his view on its position in the earth and on the character of the objects found, puts it before the beginning of the first dynasty of Ur and

[10]Cf. from 1924 the articles of P. Dhorme, *L'Aurore de l'histoire babylonienne* in *RB*, 1924, pp. 534-56; 1926, pp. 66-82; pp. 223-39; pp. 535-48. By the same author: *Abraham dans le cadre de l'histoire*, 1928, 1st articles, pp. 367-85, and 481-511. These articles, now dated, obviously need rectifying on more than one point as a result of 30 years archæological progress. Cf. R. de Vaux, O.P. *Les patriarches hébreux et les découvertes modernes* in *RB*, 1946, pp. 321-48; 1948, pp. 321-47; 1949, pp. 5-36.

[11]S. N. Kramer, *L'Histoire commence à Sumer*, French translation, Paris, 1957, p. 89; R. de Vaux, *article quoted*, 1946, p. 336.

[12]*Ur of the Chaldees*, p. 158; the description of these houses 'in the time of Abraham' is of lively interest and Woolley's drawing 'A house restored as in Abraham's period' has been reproduced in a number of popular works.

considers that it lasted about 300 years (thus, according to his chronology, from 3500 to 3200). The results of these two seasons of excavation surpassed all expectations, not only on account of the numerous and fine objets d'art found in the royal tombs, but especially the ghastly discovery of a number of human bodies heaped up close to several tombs, in particular those of king A-Bar-Gi and queen Shub-Ab: sixty-five bodies by the king's tomb, twenty-five by the queen's. All were carefully laid out alongside each other, all richly clothed; they must have been members of the court, and all meant to be companions of their king and queen in the world beyond. There was no trace of bodily violence, nor any sign of conflict. Woolley supposes that when the king was buried 'the victims walked to take up their position, swallowed a drug of some kind . . . and laid themselves down in good order; when the drug had produced its effect—either death or sleep—final adjustments to the bodies were made and the grave filled in' (*op. cit.* p. 57).[13]

The last great find at Ur, in 1927-9 was the evidence on the spot of a considerable flood that must have submerged the entire region. Beneath the layer in which the royal tombs were found, there appeared a wide layer of clay, varying from eight and a half to twelve feet in thickness, without any remains of human habitation. Then, abruptly, below this layer, clear indications of human life and activity reappeared. But these were characteristic of an earlier civilization, much inferior to that of the royal tombs, and rather like the pre-Sumerian civilization of El-Obeid. What was the meaning of this thick layer of clay, dating from the middle of the fourth millennium? Was it archæological evidence of a catastrophic inundation that lay behind the Sumerian and Assyrian stories of the flood and which is also recalled in the narrative in Genesis? It is not our business here to join in the discussion which archæologists are still pursuing. I shall mention only the hypothesis which A. Parrot, in 1952 described as 'the most probable' (*Déluge et arche de Noé*, p. 30): 'one of these cataclysms was accompanied by such ravages and made so great an impression that it became a theme in cuneiform literature. This was *the* flood; legend certainly magnified

---

[13]C. L. Woolley described this grisly discovery at once and in detail in *The Museum Journal*, London, March, 1928; this report was carefully summarized by P. Dhorme, *RB*, 1929, pp. 149-55.

its violence and destruction, for archæology indicates that not all the towns suffered to the same extent'. Biblical exegesis must consider this hypothesis and ask why this traditional story was again taken up by the inspired authors, with what historical presuppositions, and with what religious meaning?[14]

For the rest, it becomes increasingly clear that Sumerian thought, its literature and its idea of religion are of great significance for the history of human civilization and for the understanding of the oldest historical foundations of our Bible.[15] During the last fifty years or so, on the basis first of a large number of tablets from Nippur unearthed during the final years of the nineteenth century (cf. above p. 11 ff.), then on many texts discovered or studied more thoroughly in the twentieth century, knowledge of the men of Sumer has been laboriously built up and extended.[16] The inevitable repercussion of these fresh aspects on the interpretation of the Old Testament will be realized by everybody.[17]

[14]Cf. on this question two articles by G. Lambert, S.J. '*Il n'y aura plus jamais de déluge*', *Genesis XL.* 11 in the *NRT*, 1955, pp. 581-601 and 693-724. These give all the relevant literary and archæological documentation as well as a study of the religious problem involved.

[15]On Sumerian religion cf. the work of Charles F. Jean, *La religion sumérienne d'après les documents sumériens antérieurs a la dynastie d'Isin* (2186), Paris, 1931.

[16]S. N. Kramer, one of the specialists most competent in this matter, in his recent book of learned popularization, *L'Histoire commence à Sumer*, has tried to make clear to the general public, by a kind of annotated anthology of selected texts, translated or summarized, what the Sumerians understood by education, international relations, government, historiography, taxation, justice, agriculture, cosmology, religion, the moral ideal etc. Many details are of particular interest: for example: 'the first library catalogues', 'a plan of Nippur' about 1500 B.C. (reproduced), a table drawn up by the author of the origin and development of cuneiform writing from 3000-600 B.C. etc.

[17]The example of the excavations at Ur is enough for our purpose. It is easy to be perfectly informed about those made at *Tello* (the ancient Lagash) by Sarzec (1877-89; 1895-1900), Cros (1903-9), abbé de Genouillac (1931-3), in a fine book by André Parrot, *Tello, vingt campagnes de fouilles* (1877-1933), Paris Éditions Albin Michel, 1948. For those of *Warka* (the ancient Uruk: German excavations—Jordan, Nöldeke, Heinrich—in 1911, 1927-39) recourse may be had to the *annual* reports: *Uruk-vorläufiger Bericht*, Berlin, 1930s, or to the volumes that have been published of the *Ausgrabungen der Deutschen Forschungsgemeinschaft in Uruk-Warka*, Leipzig, 1936 ff. A short summary of each annual campaign regularly appeared in the *Fortschungen und Fortschritte* of Berlin from 1929-39.

I have summarily indicated above, p. 80, what the excavations of E. Mackay and S. Langdon at el-Oheimur (the ancient Kish) and very specially, near Kish, at Jemdet Nasr, have done to illustrate the proto-history of the Sumerians or pre-Sumerians. Cf. on this period of history; Contenau, *loc. cit*, vol. IV., p. 1276-2002 and Parrot's bibliography, *Archéologie mésopotamienne*, p. 367. In general, on the excavations of Mesopotamia, the work of A. Parrot, *Archéologie mésopotamienne* (1st vol: *Les étapes.* 2nd vol: *Technique et problèmes*) Paris, Albin Michel, 1946 and 1953, presents a very clear and solidly documented synthesis.

Central Mesopotamia and the region of the Tigris

Mesopotamian archæology began in the Assyrian regions, Nineveh, Kalah, etc. It was the period of the great power of Assur from the ninth to the seventh century that the explorers first discovered (cf. above pp. 10-11), but twentieth-century excavation penetrated much further back into history. The excavation at Tepe Gawra, fifteen miles east of Mosul (American expeditions directed by E. A. Speiser, and Ch Bache, 1927-38), succeeded in clearing successive layers of this site from the middle of the second millennium to the middle of the fourth and even, in certain borings, to the neolithic age. In this way a stratigraphy of the peak periods in Assyria became possible, by comparing them with the better documented sites of southern Mesopotamia.[18]

Further south, about twenty-five miles North-East of Baghdad, the site of Tell-Asmar, intensively excavated by Americans in 1930-6, under the direction of the Dutchman Henry Frankfort, made its own contribution to the clearer demarcation of the protohistorical-stages in Mesopotamia. Apart from this, the main significance of these excavations, together with the proof that the site was the ancient Eshnunna, was that they traced the history of Eshnunna back from 2300 to 1900 B.C., its buildings and the changes in the site up to the conquest of Hammurabi, king of Babylon.

Still further south, Yorghan Tepe (east of Assur, eight miles south-west of Kirkuk) was identified as Nuzi, a Hurrite town of the fifteenth century B.C. (It was called Gasur in the Accadian period). A number of American societies joined in subsidising the campaigns of excavations in 1927-31 under the direction first of E. Chiera, then of R. H. Pfeiffer and R. F. S. Starr. The cultural phases of the history of the town (proto-historical, from the beginning until 3000, period of Gasur culminating about 2500; period of Nuzi, 1500-1400) were able to be clearly defined. Hundreds of tablets were unearthed in the Accadian language—according to Chiera it was an Accadian spoken by non-Semites, the Hurrites, who had conquered the Accadian town. They reveal interesting analogies with certain laws and customs of the Old Testament, and one of the leading interpre-

---

[18]E. A. Speiser, *Excavations at Tepe Gawra.* Vol. 1. (Levels: I-VIII, Philadelphia, 1935, and the regular reports in the *Bulletin of the American Schools of Oriental Research.*

ters of the tablets, C. H. Gordon, wrote a stimulating article in the *RB*, 1935, p. 34-42 on these analogies: 'Nuzi parallel to the laws and customs of the Old Testament.'

The Valleys of the Euphrates and its tributary the Khabur

We read in the Bible (4 Kings 17. 6 and 18. 11) that after the taking of Samaria, the king of Assyria (Sargon) carried off its inhabitants and settled them in Halah on the Khabur, a river of Gozan, and in the towns of the Medes. This extremely fertile Khabur basin, formerly called Subartu, had been densely populated from the remotest times; the pottery found there seemed even earlier than the oldest Obeid period (cf. above pp. 80-1). It was in the heart of this region, at Tell-Halaf (on the present frontier of Turkey) that a German mission under the direction of Max Von Oppenheim made excavations in 1911-3 and 1927-9. Oppenheim believed he could establish that Tell-Halaf was, from the third millennium, the centre of a vast population, long civilized, the 'Subareans', a people so cultured, that he ranked their civilization as one of the three great civilizations of that age, alongside Egypt and southern Mesopotamia. Although this thesis is keenly controverted, there can be no doubt that the pottery found there is of great antiquity. These 'Subareans' were conquered by the Mittannians (of Indo-European race), whose kingdom held an important position in the Middle East during the second millennium. These were followed in the thirteenth century B.C. by the Arameans whose king Kapara (twelfth century) was the great builder. The strange, colossal monuments discovered during the excavations were regarded by Oppenheim as archaic (Subarean) monuments, put to fresh use by the monarch. Other archæologists consider them to be unfortunate experiments made by the architects of Kapara. About 1100 the Arameans were overcome by Tiglath-Pilesser I and in the ninth century the region became an Assyrian province and was called Guzana. Thus Tell-Halaf is a witness to those conflicts between empires and peoples which fill the third and second millennia B.C. in the Tigris and Euphrates regions. Haran, whence Abraham set out for Canaan about 1850 B.C. is less than 100 km. west of Tell-Halaf.

The most interesting excavations in the Euphrates valley have been those of Mari directed by André Parrot[19] from 1933-9.[20] The civilization of Mari, so far as it has been unearthed up to now, extends from the pre-Sargonic period to about 3200 B.C., until the conquest and destruction of the town by Hammurabi, king of Babylon (date still disputed, probably eighteenth century B.C.). At the foundations of the town's temples, dating from the most ancient period, were discovered the vast temple of Ishtar, the temples of Ninhursag and of Dagan. In the temple of Ishtar at least fifty statuettes were found, either whole or in fragments. Among them was the famous statue of the king Lamgi-Mari, frequently reproduced in books about Mari. On his right shoulder is the inscription: 'I am Lamgi-Mari.' This was discovered in 1934 and it settled the identification of the site.

The monument that made the excavations at Mari especially famous was the great palace whose size exceeded all expectations: 'the jewel of ancient eastern architecture' as Fr Vincent O.P. called it. Built at the end of the third millennium, it covered a site of some six acres (about 218 yds long by about 131 yds wide) and contained 260 rooms and courts.[21] Its state of preservation is particularly noteworthy; walls were uncovered to a height of sixteen feet, doors were intact, there were fittings that almost without repair could still function today. The last occupier before its destruction was king Zimrilin, a contemporary of Hammurabi.

During the excavations the royal archive room was discovered. Mari has provided eastern archæology with more than 20,000 epigraphic documents of great interest, most of them found in this room. This diplomatic correspondence (in Accadian and in cuneiform script) between the kings of Mari (especially the last of them, Zimrilin) and other rulers and royal functionaries throws light on many problems of ancient eastern history and archæology. For instance, the date of the reign of Hammurabi, king of Babylon, for

[19]Cf. A. Parrot, *Mari, une ville perdue.* 1st edn, Paris, 1936; 4th edn, 1948; the annual reports of the excavations in *Syria* and numerous articles, among others: 'Les tablettes de Mari et L'Ancien Testament' in the *Revue d'histoire et de Philosophie religieuses*, 1950, pp. 1-11.—C. F. Jean, 'Six campagnes de fouilles à Mari' in *NRT*, 1952, pp. 493-517 and 607-33, and with the same title, the *Cahier IX* of *NRT*, 1952, as well as other articles. Lastly, the official publication of the *Archives royales de Mari*, 4 vols. (G. Dossin, C. F. Jean, J. R. Kupper); texts and translations, Paris, *Coll. des Textes cunéiformes du Musée du Louvre.*
[20]Excavations began again after 1951.
[21]The striking aerial photograph of the palace buildings cleared by the excavations is often reproduced in works on Mari.

long thought to be in the twentieth century B.C., is, as a result of these letters of Mari, now put forward to the eighteenth century by a number of historians.[22] The excavation of Mari is of the first importance for the diplomatic, artistic, moral and religious history of the Middle East at the end of the third and the beginning of the second millennium B.C.[23]

Ancient Syria and Phoenicia[24]

Among the various excavations undertaken in these regions since 1918, two are of particular importance: those of Ras-Shamra (the ancient Ugarit, about eight miles north of Lattakia (Laodicea) and those of Jebeil (Byblos) twenty-eight miles north of Beirut.

The excavations at Ras-Shamra were due to the chance discovery

[22]On account of Genesis 14 Abraham has long been considered to be a contemporary of Hammurabi. But the tendency today is no longer to identify Hammurabi with Amraphel of Gen. 14. 1. 9; and hence the main argument for their contemporaneity falls.

[23]It may be of interest to give the general judgement of W. F. Albright on the results of the excavations at Mari, in his book: *The Archæology of Palestine* (Pelican Books pp. 236-7). 'The extraordinary discoveries of André Parrot at Mari on the Middle Euphrates since 1935 are in the process of yielding authentic information about the Patriarchal Age. Aided by finds of contemporary and somewhat later date made by Mallowan at Chagar Bazar in north-western Mesopotamia and by Chiera and others at Nuzu (Yaghlan Tepe) in north-eastern Mesopotamia, the tablets from Mari are illuminating all corners of the age at question; every new publication of theirs helps us better to understand the life and times of the Hebrew Patriarchs. Abraham, Isaac and Jacob no longer seem isolated figures, much less reflections of later Israelite history; they now appear as the children of their age, bearing the same names, moving about over the same territory, visiting the same towns (especially Harran and Nabor) practising the same customs as their contemporaries. In other words, the patriarchal narratives have a historical nucleus throughout, though it is likely that long oral transmission of the original poems and later prose sagas which underlie the present text of Genesis has considerably deformed the original events. This process of handing down the ancient tradition by word of mouth from generation to generation led to the omission of many details which would have interested a modern historian, but it also brought about a recasting of tradition in more dramatic form, emphasizing its religious and pedagogical values. Our gain is thus far greater than any possible loss.'

[24]Of less direct interest for the study of the Bible but most interesting are the excavations in the Hittite countries and their results: the discovery of the royal archives in 1906 at Boghaz-Keui (=Hattous, the ancient capital) by Winckler (cf. p. 11, note 5); the deciphering of the Hittite language, written in cuneiform script, by Hrozny, Friedrich, Götze, Delaporte, etc., after 1918; the discovery that Hittite belongs to the Indo-European group to which Greek and Latin are attached; the excavation of Djerablous (Karkemish) from 1912-4 (cf. p 14.); attempts to decipher Hittite hieroglyphics from 1931, etc. The following are easily accessible works: L. Delaporte, *Les Hittites*, Paris, 1936; article *Hittites* in Suppl. of the *Dict. de la Bible* IV. 1949, col. 32-110 and *Manuel de langue hittite*, 4 vols., 1929-33. A. Götze, *Das Hethiter-Reich*, in *Der Alte Orient*, Leipzig, 1928: J. Garstang, *The Hittite Empire*, London, 1929, G. Contenau, *La civilisation des Hittites et des Mitanniens*, Paris, 1934. O.R. Gurney, *The Hittites*, Penguin Books, London, 1952. C. W. Ceram, *Le secret des Hittites*, Paris, 1955.

of a peasant in 1928. While ploughing his field he encountered an obstacle, a tombstone, under which he found potsherds and some unbroken vases. The department of Antiquities of Syria and the Lebanon, directed by C. Virolleaud, was alerted and the excavations began in 1929. They were entrusted by the Academy of Inscriptions and Belles Lettres in Paris to F. A. Schaeffer. Eleven expeditions (1929-39) before the Second World War yielded results in plenty.[25] The entire hill, more than sixty acres, was far from being fully explored and only a few soundings had been made in the deepest layers. Since 1948 excavations have begun again and annual expeditions have followed (the eighteenth in 1954, nineteenth in 1955). Right at the start, the identification of the site with the ancient Ugarit, a very well-known city, attested by various documents of the second millennium, was seen to be beyond doubt. The site seems to have been occupied from the remotest times, at least from the fifth millennium, and the main lines of the city's history were established. One of its most flourishing periods was the fifteenth century B.C. Between 1365 and 1360 it was burnt by Etakana, prince of Qadesh. It soon rose again from its ruins and from the beginning of the thirteenth century enjoyed a new period of prosperity. At the beginning of the twelfth century it was laid in ruins for ever as a result of that terrible invasion of the 'peoples of the sea' which shook the near-East to its depths, ravaged Syria from top to bottom and destroyed the Hittite empire. Only the energetic intervention of Ramses II (twentieth dynasty, 1198-1166) brought it to a halt. He saved Egypt and Palestine. The establishment of the Philistines on the border of Israel is connected with these events.

Interest in the excavations quickly turned to the texts that were gradually unearthed. It soon became evident that the people of the city, during the principal periods uncovered by the excavations (fifteenth to twelfth centuries B.C.), must have been ethnically and linguistically very mixed. There was Accadian written in *syllabic* cuneiform characters already known and regarded as the inter-

[25]On the excavations at Ras-Shamra (until 1939) see the exhaustive study by R. de Langhe, *Les textes de Ras Shamra-Ugarit et leurs rapports avec le milieu biblique de l'Ancien Testament*, 2 vols, Catholic University of Louvain, Dissertationes ad gradum magistri, 1945. Cf. also R. Dussaud, *Les découvertes de Ras Shamra (Ugarit) et l'Ancien Testament*, 2nd edn, Paris, 1941; the annual reports (since 1929) of C. F. A. Schaeffer and C. Virolleaud, Paris, Geuthner; and the official publications of texts by Virolleaud or Schaeffer. Vol. VIII of *La mission de Ras Shamra*, edited by C. F. A. Schaeffer was published in 1956 by Geuthner.

national and diplomatic language of the time, appearing in many documents, mostly administrative. There were also other languages, similarly using cuneiform. But they also found at Ras-Shamra, together with these other languages, a system of *alphabetic* cuneiform,[26] reduced to thirty signs. These were deciphered, thanks to a combination of guesswork and insight, by Hans Bauer, Edouard Dhorme, Ch Virolleaud. It was then seen to have been chiefly used to express the local Semitic language, Ugaritic, belonging to the west Semitic group, and to its Canaanite branch, of which it represents the oldest stage yet known. It is in this language that the great mythological and legendary texts now famous were preserved, e.g. the Phoenician legend of Danel, the legend of Keret, king of the Sidonians, the mythical cycle of Ba'al; the songs of the Rephaim; many Ugaritic liturgical and religious texts, many commercial texts, etc. These Ugaritic texts as much as those in Accadian give valuable geographical and historical information about the near-East at this period from the fifteenth to the twelfth centuries; for example, about the Habiri, already mentioned elsewhere, but in evidence again at Ras-Shamra (what relationship have they to the Hebrews?); about Palestine regions where the story of Keret is imagined as taking place; and about the peoples neighbouring on Ugarit etc. It is natural also that this city so close to where Israel was to be established or had just been established should, by its information, its beliefs and legends, throw light on the biblical environment of the Old Testament.[27] There is a growing number of books about this. In the judgement of W. F. Albright (*The Archæology of Palestine*, p. 235) 'Light has been thrown on hundreds of . . . words (in the Hebrew Bible), including many whose meaning was inferred but not proved, as well as many whose meaning still remains somewhat doubtful.'

[26]The importance of this discovery for the history of the alphabet will be obvious, especially for that Phoenician alphabet from which the Greek and Latin alphabets—and consequently, our own—are derived. It may still seem that the Phoenician is independent of the Ugarite alphabet; nevertheless the latter at least shows an attempt to express articulations, parallel with the Phoenician invention which proved so successful.

[27]R. de Langhe studies these relations in his second volume p. 466-520; 'Quelques souvenirs d'Histoire biblique'; cf. also Th. H. Gaster, *The Ras Shamra Texts and the Old Testament* in *P.E.F. Quarterly Statements*, 1934, pp. 141-6; R. Dussaud, *loc. cit.* pp. 153-88. A. Lods, *Quelques remarques sur les poèmes mythologiques de Ras Shamra et leurs rapports avec l'Ancien Testament* in *Rev. hist. et phil. relig.*, 1936, pp. 101-31; A. Bea, S.J. *Ras Shamra und das Alte Testament* in *Biblica*, 1938, pp. 435-53; E. Jacob, *Les textes de Ras Shamra et l'Ancien Testament* in *Rev. hist. et. phil. relig.*, 1947, pp. 242-58.

Once again, it is sufficient for my purpose to have indicated the close relationship between contemporary archæology and biblical exegesis.

Byblos was considered by the ancients to be the oldest city in the world. It was known from Egyptian documents that it had enjoyed constant relations with Egypt throughout its history. According to the legend the waves had borne the body of Osiris the Egyptian god, to Byblos, and the Egyptians considered it a sacred city. For centuries it had provided Egypt with the various kinds of timber for her constant building needs. Since Renan (1860) the city has been identified with the present site of Jebeil in Lebanon, on the Mediterranean coast half-way between Beirut and Tripoli. After the First World War it was selected as a research field by French archæologists. Pierre Montet, an Egyptologist, directed the excavations from 1921-4; he was succeeded by Maurice Dunand in 1926-32. Their reports appeared rapidly and various studies have popularized their results.[28] The entire area of the site has been cleared and it has been excavated to its full depth.

Two results are of main concern to exegetes. First there is the history of the city, its monuments and its temple renowned in antiquity; the discovery of the royal tombs made right at the outset, and, reaching back to the earliest period, the clearing of the Aeneolithic cemetery (middle of the fourth millennium) carefully described by M. Dunand. From century to century the unbroken relations between Byblos and Egypt stand out, as well as the latter's influence on the art and religion of Byblos. Then, in 1923, the sensational discovery was made of the tomb of King Ahiram (contemporary with Ramses II, 1295-1225 B.C.) built by his son Ithoba'al and embellished with an inscription in Phoenician alphabetic characters on the upper border of the sarcophagus and a *graffito* on one of the sides of the entrance shaft. Until then the oldest inscription known in Phoenician characters had been the

[28]P. Montet, *Byblos et l'Egypte. Quartre campagnes de fouilles à Gebeil*, 1921-4. 2 vols in 4°, text and Atlas, Paris, 1928-9—M. Dunand, *Fouilles de Byblos*, t. 1. 1926-32, 2 vols. in 4°, text and Atlas, Paris, 1939, and 1937—M. Dunand, *Byblia Grammata. Documents et recherches sur le développement de l'écriture.* 1 vol. in 4°, Beirut, 1945—Summaries of these works are available in *Etudes*, 1930, 1. pp. 274-92 (L. Jalabert, 'L'histoire à coups de pioche'); in the *Revue apologétique*, June, 1931, pp. 670-93 (L. Hennequin); in the *RB*, 1931, pp. 276-91 (B. Couvoyer, *Byblos après quatre ans de fouilles*) and 1946, pp. 459-68 (R. de Vaux, O.P. and M. Dunand).

stele of King Mesa of Moab (ninth century). But now this was evidence of the existence of the Phoenician alphabet as far back as the thirteenth century, at the time when Moses probably entered Canaan; and it showed signs of already being old and known not only to the sculptor who incised it on the stone but also to the mere clerk of the works who hastily executed the graffito as a warning to any future violator of the tomb. This discovery is of considerable interest for the history of writing in biblical times, and also for the still unsolved problem of the origins of the alphabet and of the influences that combined to produce it.[29]

Exploration and excavations in Palestine

After 1920 excavations in Palestine were resumed at a rate and with a success hitherto unparalleled. Many sites studied before 1914 were investigated more thoroughly and with methods increasingly better adapted to the purpose. Many investigations were also undertaken. As early as 1938, L. Hennequin, in a most informative article in the *Supplément* to the *Dictionnaire de la Bible* (III, pp. 318-523: 'Fouilles et champs de fouilles en Palestine et Phénicie') was able to list eighty-six sites being excavated in Palestine and fifteen in Transjordania. The work was continued and extended until its interruption by the Second World War. It was resumed afterwards but the armed conflict between Jews and Arabs from May to December 1948 and the ensuing cold war is scarcely favourable to scientific pursuits.

Curiously enough, in Palestine, the land of the Bible, before the discoveries at Qumrân (1947-58; see below) which yielded so much in this domain, not a scrap of papyrus or fragment of pottery was found bearing anything on it from the Hebrew Bible.[30] At the most, with the help of the Gezer calendar (end of the tenth century B.C.), the ostraca of Samaria (beginning of the eighth century), the inscription of Siloah (about 700) and the ostraca of Lachish (beginning of the sixth century) an idea could be obtained of what Hebrew writing must have been like in contemporary manuscripts. But

[29]It is to this problem that Dunand's book *Byblia Grammata*, quoted above, is devoted, as well as the second part of de Vaux's study, also quoted. Books on this question continue to come out: e.g. G. R. Driver, *Semitic Writing from Pictograph to Alphabet*, Schweich Lectures, London, 1948; H. Tur-Sinai (Torczyner), 'The Origin of the Alphabet,' in *Jew. Quart. Rev.*, 1950, pp. 83-110, etc.

[30]The Nash papryus, containing a fragment of Deuteronomy, was discovered in 1902 in Egypt, in the Faiyum.

inscriptions found in Palestine are unfortunately not numerous. Similarly, hardly any *direct* information had been found in Palestine about the principal biblical figures in the history of Israel. In contrast with the Syrian and Mesopotamian excavations the yield of written texts in Palestine remained very meagre.

One of the first important results of the excavations was the certain identification of an increasing number of biblical cities. Sometimes it is an inscription which establishes the identification of a site: for example, at Tell Sandahannah (=Maresa, Josue 15. 44), at Tell ed-Duweir (=Lachish, often mentioned in Josue, 4 Kings, 2 Paralip, etc.), at Tell Djezer (=Gezer, 2 Kings 5. 25); more often it is a convergence of indications, as for example at Balata (=Sichem, frequently mentioned in the Bible; excavated by Sellin, 1913-4 and G. Welter, 1928 onwards).[31]

A further result particularly important in certain excavations is the amount of valuable information provided by the various stages of the digging. For example at Samaria the American expedition (G. A. Reisner, C. S. Fisher, D. G. Lyon: 1908-10; J. W. Crowfoot, 1931-5) cleared the palace of Omri, king of northern Israel (according to 3 Kings 16. 24 he made this city his capital); they worked out in detail the enlargements carried out by his successor Achab and traced the history of the city's monuments up to the time of Herod. Moreover, here at Samaria more than seventy ostraca were found, administrative items from the beginning of the eighth century and especially the fine ivory inlays similar to those found in Mesopotamia. The excavations at Tell ed-Duweir (=Lachish, west of Hebron) directed by J. L. Starkey (1933-8) provided much valuable historical information. Starkey was assassinated on 10

[31]These identifications are mentioned in the article by L. Hennequin, quoted above; characteristic examples of several identifications, particularly those to which he himself contributed, are to be found in U. F. Albright: *The Archæology of Palestine*, (pp. 227-9). The valuable alphabetical and documented list in vol. 2 of the *Géographie de la Palestine* by Fr Abel, O.P. (pp. 233-490) naturally lists all the results of these excavations. This geography (2 vols: I. *Géographie physique et historique;* II. *Géographie politique—Les Villes*), Paris, 1933-8, has done yeoman service. *Palästina, Die Landschaft in Karten und Bildern*, Tübingen, 1930, by R. Koeppel, S.J. is also very useful. Note also, together with the well-known Biblical atlases of G. Adam Smith and J. G. Bartholomew (1st edn, London, 1915), the *Westminster Historical Atlas to the Bible* by G. E. Wright and F. V. Filson (1st edn, Philadelphia, 1946, 2nd edn, 1956); the *Atlas of the Bible* by L. H. Grollenberg, O.P. (English translation from the Dutch original, published by Nelson); and the *Atlante Storico della Bibbia*, by P. Lemaire and D. Baldi, O.F.M., Rome-Turin, 1955. Also by Baldi: *Enchiridion Locorum Sanctorum*, Documenta S. Evangelii loca respicientia ... 2nd edn, Jerusalem, 1955.

January, 1938 near his site. His excavations are well known on account of the Hebrew ostraca (beginning of the sixth century) which have become known as the 'Lachish Letters'. They consist of seventeen letters sent by the captain of the fortress to his immediate superior, each letter a kind of memorandum scratched on a piece of pottery. They are evidence for us of the death struggle of Judah, destined to perish in 586 B.C.[32] Further ostraca were found in 1938, giving us Hebrew prose contemporary with the prophet Jeremias.

Many other explorations deserve a rapid mention, for example those at Tell es-Sultan (=Jericho) by E. Sellin and C. Waatzinger (1908-9), J. Garstang (1929-36) and Miss K. Kenyon (1952 onwards). These have retraced the stages of the city's development since the beginning of the fifth millennium, though they have failed so far to solve the problem of the exact date of the destruction of the city and its connection with Josue's campaign. The excavations of Tell el-Hosn (*Bet-Shan: Beison*), directed by C. S. Fisher, A. Rowe and G. M. Fitzgerald (1921-33) have revealed the Egyptian character of temples and fortresses. Particularly important are the unbroken series of investigations made at Jerusalem since the start of Palestinian archæology, the results of which for both the Old and New Testaments are condensed in the great books of Fathers Vincent and Abel: *Jérusalem: Recherches de topographie, d'archéologie et d'histoire*, 2 Vols 1912-26 and most recently, R. Vincent and A. M. Stève, *Jérusalem de l'Ancien Testament*, 2 Vols, 1954 and 1956 (a whole life's work).

Then there should be mention of the contribution made to prehistory by excavations in Palestine during the period 1925-35. Ten skeletons and several skulls were found at Tabgha (the lake of Geneserath), Sukhul and Tabun (region of Mount Carmel) and Djebel Kafzeh (near Nazareth). These show a mixture of typically Neanderthal characteristics with the more recent ones of *homo sapiens*, and this raises a problem for pre-historians. But from the biblical point of view there is no need to discuss explanations of this problem here.[33]

We ought also to record the progress of chronology in fixing the

---

[32]The letters of Lachish were edited by H. Torczyner (Tur-Sinai): *Lachish I. The Lachisch Letters*, London, 1938; *Te'udoth Lachish*, Jerusalem, 1940.

[33]Cf. the book by the two prehistorians who directed these investigations: McCowan and Keith, *Stone Age of Mount Carmel*, Oxford, 1939.

precise dates of archæological periods in Palestine. It is a curious fact—strongly emphasized by W. F. Albright—that whereas in Mesopotamian excavation the dates put forward by the first explorers were too remote and the 'short chronology' has gradually replaced 'the long', in Palestine the earliest archæologists such as Flinders Petrie and Macalister tended to select dates that were too modern and their discoveries have often had to be put back to a more distant past. Today, in many cases, the comparison that can be made between the various degrees of cultural evolution in those countries of the near-East where excavations have taken place[34] ensures increasingly precise and definite results.[35]

The most remarkable triumph of Palestinian archæology in the twentieth century has certainly been the discovery, since 1947, of the manuscripts of the desert of Juda. I shall describe these excavations and their results in the following section on the monuments and written documents found in the near-East.

2. *The numerous monuments and written documents* which have shed light on the history of the near-East and the Palestinian region in the time of Christ.

The excavations mentioned in this chapter have brought to light a great number of written documents which have considerably increased our knowledge of the history, the daily life and the religious thought of the ancient world. In the light of these texts, biblical problems are inevitably of a different character than they were a century ago. Clearly, the literature of Israel cannot be historically understood independently of the many written documents of the East that are either parallel with it or have even influenced it: for

[34]Cf. Fr Schmidtke, *Der Aufbau der babylonischen Chronologie*, Munster, 1952; P. van der Meer, *The Ancient Chronology of Western Asia and Egypt*, Leiden, Brill, 1947.

[35]The archæological, ethnographic, literary and religious study of Palestine has developed to such an extent since 1900 that it demands a systematic bibliography to be issued periodically. P. Thomsen has made this one of the principal tasks of his scientific work. The first volume of the series: *Die Palästina-Litteratür, Eine internationale Bibliographie in systematischer Ordnung mit Autoren und Sachregister*, appeared in 1911; volume 6 in 1953-6 (Leipzig, Hinrichs). The author died in 1954 aged 79, leaving the MSS of two further volumes. For Palestinian archæology and biblical archæology in general the reports most easily followed step by step are those that appear periodically in *RB*. The *Archiv für Orientforschung*, begun in 1923 by Professor E. Weidner, also provides full and regular information. One of the most interesting and accessible books on purely Palestinian archæology is the little volume by W. F. Albright, *The Archæology of Palestine*. (Pelican Books, 1st edn, 1949).

example, the first chapters of Genesis and the Sumerian and Accadian accounts of the creation and the flood; the story of the patriarchs and the ancient customs in the texts of Mari and Nuzi; the Mosaic legislation and the Eastern Codes—the Code of Hammurabi, the Hittite Code, the Sumerian laws; the psalms of Israel and the Accadian and Sumerian psalms (in the light of these parallels as well as of traces in the Ugaritic religious literature from the fifteenth to the twelfth centuries, objections against the age of certain psalms lose their force); the proverbs and maxims of Israel and the aphorisms of Egyptian and Sumerian widsom;[36] the literary structure of Hebrew poetry and the ordinary structure of such poetry in Sumer and Accad; Israelite chronology with its vague and general indications, and in Assyria, documents dated by astronomical facts or the succession of eponymous magistrates, the contributions to eastern chronology yielded by the excavations at Ras-Shamra, Mari, etc.; the religious institutions and beliefs of Israel and their parallels in other eastern religions, e.g. Jewish and Persian angelology; the doctrines of Ecclesiastes or of the Greek Book of Wisdom and the philosophical systems of contemporary Hellenism, etc.

The method of writing the history of Israel had remained unchanged in its procedure and conclusions from the first century A.D. to the beginning of the nineteenth, witness for example St Augustine and Bossuet in his *Discours sur l'histoire universelle*. It could only be a summary of the sacred books, together with some facts of Greek or Roman history, enlivened later by some curious legends from extra-biblical Jewish tradition. But now a century of research has brought the whole ancient East to life, and every year our knowledge of it becomes more vivid and complete. This revolution has had a twofold result: (a) a methodological result bringing into increasingly exact definition the different literary forms in which, during the centuries, the writers of Israel expressed their idea of history—for example, the epic history of origins in Genesis, a history that for long was oral; history for edification, idealized and liturgical in the Book of Chronicles (Paralipomenon); the political history of David in the Books of Samuel (1 and 2 Kings), perhaps in part the work of

---

[36]The recent book of J. A. van Dijck, *La Sagesse Suméro-accadienne. Recherches sur les genres littéraires des textes sapientiaux*, Leiden, 1953, brings out the great wealth and many sidedness of the Sumero-Accadian wisdom literature.

a contemporary courtier; (b) an historical result, setting the evolution of the ideas and beliefs of Israel in the concrete and living reality with which they were contemporary. The principle is unchanged; progressively God leads the people he has chosen towards the Messiah; he prepares the Jewish mind to become Christian. But in many ways the stages of this evolution are vastly different from what they were naïvely imagined to be. Instead of a clumsily pious, psychologically untrue and anachronistic transposition of Christian ideas into the past centuries we are confronted now with the stern reality of conditions in the ancient East with its ferocious hatreds and earthbound religious ideas but also with its slow and unwilling ascent towards a fresh ideal, powerful because it was divine.

The Manuscripts of the Desert of Juda

A chance find by a Bedouin in Palestine during the summer of 1947 led to archæological discoveries of exceptional importance: the manuscripts of the desert of Juda, also called the Dead Sea manuscripts or the manuscripts of Qumrân.

The first documents of Qumrân were found in February or March 1947 inside a cave high up in the rocks, eight miles south of Jericho, on the north shore of the Dead Sea by Mohammed ad Dhib, a fifteen-year old Bedouin. He had come across the opening by chance while searching for a straying goat. He managed to slide in and found several big jars, some intact, some broken, containing leather scrolls. The scrolls which could be unrolled were covered on their inner surface with characters written in a language unknown to the Bedouins. When the leaders of the tribe heard about this they resolved to sell them at as high a price as possible.

Transactions of this nature were not easy in that year of great disturbance in Palestine. England, unable to reach a peaceful solution with regard to Palestine's future status, gave up her mandate over the country and left the United Nations to decide. Arabs and Jews were in constant conflict; there was no security anywhere. Things became even worse after the decision of the United Nations (29 November 1947) to partition Palestine between Jews and Arabs, a decision accepted by the Jews but rejected by the Arabs, and leading to the Jewish-Arab war of 1948 which ended in victory for Israel and the successive armistices from January to July 1949.

It was during these political events that the initial stages in the history of the manuscripts of the desert of Juda took place. During the summer of 1947 the Bedouins paid a visit to the Syrian-Jacobite monastery of St Mark in Jerusalem. They believed the documents to be in ancient Syriac and hence thought that this would be the best place for a lucrative sale. The Syrian archbishop, Athanasius Yeshoue Samuel saw at once that the manuscripts were not in Syriac but in Hebrew. After various delays and incidents due to the difficulties of the political situation he decided to buy the parcel of manuscripts offered to him and acquired for his monastery five scrolls containing four works. 1. A complete manuscript of Isaias 1-66 in the square alphabet.[37] 2. A Hebrew commentary (a kind of *midrash*) on the first two chapters of the prophecy of Habacuc.[38] 3. Two scrolls brought separately by the Bedouin but originally forming only a single scroll and containing in Hebrew the rules for the organization and discipline of a community or a religious group: the title *Manual of Discipline*[39] given it by Millar Burrows, is commonly accepted. 4. Lastly a leather scroll whose leaves had become so stuck together in the course of time that for a long while it seemed as though it could not be undone without destroying it and making it illegible. On the strength of a few words that could be deciphered it was called for some time *The apocalypse of Lamech*. In the end it was opened and found to be a *Midrash on Genesis*[40]. These four

[37]A leather scroll made up of sheets sewn together: it is about 12 ft 6 ins in length and just over 1 ft broad. The Hebrew text forms 54 successive columns, still clearly legible. It is complete up to chapter 46. The writing is in square Hebrew. Comparison between its letters and those of Palestinian inscriptions of the first cent. B.C. has made many consider that it probably belongs to this period. *On the whole*, it confirms the classical Massoritic text, but *a number of differences in detail* make the discovery greatly interesting from the point of view of textual criticism. It is a remarkable fact that more than a thousand years lies between our most ancient complete Hebrew MSS of Isaias (the end of the tenth cent. A.D.) and this MS, thus dated in the first century B.C.

[38]A leather scroll 5 ft 5 ins in length (i.e. in the state in which it was found, the beginning—a column, perhaps?—is missing), and about 7 ins in its least broad parts (the bottom of the columns has frequently disappeared). The commentary on Habacuc consists of an application of his prophecies to the situation contemporary with the author. The Midrash is chiefly interesting on account of its contemporary allusions; e.g. to the Kittim, whom many believe to be the Romans of the period of Pompey's campaign in the East: to the 'Master of justice' and his enemy 'the impious priest'—those two persons appear in other documents.

[39]Hence, originally, a single scroll (five leather sheets sewn together); total length 5 ft 11 ins: breadth 9½ ins. The beginning is missing. This is a document of great interest: it contains the detailed constitution of a religious group, a communal unit.

[40]When at last it was unfolded, it was seen to be 8 ft 3 ins in length, made up of five leather sheets sewn together. It was published in 1956 in Jerusalem at the Magnes Press of the Hebrew university and the Heikhal ha-Sepher of Jerusalem by

works[41] after some unsuccessful bargaining—were bought by the government of Israel from their Syrian owners. All the great manuscripts of the first cave have been edited scientifically.

A second set of documents taken from this first cave—after a series of negotiations—[42] was offered to E. L. Sukenik, professor of archæology at the Hebrew university, who until then had not known of the existence of the first set and its sale to the Syrian monastery. The purchase was completed and the money handed over on the 29 November 1947, the day on which U.N.O. decided to divide Palestine between Jews and Arabs.

Professor Sukenik's collection contained three works, which were brought to him in six separate scrolls (four of which had originally formed a single scroll). 1. A scroll called by E. Sukenik: *The scroll of the war between the sons of light and the sons of darkness*,[43] but which Fr van der Ploeg prefers to call: *Manual for the War*. It seems to be concerned with some future war at an eschatological period. 2. Four scrolls (as noted above, these were originally only one), containing twenty hymns or psalms, usually designated by the Hebrew word *Hôdayôth* (hymns of thanksgiving).[44] The document is of great interest for the understanding of the piety and hopes of the religious group from which it came. 3. A second manuscript of Isaias (incomplete) containing the last third of the book: Chapters 38 to the end and passages from Chapters 10, 13, 19-30, 35-40. It was very difficult to open, as the leather had greatly deteriorated.[45]

Nahman Avigad and Yigael Yadin (son of E. L. Sukenik): *A Genesis Apokryphon*: *A Scroll from the Wilderness of Judaea. Description of contents of the Scroll, fascimiles, transcriptions and translations of columns II, XIX-XXII* (translated from the Hebrew by Sulamith Schwarts Nardi) pp. 48, 8 plates.

[41]Several fragments of less importance should be added to these.

[42]Millar Burrows, in his book: *The Dead Sea Scrolls*, pp. 4-19, (noted again in our bibliography below) gives the details of the wayward course of these offers, purchases, security measures, first diffusion of the news etc. during 1947-8. Fr G. Lambert in an article in *NRT*, March 1949, pp. 286-304, (followed by a supplementary note in May 1949, pp. 414-6, and in June, pp. 621-37, a translation, together with the Hebrew text of one of the psalms discovered) acquaints the readers of the review with the facts about this sensational discovery.

[43]A scroll 8 ft 10 ins in length and nearly 6 ins wide made up of 3 sheets of leather sewn together and pieces of another sheet. The scroll is almost intact, except for the lower edge which is frayed. It comprises 19 columns of text.

[44]When joined together these four scrolls are more than $6\frac{1}{2}$ ft in length and contain 12 columns, just over a foot wide, each column having more than 30 lines (maximum: 39).

[45]It seems to be even closer to the classical Massoretic text than the MS of Isaias bought by the monastery of St Mark.

It was only gradually that the news of this discovery spread to Europe and America during the year 1948. In Palestine the Israel-Arab war broke out in March 1948 and the Syrian archbishop had taken the precaution of sending the manuscripts he had acquired out of the country. This decision proved to be fortunate, for the monastery of St Mark was hit in the bombardment and Fr Boutros Suwame, the archbishop's confidant, was killed. As early as October 1948 an American Jewish exegete, Solomon Zeitlin, began to express doubts about the age of the manuscripts and his scepticism increased during the following years. In order to settle the authenticity of these first documents, to enable proper and informed discussion about their date to take place and to make ready for further and more systematic excavations, it seemed indispensable to identify the cave from which the Bedouins claimed to have taken the manuscripts they had sold.

In December 1948 a Belgian officer, Philippe Lippens, sent to Palestine as an observer for the United Nations, having before his departure read about the Palestinian discovery in the American magazine *Time*, determined to find the famous cave of the manuscripts. His official position enabled him to make contact with various persons in authority (General Lash, the commandant of the third brigade of the Arab Legion at Ramallah and his archæologist, Colonel Ashton). Colonel Ashton, assisted by information of various kinds, was the first to enter the cave, 28 January 1949. On 11 February the English archæologist, G. Harding, Fr de Vaux O.P. and P. Lippens, also arrived there. The cave was methodically examined until 5 March. Their discoveries—pieces of ancient pottery, scraps of linen of the same period, a number of fragments of leather homogeneous with the documents previously discovered and evidence given by the Bedouins, left no room for any doubt about the precise identification of the site and the value of the initial discovery.[46]

[46]A detailed report on *the identification of the cave* will be found first in Fr G. Lambert's supplementary note quoted above, (*NRT*, 1949, pp. 414-6); then, more minutely, in a later article (*NRT*, January 1950, pp. 53-65; and lastly, with special reference to the collaboration of P. Lippens, in an article in *La Revue générale Belge*, January 1950. Cf. also on this subject M. Burrows, *op. cit.* pp. 32-5. Fr de Vaux, who took part personally in this identification, gave a preliminary account of it in the *RB*, 1949, pp. 234-7, under the title: *La cachette des manuscrits hébreux*. Later in the same review (1949, pp. 586-609) he wrote a technical article: *La Grotte des manuscrits hébreux*. In it he examines the pottery and the manuscript fragments. The article is illustrated by several plates.

From this moment there began, as Fr de Vaux remarks,[47] 'a veritable hunt for manuscripts, in which Bedouins and archæologists competed and which quickly spread to the whole Desert of Juda'. From the end of 1951 and throughout 1952 finds were made which, taken as a whole, proved to be even more important than those in the first cave. During the following years, up to December 1956, the number of caves containing manuscripts, over an area of five miles north and south of the first cave, rose to eleven. Together with this exploration of fresh caves, a methodical clearing of the ancient ruin of Khirbet Qumrân was undertaken in 1951-6. Its existence had been known for some considerable time. But now an effort was made to reach certainty about its significance and purpose, the dates when it was occupied and its relation to the caves and their manuscripts.

In spite of their value, it is not the intention of this book to give an exhaustive account of the finds in the desert of Juda, but simply to note their most striking characteristics.

It was a fresh offer from the Bedouins of manuscripts from a cave of Qumrân (cave 2), quite close to the previous one, that made the archæologists decide to organize a general survey (for 4 weeks) of the cliffs in the Judean desert, covering an area of five miles, from Hadjar-el-Asba in the north to half a mile south of Ras Feshka. Twenty-five caves or clefts in the rocks were found containing pottery of the same type as in the first and two caves containing manuscripts—the one already discovered by the Bedouin and in March 1952 another (cave 3); in this cave were found together with various manuscripts two copper scrolls, the first made up of two leaves rivetted and rolled up together, the other of a third leaf which had been detached and which was also rolled up. The oxydized state of both scrolls was such that it seemed absolutely impossible to unroll them; it was necessary to utilize a method of separating them which was carried out in England at the end of 1955 and the beginning of 1956. The three leaves together formed a scroll 7 feet 10½ inches long and just over 11½ inches in width arranged in twelve successive columns each containing between thirteen and seventeen lines. The scroll was then seen to be a list in Hebrew of some sixty hiding-places where stores of gold, silver and boxes of incense were concealed. These hiding places were scattered, according to the scroll 'throughout the

---

[47]In his article in the review *La Table Ronde*, November, 1956, *Les Manuscrits de la Mer Morte*, pp. 73-84.

region from Hebron to Mount Gerizin near Neapolis (Nablus), but most of them would be in the neighbourhood of Jerusalem'.[48] Here is one of the directions given: 'In the great cistern within the pillared courtyard, in a recess at the back of it, hidden in a hole, opposite the upper opening, nine hundred talents.' The complete text has not been published. An official report has simply indicated its general purport and expresses the opinion that since the treasures emunerated amount to the startling total of 200 tons of gold or silver, it cannot be a real catalogue but rather, in Fr de Vaux's phrase (La Table Ronde, p. 78) a kind of 'guide to hidden treasure', with the characteristic 'unrealitity of folklore', such as is found in other literatures. On the other hand A. Dupont-Sommer, following Allegro, believes it to be a real inventory of the possessions of the community that were put into different places for safety's sake on account of the imminent Roman invasion, and he tries to show that the amount is not beyond the bounds of possibility for the combined wealth of a community in the circumstances of that age.

In September of that same year 1952, the Bedouins were again the first to find a cave, quite close to Khirbet Qumrân, 'in a place where the nature of the surroundings made any such find improbable'.[49] This was cave 4 which proved to be richer in documents than any in the region, superior even to cave 1. The three scientific associations that had joined forces for the exploration of the caves— the Jordanian Department of Antiquities, the French Biblical and Archæological School of Jerusalem (Ecole Saint-Etienne) and the Palestinian Archæological Museum—immediately began to make an inventory of its contents. Very near this cave 4, another (5) was discovered and a hole in the rocks containing some fragments (cave 6). In 1955, during the excavation season at Khirbet Qumrân, traces of several caves were observed on the clay shelf; they had crumbled into the ravine but some written fragments remained (caves 7-10 of Qumrân; de Vaux, art. cit. La Table Ronde, p. 75). Cave 11, a mile and a quarter north of Khirbet Qumrân, was discovered by Bedouins at the beginning of 1956; it, too, gives every promise of being of great value.

For the systematic analysis and scientific publication of this mass

[48]According to the article of A. Dupont-Sommer, Les rouleaux de cuivre trouvés a Qumrân in the Revue d'histoire des religions, January-March, 1957, pp. 22-36.
[49]R. de Vaux O.P. in the foreword to his report of September 1952, in the RB, January, 1953, pp. 83-106; Fouilles en Khirbet Qumrân.

of documents a team of specially qualified exegetes had had to be established in Jerusalem. The relevant information on this will be found in *RB*, January 1956, pp. 49-67: 'Le travail d'édition des fragments manuscrits de Qumrân.' The centre for the assembling of the fragments is the Palestinian Archæological Museum of Jerusalem (Rockefeller Foundation). It is here that the thousands of fragments are technically prepared, photographed, put under glass, pieced together and interpreted for publication.[50]

The three scientific associations mentioned above with the occasional assistance of the American School of Oriental Research undertook the organization, responsibility and carrying out of the work. The immediate direction was entrusted to Fr R. de Vaux O.P., President of the Trustees of the Palestinian Museum and Director of the French School of Archæology and to G. L. Harding, Director of the Jordanian Department of Antiquities. Publication will consist of a series of volumes entitled *Discoveries in the Judaean Desert*, printed at the Clarendon Press, Oxford. The first volume has been published; it is expected that ten will be published, of which volumes III and IV will be devoted to cave 4 alone.

In the eleven caves of Qumrân about 600 fragments of manuscripts have been found; almost 400 of these come from cave 4. Apart from the Book of Esther, all the books of the Hebrew canon of the Bible are represented, Isaias, Deuteronomy and the Psalms being the most frequent. Of special interest is the fact that the hoard contains books of the Bible in Hebrew or Aramaic, hitherto known only through the Greek translation of the Septuagint; for example, the book of Tobias is represented (cave 4) by three portions of manuscript, one in Hebrew on leather, two in Aramaic, one of them on leather, the other on papyrus. Two short fragments of the book of Ecclesiasticus in Hebrew were discovered in cave 2; it is well known that important fragments of this Hebrew text, in a medieval transcription, had been found in the Cairo Geniza (cf. above, p. 9, note 4). A few of the biblical manuscripts are in ancient Hebrew (Phoenician) writing. The gain to the textual criticism of the Old Testament from a comparison between the present text of our manuscripts with these documents, older by a thousand years or more, is

[50]Cf. the photograph of the vast room set aside for this work in M. Burrows, *op. cit.* plate VIII.

B

easy to understand. On the whole they seem to confirm the Massoretic text.

Together with the biblical manuscripts, several copies of the *Manual of Discipline* and of the Hôdayôth of cave 1 have been identified. And we may note also: 1. a number of manuscripts of the *Document of Damascus*, discovered in 1896-7, in the Cairo Geniza; 2. several Hebrew manuscripts of two apocrypha of the Old Testament, the Book of Jubilees and the Book of Enoch (but without the Parables of Enoch); 3. copies of the Testament of Levi, one copy of the Testaments of the twelve patriarchs, already known. 4. anthologies of texts, collections of Messianic texts, which verify the hypothesis, advanced by some exegetes, that certain Messianic references in the New Testament could be explained only by the existence of such *Testimonia*; 5. commentaries and paraphrases of biblical books which apply the ancient texts to the circumstances of the authors and their group; 6. liturgical books and hymns. All these writings form the 'library' belonging to this group. Some of them are their own products. They reflect the thought and religious ideas of a Jewish community living in Palestine slightly before and during the period when Jesus taught there and gathered the crowds around him. Contemporary archæology had never at one fell swoop made such a find with so great a promise of immensely valuable results.

To understand these manuscripts some knowledge of the building, the Khirbet Qumrân, the centre of this religious group, is essential. The ruin had long been known; it was marked on the detailed maps of the region, and the latest hypothesis held it to be a Roman outpost. Soon after the first discoveries, the necessity for a thorough study of it, involving clearing it and covering the foundations, became obvious. Five seasons of excavation followed each other from 1951-6. These led to the conclusion that Khirbet Qumrân was the central headquarters of a religious group who lived in a number of huts or caves scattered through the desert of Juda, and met together in the buildings of the Khirbet for prayer, community meals etc. It was made up of several buildings: an assembly room, a large kitchen, a room some twenty yards long, doubtless for general meetings and common meals, and a scriptorium etc. Great care had been taken with the water supply. Outside, there were mills, a bread oven and a vast cemetery with more than a thousand graves.

The coins found in the building and the examination of the pottery and other materials, led Fr de Vaux and other archæologists to the following conclusions:

Period I. Installation of the community at the end of the reign of John Hyrcanus (B.C. 134-104) or under Alexander Jannaeus (B.C. 103-76).

An earthquake in the spring of 31 B.C. damaged the buildings and compelled the community to give up the site for a time.

Period II. Return and restoration under Archelaus 4 B.C.-A.D. 6. Common life re-established until June A.D. 68. In face of the advance of the Roman tenth legion, the community fled, leaving its possessions behind and hiding its manuscripts in near-by caves.

What was this Jewish religious group? From the end of the second century B.C. to A.D. 68 they lived in the desert, by the shore of the Dead Sea, following a strictly regulated community life, with the poverty and asceticism that are indicated in the *Manual of Discipline*, and in the atmosphere of piety expressed in the Hôdayôth. They seem to have been faithful to the Law and to the whole religious past of Israel, but in some respects they claimed to keep apart from official Judaism. Instinctively we think of the Essenes, described by Josephus, Philo and Pliny as existing precisely at this period and localized by Pliny in the desert by the shore of the Dead Sea, north of Engaddi. This identification of the Qumrân group with the Essenes seems increasingly certain to modern interpreters. Most of them now take it for granted.

The task imposed on exegetes by these documents is obviously immense. First, they must reconstitute, so far as existing indications allow, the history of the Essenian movement in ancient Judaism, and its connection with the Hasidim (the devout) who in the second century B.C. had violently broken away from the Hasmonean kings. since, in their opinion, these latter had become too worldly. What was the function and religious status of the Master of Justice? When did he function? Who was the impious Priest who persecuted the Master of Justice? But, above all, what do these texts reveal about the fundamental religious inspiration of the movement, its theology, its piety and its eschatological hopes, with their real values and their deficiencies? It is an attempt to understand the movement from within.

Then must come the comparison with Christianity: likenesses and differences between the two doctrines; influences,—possible, probable or non-existent—of Essenism at the various stages in the establishing of Christianity, from the preaching of John the Baptist in the desert to the message of John the Evangelist at the end of the first century A.D.; and the essential originality of Christianity's core. It is not part of the purpose of this book to attempt such a comparison; in any case, it has hardly begun to be made, a large part of the documents being still unpublished and perhaps the series of discoveries not yet ended.

The frenzy of hasty and tendentious popularization which marked the first years has now fortunately calmed down; and a more solid exegetical and theological enquiry is being quietly undertaken. It should prove most useful for a better understanding of the Christian mystery. Already the bibliography of books and articles on Qumrân is considerable; the mere enumeration of their titles would fill a volume.[51]

Discoveries in the desert of Juda were not limited to the manuscripts of Qumrân and the knowledge gained of the Essenian community in that region. At the end of 1951 Fr de Vaux and G. L. Harding received offers from Bedouins of manuscripts on leather and papyrus which they felt could not have come from the caves

---

[51]The account we have given is based first of all on the articles and regular reports of *RB*, from 1949-56 and on the articles of Fr G. Lambert in the *NRT*, from 1949-52; then on the following works enumerated according to the dates of their first appearance: G. Vermès, *Les manuscrits du désert de Juda*, Tournai, Desclée, 1953; A. Vincent, *Les manuscrits hébreux du désert de Juda*, Paris, Arthème Fayard, 1955. J. Schmitt, *Les écrits du Nouveau Testament et les textes de Qumrân*, in *Revue des Sciences Religieuses*, 1955-6; M. Burrows, *The Dead Sea Scrolls*, London, Secker and Warburg, 1956; J. M. Allegro, *The Dead Sea Scrolls*, Penguin Books, 1956; Th. H. Gaster, *The Scriptures of the Dead Sea Sect*, (trans) 2nd edn, London, Secker and Warburg, 1957; J. Daniélou, *Les Manuscrits de la Mer Morte et les origines du Christianisme*, Paris, Editions de l'Orante, 1957; J. T. Milik, *Ten Years of Discovery in the Wilderness of Judaea*, (Studies in Biblical Theology 26, Naperville, Ill.) trans. A. R. Allenson, 1959; A. Dupont-Sommer, *Les écrits ésseniens découverts près de la Mer Morte*, Paris, Payot, 1959. Very useful are the regular notes by Fr van der Ploeg, O.P. in *Ex Oriente Lux* from 1949 and also the reports of the *Theologische Literaturzeitung, Der gegenwärtige Stand der Erforschung der in Palästina neu gefundenen hebräischen Handschriften* from 1949 to 1957. The bibliography dealing with the explorations in the desert of Juda is immense. It can be found arranged in the volume by Chr. Burchard, *Bibliographie zu den Handschriften vom Toten Meer* (Beihefte zur Zeitschrift Altt. Wiss., t. 76). Berlin, Töpelmann, 1957; also W. S. La Sor, 'Bibliography of the Dead Sea Scrolls, 1948-1957' Fuller Library Bulletin 31, (Fall, 1958) (Fuller Theological Seminary Bibliographical Series 2). The quarterly *Revue de Qumrân*, founded in 1958, is devoted exclusively to the Dead Sea manuscripts.

already discovered. Close questioning of the Bedouins and clever use of the first admissions finally led to their being guided to the new cave in January 1952. It was situated just over eleven miles south of the first cave of Qumrân, in the wady Murabba'at. It was much larger than the previous caves, and was in reality a group of four caves which had been inhabited at different periods. The first penetrated fifty yards into the mountain, forming a kind of tunnel, its width varying from thirteen to twenty-four feet. But it was the second cave, opening immediately to the west of the first, that yielded manuscripts of real interest. In this case the finds were not related to the Essenian community of Qumrân. These caves served as places of refuge for the Jewish partisans in the second great revolt (A.D. 132-5) during the reign of the Emperor Hadrian. They fought the Romans with the energy of despair. It was a grim guerrilla war and led to bloody repression. At Murabba'at the documents refer mainly to this period. Two authentic letters have even been found, signed by the leader of the revolt, Shimeon Ben Kosebah (commonly known as Bar Kochba, 'Son of the Star'). The documents reveal the Messianic and religious ideal of the rebels.[52]

In the same year 1952, Bedouins brought more documents from the desert of Juda, from the ruins of an ancient Byzantine monastery, Khirbet Mird, two and a half miles north-east of the monastery of Mar-Saba in the wady en-Nar. This time the find was directly connected with Christianity. A Belgian mission from Louvain university directed by Professor R. De Langhe, took charge of the investigation from February to May 1953. Among other items, the inventory contained Greek and Syro-Palestinian fragments of books of the Old and New Testaments; liturgical texts from the fifth to the eighth centuries A.D. and Arab papyri from the first centuries after the Hegira, etc.

The discoveries in the Desert of Juda are unquestionably a culminating point in the nineteenth and twentieth century history of biblical archæology as were, after 1850, the rediscovery of the Accadian, Sumerian and Egyptian civilizations. For the history of the text of the Old Testament, the more thorough understanding of Jewish religious life in the time of Christ, and a more historical

---

[52]Cf. the report in the *RB*, April 1953, by Fr de Vaux: *Les grottes de Murabb'at et leurs documents*, pp. 245-67; *Quelques textes hébreux de Murabba'at*, pp. 268-75; J. T. Milik, *Une lettre de Siméon Bar-Kokheba*, pp. 276-94 (cf. also p. 94 of his book quoted above, for the later modification of one of his interpretations).

interpretation of a number of passages in the New Testament in the light of the ideas with which they were contemporary, they give every promise of being very useful. Once again, a better understanding of man will help us to grasp the message of God as it was concretely given.

3. *The discovery of papyri in Egypt*

These have thrown considerable light on many aspects of the daily life of the ancients, increased our Greek literary inheritance, both secular and Christian and considerably assisted the understanding of biblical Greek and the textual criticism of the New Testament.

An aphorism of Mommsen is to the point: 'the nineteenth century has been the century of epigraphy; the twentieth will belong to papyrology'. Very many papyri have been found in Egypt: hieroglyphic and demotic papyri illustrating ancient Egyptian life and thought; Aramaic papyri from Elephantine (an island in the Nile) giving the beliefs of the Jews who had emigrated to Egypt in the fifth century B.C.;[53] Greek and Coptic papyri, covering a thousand years from the conquest of Egypt by Alexander to the Mohammedan Arabic invasion, and lighting up many corners of ancient history. Confining ourselves to the Greek papyri alone, we note that they have not only added several masterpieces to secular Greek literature, but have also thrown much light on the daily life of Egyptian communities: native pagans, emigré Jews, early Christian communities. There are mutual invitations to meals and celebrations; letters from parents to their children, and from schoolboys to their father or mother; bills of purchase or sale; scholastic exercises, administrative documents etc. In addition there are magic papyri, with incantations and curses, certificates of sacrifice testifying that a Christian or someone suspected of Christianity has sacrificed to the pagan divinities, fragments of Christian writings or of pre-Christian Jewish works: all this has remarkably increased our knowledge of biblical matters.

Here are some examples.

The language of the New Testament has benefited from the papyri. We need not agree with all the conclusions of Deissmann in his *Licht vom Osten* (2nd edn, 1909), and it may be admitted that there

---

[53]Cowley's edn, *Aramaic papyri of the fifth century B.C.*, Oxford, 1923, and the article: *Éléphantine* in the *Supplément* of the *Dict. de la Bible*. II coll. 962-1032.

is a certain Aramaic and Hebrew influence in New Testament language. Nevertheless, that language was essentially the popular *Koiné*, the language of the contemporary papyri. The vocabulary of the papyri has been of immense help in understanding biblical Greek and this is made very clear by a work like the lexicon of Moulton and Milligan: *The Vocabulary of the Greek Testament, illustrated from the Papyri and other non-literary sources*, London, 1914-29.

Non-Biblical Christian literature has been enriched: e.g. by the *Logia Jesu* of Oxyrrynchos (six short sayings attributed to Jesus by a copyist of the first half of the third century; fresh *Logia Jesu* (very short and mutilated; third century): a considerable fragment of the apocryphal Gospel of Peter, discovered in 1887 and published by Bouriant in 1892;[54] a fragment of a non-canonical gospel of the middle of the second century, called the Egerton papyrus;[55] *Conversations of the Risen Lord with his Disciples*, a Coptic papyrus of the end of the fourth century, found in 1895.[56]

In addition, two discoveries may be mentioned which although they are not concerned with specifically Christian writings are yet of the greatest interest for Christian literature: (1) the chance discovery in 1930 by Egyptian fellaheen at Madinet Madi, in the south west of the Faiyum, of a wooden chest containing seven scrolls, of a Coptic translation of Manichaean writings, partly by Mani himself, written in the third century A.D. and translated by Coptic scribes in the fourth century.

(2) Even more important was the gradual acquisition between 1945 and 1948 of a complete Gnostic library, in Coptic translation, discovered in a Greco-Roman cemetery in the region of Nag-Hammadi, about thirty-two miles north of Luxor, not far from an ancient monastery founded by St Pachomius in the fourth century. It consists of thirteen Codices containing forty-four Gnostic works of the first importance.[57]

[54]The best edition, with a long introduction, is by L. Vaganay: *L'Évangile de Pierre*, Paris, 1930.
[55]Published in 1935 by H. Idris Bell and T. C. Skeat, *Fragments of an unknown Gospel and other early Christian Papyri*, London. Of interest because it shows that the fourth Gospel was known and used in Egypt before A.D. 150
[56]C. Schmidt, *Gespräche Jesu mit seinen Jüngern nach der Auferstehung*, Leipzig, 1919.
[57]Cf. several articles on this discovery by J. Doresse, beginning with the announcement of the find in a report to the *Académie des Inscriptions et Belles Lettres de France*, June 17, 1949; a short account in the *Bibliotheca Orientalis* of Leiden, VI. 314, 1949, pp. 102-4; several articles in *Vigiliae Christianae*, 1948 and 1949; and a popular account in the number of *La Table Ronde*, devoted to *La Bible*

One of these Codices was acquired by the Jung Institute of
Zurich and has been named 'Codex Jung'; it is in process of publication.[58] Of the other Codices, the first alone has just been
published.[59] But to date all that these discoveries and studies
have already revealed concerning Manichaeism and Gnosticism
have shown more and more clearly that recent hypotheses about
Mandean influence on St John are improbable. It was an intellectual movement which definitely came later.[60]

As regards biblical texts on papyri found in Egypt, the following
may be noted: (1) the short fragment of St John in the Ryland's
Library at Manchester, which, from its date, proves that the Gospel
of St John was known and copied in Egypt from the first half of the
second century;[61] (2) the oldest Coptic manuscript of St John (fourth
century) discovered in 1923;[62] (3) the remarkable acquisition of
the Chester Beatty papyri (1931 ff.): 12 Codices of Biblical papyri—
3 of the New Testament from the third century, fragments of the
Gospels, 86 leaves of St Paul, 10 of the Apocalypse.[63] All these seem
to be of great value for the textual criticism of the New Testament.
(4) In 1956, V. Martin, professor at the University of Geneva,
published a papyrus recently found in Egypt and containing
fourteen chapters of the fourth Gospel (1, 1-14; 26); it dates from
around 200, and begins with the title $\epsilon\nu\alpha\gamma\gamma\epsilon\lambda\iota\nu$ $\kappa\alpha\tau\alpha$ $\iota\omega\alpha\nu\nu\eta\nu$.[64]

vivante, Paris, November, 1956, pp. 85-96: *Les gnostiques d'Égypte*—cf. also a generally
accessible account by V. R. Gold, 'The Gnostic Library of Chenoboskion' in *The
Biblical Archeologist*, December, 1952, pp. 70-88.

[58]The first volume has appeared—Coptic text, English, French and German
translations: *Evangelium veritatis*: Codex Jung, f.VIIIv-XVIv and XIXr-XXIIr,
edited by M. Malinine, H. C. Puech, G. Quispel, Zurich, 1956. On the discovery
of Nag Hammadi and the Codex Jung, of the excellent book: *The Jung Codex*,
London, 1955.

[59]Cf. on this volume of G. Garitte 'Le premier volume de l'édition photographique
des manuscrits gnostiques coptes et l'Évangile de Thomas' in *Le Muséon*, 1957,
pp. 59-73; G. Garitte, 'Le fragment géorgien de l'Évangile de Thomas' in the
Revue d'Histoire Ecclésiastique, 1956, pp. 513-20.

[60]From the Biblical point of view there is no need to examine here the contribution of papyrology to Patristic literature. On this point cf. The article by W.
Derouaux, in the *NRT*, 1935, pp. 810-43: 'Littérature chrétienne antique et
papyrologie.'

[61]C. H. Roberts, *An unpublished Fragment of the Fourth Gospel in the John Rylands
Library*, Manchester, 1935.

[62]H. Thompson, *The Gospel of St John according to the earliest Coptic Manuscript*,
London, 1924.

[63]F. G. Kenyon, *The Chester Beatty Biblical Papyri*, London, 1933ff, 15 volumes
have appeared.

[64]V. Martin, *Papyrus Bodmer II. Évangile de Jean, chap* 1-14, Cologne-Genève,
Bibliothèque Bodmer, 1956.

This is the oldest manuscript of St John of such length yet found, and it is an interesting witness to the state of the text at that period.

This leads us to the fourth indication of biblical progress in the twentieth century: the newly-found manuscripts of the Bible.

4. *The discovery and publication of new manuscripts of the Bible*

Modern textual criticism of the New Testament began with Westcott and Hort's edition in 1881. It had been preceded by a number of works, and among them that of Tischendorf. Since then a long road has been trod which, as discoveries are made, seems continually to grow longer.

There is only room to mention a few milestones[65]: (1) the discovery of the Syriac Sinaitic version in 1892, on the eve of the Encyclical *Providentissimus*; (2) increasingly penetrating research on the so-called 'Western' text; (3) study of the Latin versions and quotations made by the Western Fathers, e.g. Irenaeus, etc. (4) the discovery in 1906 of the manuscript W of the Gospels, called Freer; (5) the edition by von Soden in 1914 and the critical labours it stimulated; (6) the Farrar group and family 1, gradually leading to the identification of a new family of manuscripts, first called the 'Caesarean' text; (7) the discovery and publication of the oldest Coptic version of the Gospel of St John (mentioned above); (8) the Chester Beatty papyri, 1931 onwards (see above); (9) the beginning of the Oxford *Novum Testamentum Graece* (Mark, 1935; Matthew, 1940) which, while retaining the Westcott and Hort text, gives a very full critical apparatus; (10) the discovery of the papyrus Bodmer II, of St John 1-14 (see above); (11) an Anglo-American project (1950) for an edition of the New Testament provided with as complete and easily useable critical apparatus as possible: eight volumes are expected, apart from a volume of Prolegomena. The best specialists in textual criticism are to collaborate in it, and it will be increasingly international.

In the middle of the nineteenth century, the textual criticism

[65]In the Schweich Lectures, 1932, *Recent Developments in the textual criticism of the Greek Bible*, F. G. Kenyon has given a stimulating account of the development of the textual criticism of the Greek Bible since Westcott-Hort, down to 1932. Cf. also the excellent volume by F. Lagrange, *Critique textuelle du Nouveau Testament*, II *Critique rationelle*, Paris, 1935. Cf. the article by E. Marsaux, *État actuel de la critique textuelle du Nouveau Testament* in the *NRT*, 1953, pp. 703-26. First rate and generally useful is the recent volume by R. Devreesse, *Introduction à l'étude des manuscrits grecs*, Paris, 1954.

of the New Testament did not yet exist, it was only groping its way. By 1900 essential results had been established, essential points fixed and a method created. But fifty years of research were to reveal the full complexity of the problem, perfect the methods and increase the chances of a more immediate contact with the original text. The Encyclical *Divino afflante Spiritu* devoted a lengthy section to the method of textual criticism.

5. *An increasingly extensive and thorough study of patristic exegesis*

The great historical work of the last fifty years has been no less active in patristic matters than in scriptural. The result of many efforts has been to settle more definitely the Biblical *text* used by different Fathers—e.g. that of the New Testament as used by St Irenaeus, Tertullian, St Cyprian, St Ambrose, St Augustine, St Ephrem, etc. The study of Scriptural 'chains' has much increased the wealth of exegetical texts by the Fathers belonging to or lost or wrongly attributed works. Books wrongly assigned to others have been restored to their authors. Lost commentaries have been found, for example, by Hippolytus, by Pelagius in its authentic text, by Evagrius Ponticus, Diodorus of Tarsus, Theodore of Mopsuestia, and quite recently, Origen.[66] But the chief result has been, through a more informed appreciation of the intellectual movements of the early centuries, to establish a more precise assessment of the characteristics of the various exegetical schools or groups, of the secular influences that acted on them, their mutual relationships, the tendencies of their exegesis, and, in each group, the characteristics of individual Fathers, their originality and their personal principles of interpretation.

6. *The establishment, by many examples, of how the ancient peoples spoke, narrated and wrote*

One of the typical traits in the Encyclical *Divino afflante Spiritu* (as I have observed above, p. 71, n. 1) is its insistence on the manner in which the ancients regarded history and wrote it, and on

[66]To give detailed references would be to go far beyond the limits of this book. I shall refer merely to the account of advances in patristics in the book by the late Fr J. de Ghellinck, S.J., *Patristique et Moyen âge. Études d'histoire littéraire et doctrinale*, vol. II *Introduction et compléments à l'étude de la patristique*. Étude I. *Progrès et tendances des études patristiques depuis quinze siècles*, chapter II 'Progrès contemporain et son résultat actuel', Paris, 1947.

their methods of composition, their way of understanding and describing nature and events. After a century of archæological discovery and interpretation, both the over-literal methods of classical exegesis and the arbitrary and hypercritical construction of liberal exegesis have often been contradicted or at least corrected, made more precise or in some way qualified. It is of interest to observe that Pius XII decided to conclude his account of the progress of contemporary exegesis by noting this fact.

So an essential task for exegetes today becomes increasingly clear. By understanding eastern culture, its literary, historical and religious ideas, they must enter more thoroughly into *the concrete ways in which its writers* presented holy Scripture according to their period, their environment and the ancient psychology of the human interpreters. In short, exegetes must take into account more judiciously the human presentation of the divine message.

CHAPTER VI

BIBLICAL EXEGESIS SINCE 1918: NEW HORIZONS

I. *Protestant Exegesis*

SINCE 1918 the climate of Protestant exegetical research in Germany has fortunately been transformed in some respects. As a result of the world war, the Evangelical Churches, freed from servile dependence on the State, regained consciousness of being religious societies engaged in a common effort to recover, by surmounting nineteenth century liberalism, the religious thought of Luther and, thereby, such part of the Catholic inheritance as Luther had retained. The sufferings and final humiliations of the war awakened a deeper understanding of Christianity in many souls and more clearly defined mystical aspirations among many intellectuals. In a number of scientific commentaries, the merely technical description of Jewish or Christian doctrines, limited to historical objectivity, gave way to a direct doctrinal and theological interest, perceptibly inspired by a constructive Christian ideal. The theology of Karl Barth (a Swiss, born at Basle, 1886: his first book—*Der Römerbrief*, 1918) marking a return to a more dogmatic conception of Chistianity, exerted a profound influence on Protestant religious thought after the first war. The review *Zwischen den Zeiten* (1922 following) in which K. Barth, F. Gogarten, E. Thurneysen and E. Brunner collaborated, supported and extended this activity.

In the present study it is the general effect of these tendencies upon exegesis that concerns us. The difference between German Protestant commentaries before and after the First World War is very striking. Compare, for example, the classical pre-war commentary, the *Handkommentar zum Neuen Testament* by H. J. Holzmann, R. A. Lipsius, P. W. Schmiedel and H. von Soden with the *Theologischer Handkommentar zum Neuen Testament* published by Deichert from 1928 onwards, or *Die Schriften des Neuen Testaments übersetzt und für die Gegenwart erklärt* by J. Weiss, etc., with *Das Neuen Testament deutsch*[1] in which, since 1932, experts like P. Althanus, F. Büchsel, F. Hauck, J. Jeremias, etc. collaborate. The contrast between two epochs and two generations of exegetes, is immediately evident.[2] While losing nothing of the historical gains and scientific methods of the previous century emphasis was now laid more clearly on constructive theological synthesis and the enduring religious aspect of the problems at stake. The work undertaken since 1932 by G. Kittel: *Theologisches Wörterbuch zum Neuen Testament*,[3] both in the general tendency of this dictionary and in the choice of most of the collaborators, is a significant illustration of the trends of the period.

The same more theological and directly religious tendencies have appeared in the Protestant exegesis of other countries also: in French-speaking Switzerland, for example, in the *Cahiers théologiques* (called to begin with *Cahiers théologiques de l'actualité protestante*) published since 1943 under the direction of J. J. von Allmen, and in the *Commentaire du Nouveau Testament*, published by Delachaux and Niestlé since 1949; in German-speaking Switzerland, in the *Abhandlungen zur Theologie Alten und Neuen Testaments*, directed by W. Eichrodt and O. Cullmann published at the Zwingli-Verlag of Zurich since 1943. The works of A. Fridrichsen (at the University of Upsala in Sweden), of his collaborators or former pupils like H. Riesenfeld, B. Reicke, and others, express the same attempt to build a positive theology. The same atmosphere is to be found in certain works in English, e.g. by H. H. Rowley in England; by Millar Burrows and W. F. Albright in America—and the list could easily be extended. The growing number of Protestant theologies of the New Testament is a further expression of the concern of exegetes and of the desires of Christian people.[4]

[1] I have tried to define the characteristics of these two more recent collections in my reports in *NRT*, 1933, p. 940; 1935, p. 738; 1937, p. 533, etc., and in 1933, p. 551; 1935, p. 417; 1936, p. 770; 1938, p. 610; 1939, p. 114.

[2] I do not overlook the fact, however, that, even during the liberal period, the more theological tendency, more intent on keeping faith with Christian doctrinal values, was maintained in several sectors of Protestant exegesis; I have said so above, p. 25. But then it seemed to be the exclusive affair of a minority with little influence.

[3] Begun in 1932, the Dictionary reached, by June 1961, the fourth fascicule of the seventh volume, article σημεῖον. I have analyzed the fascicules regularly in the *NRT*, to which I venture to refer readers. An English translation of certain articles in Kitte has begun to appear in small separate books: *Bible Key Words from Gerhard Kittel's Theologische Wörterbuch zum Neuen Testament* (London, 1949-   ).

[4] They do not all express the same tendencies: R. Bultmann, in spite of the very

Turning now to the technical point of view, either historical or philological, it must first be observed that critical conclusions on the authenticity and chronology of the Old Testament, during the last eighty years, and particularly under the influence of archæology, have often become strikingly less radical than in the time of Wellhausen.[5] Certain psalms which Duhm in 1899 assigned to the second century B.C. in the time of Maccabees, Gunkel, in 1929, attributed to the period of the kings in the eighth or seventh century. Proverbs, whose first sections Wildeboer (1897) ascribed to the fourth century and not earlier, are for the most part clearly dated by Gressmann before the exile of 586. Semitic alphabetical writing which, sixty years ago, was considered to be unimaginable in the time of Moses, is since Montet's excavations at Byblos, now seen to have been fully formed in the thirteenth century B.C. A very competent and well documented account of this evolution of biblical criticism may be found in the book by J. Coppens, *Histoire critique des livres de l'Ancien Testament* first published in *NRT*, 1938, third edn, Bruges-Paris, 1942.

With regard to the exegesis of the New Testament, it would seem that since 1918 three aspects of research can be distinguished. By

personal nature of his work and his vast Scriptural knowledge, belongs in certain respects more to that historical scepticism about Christian origins which marked liberal research; nevertheless, his *Theologie des Neuen Testaments* is of value. More characteristic of the new spirit are, for the Old Testament, the theologies of W. Eichrodt (three volumes, 1933, 1935, 1950); Th. C. Vriezen (Dutch, 1949); O. Procksch (German, 1950; a posthumous work); E. Jacob (French, professor at Strasbourg, 1955); Von Rad (*Theologie des A.T., Vol* 1: *Die Theologie der gesch. Ueberlieferungen Israels*, 1957); G. A. F. Knight (*A Christian Theology of the Old Testament*, London, 1959); S. Mowinckel (*The Old Testament as Word of God*, Nashville, 1959); for the New Testament, E. Stauffer (1st edn, 1941); F. Buchsel (1935); O. Cullmann (*Die Christologie des N.T.*, 1957; English translation: *The Christology of the New Testament*); A. Richardson (*An Introduction to the Theology of the New Testament*, London, 1958).

[5]This can easily be seen in very recent introductions to the Old Testament such as *The Old Testament and Modern Study*, Oxford, 1951; A. Benzen, *Introduction to the Old Testament*, two volumes, 2nd edn, London 1951; M. Noth, *Die Welt des Alten Testaments*, 2nd edn Tübingen, 1953; O. Eissfeld *Einleitung in das Alte Testament*, 2nd edn, Tübingen, 1956. The same conclusion is to be drawn from historical accounts of Israel such as those of M. Noth *Geschichte Israels*, 2nd edn Goettingen, 1954; in English translation: *The History of Israel* (new translation by G. B. F. Brondon; New York, Harper, 1959); G. H. Gordon, *Introduction to Old Testament Times*, Ventnor, 1953; L. Kohler, *Der Hebräische Mensch*, Tübingen, 1953; H. H. Rowley, *From Joseph to Joshua*, Oxford, 1950; W. F. Albright, *From the Stone Age to Christianity* (2nd edition, with new introduction; Garden City, N.Y.; Doubleday Anchor Books, 1957); and from general histories of the East, such as that of S. Moscati, *Geschichte und Kultur der semitischen Völker*, Zurich and Vienna, 1953 (translated from the Italian.)

broadening the general outlook these have held the attention of a number of Protestant exegetes.

First, there has been a more thorough study of Jewish life and thought in the time of Christ and the apostolic period. It is indeed true that Christian exegetes had long studied attentively the writings of post-Biblical Judaism as a means to a better interpretation of the New Testament and had benefited from Jewish publications—translations of the Mishnah and the Talmud, and expositions of their own theology. To realize this one has only to turn over the pages of Schurer's bibliography in his *Geschichte des Jüdischen Volkes im Zeitalter Jesu Christi.*

At the beginning of the twentieth century the eschatology or the Old Testament Aprocrypha had been specially studied in a number of works, e.g. by R. H. Charles in England; by P. Volz and the collaborators in *Die Apokryphen und Pseudepigraphen des Alten Testaments* edited by E. Kautzch in Germany; the leaders of the eschatological schools, J. Wiss, A. Schweitzer, etc. Among Catholics, Fr Lagrange O.P., the editors of the Old Testament Apocrypha (F. Martin, E. Tisserant, J. Viteau) gave competent attention to the same problem.

After the first war, however, the study of Judaism in the last centuries of Israel and in the early days of Christianity was pursued with enthusiasm and Jewish and Christian scholars often worked together. In 1926, G. Kittel in his book *Die Probleme des palästinischen Spätjudentums und das Urchristentum* had shown once more what New Testament exegesis would gain from a thorough study of Rabbinical Judaism in the time of Christ and after. In 1931 he was able to put this into practice with the project of his *Theologisches Wörterbuch zum Neuen Testament*, in which each doctrinal word of the New Testament is studied, first in the corresponding Hebrew word of the Old Testament, then in secular Greek literature, then in its rabbinical setting and finally in the New Testament itself.

Editions of Jewish Rabbinic texts followed each other, after 1918, with increasing speed. G. Beer and O. Holzmann began the publication, in successive brochures, of the various treatises of the Mishnah, and this is still proceeding. In 1933, G. Kittel and H. Rengstorf undertook the publication of the *Rabbinische Texte*, consisting of the *Tosefta* (estimated to cover six volumes) and the *Midraschim* of the Tannaim. Goldschmidt's *Talmud of Babylon*, with its German translation, and Schwab's French translation of the *Talmud of Jerusalem* were newly edited. Danby's English translation of the Mishnah, 1933, published in a handy volume, met with great success. Other works also, e.g. those of P. Fiebig, Walker, etc., afford proof of the interest taken by exegetes in Rabbinical Judaism as a clue to the interpretation of the New Testament.

Among the aids to study then published for the use of scholars, the following should be noted: in 1927, the great work of G. Foot Moore *Judaism in the First Centuries of the Christian Era, The Age of the Tannaim*, 2 vols, Harvard University Press; from 1922 to 1928, the five volumes of the *Kommentar zum Neuen Testament aus Talmud und Midrasch* by H. L. Strack and P. Billerbeck; among Catholics, the works of P. J. Bonsirven, e.g. *Le Judaïsme palestinien au temps de Jésus-Christ*, 2 vols, 1955, and *Textes rabbinques des deux premiers siècles chrétiens*, Rome, 1955; *Le Judaïsme avant Jésus-Christ* by Fr Lagrange, etc.

From 1947, the understanding of the religious ideas of Judaism in the time of Christ has been strikingly increased by the discovery and progressively thorough interpretation of the manuscripts of the desert of Juda described above. This Essenian section of New Testament exegesis has not yet yielded its full harvest.

The study of the Hellenistic religious background in which early Christianity developed and expressed itself has been pursued with equal intensity since 1918.

It is certainly true that, from the time when historical exegesis began in the nineteenth century, the religions of the Greco-Roman world and the classical religious philosophies had been the subjects of considerable research. But at the beginning of the twentieth century, the 'history of religions' increased in subject matter and importance as already mentioned on pp. 38-9. It covered an immense field, reaching from the most primitive religions to those most remote from Christianity in time and space. Congresses of comparative religion were held, university chairs, publications and explorations were established. All these came about with increasing speed. At times comparative religion was presented in a liberalizing, popular and anti-Christian form, e.g. in series such as the *Religions-geschictliche Volksbücher*, Tübingen, Germany or *Orpheus, Histoire générale des religions*, by Solomon Reinach (Paris, 1909; thirty editions in fifteen years; English translation, London 1910) and the *Bibliothèque de propagande* of Brussels, published as brochures and very anti-Christian. In answer to this erroneous popularization, Catholics published such works as *Christus*, a manual of the history of religions edited by Fr Rousselot and Fr Huby, or the book *Où en est l'histoire des religions?* by Fr Bricout and his collaborators.

Since 1918 the history of religions seems to have been developing with more serenity and scientific probity and even with a certain respect for the phenomenon of religion and an effort to appreciate its inner meaning. It is as the background to Christianity that this domain concerns the exegete; the influences that could have acted upon it, or against which it may have reacted, the religious movements in Greco-Roman paganism that may have conditioned its development. Books on the different aspects of religious life and thought—the numerous works on the *Neutestamentliche Zeitgeschichten* or the *Pagan Background of Early Christianity*—can be counted in hundreds. They cover such subjects as the tendencies of Greek philosophy from Plato to the Stoics and their influence; Greek and Roman religions; eastern religions in Roman paganism; ancient mystery-religions and the Christian mystery; religious movements such as Orphism and Hermetism; the origins and development of Gnosticism; Christian words such as 'saviour' and 'salvation' and the corresponding words in the ancient world. Each of these headings will bring specialists in their subjects to the minds of informed readers. So wide is their range that here this mere indication must suffice.

A third, more technical aspect of research since 1918 is the *Formgeschichtliche Methode*, applied chiefly to the Gospels. It is a fact, of course, that as soon as the historical and philological character of exegesis began to be stressed in the nineteenth century, the different layers, the successive moments of the Christian tradition finally recorded in our Gospels, were bound in time to be discerned. Literary criticism working on the written sources of the synoptic Gospels (the Synoptic Problem) was connected as a rule with the attempt to distinguish the different stages of the primitive oral tradition. Many examples of this can be found in Protestant commentaries at the end of the nineteenth century, e.g. those of H. J. Holzmann, J. Weiss, etc. A. Jülicher's book *Die Gleichnisreden Jesu*, 1899, already applied the principles for the discernment of literary forms which were to be formally systematized and used by the *Formgeschichtliche Methode*. Other precursors were men like E. Norden and P. Wendland for the New Testament, and especially H. Gunkel for the Old Testament in his attempt to discover the different literary forms in the ancient narratives of Genesis and particularly in the Psalms.

The main works expounding and explicitly formulating the *Formgeschichtliche Methode* were, however, published after the First World War. These are R. Bultmann *Die Geschichte der synoptischen Tradition*, 1st edn, Gottingen, 1921; M. Dibelius *Die Formgeschichte des Evangeliums*, 1st edn, Tübingen, 1919; K. L. Schmidt *Der Rahmen der Geschichte Jesu*, Berlin, 1919; P. Albertz, *Die synoptischen Streitgespräche*, Berlin, 1921 and G. Bertram *Die Leidensgeschichte Jesu und der Christuskult*, Gottingen, 1922.

As formulated by its chief theorists R. Bultmann and M. Dibelius, the *Formgeschichtliche Methode* is based on the following principles and presuppositions: the material found in our synoptic Gospels is essentially communal popular literature which originated and developed in a collective source (the early Church) and in response to the religious needs of this collectivity. Our synoptic evangelists collected these narratives: basically they were *Sammler*, that is, those who group things together: they arranged these narratives into a framework which they devised, the historicity of which many partisans of the *Formgeschichte* deny. In any case, these exegetes consider that it is now essential to study the formation and the evolution of the particular narratives, and of the *logia*, or collections of *logia*, which constitute the *anonymous evangelical tradition* as it was before anything had been written down.

How is the path of this evolution to be retraced and its successive stages realized? By the study of the mode of expression, of the style, in the widest sense—that is, taking style or form as every way in which the reality is expressed. The form discloses the literary form which gave rise to the narrative or accompanied it, and the literary form will show the concrete historical and social situation in the interest of which this narrative was inserted in the thought and life of the primitive community. It will indicate to what cultural and religious apologetic the narrative was meant to respond and be adapted. It will fix 'the position of this narrative in the life of the community —*Sitz im Leben*'. The early Christian Church was concerned with living its Christian life and not with writing history for history's sake. We have to take the Gospel narratives and think them out again in terms of the *religious needs* of the early Church and not in terms of an overriding preoccupation with historical truth.

Since the purpose of this book is simply to supply a faithful report, it is exempted from attempting to distinguish[6] between what is sound in the method (for example, its concern to examine the words of Jesus in the setting of the thought and needs of the early Church: *Sitz im Leben*), what is excessive in it (for example, its depreciation of the personal part played by the evangelists), and the danger to historical objectivity which the method conceals (for example, subjectivism in reconstituting the stages of the oral tradition), etc. Here, then, it only needs to be noted that the *Formgeschichte*, in varying degrees and in ways that differ according to the personal presuppositions of the exegete, has been used since 1920 in most of the commentaries on the synoptic Gospels and in other evangelical studies. In the case of a scholar like R. Bultmann it may have led to a radical scepticism about the historical value of the evangelical tradition as an authentic expression of the teaching of Jesus. In other cases its results have proved fruitful, e.g. in works either by Catholics such as *Die Passion Jesu in der Verkündigung des Neuen Testaments* by K. H. Schelkle, Heidelburg, 1949, and *Les Justes et la Justice dans les évangiles et le christianisme primitif*, the degree thesis of A. Descamps, Louvain, 1950; or by Protestants—C. H. Dodd, *The Parables of the Kingdom*, London, 1935; V. Taylor, *The Gospel according to St Mark*, London, 1952; J. Jeremias, *Die Gleichnisse Jesu*, 2nd edn, Zurich, 1952.

On the morrow of the Second World War Protestant exegesis showed a notable tendency (which has continued) to bring out the profound religious unity of the Bible. This unity arises from the fact that throughout the Bible it is God's plan which is being revealed and carried into action. The Scriptures, in the totality of their meaning, present the utterance of God culminating and ending in the one who *is* that utterance itself, the 'Word' of God. This is their

---

[6]Catholic attempts at such discrimination are to be found in Fr Benoit *Reflexions sur la 'Formgeschichtliche Methode'*, art. in *RV*, 1946, pp. 481-512; Ed. Schick, *Formgeschichte und Synoptikerexegese*, Munster, 1940; A. Wikenhauser, *Einleitung in das N.T. Formgeschichte*, pp. 182-99; or among Protestants, the articles of O. Cullmann, in *Rev. d'hist. et de phil. rel.*, 1925, pp. 459-77 and 564-79, and E. Fascher *Die Formgeschichtliche Methode*, Giessen, 1924.

theological and apologetic value. This tendency is exactly paralleled in Catholic works of the same period. Books from both sides found a most favourable audience among Christian people. They were translated into a number of languages and went through several editions. Among Protestant works note: A. M. Hunter, *The Unity of the New Testament*, Philadelphia, 1944; H. H. Rowley, *The Unity of the Bible*, London, 1953; S. de Diétrich, *Le dessein de Dieu, Itinéraire biblique*, Paris-Neuchâtel, 1949 (15th thousand, by 1956); E. Hoskyns and F. N. Davey, *The Riddle of the New Testament*; A. G. Hebert, *The Authority of the Old Testament*, London, 1947; and a number of books and articles with the same tendency, e.g. those by W. Vischer, F. J. Leenhardt, C. H. Dodd, etc. The parallel movement in Catholic religious literature is mentioned below.

Having completed this summary of some new aspects of Protestant exegesis, it must be pointed out once again that no attempt has been made to provide a technical history of the subject. All that has been aimed at has been to secure a better understanding of the essential attitude towards Scripture as 'the word of God in the words of man', adopted by some interpreters of the Bible. That is what this book is about, as its title indicates.

II. *Catholic Exegesis*

After the 1914-18 war religious progress in several sections of Christian life brought a spirit of optimism into the Catholic world. Many concordats ensured fuller religious freedom in several old- or newly-established countries. The missionary spirit was intensified, the theology of missions was awakened, and in not a few missionary lands the Gospel made progress. Among Christian youth there was a marked development of the social spirit and Catholic Action promoted apostolic action. Such were some of the fruits among the Catholic élite of Pius X's eucharistic decree on frequent, even daily Communion from the age of seven.

In the realm of scriptural research, however, this trustful serenity was not immediately evident. The shock of modernism had been too violent for calm to be restored at once. Benedict XV, indeed, in his first Encyclical (1914) *Apostolorum principis* had vigorously rebuked the casting of unjustified suspicion and the morbid denunciations common in certain Catholic circles during the closing years of the anti-modernist conflict, on the eve of the First World War.[7] It is also true that soon after 1918 an intense desire became evident among those young Christians whose piety flowed from the Eucharist to go back to the primary sources of Christianity, and especially to Scripture. They wanted to get to know the Scriptures better, by means of relevant reading and by corporate exegesis in study circles. From the beginning of their movement, the Young Christian Workers turned to the Gospels in order to know Christ concretely and to be united with him. And gradually the whole Bible, Old and New Testaments, aroused a lively interest among the young in general. It raised many problems, and provoked many questions which they put to their priests and to the chaplains of their various societies.

But in these years of transition these priests often felt embarrassed, either because their training had been dogmatic and speculative rather than scriptural, or else from a vague feeling that the difficulty could only adequately be met by a broader kind of exegetical interpretation than they had been given in the seminary. The modernist crisis was only just over, the atmosphere of fear was not yet calmed. They were afraid lest they might betray their responsibility as priests by interpretations which might not coincide with the mind of the Church. They felt that there was so little help: as for the interpretation of the Old Testament as a whole, the history of the people of God, modern books were rare. Where was a safe guide to be found? Catholic books on the Old Testament written before 1900 were, in general, historically and philologically out of date. They realized this. New books by Catholic specialists in exegesis were often confined to isolated questions, not raising the great problems that were disturbing believers. The exegetes seemed to fear any general treatment that would explore the whole history of the people of God. The question of the Pentateuch, together with those about Daniel and the second part of Isaias, keenly studied between 1890 and 1907, seemed to have disappeared after that time from the exegetical horizon.

There was real and deep uneasiness among Catholic exegetes; it was to be aggravated by several ecclesiastical decisions: on 25 May 1920 a decree of the Holy Office (whose secretary from October 1914 to February 1930 was Cardinal Merry del Val)

[7] *Vide supra*, p. 73, note 8.

stated that the view put forward by Fr Touzard in his two articles
Moïse et Josué in the *Dictionaire apologétique de la foi catholique* and
Moïse et la Pentateuque in the *Revue du clergé francais*[8] was unsound
(*tuto tradi non posse*); on 12 December 1923, the *Manuel biblique* of
Vigouroux, Bacuez and Brassac, and the 12th to 15th editions of
the New Testament and 14th edition of the Old were put on the
Index, and this condemnation was followed by a most severe
explanatory letter from Cardinal Merry del Val to the Superior
General of Saint-Sulpice[9] (22 December 1923).[10]

Beyond question Catholic study of the Old Testament went
through a painful crisis between 1918 and 1930. In 1929 (*NRT*,
pp. 818-38) I tried to give some idea of this in an article whose
most relevant section I may perhaps be allowed to reproduce:

A retrospective study of these events (the archæological and
historical progress of the last sixty years) was necessary in
order to see the question with which this article is concerned
in its right perspective. That question is: *In view of all this
complex past, what is the attitude of Catholic exegesis today? In particular, as a result of those facts, what has happened, in Catholic
writing, to this attempt at a supernatural synthesis which is the soul of
the Old Testament?* From this point of view one might divide
Catholic exegetes today into three main groups. First, there are
those who are theologians rather than exegetes, barely conscious of critical problems and historical difficulties, who treat
the Old Testament almost as they would have done sixty years
ago, happy enough if they can garnish their work with a lacing
of orientalism. It is no use looking to them for any vital
description of the real religious, political and social evolution
of Israel. Their histories of Israel—few enough in any case—
are little more than a paraphrase of the Bible augmented by
some archæological illustrations and some indications as to
where sacred and profane events synchronize. Of course they

---

[8]Cf. *Acta Apostolicae Sedis*, xii, 1920, p. 158; *NRT*, 1920, pp. 495-8. This decree was
not included in *EB* 1954. But cf. in *EB*, Fr Vosté's letter to Cardinal Suhard *de
tempore documentorum Pentateuchi et de genere litterario undecim priorum capitum Geneseos*
which is a good indication of the distance travelled between 1920 and 1948.

[9]Note also with respect to German-speaking Catholics that in 1921-2 two
volumes of translations from the New and Old Testaments by N. Schloegl were
put on the Index, and in 1934 *Die Einwanderung Israëls in Kanaan* by F. Schmidtke.

[10]*Acta Apostolicae Sedis*, xv, 1923, p. 615 ff; *NRT*, 1924, pp. 181-4; *EB* (1954),
pp. 177-82.

have the spirit of faith and that saves their exegesis, but their historical sense is feeble, and in their work the history of Israel is not up to the standard of middle-eastern history today.

Others are all too conscious of the contemporary tendency to reduce all explanation to the naturalism of the present time. Their chief aim is to attack the enemy on his own battle-field, history. And so with them, refutation takes first place. Hours are spent not in scrutinizing the word of God, but in refuting Wellhausen, Stade, Duhm, Gunkel, etc. Pick up a notebook of a term's lectures devoted to the study of Genesis; there is nothing in it but refutation, not a trace of any effort to construct a positive solution of the problems. With regard to the first of our inspired books a young priest will be nourished with the knowledge that a nineteenth century German named Wellhausen interpreted it wrongly. Even supposing that such a refutation can be decisive, it does not lead on to any positive construction. Is such information the life-giving message of holy Scripture?

Lastly, many exegetes, often those most competent and penetrating, fully aware of the grave historical or theological problems raised by the Old Testament, consider that any attempt at a synthesis should be put off for a while. They specialize in one of the auxiliary subjects of the Bible—Assyriology, Hebrew Grammar, problems of style, textual criticism, the history of exegesis, or the study of a limited period or a particular book—all matters less likely to be controversial. Of course, it is a good thing that there are Catholic specialists in biblical sciences: in grammar, archæology, Semitic studies, etc. But how few are the Catholic historians of Israel! How few the Catholic exegetes of Israel's fundamental books! Perusing the reviews devoted to Scripture for these past years one finds that general problems, eagerly studied in 1900, are now pushed into the background. The dominant features are technical discussions and studies of minor points for specialist consumption. When priests or laymen want an answer to some theological or historical question raised by merely reading the Bible, they may be referred to an article of 1895 or a book of 1900 to solve their difficulties, but to nothing much within the last twenty years. Is Hebrew exegesis to continue to take refuge in its ivory tower, inaccessible to mere mortal men? Is the explanation of the Bible to educated people to be left to amateurs and to the self-taught? If so, then it is to be feared that the Old Testament will continue to lose ground in the Christian pulpit and in secondary education only to be confined to the elementary schools where it remains quite unchanged from what it was sixty years ago.

Fortunately three principal causes had begun and were to continue to transform that atmosphere of fear into one of joy in this work, causes which were to find their crown and sanction in a highly constructive act of the papal *magisterium*: I refer to the Encyclical *Divino afflante Spiritu* in 1943.

The first cause, one already mentioned, was the desire of the Christian people to make contact with the Bible, the fundamental book of the Christian faith. It had no intention of controlling or correcting the Church through Scripture as in the days of the Protestant Reformation. It was a spirit of faith eager to understand God's plan preparing for Christ by means of the Old Testament, eager to know Christ better by the Gospels and to assimilate that knowledge which St Paul, St John and the other New Testament writers had of him. Such a desire commanded respect, and imposed on Catholic exegetes a duty of going on from technical studies to produce works of general value for Christians today. It required suspicious conservatives, confined within the co-called tradition of the manuals, to make a careful and personal study of contemporary exegesis, the result of a hundred years of historical and archæological research, and of the thought of contemporary minds in their religious aspects. In this way they might cease to be an obstruction between the message of God and Christian souls. Once again in the Catholic Church, the priesthood and the laity was going to share a common intellectual interest, under the direction of the hierarchy, a mutual effort to come to grips with the entire content of faith. It was an authentically Christian impulse, in which authority could place a confidence that was impossible during the modernist crisis.

The second cause was the very definite change in the approach of Protestant exegesis.

It was observed above that owing to archæological discoveries, Protestant criticism of the Old Testament, on points of authenticity, dates and literary criticism, had become less radical or more qualified. Many issues could now be discussed more temperately between different denominations than was possible eighty years before.

Moreover, Protestant exegesis, at least in some of its sections, had shown a more religious tendency, a greater concern for living theology, than in the days of 'historicist' liberalism at the end of the nineteenth century.

The third, most direct and immediately active cause was the persevering, enlightened and solid work of the more able Catholic exegetes since 1890. The different aspects of this Catholic effort from 1890-1914 have been described above (pp. 40-60), and the main centres of their work indicated (pp. 44-5, 50). These were university faculties of Catholic theology, theological colleges of religious orders, outstanding among them being the École biblique Saint-Étienne of the Dominicans in Jerusalem founded and for many years directed by Fr M. J. Lagrange O.P., and towards the end of this period, in 1909, the Pontifical Biblical Institute founded by Pius X and entrusted to the Jesuits. The grave difficulties encountered by exegetes during this time have been mentioned, as well as the constructive soundness of their work. The results of this long and difficult work, continued and increased since 1918, had been sanctioned, approved and guaranteed for the future by Pius XII in his Encyclical *Divino afflante Spiritu*, 1943.

From 1890 to 1914, this first generation of Catholic exegetes, in spite of the troubles of the times, secured its rightful place to the historical method and its problems and in the seminaries and theological colleges gradually prepared an atmosphere favourable to an historical approach to the interpretation of Scripture. No doubt after the salutary repudiation of modernist exegesis by the Decree *Lamentabili*, many Old Testament problems were still very obscure. But after the setback of the First World War, in calmer circumstances, exegesis was able to begin again in a more effective way. It was necessary to comply with the desires of Catholics in every country. At this time, H. Vogels says, they 'showed an interest in biblical questions unparalleled since the Reformation, at least in Catholic Germany' (*Theologische Revue*, 1914, col. 193).

Writings on the New Testament after the 1914-18 war were plentiful and they were often aimed at the educated public. As in the previous period, Fr Lagrange O.P. was in the forefront. His great works on the Old Testament had led to disputes and mis-understandings. So, during the modernist crisis, he turned to the New Testament. In the *Études bibliques* he published in 1910 his commentary on St Mark, a large volume of more than 500 pages; in 1915, a commentary on the Epistle to the Romans; in 1918, on Galatians; from 1921-5, the three commentaries on St Matthew, St Luke and St John; in 1928, *L'Evangile de Jésus-Christ*, a kind of life of Jesus, adapting the results of the four previous volumes for public consumption; in 1931, *Le Judaisme avant Jésus-Christ;* at the beginning of his seventy-eighth year he undertook, on the basis of a life's research, an *Introduction à l'étude du Nouveau Testament*, of which he published in 1933 the *Histoire ancienne du Canon du Nouveau Testament*, in 1935, *Critique textuelle*, and in 1937, *L'Orphisme*. He died on 10 March 1938, aged eighty-three. Since the foundation of the Biblical School in Jerusalem, through his own work, through the *Études bibliques* (studies of abiding value, coming one after an-other since 1902, forty of them by 1958; Paris, Gabalda), through the *Revue biblique*, which was from the start, and now in its sixty-eighth year still remains, the supreme Catholic review devoted to the Bible, he had been the principal master and the greatest benefactor of Catholic exegesis.

There is no room here to list all the works that were published between 1914 and 1939 with the intention of establishing and deepening the vital relationship between the New Testament and Catholic priests, seminarists and believers. A few indications must suffice to illustrate the intensity and efficacy of Catholic exegetic work during this period.[11]

SERIES OF COMMENTARIES:

In French: Études bibliques; *Verbum salutis* (sixteen volumes by 1958, Paris, Beauchesne), begun by Fr Huby, S.J. in 1924 and directed by him until his death; *La Sainte Bible*, Latin text, French translation (Old and New Testaments) by L. Pirot, fourteen volumes published, Paris, Letouzey.

In German: Die heilige Schrift des Neuen Testaments (Bonner-Bibel) begun in 1912 by F. Tillmann (ten volumes, Bonn, Hanstein); *Die heilige Schrift des Alten Testaments*, begun in 1923 by F. Feldmann and H. Herkenne (twenty-five volumes, Bonn, Hanstein); *Die heilige Schrift für das Leben Erklärt*, begun in 1935 under the direction of E. Kalt and W. Lauck (more than twenty volumes by 1958: Old and

[11]For most of the works to be quoted now, may I refer readers to the regular reports on them in the *NRT*: they can easily be found thanks to the general tables of the review, 1914-39, and 1940-55.

New Testaments, Freiburg, Herder); *Das Neue Testament* begun in 1938 under the direction of A. Wikenhauser and O. Kuss (The Ratisbon Bible, Pustet, nine volumes up to 1958.

Similar efforts have been made, though less vigorously, in other Catholic regions.

In Catalan: La Biblia, begun in 1926 by the Benedictines of Montserrat on the initiative of Dom Ubach (eight volumes of commentary and two remarkable volumes of biblical illustrations of Genesis, Exodus and Leviticus, from 1926 to 1936; the work was begun again in 1948).

In Italian: Fr Sales O.P. began a new collection *La Sacra Bibbia* in 1935 which was continued by Fr Girotti O.P. It could not be carried on, and was only recommenced in 1955.

After the war in 1940 these series of commentaries became increasingly numerous in Catholic countries.[12]

INTRODUCTIONS TO THE BIBLE

Old and New Testament introductions were always required for Scriptural teaching in Catholic seminaries. After the Vigouroux-Brassac *Manuel-Biblique* had been put on the Index they became more necessary than ever. Some of those that have been frequently republished may be mentioned:

In Latin: Institutiones biblicae scholas accommodatae (Rome, The Biblical Institute, several volumes from 1925); H. Höpfl O.S.B. *Introductionis in sacros utriusque Testamenti libros compendium* (Rome, College of San Anselmo, several volumes from 1920); Adr. Simon, C.SS.R. (d. 1927) and J. Prado C.SS.R., *Praelectiones biblicae* (in several volumes, Turin and Madrid, from 1920); L. Balestri, O.E.S.A., *Biblicae introductionis generalis elementa*, Rome, 1932; P. Gachter, S.J. *Summa introductionis in Novum Testamentum*, Innsbruck, Rauch, 1st edn 1938; and new editions (in Latin and French) of the old *Introductionis in S.Scripturae libros compendium* by Cornely-Merk S.J. (Paris, Lethielleux).

In French: In addition to the introductory volumes by Fr Lagrange, quoted above, Fr Cheminant *Précis d'introduction à la lecture et à l'étude des saintes Écritures*, 1st edn, two volumes, Paris, Blot, 1930; J. Renié, *Manuel d'Écriture sainte*, several volumes, Lyons, Vitte, 1st edn 1930; Abbés Lusseau and Collomb, *Manuel d'études bibliques*, several volumes, Paris, Téqui, 1st edn, 1930. *Initiation biblique: Introduction à l'étude des saintes Écritures*, under the direction of A. Robert and A. Tricot, Tournai-Paris, Desclee, 1st edn 1938.

In German: J. Goettsberger, *Einleitung in das Alte Testament*, Freiburg, Herder, 1st edn 1928; J. Sickenberger, *Kurzgefasste Einleitung in das Neue Testament*, Freiburg, Herder, 3rd edn 1925 (the author died in 1945); M. Meinertz, *Einleitung in das Neue Testament*, Paderborn, Schöningh, 1st edn 1933; K.Th.Schäfer, *Grundriss der Einleitung in das Neue Testament*, Bonn, Hanstein, 1st edn 1938. In 1953 A.

---

[12]Note for example. after 1940 in Germany the *Echter Bibel* of Wurzburg directed by F. Nötscher (Old Testament) and K. Staab (New Testament); in Italy, *La Sacra Bibbia* of Turin (Marietti), directed by Mgr Garofalo; in Holland, *De Bocken van het Oude Testament*, Ruremond and Maaseik, collection directed by A. van den Born, W. Grossouw and J. van der Ploeg; in England, a single volume in collaboration, *A Catholic Commentary on Holy Scripture*, 1st edn 1953, London and New York (Nelson): new edn in preparation.

Wiekenhauser's valuable *Einleitung in das Neue Testament*, Freiburg, Herder, 2nd edn 1956, translated into English, *New Testament Introduction*, by T. Cunningham, New York, 1958. Although not what would be called an 'Introduction to holy Scripture' this list may well be concluded by the remarkable *Supplément du Diction-naire de la Bible*, edited successively since its foundation in 1928 by L. Pirot, A. Robert and H. Cazelles, which supplies everything that is to be expected from an introduction to the Bible.

Finally, as an indication of Catholic interest and of the work of exegetes from 1918-39, the lives of Jesus or related works, published during this period, and of which many editions have been issued. *In French*: the valuable apologetical study by Fr de Grandmaison *Jésus-Christ, sa personne, son message, son oeuvre*, completed by Fr de Grandmaison just before his death (1927) and published in 1929, two volumes (Paris, Beauchesne)—English translation Sheed and Ward, 1930; M. J. Lagrange O.P., *L'Évangile de Jésus-Christ* (Paris, Gabalda, 1st edn 1928—English translation London 1938; J. Lebreton S.J., *La vie et l'enseignement de Jésus-Christ, notre Seigneur*, Paris, Beauchesne, two volumes, 1st edn 1931; F. Prat, S.J., *Jésus-Christ, sa vie, sa doctrine, son oeuvre*, Paris, Beauchesne, 2 volumes, 1st edn 1933; and during the Second World War, the two books of Daniel-Rops, *Histoire Sainte* and *Jésus en son temps* were published (English translations, London 1956); they enjoyed a success unprecedented in twentieth-century religious literature and this result has turned the author to a vivid study of Christian history which is of great service to the Church. Other lives of Jesus could easily be added to this list, as well as doctrinal or apologetical studies of his message and personality.

In German there are the remarkable studies by Karl Adam (professor of theology at Tübingen) on Christ and by Romano Guardini on the Lord; the apologetic studies on Christ's divinity by H. Felder, O.F.M.Cap. and its abbreviation *Jesus von Nazareth, ein Christusbuch*, 1936; the life of Jesus by F. M. Willam, *Das Leben Jesu im Lande und Volke Israël*, 1933, etc. *In English*, Mgr Goodier, *The Public Life of Our Lord Jesus Christ*, two volumes, London, 1930. *In Italian*, J. Ricciotti *Vita di Jesu Christo*, Milan, 1941. *In Dutch*, P. van Imschoot, *Jesus Christus*, Ruremonde, 1941.

These three groups of examples, (series of commentaries, introductions to the Bible, lives of Jesus) have been chosen to bring out both Catholic exegetical activity in this period between the two wars, and its attempt to meet the growing interest of the Catholic public in Scripture and, at that time, particularly in the New Testament. Examples of more technical exegesis could have been added, specialist work by Catholics in the different branches of the Bible, textual, literary and historical criticism, biblical archæology and geography, oriental language, etc. But that would have been outside the purpose of this book.

After the second world war the biblical movement among Catholics grew in intensity and depth. It is intimately associated, through a most significant interpenetration of ideas and feelings, with several other trends of thought characteristic of our time: the doctrine of the 'Mystical Body', which opens the way to a better understanding of the Church and to a more personal idea of the individual incorporation into Christ;[13] the ecumenical movement which, as a result of world atheism and the consequent threat to religion, realizes the need of closer collaboration in prayer and action of all those who believe in Christ and his redemptive Incarnation; the liturgical sense that is awakening the need for more effective, concrete and vital participation of everyone, laity as well as priests, in the fathomless resources of Catholic worship and especially in the sacrifice of the Mass.

Three papal Encyclicals, *Mystici Corporis Christi* (29 June 1943) on the Mystical Body of Christ, *Divino afflante Spiritu* (30 September 1943) on biblical studies, and *Mediator Dei* (20 November 1947) on the liturgy, by enlightening and directing Catholic thought, have powerfully confirmed and deepened these fortunate and eminently Christian tendencies in the Catholicism of our time. Here in this book, only the Encyclical *Divino afflante Spiritu* has to be considered. For Catholic exegesis it is what *Rerum novarum* was for the social question in 1891. It was an act of liberation, rich in lasting results, coming exactly at the right time, the result of long years of preparation by Catholic exegetes who patiently carried on their work amidst difficulties and who now saw their efforts sanctioned and ratified, in the same way that *Rerum novarum* had sanctioned and ratified the constant social work of a great number of bishops, priests and laymen. The immediate results of the encyclical for the history of Catholic exegesis were of capital importance; they will be no less so in the future. All the more because this first clarifying of the official attitude was to be followed by others equally important and exactly in the same line: the letter from the secretary of the Biblical Commission, Fr Vosté to Cardinal Suhard (16 January 1948) on the dates of the documents of the Pentateuch and on the literary form of the first eleven chapters of Genesis (A.A.S. xl, 1948,

[13]Since 1918 there have been many books on the doctrine of the Mystical Body, but the most intelligent and fruitful work in these spheres was that done by Fr Emile Mersch, S.J. (1890-1940) in his great books *Le Corps Mystique*, two volumes, 1st edn 1933, 2nd edn 1951; *Morale et Corps Mystique*, 1st edn 1937; 4th edn 1955; *La théologie du Corps Mystique* (a posthumous work), 2nd edn, 1944; 4th edn 1954; and in his many articles on this subject. It was his life's work.

pp. 45-8; *EB* 2nd edn, n.577-81); clarifications on the interpretation of Scripture in the Encyclical *Humani Generis* (A.A.S. xlii, 1950, pp. 561-78; *EB*, 2nd edn, n.611-20); the declarations of the secretary and under-secretary of the Biblical Commission on how the Commission's decrees issued during the modernist conflict are to be understood today. The next chapter will constitute a consideration of these documents as a whole.[14]

[14]The following chapter is largely a reproduction of a commentary on *Divino afflante Spiritu* published in 1946 in *NRT*, and then as a pamphlet which was soon out of print. As it stands perhaps it will prove excessively long for the needs of some readers. It is really intended for fellow teachers in Scripture. The wide implications of this particular document of the magisterium, unique in the history of Catholic exegesis, would seem to demand a thorough interpretation.

CHAPTER VII

THE ENCYCLICAL *DIVINO AFFLANTE SPIRITU* (1943) AND RECENT DIRECTIONS OF THE MAGISTERIUM

The Letter from the Biblical Commission 20 August 1941

THE SPIRIT and basic conclusions of the Encyclical *Divino afflante Spiritu* were presaged in an important document, the letter of the Biblical Commission dated 20 August 1941. This letter was provoked by an incident in the life of the Church in Italy. Under the pseudonym Dain Cohenel an Italian priest, now known to have been Fr Dolindo Ruotolo, in a forty-eight page pamphlet entitled *Un gravissimo pericolo per la Chiesa e per le anime. Il sistema critico-scientifico nello studio e nell'interpretazione della Sacra Scrittura, le sue deviazioni funeste e le sue aberrazioni*, violently attacked the employment of scientific, historical and critical methods in the study and interpretation of holy Scripture. This pamphlet was sent simultaneously to the pope, the cardinals, all the Italian bishops and certain superiors of religious Orders. Its author had previously published a series of commentaries on Holy Scripture (in thirteen volumes, from Genesis to Ecclesiasticus) under the title *La Sacra Scrittura, Psicologia-Commento-Meditazione* which often showed great devotion, but were totally devoid of signs of historical knowledge and in several places defective from the theological point of view. The whole series was put on the Index *donec corrigatur* by a decree of the Holy Office dated 20 November 1940. The author submitted, and his submission was announced in the *Acta Apostolicae Sedis* for 1940 (p. 554), but he then contrived to defend his point of view indirectly by denouncing as disastrous for the Church the critical movement, which he regarded as diametrically opposed to the principles of his own exegesis.

In his pamphlet he stigmatized as semi-rationalists and modernists, and as endangering holy Scripture, a group of Italian Catholic exegetes who were endeavouring to base their interpretations of Scripture on a soundly conceived system of historical cricitism as well as on respect for Catholic tradition. His attack was directed especially against the Pontifical Biblical Institute. The Biblical Commission felt compelled to reply to this sharp attack in a letter dated 20 August 1941, signed by its president, Cardinal Tisserant, and its secretary, Fr Vosté O.P., and addressed to all the archbishops and bishops of Italy. It was published in the *Acta Apostolicae Sedis* for 1941 (p. 465 f.) and numerous similarities in approach and form show that it was as it were the first draft of part of the Encyclical.

To make it easier to understand the full scope of Pius XII's instructions in the Encyclical *Divino afflante Spiritu* it will be worthwhile in the first place to set out a short summary of the chief points in this letter.

The letter is severe in its description and condemnation of Dain Cohenel's pamphlet.

Under the pretext, says the letter, of defending a better kind of exegesis, called the exegesis 'of meditation', the pamphlet is primarily a virulent attack on the scientific study of holy Scripture. It calls the philological, historical and archaeological examination of the Bible naturalism, rationalism, modernism, scepticism and in their place it advocates giving free reign to the mind, as though each individual ought to receive from the Holy Ghost special enlightenment as the first Protestants claimed. With extreme violence, it attacks the pontifical scientific institutes, and sees at work in the scientific study of the Bible the spirit of pride and presumption and a hypocrisy scrupulously anxious about the letter. It scorns all learning and any knowledge of oriental languages and auxiliary sciences, and falls into grave errors regarding the fundamental principles of inspiration and Catholic hermeneutics, by misunderstanding the doctrine regarding the meanings of Scripture and treating the literal meaning and accurate research into it extremely slightingly. Moreover, it defends a wrong theory of the authenticity of the Vulgate.

Having regard to these errors the Biblical Commission, the letter continues, has decided to draw attention to the most recent of papal directives concerning the scientific study of holy Scripture since Leo XIII, setting them out under four headings: (i) the literal sense, (ii) the use of the Vulgate, (iii) textual cricitism and (iv) the study of eastern languages and auxiliary sciences.

These are—but in reverse order—the directives again referred to in the first two sections of the second part of the Encyclical *Divino afflante Spiritu*.

(i) *The literal sense.* While admitting for form's sake that the literal sense is the basis of biblical interpretation, the anonymous author in fact extols a completely subjective and allegorical interpretation, according to the personal inspiration or, rather, imagination, of each individual. It is of course an axiom taught by faith that holy Scripture has, as well as a literal sense, a spiritual or typical sense. But not every sentence or narrative has a typical sense, and it was a serious exaggeration of the Alexandrian school that they tried to find a typical sense everywhere, even at the expense of the literal and historical sense. The typical sense, besides being based on the literal sense, should be founded either on the usage of our Lord, the apostles and the inspired writers, or on the traditional custom of the holy Fathers and the Church (especially in the liturgy, for *lex orandi, lex credendi*). A wider application of the sacred text might be justified by its employment for the purposes of edification in preaching or ascetical writing, but meanings thus obtained cannot really and strictly be called the meaning—the inspired meaning—of the Bible. On the basis of these principles, the Biblical Commission sets out in detail the errors and unjust attacks in this anonymous pamphlet, setting against them in addition to the well-known text from St Thomas Aquinas *Omnes sensus fundantur super unum, scilicet literalem, ex quo solo potest trahi argumentum* (All meanings are based on one, and that is the literal, from which alone argument may be drawn— *Summa Theologica* Ia, qu. 1, 10 ad 1), various passages from the Encyclical *Providentissimus* (*EB*, 2nd edn, n. 107 and 112),[1] and the Encyclical *Spiritus Paraclitus* by Benedict XV (*EB* n. 485 and 487) as well the authority of St Jerome (*EB*, n. 106 and 487).

(ii) *The use of the Vulgate*. Still more obvious is the anonymous writer's error regarding the meaning and scope of the Tridentine decree about the Vulgate. It was the intention of the Council of Trent to sanction the use in the Western Church of the common Latin version used for centuries in the Church, so countering the confusion occasioned by the use of the new Latin and vernacular language translations then being published. But by doing so it had no intention of lessening the authority of the ancient versions followed in the Eastern Churches, especially the Septuagint used by the apostles themselves, and still less the authority of the original texts. Indeed, it resisted endeavours made by some of the assembled Fathers who desired to see the Vulgate used exclusively as the only authoritative text. This anonymous author, however, interprets the Tridentine decree as though it conferred a unique authority on the Vulgate making it superior to any other text; he would forbid straying from it in any passage; the practice of textual criticism in his view, is 'to multilate holy Scripture' and use of another text is 'to substitute one's own research for the authority of the Church'. To talk in this way is not only to offend against common sense, which could never admit the superiority of a version over the original text, but also to falsify the mind of the Fathers of the Council as it appears in the official acts. Indeed, the Fathers recognized the need for a revision of the Vulgate itself, and entrusted its execution to the pope. Moreover, they made provision for and decided on the preparation of new editions of the Septuagint, the Hebrew text of the Old Testament and the Greek text of the New. To speak as this author does is to contradict the very teaching of the Encyclical *Providentissimus* itself (see *EB*, n. 106). Briefly the Council of Trent declared the Vulgate authentic in the legal sense, in relation to the *vis probativa in rebus fidei et morum*, but by no means excluded the possibility of divergences in it from the original text and the texts of the ancient versions.

(iii) *Textual criticism*. In view of his principles regarding the Vulgate and other texts, it is natural that the anonymous author should deny the necessity and utility of textual criticism. 'To criticize textually is to treat the divine book as

---

[1]The Letter appeared in 1941 and references in it are therefore all to the 1st edn of *EB* (1927). For them I have substituted here and throughout this chapter references to the 2nd edn (1954) in general use today.

though it were a human book', it is to 'massacre' the Bible. Thence arise this author's violent invectives against 'scientific criticism', 'naturalism' and 'modernism'. With such obtuseness the Biblical Commission contrasts the attitude of Catholic biblical scholarship from Origen and St Jerome to the Commission for the revision of the Vulgate set up by Pius X and the declarations of Leo XIII (*EB*, n. 142), the decrees of the Biblical Commission on the Psalms (*EB*, n. 349) and the Penateuch (*EB*, n. 184), and the decrees of the Holy Office dated 2 June 1927 on the Johannine Comma (*EB*, n. 136) etc.

(iv) *The study of eastern languages and auxiliary sciences.* For this anonymous author Hebrew, Syriac, and Aramaic are only 'a source of pride' to the *scientifici*, orientalism has become 'a fetish', etc. Such language, well adapted to discouraging the real and difficult labour of study, and encouraging to lack of thought and restraint in exegesis, is in complete contrast with the instructions of the Church from St Jerome to our own times. The Biblical Commission proves this with a series of quotations from Leo XIII (*EB*, n. 118 and 140), Pius X (*EB*, n. 178) and Pius XI's Constitution *Deus Scientiarum Dominus* (art. 33-4). To exegetes, the study of eastern languages and the auxiliary sciences is not, of course, an end in itself, but a way to the understanding and clear and accurate exposition of the word of God: in its application it can be abused and exaggerated, but *abusus non tollit usum.*

In four further pages the anonymous author tries to invoke for his teaching the special patronage of Pius X and the Encyclical *Pascendi*. He is oblivious of the fact that, although it was Leo XIII in his Encyclical *Providentissimus* who gave exegesis its *Magna Carta*, it was Pius X who, as early as 1904—a few months after his election—proposed a centre for higher biblical studies and, after various preparatory steps, finally founded the Pontifical Biblical Institute in 1909; and it is well known how much this Institute has done for the advancement of biblical studies. It was Pius X who finally gave their definitive form to the directives about scriptural studies in seminaries (27 March 1906; *EB*, 162-80), and so on.

The document ends with an exhortation to continue the study and teaching of Scripture in accordance with the directions of the popes just named, and contrary to the suggestions of the anonymous author. In an audience on 16 August 1941, the pope was pleased to approve this letter and order its distribution.

What makes this letter interesting is less its refutation of Ruotolo's ideas—they are so far-fetched that they could only be rejected—than its assertion of two principles, of two mental attitudes towards the Bible which were to be equally predominant in the Encyclical:

1. The first of these is that the interpretation of the Bible demands, as one of its constituent elements, human knowledge, natural scientific work. Of course, the Church has always maintained, and will always maintain, that *animalis homo non percipit ea quae Dei sunt:* all natural knowledge, even the maximum of natural knowledge, will never succeed in understanding the Word of God as it should be understood, in penetrating it in such wise as to see perfectly its

definitive truth and to live according to its religious implications, if
the light of grace and the holy desire for what is good, inspired by
grace, do not enlighten and animate the reader of the Bible. The
vitally essential and eternal content of the divine message can be,
and normally is, more clearly perceived by a simple and upright
soul responding to God's call and seeking him with all its powers,
than by a very erudite and, humanly speaking, very acute scholar
who is impervious to the things of God. This is incontestable. To
reach the God who is revealed, knowledge must become religious,
supernaturally religious. Otherwise it will never achieve its end.

But while the Church asserts all this, she also asserts equally
energetically the rights and authority of science, and especially of
history in the study of the historical facts on which Christianity is
based. As events happening at definite moments in time and at
definite places in our world these facts must be examined with all
the resources and all the thoroughness of ever-advancing science,
and proportionately to that advance itself. There are not two
Christianities, the Christianity of faith, and the Christianity of
history. There is only one Christianity, which is simultaneously that
of faith and history. Nor is Christianity a simple groundwork of
individual religious experiences; its sacred books are not simply the
means of arousing salutary feelings in souls through the uncontrolled
reading of the sacred texts.

The Christian religion in all its parts, including the scriptural
part, is simultaneously a human and divine work, brought into being
here on earth; to be understood it requires the exacting effort of the
whole man, with all his natural powers, as well as with all the help
afforded him by supernatural strength. Ruotolo's theses not only
conflict with the directives of recent popes (as the letter of the
Biblical Commission clearly shows), they contradict the very
principles of Christian humanism, as these are to be discerned in the
whole life of the Church.

2. The second principle, immediately obvious in the Biblical
Commission's letter, and later asserted equally clearly in the
Encyclical, is that of the primacy of the literal sense in biblical
exegesis. Thus the two documents confirm and sanction the distinct
movement which for long, but especially during the previous fifty
years, had been leading Catholic exegetes in the same direction.

Everyone, of course, admits the existence of a spiritual sense in

Scripture and the Italian letter of 1941 uses an especially strong formula to affirm its existence: *è propositione di fede da tenersi per principio fondamentale;* but there are certain conditions which must be fulfilled if it is to be recognized *as the inspired sense*—the conditions set out in the letter of the Biblical Commission and repeated in almost identical words in the Encyclical. We shall return to them below. In addition, the letter resists the notion that an allegorical sense may be sought in every passage of Scripture, and blames Alexandrian exegesis for having attempted this very thing. Repeating St Thomas's words *Omnes sensus fundantur super unum, scilicet litteralem, ex quo solo potest trahi argumentum,* it requires that the spiritual sense 'should be based on the literal meaning' (*fondarsi sopro il senso letterale*).

In quite recent years there has indeed appeared a movement in reaction against the narrow rationalism which, among supporters of liberal critical methods, has tended to 'water down' the Bible and deprive it of what is of primary value in it (that is, its religious teaching); it is a movement in favour of a return to as wide an allegorical interpretation as possible. Doubtless this movement has avoided Ruotolo's exaggerations: inspired by men of eminence, like the writer Paul Claudel,[2] it is full of delicate light and shade, subtle, often rich in poetry and imbued with a very lofty religious sensibility.

But unfortunately these writers do not seem to possess sufficient understanding of the wealth of the literal meaning of the Bible, understood theologically in the light of Christian doctrine as a whole. Mesmerized by the narrowness of rationalist critical exegesis, they do not see sufficiently the religious and theological profundity of the slow doctrinal ascent of the Old Testament towards its perfection and its crown in the New (*Vetus Testamentum in Novo patet*); nor do they perceive the riches of the traditional typology based on the literal meaning.[3] As a consequence there are instances in their

---

[2]*Introduction au livre de Ruth,* complete text of the book by Fr Tardif de Moidrey (1828-79), Paris 1938. See also the review *Dieu vivant* n. 1, pp. 83-92. It will be worth consulting also on some of the ancient writers whose authority is invoked by this movement: H. de Lubac S.J. on Origen in *Dieu vivant* II, pp. 101-13, for example, or J. Daniélou, S.J. *Grégoire de Nysse, Vie de Moïse,* Introduction, especially pp. 22-7 (Paris 1941).

[3]Mgr Cerfaux records some of these in his study of Pius XII's Encyclical entitled *Encyclique sur les études bibliques,* pp. 23-6, 98-100, Brussels, 1945. For further examples, see also V. Laridon's articles on the Encyclical in *Collationes Brugenses* 1945-6, January 1946, pp. 3-11; and V. Jacques *art.* in *Coll. Namurcenses,* 1945, pp. 167-71.

writings of exaggerated, even indefensible, expressions about the literal sense, and there is an excessive cult of artificial and fantastic allegories carrying exegesis back to the worst days of Alexandrianism. The principles laid down by the Biblical Commission's letter and afterwards by the pope's Encyclical at least offer a practical guide to this movement, and at the same time form a valuable safeguard against deviation and error. True progress is to be found in the direction indicated by the Encyclical, and not in an artificial return to outmoded methods.

The Encyclical Divino afflante Spiritu

The occasion and purpose of the Encyclical Divino afflante Spiritu

The Encyclical *Divino afflante Spiritu* appeared fifty years after the Encyclical *Providentissimus*, and refers to it quite explicitly. The pope's intention was to celebrate the fiftieth anniversary of the earlier Encyclical 'which is regarded as the great charter of scriptural studies';[4] he thought it opportune 'to confirm and endorse the wise injunctions of our predecessor as well as the prudent measures taken by his successors for the establishment and crowning of his work, and also ourselves to set forth such instructions as the present time seems to demand, so that all the children of the Church who devote themselves to these studies may receive added encouragement in so necessary and laudable a task'.

As a result of the complex evolution of exegesis, there were many points in the former papal instructions needing confirmation and definition and even completion. Not in vain had Catholic science been toiling, gradually improving its methods and principles during the previous fifty years. The Encyclical came, so to say, as the approbation, the ratification, of a vast effort, and, as such, was received with profound gratitude by all Catholic exegetes.

Apart from this fundamental purpose, the Encyclical, or at least some parts of it, seems also to have been called forth by Dain

---

[4] *Divino afflante Spiritu* is quoted here from Mgr Canon G. D. Smith's translation, published by the Catholic Truth Society, London, under the title *Biblical Studies*.

Cohenel's pamphlet: it seemed necessary to react against the erroneous tendencies there revealed not only in regard to Italy but also to other countries where a similar narrowness of outlook was to be seen.

Finally, the Encyclical, in the pope's own words, seemed to him to be necessary because of the vast technical, archæological and historical progress made since the Encyclical *Providentissimus*. Pius XII frequently emphasized the discoveries made during the previous fifty years and the strict discipline in method that emerged from them.

The Encyclical appeared during the Second World War. At that time a discussion of authentic exegetical methods seemed far removed from the worldwide concerns of mankind. But even this contributed to the beneficial effect of the Encyclical, for it resulted in the new instructions being applied by Catholic exegetes quietly, without excitement—the excitement was elsewhere—step by step, gradually, as it became possible in the various countries to take up scientific work again. Research was continued along the lines already followed by the best workers, and henceforward workers were aware of the certainty of the approval of their work by the Church. The ability to work peacefully, safe in this knowledge, is an essential condition of true progress.

Outline of the Encyclical

After an introduction indicating the occasion and purpose of his Encyclical, Pius XII reminds his readers in the first and historical section of what Leo XIII and his successors did regarding biblical studies, emphasizing certain points and bringing out clearly their full significance. He enumerates the results obtained by these documents and through the work of Catholic exegetes loyal to the directives they contain.

In a second, doctrinal section, in some sort a methodology of holy Scripture, he first sets out succinctly the chief scientific advances made in biblical sciences in the previous fifty years. Consequently he states clearly the necessary conditions for a biblical exegesis at once both scientific and Christian. These conditions are:

(1) *A return to the original texts*. This requires a profound knowledge of the languages of the Bible and of the purpose and technique of textual criticism. It in no way conflicts with the decree of the

Council of Trent regarding the official character of the Latin Vulgate.

(ii) A proper interpretation of the sacred books based on the literal sense considered from every point of view, in its philological, archæological and historical bearing, but also and above all in its theological implications. With regard to this literal sense, the pope defines the legitimate approach to the 'spiritual' sense of Scripture. He lays stress on the help to be obtained by the modern exegete for a full understanding of the authentic meaning of the Bible from knowledge of the Fathers and Doctors and great exegetes of the Catholic past.

(iii) Special tasks face modern commentators as a result of present progress in history and historical method. They must (a) take into account the personality of the inspired writer (his psychology, the influence of his own period, his sources, stylistic method and aim), (b) take into account literary forms, particularly with historical material—none of the 'forms of expression' used in human speech among eastern peoples was excluded from the Bible unless it was repugnant either to the holiness or truth of God: in speaking with men, God uses human speech forms; and (c) promote a more profound study of biblical antiquities and everything that might throw light on them—archæology, history and the literature of ancient peoples.

(iv) As in the past, so also today, exegesis is faced with serious difficulties: if, through the endeavours of modern scholars, some former difficulties have now been solved, others still remain and some of them will perhaps always remain. In one of the most original passages of the Encyclical, the pope speaks of the spirit of freedom and mutual charity which, as well as fidelity to the Church, befits the pursuit of these difficult solutions: he shows how important it is not to exaggerate the number of passages—in fact, there are very few—whose meaning has been defined by the Church or fixed by the unanimous consent of the Fathers. There is a wide field in which research workers are still free—and freedom is an essential condition of scientific advance.

(v) After these scientific directives, the pope lays down the rules for the use of holy Scripture in the teaching of the faithful. He defines the various ways in which it may be used in the sacred ministry and especially the form to be taken by the course in

Scripture at seminaries. With a glance at the times in which the Encyclical was published, he reminds his readers of the great importance of Scripture in time of war.

The conclusion is an ardent and encouraging appeal addressed to Catholic exegetes responsible for the important mission of interpreting the Word of God, and to all those whose duty it is to pass on the riches of Scripture to the faithful: they will be greatly rewarded.

The Characteristics of the Encyclical

The Encyclical is positive and constructive. It contains instructions for future work rather than warnings against dangers. Ordinarily, a pope is led to intervene doctrinally in the evolution of ideas either to ward off error or grave dangers threatening the faith —as for example in the Encyclical *Pascendi* (against modernism) *Divini Redemptoris* (against atheistic communism), or *Mit brennender Sorge* (against National-Socialistic totalitarianism)—or to explain a doctrine to the minds of Christians or indicate a line of conduct to their wills—as for example in the Encyclicals *Mystici Corporis* (on the mystical Body), *Rerum novarum* (on the social question), or *Divino afflante Spiritu* (on the study of the Bible). Moreover, the two purposes are often combined.

All were struck by the positive character of *Divino afflante Spiritu*, seeing it as an optimistic and trusting exhortation to work freely and fruitfully in the field of Catholic exegesis. They felt that the pope was conscious of being able to depend unreservedly on the numerous groups of Catholic research scholars, and able to allot them their tasks without fear of seeing his thought distorted either by daring excess or narrowness.

As soon as it was published it was seen at once that the Encyclical was progressive and liberalizing. For Catholic exegetes it was what *Rerum novarum* had been in 1891 for Christians concerned with social problems. It touches on and solves with a clarity hitherto unattained various problems such as the value of the Vulgate, the importance of the literal sense (and the inevitable limitations of the spiritual sense), the importance of 'literary form' in the interpretation of historical narratives, and so on. The Encyclical contains many trenchant passages which were immediately noticed; for example, on the fewness of scriptural texts whose meaning has been defined by the Church or is imposed by the unanimous consent of the

Fathers, or on the charity and trust which must be shown to exegetes seeking solutions to problems, and in many other similar passages.

On the other hand careful reading of the Encyclical shows it to be very circumspect, as precise as it is balanced in its demarcation of the limits of each of the rules that it lays down. To remove some of the more liberal exegetical formulas from their context and set them up as absolute standards, valid in all cases and circumstances, would be to misrepresent the mind of the pope. As I have just said, the whole of the Encyclical is an act of confidence in Catholic exegetes' prudence and farsightedness such as has been shown by many during the previous fifty years, and which the pope has the right to expect from them in the future. The cause of real critical exegesis among Catholics could not but suffer as the result of exaggeration and foolhardiness, which are both contrary to papal intentions and inimical to solid scientific progress.

In this study I intend to survey the various parts of the Encyclical one by one, analyzing and commenting on the more important passages, and summarizing the rest, in order to grasp the pope's thought as perfectly as possible, both in itself and in the circumstances which show its trend and timeliness.

The Introduction to the Encylical

Since holy Scripture, written under the inspiration of the Holy Ghost, is the Church's treasure, it has always been the object of her greatest solicitude. So, for instance, the Council of Trent drew up a definition of the Canon of Scripture (DZ 783 f.; *EB*, 2nd edn, 57-60), and the Council of the Vatican a decree of inspiration (DZ 1787; *EB* 77), and when controversies seemed to be limiting the inspiration and inerrancy of Scripture to matters of faith and morals alone, there was published the Encyclical *Providentissimus* (18 November 1893). In our own times, on this the fiftieth anniversary of that Encyclical, Pius XII's intention as the passage reproduced above shows, is on the one hand to recall and confirm what Leo XIII and his successors had done with regard to the Bible (and this is the subject of the first part of the Encyclical), and on the other, to indicate what 'the present time seems to demand' (and this is the subject of the second part). The final aim is the further encouragement of all the sons of the Church devoting themselves to biblical studies.

PART I:

Historical Papal Acts, 1893-1943

In this enumeration of the acts of former popes Pius XII seems deliberately to have chosen on the one hand to recall and confirm clearly those passages which laid down the immutable principles of Catholic exegesis, those it is important constantly to emphasize in order to safeguard the Church's dogmatic treasures and on the other hand to select and accentuate in the field of special directives those which seem more progressive and, used wisely, capable of wider application. This twofold concern for firmness on essential principles and a deliberate, intentionally broader tendency in the special directives I believe to have been the inspiration of the whole of this first section.

The Acts of Leo XIII

The first was the Encyclical *Providentissimus*[5] of 18 November 1893. From it Pius XII repeated those essential principles of the total

[5]It would be very interesting and useful to set out in parallel columns the passages in the two documents dealing with the same subjects. Despite the identity of their essential principles on the total inspiration and inerrancy of Scripture, they would obviously show very significant differences on many specific points— a clear indication of the influence of a fifty years' gap on the way problems are stated and solved.

Where Providentissimus said: 'The teacher must use the Vulgate version . . . But we do not mean that no attention should be paid to the other versions used praiseworthily by Christians of the first ages, and especially the primitive texts', *Divino afflante Spiritu* says 'the interpreter must explain the original text, for this, being the actual work of the sacred writer himself, has greater authority and weight than any translation, however excellent, be it ancient or modern'. In a long passage it explains that this is in no way contrary to the mind of the Council of Trent on the Vulgate. Although reference to the original texts is approved and praised in both documents, it is formulated very differently in the two texts, the emphasis in the first being very noticeably on the Latin Vulgate and in the other on the primitive text. What looks like authorization or permission in *Providentissimus* becomes a directive and a rule in *Divino afflante Spiritu*. The same kind of explanation, the same evolution to greater clarity of expression, I think, can be observed at many points—as, for example, in the relation between the literal sense and the spiritual sense, in the question of the exegete's obligation to follow the morally unanimous interpretation of the Fathers, and on the problem of the interpretation of historical facts in terms of literary form etc. There is a strong bond of continuity between the two Encyclicals, and the influence of the earlier upon the later is obvious throughout, but it seems indisputable that after fifty years of scientific progress the Church has adapted its language to suit a Catholic exegesis that is now more adult and better armed against the peril of rationalism.

inspiration and inerrancy of Scripture: 'It is absolutely unlawful "either to restrict inspiration to certain parts of sacred Scripture alone, or to admit that the sacred writer himself has erred," inasmuch as divine inspiration "of itself not only excludes all error, but as necessarily excludes and repudiates it as God, who is the supreme Truth, is necessarily unable to be the author of any error whatsoever. This is the ancient and unchanging faith of the Church".' This doctrine, taught forcefully by Leo XIII (*DZ* 1950-1; *EB*, 124), is reaffirmed by Pius XII in the words: 'We now set forth this by our authority also, enjoining that it be scrupulously maintained by all.'

In the same passage, Pius XII recalls the principle laid down in the Encyclical *Providentissimus* which at that time set scholars free from the trammels of the unhappy attempts to bring Scripture into concord with the natural sciences. It was established that 'no error whatsoever exists in those cases in which the sacred writer, when treating of special matters "followed sensible appearances" . . . expressing himself "either metaphorically or in the common manner of speaking current at that time" . . . for "the sacred writers—or more properly, as St Augustine says, the Holy Ghost who spoke through them—did not intend to teach men those matters (namely, the inner constitution of visible things), which are in no way profitable to salvation".'

Pius XII immediately adds to this quotation the famous phrase from the Encyclical *Providentissimus*, which has given rise to so many controversies: *Quod quidem 'ad cognatas disciplinas, ad historiam praesertim, iuvabit transferri'*: a principle which 'will usefully be applied also to cognate sciences, and especially to history'. Thus with Leo XIII he explicitly invites us to seek, for the historical sciences, a principle for the solution of problems analogous to that proposed for those in the natural sciences.[6] What solution? The pope does not say exactly, but with a concern to maintain the continuity of the Church's teaching, to complete Leo XIII's thought he uses the very words used by Benedict XV in the Encyclical *Spiritus Paraclitus*: 'a principle which will usefully be applied to cognate sciences, and especially to history, that is to say, "a similar method of refuting the fallacies of opponents and defending the historical credit of the sacred Scripture against their attacks" ' (*Spiritus Paraclitus, DZ* 2187, *EB* 458). But Pius XII did not repeat the whole section from *Spiritus*

[6]On this point see the commentary on *Providentissimus*, pp. 64-5 above.

Paraclitus (*EB* 456-60) from which the words in double quotation marks are taken—a section which, when it was first published, attracted some notice, and provoked considerable commentary; in it Benedict XV rejected the theory of a twofold truth, absolute and relative that, it was claimed, could be deduced from Leo XIII's own words.[7] Set out in this way, and joined to part of a comment by Benedict XV, Leo XIII's famous phrase remains an intricate matter of interpretation. The Encyclical does not at this point dispel existing obscurities; it does so more completely in the second part, in dealing with the importance of literary form in history.

Pius XII next recalls in passing two other, secondary reasons set out in the Encyclical *Providentissimus* why no error should be imputed to Scripture, namely, the possibility of accidental mistakes by copyists in transcription, and the possibility that the meaning of a passage might still, even now, be obscure to us. But his *chief* concern is to emphasize Leo XIII's *chief* and essentially constructive aim in his Encyclical, which was the positive promotion among Christians, and especially among priests,[8] of an ever more perfect knowledge of Scripture. This was the fundamental purpose of the Encyclical *Providentissimus*, and in *Divino afflante Spiritu*, Pius XII ratifies it and makes it his own.

Pius XII next recalls and lays stress on two other acts of Leo XIII. When we remember the attacks and suspicion to which the École Biblique Saint-Étienne in Jerusalem was subjected from time to time by various groups of Catholics the very high praise of this school and the reminder of Leo XIII's eulogy of it are in this context highly significant of Pius XII's desire to approve the achievements and tendencies of the school founded and for long presided over by Fr Lagrange.[9]

[7] It may be that Pius XII deliberately chose to exclude the idea of two kinds of truth from his exposition. In fact, in exegetical research these words have designated two very different types of interpretation: the first, that of Loisy, according to which everything in dogma and theology is 'relatively' true (this interpretation springing from his relativist philosophy, which was destructive of all Christian revelation); and a second in which the phrase 'relative truth' might be used to qualify an exposition in keeping not with the reality of the facts, but with what popular contemporary opinion said on a subject. The fact that part of the truth might be contained in this second interpretation is in practice echoed in the theory of 'literary form'. It was better to drop equivocal expressions.

[8] Cf. pp. 61 and 69-70 above.

[9] The Apostolic Letter *Hierosolymae in coenobio*, 17 September 1892 (*Leonis XIII Acta*, XII, 239-41, cf. p. 240).

There next follows a reference to the foundation of the Biblical Commission by Leo XIII on 30 October 1902, during the last year of his pontificate.[10] Here again, the purpose of the Encyclical is clearly to emphasize broadly and frankly the constructive nature of Leo XIII's new institution. And indeed it is certain, both from the circumstances of its foundation and from the programme assigned to its members (as well as from the choice of those first members themselves), that Leo XIII envisaged for the Biblical Commission, as well as the necessary duties of vigilance and defence, a very large part in the maintenance, encouragement, and advancement of Catholic exegesis.

The acts of the successors of Leo XIII

The Encyclical *Divino afflante Spiritu* does not mention everything in the work of Leo XIII's successors concerned with the study or defence of the Bible, but only the positive steps in support of the teaching and diffusion of the holy Scriptures. The pope does not go back over the struggle against modernism, or the condemnation in the Encyclical *Pascendi*, the decree *Lamentabili* and the various decrees of the Biblical Commission of the scriptural errors of Loisy and other exegetes; even Benedict XV's Encyclical on St Jerome is not mentioned in its chronological position between the work of Pius X and that of Pius XI, but is placed in the following paragraph in connection with papal concern for the use and propagation of holy Scripture.[11]

The following acts of Pius X are mentioned: the Apostolic Letter dated 23 February 1904, establishing the degrees of licentiate and doctor of biblical sciences, degrees to be conferred by the Biblical Commission;[12] the Apostolic Letter dated 27 March 1906 on the organization of scriptural studies in seminaries;[13] and the founda-

---

[10]Cf. p. 70, *supra*: *EB*, 137-48.

[11]Nevertheless, in referring to this Encyclical to quote from it the passage exhorting Christians to read holy Scripture, Pius XII does in fact recall the doctrinal passages in this letter: *Benedictus XV . . . postquam tum eiusdem Doctoris (i.e. St Jerome) praecepta et exempla, tum principia ac normas a Leone XIII et ab Se datas religiosissime inculcavit, atque alia hoc in rerum genere maxime opportuna neque unquam oblivioni tradenda commendavit . . .* (Benedict XV . . . by carefully inculcating the teaching and example of that Doctor (St Jerome) as well as the principles and regulations set forth by Leo XIII and by himself; and besides other most opportune and memorable recommendations on this subject . . .)

[12]*EB*, 149-57.

[13]*EB*, 162-80.

tion in 1909 of the Pontifical Biblical Institute, entrusted to the
Society of Jesus, so that there might be in Rome 'a centre of higher
scriptural studies to promote biblical learning and subsidiary
sciences as effectively as possible and in accordance with the spirit
of the Catholic Church'.[14]

Of the acts of Pius XI, those principally recalled include: the
Motu proprio of 27 April 1924 requiring that those who teach holy
Scripture in seminaries should possess academic degrees either from
the Biblical Commission or from the Biblical Institute, and exhorting
the general superiors of religious Orders and the bishops to send the
most suitable of their students to attend the courses at the Biblical
Institute[15]; and the Apostolic Constitution *Inter praecipuas*, dated 13
June 1933,[16] founding in Rome the monastery of St Jerome for the
Benedictine monks who, in 1907, had been entrusted by Pius X
with the revision of the Vulgate.[17]

The popes have shown a like concern for the use and widespread
diffusion of the Scriptures among the faithful. Two documents
from among the many are evidence of this, first the encouragement
given by Pius X (1907)[18] to the Society of St Jerome for the propagation of the Gospels, and secondly those passages of Benedict XV's
Encyclical *Spiritus Paraclitus* (1920) especially devoted to this
subject.[19]

Conclusion of the First Section

In a final paragraph, Pius XII bears witness to the great advance
made during the previous fifty years in the biblical field both in
scientific study of holy Scripture among Catholic exegetes and in
its intelligent use in preaching, ascetics and the Christian life. The
picture he draws is extremely optimistic and encouraging, particularly for exegetes. More than once during previous pontificates
they experienced anxious moments and at times felt that higher
authority regarded them with suspicion. It might well be thought
that it was Pius XII's wish here to offset all these painful memories
with the warmth and intensity of his praise and encouragement.

[14]*EB*, 297-310.
[15]*EB*, 505-12.
[16]*Acta Apost. Sedis* XXVI, 1934, pp. 85-7.
[17]*EB*, 289-90.
[18]*Pii X Acta*, IV, pp. 23-5.
[19]*EB*, 444, 482, 484, 478.

PART II:

The Doctrinal Section
The Study of Holy Scripture in Our Own Times

The present state of biblical sciences

Pius XII draws a composite picture of remarkable progress made in the sciences auxiliary to the Bible and in biblical studies since the Encyclical *Providentissimus*. His purpose is to reveal 'how deeply the better and fuller understanding of the sacred books is indebted to such investigations'. In these advances he sees a hidden design of Providence as well as an effective stimulus to exegetes to further work.

In the earlier pages of the present study I endeavoured to set out accurately the details of these new aspects of the biblical problem, especially in Chapter I (pp. 7-20) and Chapter V (pp. 77-113). In Chapter V, I intentionally followed the plan adopted here by Pius XII, so that it could easily be used as a commentary.[20] I venture therefore to refer the reader back to the sections of that chapter in connection with each of the six points made by Pius XII, and consequently confine myself now to a simple transcription of his words:

> It is obvious that the conditions of biblical science and of subsidiary studies have changed considerably in the course of the past fifty years. To mention only a few examples, at the time when our predecessor published his Encyclical *Providentissimus Deus* only one or two places in Palestine had been explored by excavations for the purposes of this study. But now explorations of this kind have become much more frequent and, being conducted by stricter methods and with experienced skill, are providing much more abundant and reliable information. How deeply the better and fuller understanding of the sacred books is indebted to such investigations is well known to experts and to all those who devote themselves to these studies.[21] Their importance is increased by the frequent discovery of

[20]Cf. pp. 77-8, above.
[21]On these archæological excavations, see Chapter I, p. 7 for the period 1850-1914, and Chapter V, section 1, for the period after 1914.

written records which contribute greatly to our knowledge of
the languages, literature, events, customs and cults of very
ancient times.[22] Equally noteworthy is the discovery and
examination, so frequent in our own day, of papyri, which
have given us very valuable information concerning the literature and institutions, public and private, especially of the time
of our Saviour.[23] Moreoever, ancient manuscripts of the
sacred books have been discovered and edited with skilful
care;[24] wider and deeper study has been devoted to the
exegesis of the Fathers of the Church;[25] and innumerable
examples are throwing light upon the forms of speech, writing,
and narrative in use among the ancients.[26]

All these are benefits granted by divine Providence to our
age, and they serve as a stimulus and an encouragement to
interpreters of Holy Writ to make eager use of the great light
thus afforded for a closer examination, a clearer explanation,
and a more lucid exposition of sacred Scripture. The fact that
the said interpreters have already responded and are still
responding with alacrity to this challenge[27]—a fact which we
observe with great consolation—is by no means the last or the
least of the fruits of the Encyclical *Providentissimus Deus*, in which
our predecessor, Leo XIII, as though foreseeing this new development of biblical science, both summoned Catholic exegetes
to their task and also wisely traced out for them its method
and programme.

To assure the uninterrupted continuance of this work and
its more and more successful advancement is our object in this
Encyclical, in which we intend especially to indicate to all
what still remains to be done, and in what spirit the Catholic
exegete ought today to approach this great and noble task,
and also to stimulate and encourage anew the labourers who
are working so strenuously in the Lord's vineyard.

[22]On the written records, see Chapter V, section two, p. 95.
[23]On the discovery and examination of the papyri, see Chapter V, section three.
p. 108.
[24]On the discovery and publication of biblical manuscripts, see Chapter V,
section 4, p. 111.
[25]On advances in patristic exegesis, see Chapter V, section 5, p. 112.
[26]On new light on forms of speech, writing and narrative in use among the
ancients see Chapter V, section 6, p. 112.
[27]I tried to illustrate this point in Chapter III, p. 40 *Catholic Exegesis from
1880-1914* and Chapter VI, p. 114 *New Aspects in Catholic Exegesis after* 1918.

The Instructions regarding exegesis in the Encyclical

For the plan of the Encyclical see pp. 140-2. In short, it follows the natural pattern of any hermeneutic work, starting from the lowest steps—a word, a phrase—to ascend gradually to the loftiest heights in interpreting and teaching the word of God.

The main outline of this plan is here resumed, not for the sake of repetition, but to complete what was said earlier by pointing out the similarity between this plan and the logical arrangement of all proper methods of interpretation.

1. The philosophical study of the text: of words and phrases, implying recourse to the original Hebrew, Greek or Aramaic texts rather than to the Latin, and presupposing, therefore, thorough knowledge of the languages of the Bible and of the science and art of textual criticism.

2. The determination of the literal sense, in all its aspects, and especially in all its theological significance: this implies not only an adequate knowledge of philology, but also acquaintance with the vast body of historical, archæological and religious facts indispensable to the understanding of any theological text from the past.

3. When the author's thought has been sufficiently grasped there follows historical criticism[28] of his statement. Even with the Bible, although it is safeguarded by the privileges of inspiration and inerrancy, it is impossible completely to understand the authentic message of the sacred writer, speaking in God's name, without taking into account his personality, and the literary form he uses, as well as the historical milieu in which he lived.

4. Are not the results, to which this strictly historical path leads us, certain to raise grave problems, either with regard to the inerrancy of Scripture, or to the history of the divine revelation in the Old and New Testaments itself? How, within the atmosphere of Christian concord, can we work towards an orthodox and completely historical solution of such problems as these?

5. Finally, the primary end of Scripture being the furtherance of the Christian life, how can it be taught to the faithful, and how, above all, can it be taught to the priests whose task it is to transmit its saving influences to the world?

---

[28]The Encyclical does not use this expression, to avoid, probably, erroneous or exaggerated interpretations.

1. Recourse to the Original Texts

The Encyclical states that recourse to the original texts and the study of ancient languages was being recommended in Christian antiquity by the Fathers of the Church, and especially by St Augustine. Yet there is a great difference between our day and former times, not only with regard to knowledge of Hebrew and other eastern languages, but even regarding knowledge of Greek among the greatest of the medieval Doctors. In our times, 'so many facilities are now available for the learning of these languages that the biblical exegete who failed to make use of them, and thus denied himself access to the original texts, could certainly not escape the stigma of levity and negligence'.

Hence it is the exegete's duty 'with the greatest care and veneration to seize eagerly upon every smallest detail of what has flowed from the pen of the sacred writer under God's inspiration'. He must therefore 'use every diligence to acquire a more and more thorough knowledge of biblical and other oriental languages, and assist his works of interpretation with all the aids that any branch of philology may supply'.

St Jerome and the great exegetes of the sixteenth and seventeenth centuries made every effort to acquire this mastery so far as the state of knowledge in their times allowed. 'By this means, then, the interpreter must explain the original text, for this, being the actual work of the sacred writer himself, has greater authority and weight than any translation, however excellent, be it ancient or modern.'

This statement is, I think, the clearest that has ever appeared in an ecclesiastical document giving the original text the priority due to it in study, and hence in exegetical teaching, and so relegating all versions, even the official Vulgate version, to second place. Undoubtedly it is the outcome of a lengthy and slow evolution in discipline, a final clear statement of what was only virtually established fifty years beforehand.

The importance of Textual Criticism

It is impossible to reach the original text without the employment of textual criticism. In the first centuries, St Augustine laid it down as the exegete's duty. Today 'precisely because of reverence due to the word of God' the exegete in his study of the sacred books must profit from the advances made in textual criticism 'employed with great brilliance and success in the editing of profane writings'. Equally, this is required of us by the 'filial gratitude' we feel towards God 'who has . . . sent us these books . . . as the letters of a Father to his own children'.

Of course, there is an unjustifiable kind of textual criticism which 'a few decades ago was employed by many in a completely arbitrary manner, and frequently in such a way that one would have said that they were using it as a means of introducing their own pre-conceived opinions into the text'. Probably the Encyclical is here referring to that strange freedom with which the poetical texts of the Old Testament were modified off-handedly by corrections, additions and omissions, (e.g. Duhm and Gunkel etc.) to accommodate them to the rhythm and logic considered more fitting by us in the twentieth century. In the New Testament, it was this same liberty which was so ingenious in the discovery of successive editorial strata, for example in the fourth Gospel, or found so little difficulty in postulating interpolations (as for example, Harnack and others at Luke 1. 34-5) or alterations (as Harnack at Matt. 16. 18).

Subjectivism of this kind is becoming increasingly unfashionable. As a direct result of technical progress, the present tendency in textual criticism is towards the most circumspect objectivity. The Encyclical bears witness to this in the words that nowadays 'it has achieved such stability and sureness that it has become an excellent instrument for producing a purer and more accurate edition of the word of God; any abuse of the art can now easily be detected'.

The optimism displayed by the Encyclical with regard to textual criticism must be properly understood.[29] All exegetes know that at the present time an absolutely definitive text of either the Old or New Testament is still not possible. Too many problems remain to be solved: thus in the New Testament, that of the origins, history and real value of the text formerly known as 'Western', or that of the origins and characteristics of the revisions which gave rise to the chief families to which our texts belong, or again, that of the value of the patristic readings from the first three centuries, and so on. But there is no doubt that textual criticism since the Westcott-Hort

[29]At first sight this optimism astonished many interpreters of the Encyclical, among them, for example, Fr Vaccari in *Periodica de re morali et canonica*, 1944, p. 122, who demonstrates why and in what way such optimism is legitimate, but points out that it must not be taken further than Pius XII intends.

edition of 1881 has made a continual and very signficant progress marked by a wealth of new materials and improvements in method. An account of these advances appears in section four of chapter V (pp. 111-112), and the reader is referred to it for a commentary on this part of the Encyclical.

But while awaiting the establishment of the ideal text, we must profit now from the results already achieved: this part of the Encyclical ends with an urgent appeal for the appearance 'as soon as it is possible and opportune' of 'editions of the sacred books and of the ancient versions—prepared by Catholics[30] in conformity with these critical standards; editions, that is, in which a scrupulous observance of all the laws of criticism shall be combined with the deepest reverence for the sacred text'.

The significance of the decree of the Council of Trent on the Vulgate. Translations into modern languages

An objection must be considered at this point. Is not this insistence on the original texts in conflict with the pre-eminence of the Latin Vulgate as it was proclaimed by the Council of Trent? Is not the Vulgate the official text in the Catholic Church?

The Encyclical answers this objection as it was answered by the Biblical Commission on 20 August 1941. Use of the original texts in this way is no sort of contradiction of the wise decrees of the Council of Trent regarding the Latin Vulgate. In the first place, indeed, the Council itself demanded the publication of a corrected and official text not only of the Latin version, but also of the Greek and Hebrew texts: what could not then be achieved would be possible today. Moreover, this decree affected only the Latin Church. And lastly, it in no way lessened the authority and standing of the original texts, but merely indicated the Church's choice, among the Latin versions circulating at the time 'among which the Council rightly decreed preference to be given to that version which "has been approved by long use in the Church for so many centuries".'

'This pre-eminent authority, or "authenticity", of the Vulgate was determined by the Council not primarily on critical grounds, but rather by reason of its legitimate use in the churches, through

---

[30]Such as, for example, the excellent small Catholic editions of the Greek New Testament by Merk, Vogels and Bover, and the critical edition of the Vulgate by the Benedictines of the Monastery of St Jerome.

the course of so many centuries, a use which proves this version to be entirely immune from any error in matters of faith and morals; so that, by the very witness and approval of the Church, it may safely and without danger of error be cited in discussions, lectures, and sermons. Its authenticity is therefore more properly called *iuridical* than *critical*.'

These sentences state what has become common teaching in Catholic seminaries. They give it the official ratification of ecclesiastical authority with a clarity of expression hitherto never attained.

Two recent pronouncements lend even clearer support to the movement for a return from the Latin Vulgate back to the original texts. First came the decree of the Biblical Commission dated 22 August 1943 (*EB.* 535-7): this was a discreet clarification of an earlier decree (30 April 1934) which might have appeared unfavourable to modern translations of Scripture made from the original text. The second was the official publication (*Motu proprio* dated 24 March 1945, *EB.* 571-5) of a new translation of the Psalter, made directly from the Hebrew, and sanctioned for immediate use in the Divine Office. This revision also embraced the canticles of the New Testament, such as the *Benedictus* and *Magnificat*.

From the respective value of the original text and the Vulgate the Encyclical also draws another conclusion about translations of the Bible in modern languages: 'Nor, finally, does this same decree of the Council of Trent prohibit translations into the vernacular, made even from the original texts themselves, to be provided for the use and benefit of the faithful and for the easier understanding of the word of God, as we know to have been done in many places laudably and with the approval of ecclesiastical authority.'

2.   *The Interpretation of the Sacred Books*

The value and investigation of the literal sense

At this point we meet again clearly enunciated the two principles deduced above from the letter of the Biblical Commission: the need for human scientific work, and the primacy of the literal sense in biblical exegesis.

Well equipped then with a knowledge of ancient languages and with the aids afforded by the critical art, the Catholic exegete must approach the most important of the tasks imposed upon him; that of discovering and expounding the genuine sense of the sacred books. In discharging this function interpreters should bear in mind that their chief aim must be to discern and determine what is known as the *literal* sense of the words of the Bible, 'from which alone', as Aquinas excellently observes, 'an argument can be drawn'. This literal meaning of the words they must investigate with every care by means of their knowledge of languages, using the help also of the context and of comparison with parallel passages—aids which are all commonly employed also in the interpretation of profane writings for the clearer understanding of the author's meaning.

There is no difficulty about the meaning of these directives. They demand complete philological interpretation in every field.

To them the Encyclical adds two principles peculiar to scriptural exegesis: (1) because it deals with inspired writings 'whose guardianship and interpretation have been entrusted by God himself to the Church', exegetes 'must take into equally careful consideration the explanations and declarations of the teaching authority of the Church, the interpretation given by the holy Fathers, and also the 'analogy of faith' as Leo XIII wisely enjoins in his Encyclical *Providentissimus Deus*.[31]

What we have here is a statement of the important law of the unity of the faith. God, the principle Author of Scripture, as also of the definitive teaching of the Church, cannot contradict himself: there are not two Christian doctrines. Every scriptural passage on faith or morals, of course, has its own historical and philological context determined in some given writing, and in a particular climate of thought. The real historical method requires that it shall be interpreted in close relation to that context, and that the exegete shall try as far as possible to determine the degree of clarity and maturity that this or that truth appears to have attained at that given moment in time in the mind of the human writer. But at the same time, the text under consideration belongs to another theo-

[31]This passage in the Encyclical *Providentissimus Deus* is famous. See *Leonis XIII Acta*, pp. 345-6; *EB*, 109-11, where the fundamental principle is expressed in the words *In ceteris* (that is, in passages of which the true meaning has not been defined by the Church) *analogia fidei sequenda est, et doctrina catholica, qualis ab auctoritate Ecclesiae accepta, tamquam summa norma est adhibenda*. Leo XIII laid down the same precept in the Apostolic Letter *Vigilantiae* (1902) *EB*, 136.

logical and religious context, that of the totality of Christian dogma
as it is taught by the Church. If our faith is true, the teaching of St
Paul cannot contradict that of St James; the mysticism of St John
cannot be in conflict with that of St Paul, any more than dogma of
today can deviate from that taught by Paul, John or James.

The Catholic exegete must be capable of rethinking his historical
conclusions in the light of a theological synthesis as penetrating and
accurate as possible. This very difficult task requires of him sincerity in two directions; the sincerity of the historian, who would
remain objectively and scrupulously loyal to the data revealed by
the facts (while never forgetting the subjective element subsisting
in any statement of fact), and then the sincerity of the believer who,
conscious of the inspired nature of the Word of God, never loses
sight of the Church's dogmatic synthesis as a whole into which the
individual passage fits. If he keeps this twofold sincerity firmly
anchored in his mind and will, he will safeguard himself against
hurriedly made concordances, sacrificing the data of history to the
premature conclusions of a transitory theology, and also against that
religious recklessness that compromises the eternal faith on account
of particular historical difficulties which may well vanish tomorrow.
And if he has to wait, and leave the resolution of apparent difficulties
between history and faith to the following generation, he will yet have
the courage to keep the problem in all its truth before him so that
when later it is studied more closely its true solution may be found.

Thus essentially biblical exegesis transcends the bounds of profane philology. It can never be said often enough (as recent popes,
and especially Pius X, have declared continually) that the exegete
must be a theologian, but a theologian who applies himself to
separating essentials from inessentials, who does not obtain all his
doctrine from some present or past scholastic manual, but from the
very sources of everlasting Christianity. (2) The same spirit imbues
the Encyclical's second directive: it requires that the teaching of
holy Scripture should be principally theological.

> And let them be especially careful not to confine their
> exposition—as unfortunately happens in some commentaries—
> to matters concerning history, archæology, philology and similar
> sciences. These should indeed to be given their proper place so
> far as they may be of assistance to the work of interpretation;

but commentators must have as their chief object to show what is the theological doctrine touching faith and morals of each book and text, so that their commentary may not only assist teachers of theology in expounding and corroborating the dogmas of faith, but also be useful to priests in their work of explaining Christian doctrine to the people, and help all the faithful to lead a holy and Christian life.

Pius XII is here thinking of the theological sense which immediately becomes apparent from literal exegesis, and of the religious interpretation genuinely based on the literal meaning of the texts: here resides, according to the Encyclical, the primary spiritual sense of the Bible. Again, to discover it and make it the chief object of his teaching, the mind of the exegete must be sincerely turned towards this spiritual and religious understanding of holy Scripture and should not be attracted exclusively by the problems of history and literary criticism.

In Chapter II (pp. 21-39) I endeavoured to show the form taken by literary and historical criticism of the Bible under liberal Protestantism between 1870 and 1914, and in Chapter III (pp. 40-60) what constructive work was done by Catholic exegesis in the same period and the fearful ordeal imposed by modernism. Throughout this period the Church strove continually to remind exegetes of the religious nature and theological aspects of scriptural interpretation (Chapter IV, pp. 61-76). After the unhappy period of the 1914-18 war, both in modern Protestantism and, of course, in Catholic exegesis, the living religious meaning and theological value of holy Scripture were increasingly esteemed (Chapter VI, pp. 114-122 and 122-132) though full account was taken of the immense advances in archæology, history and philology, the result of a century's exegetical labour. In this new atmosphere, Pius XII's insistence on the Christian duty of theological and religious interpretation assumes particular importance. In addition, viewed in the context of the constant papal endeavour since 1893, it is a clear sign of the advantage of a supreme religious authority in the chaos of human opinions and hypotheses.

Pius XII concludes this passage by stating clearly that the use of 'theological interpretation' of this kind, based securely on the literal sense, is the best reply to those who, like Dain Cohenel, dream of a return to Alexandrian allegorism. 'By giving an interpretation such as we have described, that is, one primarily theological, they will effectively silence those who assert that in biblical commentaries they can find hardly anything to raise their minds to God, nourish their souls, and foster their interior life, and therefore maintain that recourse should be had to a spiritual and so-called mystical interpretation.'

The right use of the spiritual sense

It may occasion some surprise that on this subject of the spiritual sense of Scripture the Encyclical is far vaguer in its explanation than the Biblical Commission's letter, or for that matter most Catholic interpreters. It does not mention the term 'typical' sense used in the 1941 letter, an expression based on the teaching of St Thomas Aquinas.[32] Nor does it refer to the profitable principle laid down in 1941: 'the spiritual sense must be based on the literal sense'. But it does emphasize the other principle, 'God alone knows and can reveal this spiritual sense to us'; far from being contradictory, these two statements, I consider, are complementary.

However, it links up directly with the earlier document in the enumeration of the arguments which alone buttress and guarantee the spiritual sense; the teaching of Christ or the apostles, the continuing tradition of the Church, and liturgical use whenever the well-known tag *lex orandi, lex credendi* is applicable. Hence it is clear that in the Encyclical there is no intention of adopting a definite position in face of the different Catholic attempts to define the various 'senses' of Scripture. The Encyclical does not seek to elaborate a doctrine of the spiritual sense and justify it to reason enlightened by faith. It is content to affirm that it exists, and to remind us of the principle accepted by all Catholics: 'what was said and done in the Old Testament was wisely so ordained and disposed by God that the past would spiritually foreshadow what was to happen in the new covenant of grace'.

Thus the directives of the Encyclical on this matter may be summarized in two points: firstly, it is the duty of exegetes to 'discover' the spiritual meaning of Scripture, and 'expound' it 'on condition of its being established that such a meaning has been

---

[32]The standard texts from St Thomas are very familiar: *Quodlib.* VII, art. 14 et 15; *Summa Theol.* Ia. qu. 1, art. 10.

given to it by God', 'with the diligence which the dignity of the word of God demands'. But secondly, they should nevertheless 'be scrupulously careful not to propound other metaphorical meanings as though they were the genuine sense of sacred Scripture'. Although, especially in preaching, 'a somewhat wider use of the sacred Text in a metaphorical sense may be profitable', with moderation and prudence, 'it must never be forgotten that such a use of the words of sacred Scripture is, as it were, extrinsic and adventitious to holy Writ. Moreover the practice is not without its dangers, especially today, since the faithful, and particularly those who are learned in both sacred and profane sciences, want to know what it is that God himself means to say to us in the sacred Scriptures, rather than what some eloquent speaker or writer is expounding with a dexterous use of the words of the Bible.'[33]

An exhortation to the study of the Fathers and Great Commentators

The Encyclical also suggests one last means whereby the exegete may grasp the whole of the meaning of the sacred texts; this is by a thorough study of the Fathers and Doctors of the Church, and of the great exegetes who have commented on Scripture. They did not possess, of course, the resources of erudition and linguistic knowledge available today, but by their 'delicate perception of heavenly things' and ' wonderful keenness of understanding' they were enabled to 'penetrate far into the depths of the Word of God and bring to light all that can contribute to explaining the teaching of Christ and to promote sanctity of life'. Pius XII regrets the fact that 'these precious treasures of Christian antiquity are only too little known to many of our modern writers' and hopes that Catholic exegetes will study them closely 'drawing upon the almost unlimited accumulation of riches which they contain' in the hope of encouraging modern interpreters to have recourse to them more frequently. 'Thus will come about a happy and fruitful combination of the learning and spiritual unction of the ancients with the greater erudition and maturer skill of the moderns.'

3.   *The special tasks of contemporary interpreters*

With the conclusion of the strictly philological task a further and

[33]The section of the Encyclical paralleling the Biblical Commission's letter ends with this paragraph.

more important duty faces the exegete, that of interpreting and weighing up by severely historical critical methods the human evidence belonging to the specific period, whose meaning he has just understood. The Encyclical avoids the phrase 'historical criticism' lest the impression be obtained that 'criticism' is implied and consequently some questioning of the truth of the Word of God, which is unblemished by error. Nonetheless, it sets out the principles of an authentic historical criticism that are reconcilable with the standards of inspiration.

This is one of the sections of the Encyclical which has attracted the widest attention, and indeed it appears to be the last word, spoken by authority, in the frequent controversies and the very many attempts at interpretation that have been characteristic of the last sixty years. I endeavoured to give a summary description of these conflicts of ideas among Catholics in Chapter III of this book, (*Catholic Exegesis* (1880-1914)), and especially in the second part of that chapter: *Conservative and Ecclesiastical Objections and the Catholic Effort at a Solution*, (pp. 51-60). These discussions, which were sometimes extremely bitter, gradually led to the emergence of the final conclusion, sanctioned by the authority of Pius XII, namely, that God speaks to us through human beings, and that it is through this human language, in all its diverse forms, and within its inescapable limitations, that the divine message must be grasped, understood and accepted as infallible.

As always in human controversy, the real principle did not emerge at once, even in the minds of its best defenders. There were exaggerations followed by reactions. There were bitter arguments and interventions by ecclesiastical authority.

I shall do no more than indicate a few well-known dates in this series of events.[34] Between 4 November and 11 November 1902, Fr Lagrange gave a series of six conferences at the Institut Catholique at Toulouse (soon afterwards published as a book with the title *La Méthode historique, surtout dans l'exégése de L'Ancien Testament*) in which he gave concrete expression to his theory of literary forms in historical narratives that had already been put forward in 1896 (*RB*. V, 1896, pp. 606-18). From 1902 onwards there were lively discussions about 'literary forms' with important contributions from

[34]Cf. Fr Höpfl, O.S.B. art. 'Critique biblique' (n. 5) in Pirot's *Supplément du Dictionnaire de la Bible*, vol. II, pp. 202-20.

Holzhey and Peters in Germany, Hackspill and Prat in France and
Poels in Holland, and severely critical interventions by Brucker in
France, L. Fonck in Austria and L. Murillo in Spain. In 1904 there
appeared the systematic study of von Hummelauer, S.J., *Exegetisches
zur Inspirationslehre*, which followed Fr Lagrange's line of thought.
Then came the decree of the Biblical Commission dated 23 June
1905 (the last decree signed as secretary of the Biblical Commission
by the Irish Franciscan, Fr David Fleming, *EB*, n.154, *DZ*, 1980)
disallowing the application of the theory of literary forms to strictly
historical narratives as a general principle of interpretation, but
allowing it in certain clearly restricted cases. The discussions came
to a momentary halt after the publication of the Encyclical *Pascendi*
and the Decree *Lamentabili* in 1907. In 1920 came Benedict XV's
Encyclical *Spiritus Paraclitus*, with its more explicit acceptance of the
principle of literary forms in historical narratives, but censuring its
excessive use (*rectis quidem, si intra certos quosdam fines contineantur,
principiis sic abutuntur . . . Nimis facile ad citationes, quas vocant im-
plicitas, vel ad narrationes specie tenus historicas confugiunt; aut genera
quaedam litterarum in Libris Sacris inveniri contendunt, quibuscum integra
ac perfecta verbi divini veritas componi nequeat*). Persevering work by
Catholic exegetes led them ever more clearly to postulate the theory
of literary forms as absolutely necessary for the true interpretation
of many of the historical narratives in the Old Testament. Finally,
this long evolutionary process was successfully concluded by the
passage under discussion in the Encyclical *Divino afflante Spiritu*.

Obviously, these pages in the Encyclical must be read and
understood in the light of the preceding controversies. Hence, it is
impossible to ignore the course of events between the decree of
23 June 1905, and the section on this subject in the Encyclical
Spiritus Paraclitus (1920) and so on to 1943 and the passage under
discussion here. Progress was all in the same direction, and without
a single setback: as early as 1905 some applications of the theory
of literary forms had been recognized as legitimate, but it was only
in 1943 that it was put forward by authority itself as the most
important means of providing 'a solution to many of the objections
made against the truth and historical accuracy of Holy Writ'.[35]

---

[35]At a distance of forty years, this phrase seems to echo that used by Fr Lagrange
in the book already quoted (p. 94): 'It (the theory of literary forms) still seems to
me the most fitting for the resolution of the difficulties raised against the veracity
of the Bible.' It will moreover have been noticed that the Encyclical uses precisely

Having now considered this passage of the Encyclical in its context of earlier discussions and investigations which explain it and endow it with its full meaning we can follow step by step the teaching it sets out before us. It is made up of an introduction and three fundamental directives.

Introduction: The present state of exegesis

In accordance with the method adopted in the Encyclical from the beginning this introduction has to establish the necessity for new rules adapted to our times as a result of progress made in exegesis. Today's problems are historical. 'There are many matters, especially historical, which were insufficiently or hardly at all developed by the commentators of past centuries, because they lacked nearly all the information necessary for elucidating them'; and two examples are given of fields in which information was formerly insufficient. In addition, 'There are also other sacred books or texts in which difficulties have presented themselves only in recent times, now that deeper archæological research has given rise to new questions offering occasion for a closer investigation of the subject'.

Hence it is a mistake to say that 'nothing remains for the modern Catholic exegete to add to the achievements of Christian antiquity'. On the contrary: a very large number (*adeo multa*) of problems are being raised by modern progress, problems calling for further study and investigation (*quae nova investigatione novoque examine indigeant*). The following paragraph begins with an equally emphatic reference to the newness of 'aids and helps' to be used in solving the new problems: 'For if our age accumulates new problems and new difficulties it also supplies by God's bounty, new aids and helps to exegesis.'

The principle underlying the three subsequent directives

We shall start with a statement of the principle obviously underlying these three directives and formally enunciated in the course of their elaboration. Holy Scripture, the word of God, is communicated to us through the medium of human language. If we would

the word suggested by Fr Lagrange in the 1904 edition of his book, (p. xii, p. 187), 'approximations', to characterize certain forms of historical narrative encountered in Hebrew antiquity.

know what God is teaching us, we must understand as concretely as possible what the man inspired by God has said, what he thought as an actual man, at a given place and moment in history. Pius XII affirms this several times in the course of this section, and especially in the following sentences:

> 'In the Divine Scripture,' observes St Thomas, with charac-
> teristic shrewdness, 'divine things are conveyed to us in the
> manner to which men are accustomed.' For just as the substan-
> tial Word of God became like to men in all things, 'without sin',
> so the words of God, expressed in human language, became in
> all things like to human speech, except error.

The argument is precisely that of the doctrine of the Incarnation. In the man Jesus the Christian must recognize the Son of God, the eternal Word, and Docetism of any kind is alien to Christian truth. Similarly, God speaks to man in Scripture through human speech, and here too it would be a kind of Docetism to refuse to see the depth of his penetration into humanity.

The First Directive: Take into account the personality of the sacred writer
If we must attain the divine message through knowledge of human language, it is important that we should understand the personality of the sacred writer with as much insight as possible. Every sound philological system requires that this psychological and historical study should be as thoroughgoing as possible if it is desired to 'understand' his language. At this point, theology links up perfectly with history, as the Encyclical points out: 'Catholic theologians, following the teaching of the holy Fathers and especially of the Angelic and Common Doctor, have investigated and explained the nature and effects of divine inspiration better and more fully than was the custom in past centuries.' According to this now classical doctrine of inspiration, the man, 'the *organon* of the Holy Spirit, and a living and rational instrument' . . . 'under the influence of the divine motion . . . uses his own faculties and powers in such a way that from the book which is the fruit of his labour all may easily learn "the distinctive genius and individual characteristics and features" of each author'.
The exegete's duty, therefore, is obvious: 'Let the interpreter

therefore use every care, and take advantage of every indication provided by the most recent research, in an endeavour to
discern the distinctive genius of the sacred writer, his conditions of
life, the age in which he lived, the written or oral sources he may
have used, and the literary forms he employed' (*dispicere enitatur,
quae propria fuerit sacri scriptoris indoles, ac vitae condicio, qua floruerit
aetate, quos fontes adhibuerit sive scriptos, sive ore traditos, quibusque sit
usus formis dicendi*).

Second Directive: The importance of literary form, especially in history

We come now to one of the most novel of the directives in the
whole of the Encyclical, the one which clearly invites Catholic
exegetes to adopt the theory of literary forms in their interpretations
of Scripture and particularly of historical sections of Scripture.

Obviously, every interpreter of Scripture since patristic times has
always and spontaneously followed part of this directive. In every
age, the parables of the Gospel have been interpreted according
to their literary form: their truth consists in the moral or religious
lesson inculcated, not in the historical reality of the event described.
It has always been recognized that in the Bible there are didactic
writings, giving moral or religions teaching, which must therefore
be understood and explained as such. The only controversy on this
point has been on whether side by side with Proverbs and Wisdom
other books, like Job, which is obviously of this literary form, could
be given this classification. Similarly, it has always been known that
a poetical text cannot be interpreted like a historical narrative, and
that the song of Debbora (Judges 5) or the description in Wisdom
(16-19) of the plagues of Egypt does not contain the same kind of
truth as a historical document.

But what had been under discussion since the Encyclical *Providentissimus* had been the question of literary forms in historical
narratives. In 1896, Fr Lagrange (in *RB*, p. 510) pointed out three
possibilities. First, that it was the author's intention that his narrative
should be only apparently historical; in the guise of history his aim
was to teach a truth, defend a thesis or proffer a moral or religious
ideal; he writes an edifying tale: thus, the book of Tobias may have
been written not to assert the facts it reports, but to present in Tobias
a model of the great virtues of ancient Judaism. Secondly, it may
be the author's intention to write history. But we know that even

the best-documented history can only come as close as possible to the reality of events, and that, along with the substance of the narrative, which the author means to guarantee absolutely, there are many details that he reports without being able to guarantee. The evangelists are in agreement in saying that Peter denied Christ three times, but they differ about the circumstances and this is in no way surprising in history written by men. If instead of accepting what common sense tells us is true, we presume to add together all the various denials mentioned by the evangelists, we finish by attributing six or seven denials to Peter. Is this any nearer the truth? Thirdly, there is the history of origins: 'No nation in antiquity completely penetrated the mystery of its historical origins. There are memories which are certain, and these are the basis of history, but there are also legends which cannot be verified. In this case, although the historian collects the narratives circulating in his own day to preserve them for future generations, he gives them only for what they are worth. Everyone is very familiar with this form of history.' Lagrange wondered whether this form, common to all the peoples of antiquity, could be applied to various narratives of Genesis.

Fr Lagrange's very general distinctions might well be given greater precision. Fr von Hummelauer (1904) and many others tried to do so, but all their attempts cannot be mentioned here. It can only be observed that the three literary forms mentioned by Fr Lagrange can be further differentiated into several categories. For example, can we, within the 'history of origins', put on the same level the history of the beginnings of the world and of mankind (Gen. 1-11) and the history of the patriarchs (Gen. 12-50)? Is it not at once obvious that the relationship of the writer to his sources, and through them to the events related, is essentially different in these two groups of narratives? Will not the mode of their statement be fundamentally different? And there are very large differences too between the books of the second category: must we not 'understand' and 'interpret' the history of the reign of David in the Books of Samuel (1 and 2 Kings), probably written by a contemporary at the court, and hence to be read as 'the memoirs of an eye-witness', by completely different standards from those by which we understand and interpret the Books of Kings (3 and 4 Kings), written long after the events they describe, but based on earlier documents and books, some of which are explicitly quoted? Or again, how many distinctions is it possible to draw on the boundary line between history properly so called and the edifying story, as well as in the sphere proper to the latter? What shades of distinction should we make between 1 and 2 Paralipomenon and Tobias, Judith and Esther? Here again there are many forms to be distinguished: edifying religious history, epic or poetic history, haggadic midrash, and so on.

It is important to understand fully that this method of literary forms is not a subjective process carried out by modern exegetes, examining the past by reference to their own modern patterns of thought, but is an objective investigation of the intentions of the authors of times past, and of the mental climate in which they lived. What the proponents of this method ask is to be able to study the inspired writers exactly as they were, by accurately determining the level of culture they had attained, the written sources they used, the way in which they considered an account of some past event, and the purpose guiding them in recounting it. Only then can they be understood perfectly and hence, only then can what God wanted to say to us through them be understood.

There is, then, no question of introducing, under the pretext of distinguishing between literary forms, a subjective element into biblical exegesis, or of taking the liberty of considering this or that story as a legend or fable according to personal inclination. It is a question of reaching back more objectively to the men of the past as they really were, in accordance with the exact degree of their cultural, intellectual, moral, and religious development, and of seeing their writings as they themselves envisaged them and intended them to be, in order then to compare them with our present needs.

Thus the purpose of this system of distinguishing between literary forms in historical narratives is to determine accurately the kind and degree of historical statement that can and should be recognized in the author of an inspired writing by virtue of the form to which his writing belongs. The principle underlying the method is indisputable, and is indeed that guiding all sound profane historical criticism; at the same time it is a legitimate extension of the Thomist idea of inspiration as it is universally understood today. God speaks to us through a real man, as he was in his world and in his own age. Any literary form as long as it is intrinsically moral can convey the divine message. But although the principle is unquestionable, its application is singularly difficult. Properly understood, it can be the beacon-light of exegesis; badly understood, it can be the occasion of all sorts of capricious and reckless mistakes. There can be no doubt that it was this disturbing alternative that for long delayed the clear statement of the principle by the authorities of the Church who, even now, probably intentionally, in this important passage of the Encyclical maintain a certain obscurity.

In fact, there is at this point in the Encyclical a marked lack of proportion between the breadth of the principles laid down—which profoundly affect important and fundamental parts of the Old Testament—and the simplicity, indeed the banality, of the examples occasionally brought forward.[36] No doubt, as was proper, this passage was closely examined and carefully worked over, taking various opinions into account, with a view to making exaggerated interpretation in any direction impossible. It must be concluded, I think, that by giving clear approval to the method of distinguishing between literary forms, there is no intention in the Encyclical of giving exegetes a free hand as far as the extent and breadth of their applications of it are concerned. It is for Catholic exegetes themselves to steer a course that is so straight, true and right that it will never need correction. Here again, the Encyclical shows confidence in them. It is for them to guarantee the future of authentic Christian interpretation.

After these observations on the historical context of this section of the Encyclical, I need do no more than transcribe the essential paragraphs. They are immediately self-explanatory.[37]

But frequently the literal sense is not so obvious in the words and writings of ancient oriental authors as it is with the writers

[36]For example: 'The sacred writers, like the other ancients, employ certain arts of exposition and narrative, certain idioms especially characteristic of the Semitic languages (known as "approximations") and certain hyperbolical and even paradoxical expressions designed for the sake of emphasis.' The problem of literary forms as the Encyclical raises it in the light of former controversies while including less important matters like 'idioms' and 'parabolic expressions' certainly goes far beyond them.

[37]This passage from the Encyclical on literary forms is that which has most engaged the attention of interpreters. See, for example, De Witte 'Du nouveau en matière d'Écriture Sainte' in the Collectanea Mechliniensia, 1945, pp. 375-88; J. Heuschen 'Encore la question biblique' in the Revue Ecclesiastique de Liège, May 1945, pp. 184-97 and November 1945, pp. 381-99; V. Laridon in Coll. Brug., 1946, pp. 97 ff; pp. 172 ff; J. Coppens in Ons Geloof, 1945, pp. 155-6; B. Alfrink in the first of his two articles in the Ned. Kath. Stemmen, 1946, pp. 230 ff: A. Vaccari in Periodica, 1944, pp. 124-6; A. Bea in Biblica, 1943, p. 319.

of today. For what they intended to signify by their words is not determined only by the laws of grammar and philology, nor merely by the context; it is absolutely necessary for the interpreter to go back in spirit to those remote centuries of the East, and make proper use of the aids afforded by history, archæology, ethnology, and other sciences, in order to discover what literary forms the writers of that early age intended to use, and did in fact employ. For to express what they had in mind the ancients of the East did not always use the same forms and expressions as we use today; they used those which were current among the people of their own time and place; and what these were the exegete cannot determine *a priori*, but only from a careful study of ancient oriental literature.

This study has been pursued during the past few decades with greater care and industry than formerly, and has made us better acquainted with the literary forms used in those ancient times, whether in poetical descriptions, or in the formulation of rules and laws of conduct, or in the narration of historical facts and events. It has now also clearly demonstrated the unique pre-eminence among all the ancient nations of the East which the people of Israel enjoyed in historical writing, both in regard to the antiquity of the events recorded and to the accuracy with which they are related—a circumstance, of course, which is explained by the charisma of divine inspiration and by the special purpose, the religious purpose, of biblical history.

At the same time, no one who has a just conception of biblical inspiration will be surprised to find that the sacred writers, like the other ancients, employ certain arts of exposition and narrative, certain idioms especially characteristic of the semitic languages (known as 'approximations') and certain hyperbolical and even paradoxical expressions designed for the sake of emphasis. The sacred books need not exclude any of the forms of expression which were commonly used in human speech by the ancient peoples, especially of the East, to convey their meaning, so long as they are in no way incompatible with God's sanctity and truth . . .

Consequently, if the Catholic exegete is to meet fully the requirements of modern biblical study he must, in expounding sacred Scripture and vindicating its immunity from all error, make prudent use also of this further aid: he must, that is, ask himself how far the form of expression or literary idiom employed by the sacred writer may contribute to the true and genuine interpretation; and he may be sure that this part of his task cannot be neglected without great detriment to Catholic exegesis . . .

Thus a knowledge and careful appreciation of ancient modes of expression and literary forms and styles will provide a solution to many of the objections made against the truth and historical accuracy of holy Writ; and the same study will contribute with equal profit to a fuller and clearer perception of the mind of the sacred author.

The Third Directive: Promotion of the study of biblical antiquities

Understanding of a writer's work implies understanding of his personality, knowledge of the type of literature to which his work belongs and keen acquaintance with the milieu in which he lived; it is this he describes to us, and it conditioned his thought and work. In other words, the study of biblical antiquity is indispensable for the exegete: 'To this matter also, then, biblical scholars must pay due attention, neglecting no new information which archæology, ancient history or the study of ancient literature may provide, and which may serve to throw further light upon the mentality of ancient writers, their processes of thought, and their historical and literary methods, forms and devices.'

Hence, by corollary, any study of eastern antiquities is of great value in the advance of the biblical sciences, and the Encyclical praises at this point Catholic laypeople who devote themselves to them: 'they will not only be making a contribution to the advancement of profane knowledge, but also rendering a very great service to the Christian cause'.

4.   *Dealing with the more difficult questions*

At this point in its development, having passed from the study of word and phrase to the higher reaches of research, the Encyclical comes, in this fourth paragraph, to the more general problems of the Christian synthesis of history, to the whole question of the authenticity, antiquity, integrity, general historical truth and fundamental theological doctrines of the sacred books. Obviously the Encyclical did not mean to give at this point a general view of the present position regarding these fundamental questions, but adopting the standpoint of the agreement between history and orthodox faith, it says, with justifiable optimism, that many of the old difficulties have been fully resolved during the past fifty years by thorough research into history either by Catholic exegetes or the independent critics themselves, and suggests that this gives grounds for hope for the future. Further, with a very proper sense of reality and human possibilities, it acknowledges that there are still serious difficulties in exegesis, as in every branch of profane knowledge; this indeed is an essential condition of progress in this world, for such difficulties are the main stimulus to effort as well as the necessary foundation for true awareness of our limitations as human beings; some matters will remain obscure for centuries, and perhaps even for ever. Lastly, with great confidence in Christian freedom, the basis of all true progress, it expresses the hope that future research may be carried out in a climate of freedom and charity, and that while exegetes are striving for perfect sincerity both as historians and as believers, others will show towards them a trusting charity, founded on open-mindedness and understanding of what, of necessity, is new.

In this connection the Encyclical shows that Catholic freedom in research is much wider than has sometimes been claimed, and that the passages in Scripture whose sense has been declared by the authority of the Church or unanimous tradition remain very few.

These, then, are the three parts of the explanation; they can now be surveyed one by one.

The difficulties successfully resolved by recent research

'The progress in the investigation of oriental antiquities which we mentioned above, and the more careful study of the original texts, as well as the wider and more exact knowledge of biblical languages and of oriental languages generally, have with God's help borne fruit in the final solution of many of the objections which, in the days of our predecessor of immortal memory, Leo XIII, were being raised by non-Catholic or even anti-Catholic critics against the authenticity, antiquity, integrity, and historical authority of the sacred books.'

The Encyclical states that this result may be seen from two points of view; there is the work of Catholic exegetes, who, making use of all the resources of modern science 'have propounded interpretations which, while being in accordance with Catholic teaching and true traditional thought, appear at the same time to have met the difficulties which have either arisen from recent research and recent discoveries or had been left for our solution as a legacy from ancient times'. On the other hand, there is the work of certain non-Catholic writers 'who have been led by a serious and impartial examination to abandon the views of the moderns and to return, in some cases at least, to the older opinions'.

Pius XII is no doubt referring here to that 'return to tradition'[38] which during the past sixty years has frequently been a mark of research work in the problems of literary criticism, especially those concerning authenticity and date. Here are a few examples: in the New Testament there has been the recognition of the authenticity of the two works of St Luke, the Gospel and the Acts, by a growing number of liberal exegetes, since Harnack's *Lucas der Arzt* was published in 1906; the increasingly general agreement on the authenticity of 2 Thessalonians, Ephesians, etc.; the rejection of former Protestant interpretations of the eucharistic texts, and of the text on the primacy of St Peter, etc. In the Old Testament, there has been the abandonment of several of the principal positions adopted in Wellhausen's system, the restoration of earlier dates for Proverbs and many of the Psalms, and a wider recognition of the antiquity of the Messianic hope, etc.[39]

But Pius XII seems to have been more directly concerned with the progress made by Catholic exegesis itself. He was thinking no doubt of the more balanced and accurate historical positions, close to the text and no longer dictated by dogmatic presuppositions, which have become habitual to a growing number of Catholic interpreters, such as for example, besides many others, those who collaborated in the series quoted above (pp. 46-50 and pp. 127-130). Catholic exegesis no longer restricts its endeavours to the refutation of opponents: backed nowadays by a better training from the Catholic

---

[38]The famous expression *Zurück zur Tradition* used by the liberal Protestant author Adolf Harnack at the beginning of the twentieth century is familiar to everyone.

[39]On this point see Professor Coppen's book already quoted above *L'Histoire critique de l'Ancien Testament* (3rd edn, 1942).

universities and faculties of Europe and America, from the Biblical Institute in Rome and the École biblique in Jerusalem, it is striving now to work 'constructively'; it possesses men of real ability in all fields from the various branches of Hebrew grammar or biblical Greek and textual criticism, to the various aspects of biblical theology.

'The result has been,' the Encyclical concludes, 'that confidence in the authority and historical truth of the Bible, which, in the face of so many attacks, had in some minds been partially shaken, has now among Catholics been wholly restored.'

Difficulties still unsolved or insoluble

The Encyclical observes that there are difficulties and problems in holy Scripture with which 'the minds of Catholic exegetes are still exercised'. Inevitably, in every field of human knowledge 'it is only after much labour that the harvest can be reaped'. But just as some questions, controversial in times past, 'have in our own day at last, with the progress of research, been successfully answered,' so one day even those questions 'which now appear to be most complicated and difficult,' will be fully elucidated.

It is however possible that we shall have to wait for their solution. Difficulties themselves, however, have the good effect of stimulating us 'to study and examine them (i.e. the sacred Scriptures) with closer attention' whilst keeping us humble. 'And so we should not wonder should it happen that one or other question never finds a really perfect answer.' There may be things in history 'obscure, and too remote from our times and experience'. Besides, all the profound sciences have their mysteries.

How positive solutions should be sought

But nonetheless it remains the duty of the Catholic interpreter 'prompted by a practical and ardent love of his science, and sincerely devoted to holy Mother Church, to grapple perseveringly with the problems so far unsolved, not only to repel the attacks of opponents, but also in the effort to find an explanation which will be faithfully consonant with the teaching of the Church, particularly with the traditional doctrine of the inerrancy of Scripture, while being at the same time in due conformity with the certain conclusions of the profane sciences'.

Thus the exegete's endeavours will be guided by his twofold love for his science and the Church. Their purpose will not be mere negative refutation, but positive and constructive, and they will come to an end only when he has found a solution which is at once theologically orthodox and historically certain and sincere.

But painful and demanding labour of this kind is possible only in an atmosphere of freedom and charity, and one of the most impressive and original passages of the Encyclical extols charity and freedom, the two essential prerequisites for exegetical research.

First charity, but based on openmindedness and keen understanding of necessarily new ideas: 'And let all other children of the Church bear in mind that the efforts of these valiant labourers in the vineyard of the Lord are to be judged not only with fairness and justice, but also with the greatest charity; they must avoid that somewhat indescreet zeal which considers everything new to be for that very reason a fit object for attack or suspicion.'

This statement seems particularly forceful when we recall the unjust campaigns of suspicion and delation which, between 1907 and 1914, cast a shadow over the life of more than one completely orthodox exegete, deeply devoted to the Church, campaigns against which Benedict XV protested in his first Encyclical in November 1914, *Ad beatissimi Apostolorum principis*.

Then liberty, the liberty of the sons of God, whose characteristics are defined by the Encyclical: freedom in sincerity of devotion both to the Church and to scientific truth; on these conditions it will be fruitful and stand revealed as increasingly necessary. No scientific progress is possible without wholesome freedom of research. 'This true freedom of the sons of God, loyally maintaining the doctrine of the Church, and at the same time gratefully accepting as a gift of God and exploiting every contribution that profane knowledge may afford, must be vindicated and upheld by the zeal of all, and is the condition and source of any real success, of any solid progress in Catholic science.'

But is not Catholic exegesis tied from the outset by the many interpretations—some given by ecclesiastical authority and others by patristic or scholastic tradition? Even before the historical problems were raised in all their complexity had not the Church given irrevocable theological interpretations, so making any serious historical study useless from the start?

The Encyclical's reply to these questions is given at this point with a clarity which, I believe, has never before been attained in an official document. In the exegetical controversies of the beginning of the twentieth century appeals to the official interpretation of the Church, and especially to the unanimous tradition of the Fathers, too often assumed in the writings of fundamentalist or conservative theologians the aspect of a vague, ill-defined threat, though all the more negative and frustrating on that account. Everything said by the Fathers, even on essentially historical problems, was made to appear as necessarily unalterable so that as a result the sphere of free research became extremely narrow and restricted. The Encyclical resolves the problem very lucidly by laying down a fundamental distinction: 'Let them remember above all that the rules and laws laid down by the Church are concerned with the doctrine of faith and morals; and that among the many matters set forth in the legal, historical, sapiential, and prophetical books of the Bible there are only a few whose sense has been defined by the authority of the Church, and that there are equally few concerning which the opinion of the holy Fathers is unanimous. There consequently remain many matters, and important matters, in the exposition and explanation of which the sagacity and perception of Catholic interpreters can and ought to be freely exercised.'

This is a passage that requires to be understood aright. At first sight, it seems astonishing: for centuries the Church has been laying down, with some insistence both in her ordinary teaching and in her official documents, especially the more recent of them, that the exegete must interpret Scripture in accordance with the mind of the Church and in conformity with the unanimous tradition of the Fathers. She had inserted a promise of compliance with this duty in the anti-modernist oath imposed on all her priests. Did this mean no more than abiding by the authorized interpretation of a small number of texts?

It is important here to avoid a possible misunderstanding at the outset. In fact a distinction must be made between the general spirit of scriptural interpretation, and the interpretation of definite and specific passages of Scripture. In other words, there is a Christian way of looking at holy Scripture, which sees in the Old Testament the preparation, willed and guided by God, for the New Testament, a foreshadowing and obscure announcement of the reality to come. *Novum Testamentum in Vetere latet, Vetus in Novo patet* (the New Testament is hidden in the Old, the Old made manifest in the New). This Christian way finds in the New Testament the unity and transcendence of a definitive revelation, originating from the only begotten Son of God; it is essentially different from the rationalist view, and this radical difference may be clearly seen not only in certain specific texts, but throughout biblical exegesis. The Encyclical has already given prominence on several previous occasions to 'the nature of Christian interpretation,' and emphasizes it again later when it speaks of teaching in seminaries. It is this attitude of mind that is constantly inculcated in papal documents; it is this we should acquire from our close communion with the mind of the Church and our spiritual contact with patristic exegesis; it is this that was increasingly lacking in such exegetes as Loisy and caused their downfall.

The Encyclical is concerned here with a much more limited point. All teachers of dogmatic theology know very well that there are very few passages of Scripture whose meaning has been defined by the Church. The Church has shown herself extremely reserved in this respect. Thus, for example, at Trent she explicitly refrained from making the eucharistic interpretation of John 6 definitive, although it was then universally admitted, except for a few interpreters such as Cajetan. (In our own times it is accepted almost unanimously by exegetes, whether liberal, Protestant or Catholic.)

Equally, there are very few passages to which the Fathers have in their teaching unanimously ascribed a fixed theological interpretation as imposed by faith. But it is this that is important, and it will be noticed that the Encyclical says very clearly here that the argument from patristic unanimity ought not to be invoked in purely historical or literary questions, but only where the discussion is concerned with 'doctrine concerning faith and morals'.

A 'sense of the Church' and a 'sense of patristic tradition' are an aid to the Catholic exegete, a light, a guiding principle to deeper thought. They should not be seen as an impediment, a restriction, something narrowing the field of view. This, I think, is the teaching of the Encyclical.

5. *The use of sacred Scripture in the instruction of the faithful*

This fifth section forms as it were a third part of the Encyclical. In the four earlier sections Pius XII's instructions were really concerned with the scientific study of holy Scripture in the fields of both theology and history. It is a question now of its presentation and adaptation both for the faithful in preaching and in books, and for the clergy in biblical teaching in seminaries. The first two parts of this present section are concerned wholly with these two groups of people, while the third, very much to the point in September 1943, speaks of the value of the Word of God in times of great trial, such as a war.

The various ways of using holy Scripture in the Church's ministry

As the Church has always taught, and as St Paul instructed his disciple Timothy (2 Tim. 3. 15-17) attentive study of holy Scripture is a 'grave obligation' of the faithful, and especially of priests, both in connection with their personal formation and for the various forms of the apostolate. Priests should therefore first 'study with earnestness' the sacred books, assimilating them 'by prayer and meditation', and then 'zealously display the supernatural riches of the Word of God in their sermons, homilies and exhortations'. Their teaching of Christian doctrine should be based on the words of holy Scripture, illustrated by examples drawn from the Bible and especially from the Gospels. Their use of the Bible should be sound, with scrupulous avoidance of those accommodative, artificial and fantastic interpretations 'which are an abuse rather than a use of the Word of God'. It should be attractive and perfectly lucid, so that the faithful will 'conceive in their minds a deep veneration for sacred Scripture'.

The Encyclical asks that bishops will do everything possible constantly to increase among Catholics respect and love for the Word of God, encouraging any step taken to make it better known and loved. They should support pious associations 'whose object is to circulate copies of the Bible, and especially of the Gospels, among the faithful, and to encourage Christian families in the habit of reading them devoutly every day'. They should encourage the publication with ecclesiastical authorization of translations of holy Scripture in the common tongue, conferences or public lectures on biblical subjects, and the maintenance of periodicals 'either for the scientific treatment and exposition of questions or for adapting the fruits of such research to the sacred ministry or to the profitable use of the faithful'.

The whole of this passage is a vibrant appeal that holy Scripture shall occupy its rightful place in Catholic life, that it may be the soul of the thought and activity of all, and especially of priests.

What a difference there is between an appeal of this sort and the anxious precautions taken by the Church in this matter at the time of the Reformation! How fundamentally the situation has changed! Today Scripture is no longer exposed to the hazards of unrestricted, unenlightened study at a period of fundamental controversy concerning the Church and the Bible. Scripture is passed on to the faithful enriched by centuries of increasingly sound and objective Catholic interpretation, improved by the advances made in the historical sciences of the last eighty years, and protected by that growing confidence in the Church characteristic of true Catholics. But above all, in our time, Scripture intervenes in a world no longer hesitating between orthodoxy and heresy or schism, but in a world which must choose between Christianity and irreligion, between belief in God and materialistic atheism.

Bible teaching in the seminaries

But Scripture cannot be passed on to the faithful as it should be unless future priests have been taught in their seminaries to know and love it. To this end, the pope here gives very definite instructions for seminary professors.

Without mentioning it explicitly, these instructions imply a very opportune and necessary fundamental principle: the teaching of Scripture in a seminary is not and cannot be a course of technical instruction intended to train specialists in exegesis. The seminary professor, himself trained at a university, would be mistaken if he passed on to his students the instruction he himself received in the form he received it. His teaching, of course, is to be solidly scientific and should develop in seminarians the critical sense, the feeling for objective, literal, accurate and firmly based exegesis. The Encyclical has laid this down from the outset, and repeats it here: 'and let them set forth this literal sense so soundly . . . etc.' But the teacher should not involve his students in all the discussions and controversies by which exegesis has made its way towards a definitive solution of problems; he is to avoid 'superfluous discussions' and omit 'what serves more to satisfy curiosity than to promote true learning and solid piety'.

Then, the principal characteristic of seminary teaching should be its theological nature: 'let them set forth this literal, and especially theological sense so soundly . . .'. What we ought to look for in Scripture is the doctrine of life, the expression of the divine revelation.

Finally, instruction in Scripture should be beneficial and uplifting. Pius XII does not of course ask that the lacunae, shortcomings and mistakes of the great men of Israel in comparison with the Christian ideal should be concealed, nor does he ask that what was incomplete, unpolished or even uncouth in their faith and piety should be obscured. He asks that God's work in the midst of man's wretchedness should be given such clear prominence that Scripture will always, for every student, be 'a pure and perennial source of their own spiritual life, and at the same time food and strength for the office of preaching which they are to undertake'. He asks that professors should 'urge' the theological sense of Scripture 'with such unction . . . that their students may in some sort share the experience of the disciples of Jesus Christ on the way to Emmaus who, having heard the words of the Master, exclaimed: "was not our heart burning within us while he opened to us the Scriptures".'

The significance and scope of the Word of God in time of war

The Encyclical is dated September, 1943, during the great sufferings occasioned by the war. Pius XII reminds both suffering victims and fighting soldiers that Christ is the only solid foundation both for justice and for peace on this earth, and that the more men study and meditate on the Scriptures, and especially the New Testament, the more fully will they find Christ. From it the afflicted may draw real consolation, belligerents the sense of justice and all men the secret of true charity.

Conclusion: An exhortation to those who devote themselves to biblical studies

This is an extremely encouraging section addressed to Catholic exegetes. Pius XII congratulates them on the lofty mission entrusted to them and encourages them to carry it out with all their strength and zeal. What could be more wonderful than to live as they are able to do constantly in the world of Scripture! 'Let them pray that they may understand. Let them labour to penetrate ever more deeply into the secrets of the sacred pages; let them teach and preach to unlock the treasures of God's word to others also.' Let them try to follow as closely as possible the example of the great Catholic interpreters of the past. Their reward will be great in heaven.

The Encyclical *Divino afflante Spiritu* is a message of encouragement to Catholic exegetes. In it the Vicar of Jesus Christ extols the supernatural grandeur of their mission, tells them of his high regard for the work accomplished in the previous fifty years, of his desire to procure for their investigations an atmosphere of freedom and charity, and of his trust in their Christian sense and their scientific endeavour.

It is also a scheme of work: the pope outlines for them a wide and difficult programme, setting before them an ideal of profound theological training and complete historical preparation which can only arouse their zeal and lofty ambition.

It is a call to go forward: on every page, Pius XII speaks of new conditions in exegetical work, of new resources put at the disposal of the workers, and of new solutions to be sought and found. His insistence on newness, in fidelity to the fundamental propositions of dogmatic tradition, is one of the characteristic marks of this Encyclical, and shows the vast extent of the progress he saw as both possible and necessary.

Above all it is an act of faith in the undoubted Christian reconciliation of faith and history. Between Leo XIII's Encyclical *Providentissimus* and Pius XII's *Divino afflante Spiritu* Christian thought was imperilled by a very dangerous threat, the modernist heresy, which was to a large degree the child of scientific discouragement. The modernists despaired of being able to reconcile faith and history, thinking that in future a distinction would have to be made between the Christ of faith and the Christ of history. This danger has now past. Full of confidence in the future, Pius XII asks exegetes to be more objective, more sincere and more exacting than ever as historians. Only a more profound, complete and genuine knowledge of history can unite with the faith in a total, frankly Christian and sincerely scientific synthesis.

The letter from the Secretary of the Biblical Commission to Cardinal Suhard
(16 January 1948. On the date of the documents comprising the Pentateuch
and the literary form of Genesis 1-11).

A few years later the following letter was sent to Cardinal Suhard,
Archbishop of Paris, in the name of the Biblical Commission and
signed by its secretary Fr J. M. Vosté, O.P. It is concerned with the
problems of the sources of the Pentateuch and of the literary form
of Genesis 1-11. The letter clearly follows the progressive line adopted
in 1943 by the Encyclical *Divino afflante Spiritu*, constituting as it
were its first concrete application.[40]
To anyone who followed the investigations of the previous eighty
years the letter will be perfectly clear. Moreover, as I wrote in
1948[41] its aim is not to put forward or suggest solutions to a complex
problem. Its principal purpose is to remove the fears and suspicions
that for too long paralysed Catholic exegesis of the Pentateuch;
it will enable the questions of the origin of the Pentateuch
and the nature of the first chapters of Genesis to be studied
henceforward in an atmosphere of greater freedom and fuller
intellectual calm 'in perfect accord with the doctrine of the
Church'.
Here is the complete text of the letter:

Eminence,
The Holy Father graciously entrusted to the Biblical Commission the examination of two questions recently submitted
to His Holiness concerning the sources of the Pentateuch and
the historicity of the first eleven chapters of Genesis. Together
with their basis and implications, these two questions have been
the object of the most attentive study of the most reverend
consultants and eminent Cardinals, members of the said commission. As a result of their deliberations His Holiness has

---

[40]In Chapter II I tried briefly to set out the problem of the origins of the Pentateuch in the form in which it arose and was bitterly discussed particularly from 1878
onwards. On pp. 30-33, I mention some of the special characteristics of Genesis
and on p. 123 there is a reminder of the decree of the Holy Office declaring unsafe
Abbé Touzard's teaching on the Mosaic authenticity of the Pentateuch (a decree not reprinted in *EB*). Knowledge of these controversies and occurrences is a
useful aid to understanding the whole scope and background of this letter of January
1948.
[41]*NRT*, 1948, p. 655.

deigned to approve the following reply at an audience granted to the undersigned on 16 January 1948.

The Pontifical Biblical Commission is pleased to pay homage to the feeling of filial respect which inspired this step and desires to match it with a sincere effort to promote biblical studies by assuring to them the most complete liberty within the limits of the traditional teaching of the Church. This liberty has been proclaimed in explicit terms by the present pope in his Encyclical *Divino afflante Spiritu* in the words: 'Prompted by a practical and ardent love of his science, and sincerely devoted to Holy Mother Church, the Catholic exegete must grapple perseveringly with the problems so far unsolved, not only to repel the attacks of opponents, but also in the effort to find an explanation which will be faithfully consonant with the teaching of the Church, particularly with the traditional doctrine of the inerrancy of Scripture, while being at the same time in due conformity with the certain conclusions of secular sciences. And let all other children of the Church bear in mind that the efforts of these valiant labourers in the vineyard of the Lord are to be judged not only with fairness and justice, but also with the greatest charity; they must avoid that somewhat indiscreet zeal which considers everything new to be for that very reason a fit object for attack and suspicion.' (A.A.S. 1943, p. 319.)

The three official replies previously given by the Biblical Commission in connection with the above-mentioned questions, namely on 23 June 1905, on the narratives in the historical books of holy Scripture that are only apparently historical (*EB*, 2nd edn, p. 161), on 27 June 1906, on the Mosaic authenticity of the Pentateuch (*EB*, 2nd edn, pp. 181-4) and on 30 June 1909, on the historical character of the first three chapters of Genesis (*EB*, 2nd edn, pp. 336-43), should be understood and interpreted in the light of this recommendation by the Sovereign Pontiff. It will then be agreed that these replies are in no way an obstacle to a further truly scientific examination of these problems in accordance with the results achieved in these last forty years. Consequently, the Biblical Commission does not think that there is a need, at any rate at the moment, to promulgate new decrees in connection with these questions.

As regards the composition of the Pentateuch, in the above-mentioned decree of 27 June 1906 the Biblical Commission has already recognized that it could be maintained that Moses 'used written documents or oral traditions in composing his work' and also admitted the possibility of modifications and additions posterior to Moses (*EB*. 2nd end, pp. 183-4). No one today doubts the existence of these sources or rejects the gradual increase of Mosaic laws as a result of social and religious conditions in later times, a process manifest also in the historical narratives. However, even among non-Catholic exegetes very diverse opinions are held today concerning the nature and number of these documents, their names and dates. There are even authors in various countries who for purely historical and critical reasons, quite unconnected with any religious purpose, resolutely reject the theories hitherto in favour and seek the explanation of certain editorial peculiarities in the Pentateuch not so much in the alleged diversity of documents, as in the special psychology and peculiar mental and literary processes (better understood today) of the ancient orientals, or again in the different literary forms required by the diversity of subject-matter. We therefore invite Catholic scholars to study these problems with an open mind in the light of sane criticism and of the results achieved by other sciences concerned with these matters, and doubtless such study will establish the large part and profound influence of Moses as author and legislator.

The question of the literary forms in the first eleven chapters of Genesis is much more obscure and complex. These literary forms do not correspond with any of our classical categories and cannot be judged in the light of Greco-Roman or modern literary forms. Their historicity as a whole can neither be denied nor affirmed without unduly applying to them the norms of a literary form under which they cannot be classified. If it is agreed not to see in these chapters history in the classical or modern sense it must also be admitted that scientific facts at present known do not allow the giving of a positive solution to all the problems they pose. The first duty in this matter incumbent on scientific exegesis consists in the careful study of all the literary, scientific, historical, cultural and religious problems connected with these chapters; then, there is required a close examination of the literary processes of ancient eastern peoples, of their psychology, their way of expressing themselves and even their notion of historical truth. In a word, what is needed is to assemble without presuppositions all the material afforded by the palaeontological, historical, epigraphical and literary sciences. Only thus is there hope of seeing more clearly into the nature of certain narratives of the first chapters of Genesis. To declare *a priori* that these narratives do not contain history in the modern sense of the word might easily be understood as meaning that they do not contain it in any sense, although they relate in simple and figurative language, adapted to the understanding of mankind at a lower stage of development, the fundamental truths presupposed by the economy of salvation, as well as the popular description of the beginnings of the human race and the chosen people. In the meantime it is necessary to practise the patience that is part of prudence and the wisdom of life. This is also inculcated by the Holy Father in the Encyclical already quoted: 'But it should cause no surprise to find that every difficulty has not yet been clarified and overcome . . . This, however, is no reason for discouragement. It should not be forgotten that with the branches of human knowledge it is very much as it is with nature: the growth of undertakings is gradual, and it is only after much labour that the harvest can be reaped . . . It is to be hoped therefore that those difficulties which now appear to be most complicated and arduous will also, with perservering efforts, at some time find complete elucidation. (*EB*, 2nd edn, p. 318).

The Encyclical Humani Generis (12 *August* 1950) [42]

There are only a few passages in this Encyclical concerned with

[42]*Litterae Encyclicae 'Humani Generis' die* 12 *Augusti* 1950 *datae de nonnullis falsis opinionibus quae catholicae doctrinae fundamenta subruere nituntur, A.A.S.* 1950, *XXXXII*, pp. 561-78 Cf. the Latin text and the English version by Mgr R. A. Knox, *False Trends in Modern Teaching*, The Catholic Truth Society, London, 1959. Cf. the official French version in vol. VIII of *Nouvelle Revue Théologique*, with a commentary by six authors. On holy Scripture cf. the fourth article, G. Lambert, 'L'encyclique et l'Écriture Sainte'.

holy Scriptures and they recall the earlier directives, recently re-
stated in the Encyclical *Divino afflante Spiritu*.

In the first part of the Encyclical, four scriptural errors are listed
and prescribed. The first three had already been condemned
several times: the limitation of scriptural inerrancy to the truths of
morality and religion; the illegitimate distinction between the divine
meaning, hidden in Scripture and said to be alone infallible, and the
human meaning; exegetical interpretation which takes into account
neither the analogy of faith nor the tradition of the Church: 'they
would make the holy Scripture, interpreted by scholars each after
his own human fashion, the norm by which to measure the teaching
of the Fathers and of the Church, when they ought to be interpreting holy Scripture according to the mind of the Church, since the
Church, by our Lord's own appointment, is authorized to guard and
interpret the whole deposit of divine revelation'. In a fourth point,
Pius XII confirms and lays stress on the position which had previously been taken up in the letter of the Biblical Commission in
1941 and the Encyclical *Divino afflante Spiritu* in favour of the literal
interpretation of Scripture as the basis of all sane exegesis: he
again reproves the false principle which claims that symbolic and
spiritual exegesis should replace this literal interpretation (*EB*,
612-3).

In the third section of the Encyclical the question of the origin
of the human body within the pattern of the general evolution of
living organisms and the question of monogenism and polygenism
naturally lead to the problem of the interpretation of the first eleven
chapters of Genesis. Pius XII refers back to the recent letter of the
Biblical Commission (16 January 1948, reproduced above) and
gives its official interpretation. His interpretation in no way restricts
the meaning and scope of this document in any direction, but does
clearly define the exegetes' task in this field. The passage in the
Encyclical on this subject reads:

> As with biology and anthropology, so with history; there
> are some who make bold to overstep the rules of prudence which
> the Church has laid down. One especially regrettable tendency
> is to interpret the historical books of the Old Testament with
> overmuch freedom. In vain do the exponents of this method
> appeal, for their defence, to the letter recently received by the

Archbishop of Paris from the Pontifical Commission on Biblical Studies (die 16 januarii 1948; A.A.S. xl, pp. 45-8.) It was clearly laid down in that letter that the first eleven chapters of Genesis, although it is not right to judge them by modern standards of historical composition, such as would be applied to the great classical authors, or to the learned of our own day, do nevertheless come under the heading of history; in what exact sense, it is for the further labours of the exegete to determine. These chapters have a naïve, symbolic way of talking, well suited to the understanding of primitive people. But they do disclose to us certain important truths, upon which the attainment of our eternal salvation depends, and they do give a popularly written description of how the human race, and the chosen people in particular, came to be. It may be true that these old writers of sacred history drew some of their material from the stories current among the people of their day. So much may be granted; but it must be remembered on the other side that they did so under the impulse of divine inspiration, which preserved them from all error in selecting and assessing the material they used.

These excerpts from current stories, which are found in the sacred books, must not be put on a level with mere myths, or with legend in general. Myths arise from the untrammelled exercise of the imagination; whereas in our sacred books, even in the Old Testament, a love of truth and of simplicity shine out, in such a way as to put these writers on a demonstrably different level from their profane contemporaries.

The articles by the Secretary and Under-secretary of the Biblical Commission
(1955)

These concern the new (1954) edition of the *Enchiridion Biblicum* and the meaning and interpretation of the decrees of the Biblical Commission reprinted in the *Enchiridion*.

In the light of the Encyclical *Divino afflante Spiritu*, which records and interprets the wonderful advance made in exegesis in the last fifty years, it began to appear ever more necessary to define, clarify and adapt the pre-1914 decrees of the Biblical Commission. The need for this had frequently been felt by many Catholic exegetes and on the eve of the preparation of the new *Enchiridion Biblicum* the problem had naturally occurred to the responsible authorities. All those who had given information and help to Pius XII in the preparation of the Encyclical *Divino afflante Spiritu* were anxious to see the task of broadening and deepening investigation in Biblical studies achieved in 1943 continued along the same lines. Fr Vosté's letter in 1948 to Cardinal Suhard was, as we have said, the first concrete application of the directives of the Encyclical.

For the assistance of Catholic exegetes a further statement dealing with the early decrees of the Biblical Commission issued during the modernist crisis was unobtrusively prepared in 1955 by official interpreters of the Biblical Commission itself. At the time of the publication of the new edition of the *Enchiridion Biblicum* this statement was published in the form of two review articles, the first by Fr Athanasius Miller, O.S.B., secretary to the Biblical Commission, in the *Benedictinische Monatschrift* (1955, p. 49 ff.), and the second by Fr A. Kleinhans, O.F.M., the under-secretary, in *Antonianum* (1955, pp. 64 ff). In their judgement of the earlier replies of the Biblical Commission these two statements are almost textually identical and, taking into consideration the official status of their authors, it would appear that they ought to be taken as an unobtrusive way of informing Catholic exegetes of semi-official permission to interpret these replies—given at a very difficult period in the modernist crisis —more liberally.

Fr Miller's text read:

From this point of view the decrees of the Biblical Commission really are of great interest. However, in so far as matters are treated in these decrees, concerned neither directly nor indirectly with the truths of faith or morals, the research worker can obviously continue his investigations with complete freedom and make use of his conclusions, although always and in everything without prejudice to the teaching authority of the Church. It is today very difficult to imagine the situation in which Catholic scholars, for example, found themselves at the turn of the century—the danger in which, indeed, Catholic teaching on Scripture and its inspirations itself was, when the flood of liberal and rationalist criticism threatened to sweep away all the bounds of the traditions hitherto held sacred. Today, when the struggle has substantially slackened, when not a few of the opposing forces have been peacefully subdued, and many problems appear in an entirely new light, it is proper to smile at the 'constraint' and 'narrowness' that ruled at that time.[43] Fr. Kleinhans wrote:

But sacred Scripture has always been in the Church as it were the fount and foundation of the truths of faith and morals, and of their evolution. Thus the importance of the *Enchiridion* for the history of dogmas is clear. But at the same time this work also shows us the continual struggle which had to be faced by the Church in almost every age to preserve the Word of God intact and pure. Now in this respect the decrees of the Pontifical Biblical Commission are of great importance. Inasmuch, however, as there are opinions in these decrees concerned neither directly nor indirectly with the truths of faith and morals, the interpreter of sacred Scripture may carry on his scientific investigations in complete freedom and benefit from them, but always without prejudice to the teaching authority of the Church. It is hardly possible today to conceive of the position of Catholic interpreters or of the great danger in which the Catholic doctrine of sacred Scripture itself and its inspiration stood some fifty years ago when liberal and rationalist criticism was trying to break through all the limits set by tradition. Today, however, when these struggles have lessened, and not a few controversies have been settled peaceably, and many questions

---

[43]'Unter diesem Gesichtspunkt sind gerade die Dekrete der päpstlichen Bibelkommission von hohem Interesse. Insofern indes in diesen Dekreten Ansichten vertreten werden, die weder mittelbar noch unmittelbar mit Wahrheiten des Glaubens und der Sitten zusammenhängen, kann der Forscher selbstverständlich in aller Freiheit seine Untersuchungen fortsetzen und die Ergebnisse verwerten, allerdings immer mit Vorbehalt der kirchlichen Lehrautorität. Wir können uns heute kaum mehr eine rechte Vorstellung machen, in welcher Situation z. B. die katholischen Gelehrten um die Wende des Jahrhunderts sich befanden, ja in welcher Gefahr die katholische Lehre über Schrift und Inspiration selbst sich befand, als die Flut liberaler und rationalistischer Kritik alle Schranken bisher heilig gehaltener Traditionen wegzuschwemmen drohte. Heute, da der Kampf wesentlich abgeflaut ist, da nicht wenige Gegensätze friedlich überwunden, und manche Probleme in einem völlig neuen Licht erscheinen, ist es bequem, über damals herrschende "Gebundenheit" und "Enge" zu lächeln.'

have taken on a new aspect, it is an easy matter rashly to judge those times for too great narrowness of mind.[44]

Fr E. Vogt, rector of the Pontifical Biblical Institute at Rome, followed up these remarks by the secretary and under-secretary of the Biblical Commission with the following commentary (in *Biblica*, 1955, p. 565):

> Thus from those decrees dealing with matters concerning the faith, which therefore still stand, there are to be distinguished decrees which are in no way connected with faith and on that account do not take away our freedom. Very many of them referred explicitly to the situation in which biblical science then found itself. Among these especially are those which are concerned with literary criticism, that is, with authenticity (genuineness) or the identity of inspired authors. They were indeed made in defence of the faith, but today these questions have 'taken on a new aspect' since it is now more clearly seen that the inspiration of any biblical text is entirely safeguarded, whoever its human author may have been.   In order to judge these decrees fairly, we must bear in mind the circumstances then existing which today are changed. These decrees, now published again by the authority of the Biblical Commission, have an historical and apologetic importance, for they show that the Church is ever vigilant and diligent in the defence of sacred Scripture.[45]

[44]*S. Scriptura autem semper in Ecclesia habita est tamquam fons et fundamentum veritatum fidei et morum earumque evolutionis. Ideo patet momentum Enchiridii pro historia dogmatum. Simul autem illud nobis monstrat luctam continuam, quae Ecclesiae omnibus fere temporibus sustinenda erat ad verbum Dei intactum et purum conservandum. Sub hoc autem respectu ipsa decreta Pontif. Commissionis de Re Biblica magni sunt momenti. Quatenus vero in iis proponuntur sententiae, quae neque mediate neque immediate cum veritatibus fidei et morum cohaerent, interpres S. Scripturae plena libertate suas investigationes scientificas prosequi earumque fructum percipere potest, salva semper auctoritate magisterii Ecclesiae. Vix hodie cogitari potest, quibus in condicionibus interpretes catholici ante circa 50 annos versarentur et quanto periculo doctrina ipsa catholica de S. Scriptura eiusque inspiratione exposita fuerit, cum critica liberalis et rationalistica omnes traditionis terminos rumpere conaretur. Hodie tamen, cum illa certamina diminuta et nonnullae controversiae pacifice compositae sint pluresque quaestiones sub novo aspectu appareant, facile est negotium de nimia mentium angustia illorum temporum temere iudicare.*

[45]*A decretis igitur, quae de rebus cum fide cohaerentibus agunt ac proinde firma manent, distinguenda sunt decreta, quae quaestiones cum fide nullo modo connexas tractant ideoque libertatem non tollunt. Pleraque ex eis referebantur expressis verbis ad statum, in quo scientia biblica tunc versabatur. Inter ea sunt praesertim illa quae ad criticam litterariam i.e. ad*

Naturally these explanations of 1955 caused a great sensation in exegetical circles (cf. e.g. *RB*, 1955. pp.414-9 art. 'A propos du nouvel Enchiridion Biblicum'). They were a further clear indication of the advance made in the Encyclical *Divino afflante Spiritu* in comparison with earlier ecclesiastical decisions.

authenticitatem (genuinitatem) seu identitatem auctorum inspiratorum spectant. Data sunt quidem ad fidem defendendam, sed hodie hae quaestiones 'sub novo aspectu apparent', cum iam clarius perspiciatur inspirationem alicuius textus biblici omnino salvam manere, quicumque fuerit eius auctor humanus. Ut de his decretis aequum iudicium feratur, prae oculis habenda sunt adiuncta quae tunc existebant, hodie vero mutata sunt. Decreta haec, nunc iterum auctoritate Commissionis Biblicae edita, habent momentum historicum et apologeticum, nam monstrant Ecclesiam ad defendendam S. Scripturam semper vigilem et diligentem esse.

CONCLUSION TO PART I

THE CATHOLIC BIBLICAL MOVEMENT TODAY

AT THE deepest level, the inspiration of the modern biblical movement is the lively desire for a more personal and vivid understanding of Christianity in its supernatural, suprarational aspect based on revelation. Nowadays we have travelled far from the practical concept of Christianity as a simple, rational form of theism, sanctioned by God and forming the basis of the natural moral law, an idea which was often all too prominent in the eighteenth century under the pressure of the controversy with the 'libertines' of that time. The effect of this controversy endured for too long and its influence was felt into the nineteenth century. Today a Christian élite longs for a better understanding of the divine 'revelation', of God's 'message', of God's concrete 'plan' for mankind, so that they may live it more intensely. These Christians have become more sensitive, and are more open to the 'mystery' of God, the Christ proposed from all eternity, and now made manifest, set out before us in Ephesians (Chapters 1-3) as well as in all the Epistles of St Paul and the work of St John. By virtue of its very profundity, this movement needs to be understood properly, elucidated theologically and guided wisely in the light and under the authority of the Church.

It is easy to distinguish the many signs of this movement.

For a long time there was available to French-speaking Catholics almost no handy Bible except the *Bible de Crampon* published in 1905 by Société Saint-Jean l'Evangéliste (*Desclée et Cie*, Tournai, Paris, Rome), which after that date was periodically re-edited and adapted, and possessed the monopoly of the Catholic Bible reading public. Immediately after the second world war 'Bibles' for the use of the faithful increased in number, and quickly went through new editions. They included the *Bible de Maredsous*, published in 1949 (Éditions de Maredsous) and since republished in various formats, the *Bible de Lille* (*La Sainte Bible*, Sociep, Paris, 1951, 2nd edition 1955); the *Bible de Crampon* re-published in an entirely new form in 1952, and the *Bible de Jérusalem* published in separate fascicules between 1948 and 1954, and in one volume (a volume which soon required reprinting) in 1956.

Works of synthesis and interpretation on Christian reading of the Bible have enjoyed a growing success, and have included for example J. Guitton *Le Développement des idées dans l'Ancien Testament* (Aix-en-Provence 1947); A. Gelin *Les idées maîtresses de l'Ancien Testament* (Paris, 1948); H. Duesberg, O.S.B., *Les valeurs chrétiennes de l'Ancien Testament* (Maredsous, first published 1948); J. Guillet, S.J., *Thèmes bibliques* (Paris, first published 1950); Dom Charlier, O.S.B., *La lecture chrétienne de la Bible* (Maredsous, first published 1950); and in collaboration with other writers, *L'Ancien Testament et les chrétiens* (Paris, 1951), *La Bible et le Prêtre* (Louvain, 1951); Paul-Marie de la Croix, O.D.C., *L'Ancien Testament, source de vie spirituelle* (Paris and Bruges, 1952); L. Bouyer, *La Bible et l'Évangile* (Paris, first published 1953); G. E. Closen, S.J., *Clefs pour la Sainte Écriture* (from the German, Bruges, 1954) and *Initiation biblique* (3rd edition, Paris, 1954), translated into English as *Guide to the Bible* by E. P. Arbez and H. R. P. McGuire, vol. 1, 2nd ed., New York, 1960; J. Coppens, *L'efflorescence des études bibliques sur le vieux continent* (Louvain 1954); G. Auzou, *La Parole de Dieu* (Paris, 1956, 2nd edn, 1960); *Introduction à la Bible* under the direction of A. Robert and A. Feuillet (vol. 1, Tournai, 1957, 2nd edn; and vol. II (New Testament) 1959); and G. Auzou, *La tradition biblique* (Paris, 1957).

New series devoted to the Bible have appeared, all intended, on different levels, to adapt the Bible to suit the different classes of Christians. They have often proved very popular. They include *Lectio divina*, started in 1946 by the Dominican Fathers and published by the *Editions du Cerf*, often works of the very highest quality; *Analecta Lovaniensia biblica et orientalia*, founded and edited since 1947 by Professor J. Coppens of Louvain (and replacing the *Bulletin d'Histoire et d'exégèse de l'Ancien Testament*, 1934-7), *Recherches Bibliques* (annual volumes containing the conferences of the 'Journées bibliques' held at Louvain, beginning in 1948); *Témoins de Dieu*, a series in small format, begun in 1942, also by the *Editions du Cerf*; and also very trustworthy and illuminating, the collection *Textes pour l'histoire sacrée* undertaken by Daniel-Rops with various collaborators and comprising valuable works of biblical study, including *La Bible, livre d'histoire*; *La Bible, livre de prière, etc.*; the series of pamphlets entitled *Évangile: Cahiers bibliques trimestriels*, published since 1951 by the Ligue Catholique de l'Evangile (Rue de la Planche, Paris) and the biblical series of the Abbey of Saint-André at Bruges (*Pas à pas avec la Bible*, *Fichier biblique*, etc.); Albert Gelin's wonderful series of lessons on the Bible in the review *Catéchistes* (1950-5) entitled *A la découverte de l'Ancien Testament*, and, since 1955, those by Jean Duplacy, *A la découverte du Nouveau Testament*; whilst for young people of the Youth Section of French Catholic Action there has been the series of 4-8 page tracts called *Éléments de doctrine spirituelle*, *Étapes du peuple de Dieu* (A.C.J.F., Paris, 1948-9) and the pamphlets *Figures bibliques* and *Jésus et* (various second titles) . . . by the Oeuvre de Tracts (Rue Washington, Brussels); and for the Équipes enseignantes, books of guidance and information such as that excellent work by A. George, *L'évangile de Paul. Guide de lecture pour les épîtres de saint Paul* (Paris, 1954). We may also mention two excellent collections, which give the fruits of recent Biblical conferences:

Sacra Pagina. Miscellanea Biblica Congressus Internationalis Catholici de Re Biblica. Ediderunt J. Coppens, A. Descamps, E. Massaux. Coll. Bibliotheca

Ephemeridum Theologicarum Lovaniensium. XII-XIII. 2 vols., Gembloux, Duculot, 1959.

Studia Biblica et Orientalia. Volumes published for the 50th Jubilee of the Pontifical Biblical Institute. 2 vols., Rome, Pontificium Institutum Biblicum, 1959.

Notice the growing emphasis on the Old Testament—a pleasant contrast with the silence and constraint of the years 1907-30. In most of these works there appears to be a sustained effort to see the Old Testament in the realism its period and milieu and, at the same time, to find in it, by the light of Christ as the Catholic Church has always done, the divine plan preparing down the centuries for the coming of the Word, his message and his work. It is equally interesting to notice here the parallelism between these works and those of Protestants, such as S. de Dietrich, *Le dessein de Dieu. Itinéraire biblique*, or those of Hunter, Hoskyns and Davey, Dodd, etc. (*v.supra* pp. 121-2), and the influence of these writings from different religious backgrounds upon one another. Such mutual influence is beneficial wherever it directs our thinking towards the fullness of Christian supernatural truth and away from the naturalist concepts of critical liberalism.

The increasingly prominent place given to the Old and New Testaments in Catholic manuals of religious instruction must also be mentioned. This is easily realized if we examine modern methods of catechesis: I shall do no more here than recall the review *Lumen Vitae* started in 1946 and the manuals and courses published by the *Centre international d'études de la formation religieuse* (Rue Washington, Brussels). The very greatly increased importance given to holy Scripture in reviews concerned with spirituality and Christian education must be pointed out: the Dominican *Vie Spirituelle* (Paris), the Jesuit review of the spiritual life *Christus* (founded in 1954), *Lumière et Vie* (Lyons and S. Alban, started in 1952), and *Bible et Vie Chrétienne* (founded in 1953 at the Benedictine monastery at Maredsous). The longing so frequently expressed by the faithful today to hear sermons more firmly based on Scripture and to be in a position to understand the biblical parts of the liturgy, the Epistle and Gospel at Mass, should also be remembered. Another point it might be useful to make is that Bible Weeks or Days, and societies and circles for study of the Bible etc. have multiplied to such a degree that quite recently (15 December 1955) an Instruction had to be sent to Ordinaries by the Biblical Commission to ensure for them a more certain and effective result by applying to them certain rules dictated by prudence.

I have outlined the form taken by the Catholic Biblical movement in French speaking countries, because that was essential to the purposes of this book. I now add some indications of a comparable and parallel growth in the English-speaking countries. (The same thing, of course, might be done for Italy, Germany, etc.).

For almost three and a half centuries, there was one translation which reigned supreme among English-speaking Catholics; this was the Douai-Rheims Bible. The New Testament was issued at Rheims, where priests prepared for the English Mission, in 1582; a complete Bible appeared in 1610 at Douai. This was a translation from the Latin Vulgate. Revised by Bishop Challoner in mid-seventeenth century, this was the Bible best known until the twentieth century, when rivals began to appear. Fr F. A. Spencer, O.P. published a New Testament, translated from the Greek; Cuthbert Lattey, S.J. was the editor of the *Westminster Version*, which appeared from 1913-35, the New Testament complete, translated from the Greek, and some of the Old Testament books, translated directly from the Hebrew. Monsignor Ronald Knox translated the entire Bible from 1944-50; the New Testament from the Vulgate, with reference to the Greek original, and the Old Testament from the Vulgate, with reference to the Hebrew: a translation by a master of English style. In the United States, the Confraternity of Christian Doctrine published a revision of Bishop Challoner's edition in 1941, in the *Confraternity of Christian Doctrine New Testament*. Frs J. A. Kleist and J. L. Lilly published an interesting translation of the New Testament from the Greek in 1954; this is especially good for the Gospels. And finally, the Confraternity, through its episcopal committee, is now sponsoring a completely new translation of the Bible, from the original texts. Vol. I (1953) Genesis-Ruth, Vol. III (1959) Wisdom Literature, have appeared.

For syntheses, *Guide to the Bible*, the English translation of *Initiation Biblique* (translated by Edward Arbez and Martin R. P. McGuire; two Vols., New York, Desclée, 1960-1) will serve as the best guide for the biblical student. The Catholic Biblical Association had already published its *Commentary on the New Testament* in 1942; and in England, *A Catholic Commentary on Holy Scripture* was edited by Dom Orchard, Father Sutcliffe, S.J., R. C. Fuller and Dom R. Russell, in 1953. Dom Charlier's *La Lecture Chrétienne de la Bible* has been translated into English (*The Christian Approach to the Bible*, London, Sands & Co., 1958); the Abbot of Downside, Dom Christopher Butler, discusses the biblical movement in his book *The Church and the Bible* (Baltimore, Helicon Press, 1960).

Among the periodicals, *The Catholic Biblical Quarterly* (Washington, D.C., 1939), *Theological Studies* (1940-) and *Scripture* (London, Edinburgh, 1946-) show by their recent beginnings, the growth in biblical-theological interest. *Worship* (Collegeville, Minnesota, formerly *Orate Fratres*) helps to relate the Bible and the liturgy. Cf. also *Catholic Biblical Encyclopedia—New Testament*, by John E. Steinmueller and Kathryn Sullivan, (New York, 1950).

The Old Testament has attracted much attention among English speaking Catholics, also. We may note the reviews of work in Scripture in an article by Father James Coleran, S.J. in *Theological Studies* of 1944 (Vol. V), pp. 86-98, in which the progress of Scriptural Studies from Leo XIII to Pius XII is reviewed; the *Bulletins of the Old Testament*, articles by Fr Frederick Moriarty, S.J., (*Theological Studies* XII (1951), pp. 320-342; *TS* XIV (1953) pp. 402-429) describe work done in the field of the Old Testament by Catholics and non-Catholics. These articles will help as a general orientation. *The Catholic Biblical Quarterly*, with its features, 'Survey of Periodicals', 'Biblical and Archeological News,' will also assist the reader. Fr John McKenzie wrote his excellent *The Two-Edged Sword* (Milwaukee, 1956; London 1959) because, 'Catholics have felt no need to read the book and because the book repelled them even if they tried to read it, Catholics have left the Old Testament alone'. That is no longer true, as the contemporary biblical movement gains ground in English speaking countries. The English reader will find in Fr Bruce Vawter's *A Path Through Genesis* (Sheed and Ward, London, 1957) an excellent guide to that difficult book, and in the same author's recently published *The Conscience of Israel*, a fine introduction to the prophets.

For the New Testament: again the bulletins in *Theological Studies* give bibliographies, and an account of progress in this field. See the bulletins by Fr John Collins, S.J. in *TS* XIII (1952) pp. 205-219; *TS* XV (1954) pp. 389-415; and by Frs Collins and David M. Stanley, S.J. in *TS* XVII (1956), pp. 516-548. Invaluable for bibliography is the new venture, *New Testament Abstracts* (Weston College, Weston, Mass. 1956-) which reviews the literature published on the New Testament, both Catholic and non-Catholic, in a variety of languages.

We can but rejoice at the ever clearer prospect of a general orientation of Catholic faith and devotion towards a deeper understanding of holy Scripture, for the movement is one of religious advance both in breadth and depth.

Of course a movement of this kind—like any other movement in ideas in our poor human world—can turn aside either in the direction of superficiality, of one-sided narrowness that would shut itself off from the endeavour of dogmatic and theological thought, or that of free examination of Scripture, claiming freedom from (and indeed even often setting itself up against) the Catholic synthesis of our faith. Understanding holy Scripture is a complicated and difficult task, demanding arduous, humble and collective labour. Only the whole Church, guided gradually through the centuries by the Holy Ghost, is able progressively to understand the divine plan, God's message realized in the redemptive incarnation and given expression in Scripture.

By way of conclusion I shall attempt to define the three apparently essential conditions for the preservation of the modern Catholic biblical movement in all its pristine purity within the framework of the faith.

In the first place, the attempts at synthesis, already clearly manifest in the contemporary biblical movement—indeed one of its most encouraging aspects—should be loyally and increasingly continued.

It is pleasant to remark that works of biblical theology, for long all too rare among Catholics, have reappeared among our Catholic books since the second world war. Recent works in this field include: Paul Heinisch *Theologie des Alten Testaments* (Bonn, 1940); P. van Imschoot *Théologie de l'Ancien Testament* (2 vols, Paris and Tournai, 1954 and 1956); Max Meinertz *Theologie des Neuen Testaments* (2 vols, Bonn, 1950); J. Bonsirven *Théologie du Nouveau Testament* (Paris, 1950) and his other theological studies *Les enseignements de Jésus-Christ* (Paris, 1946) and *L'Évangile de Paul* (Paris, 1948). There are also studies of the theology of St Paul by Mgr Cerfaux (*La théologie de l'Église suivant saint Paul*, 1st edn, Paris, 1942; 2nd edn, Paris, 1948; and *Le Christ dans la théologie de saint Paul*, Paris 1951) and Fr St Lyonnet (the duplicated series *Theologia biblica Novi Testamenti*). There has been an ever-increasing number of books and articles intended to set out and adapt for the Catholic public the whole of the teaching or the characteristic marks of one of the inspired authors, either of the New Testament—for example St Paul (P.Thils, *Pour mieux comprendre saint Paul*, 2nd edn, Bruges 1942; Tresmontant, *Saint Paul et la mystère du Christ*, Paris, 1956, etc.) or St John (the many articles by Fr Braun setting out the various aspects of a theology of St John; J. Dupont, *Essais sur la Christologie de saint Jean*, W. Grossouw, *Pour mieux comprendre saint Jean*, etc.) or of the Old Testament (J. Steinmann, *Is àie, Jérémie*).

The same attempt at synthesis has been shown in the study of Old Testament history as a whole. As we have already said, the aim is to see how it is a preparation for the New Testament, to interpret it, as St Paul said, as 'the economy of the promise of God' to be realized in Christ, and to watch the Jewish soul being prepared gradually through the centuries to become the Christian soul (cf. Eph. 1, 12: *nos qui ante speravimus in Christo*). Such has been the basic aim of the works listed above.

The deeper study of some of the biblical concepts essential to our faith has also been carried on with a view to this synthesis: see, for instance F. X. Durrwell, C.SS.R. *The Resurrection*, (translation, London, New York, 1961), or the studies of the Christian concepts of ἀγάπη (C. Spicq, O.P. 1956) γνῶσις (J. Dupont, O.S.B., 1949), δίκαιος and δικαιοσύνη (Mgr Cerfaux and A. Descamps, 1950), ἐλευθερία (R. Egenter, in *Von der Freiheit der Kinder Gottes*, 1949)—the list could be extended to cover every letter of the Greek alphabet.

The English reader will be interested by the thoughtful article by the present editor of *Scripture*, Fr Thomas Worden: 'Is Scripture to remain the Cinderella of Catholic Theology?' (*Scripture* VIII, 1956, pp. 2-12), discussing the relations of Scripture and dogma, and progress in Scripture; numerous translations of the books cited above: Heinisch, *Theology of the Old Testament* translated by W. G. Heidt, O.S.B., (Collegeville, Minnesota, 1950); Mgr Cerfaux's two books on St Paul, translated into English and published by Herder and Herder; and Fr Durrwell's book *The Resurrection*, translated by Rosemary Sheed (Sheed & Ward, 1960). Finally we may cite an interesting article by Fr David M. Stanley, which shows the progress being made in elaborating a biblical theology: 'The Concept of Our Gospels as Salvation History' *Theological Studies* XX (1959), pp. 561-589, and his book *Christ's Resurrection in Pauline Soteriology*, (Anal. Bibl, n. 13, Pont. Inst. Biblicum., Rome, 1961).

As long as this work of synthesis is held in esteem in Catholic exegesis and continues to hold the interest of the élite among the faithful, and particularly of priests, there is no danger that the biblical movement will dissipate itself in superficialities prompted by snobbishness or fashion.

The second condition, closely connected with the first and essential if the biblical movement is to continue along the right lines, seems to us to be that it must show an enlightened understanding of and profound respect for Catholic doctrine. Dogma and Scripture, theology and exegesis must always seek to be linked together. Several of the studies in this book are devoted to this essential aspect of Catholic research into the fullness of divine truth. At this point I shall do no more than mention it briefly, but return to it below.

Of course, both theology and exegesis have their own rules which cannot be ignored if sincerity and objectivity are to be preserved. Premature concordances will always remain a great danger in theology, and with the advances effected in exegesis and theology it is possible that their point of encounter may not occur where it was found to be sixty years ago. It is possible, too, that fresh problems in reconciling the conclusions of the two disciplines, problems unforeseen by former works in these fields, will arise, and that each of the two disciplines will have to consider more closely, draw finer distinctions or even correct, in loyalty to its own method, this or that conclusion made in the past. A mind clinging fiercely to all the formulas of the manuals of its youth, without ever agreeing to rethink them in accordance with advances in the religious sciences, is not mature and, if it belongs to one who has pastoral or administrative responsibilities, may damage and weaken the faith or peace in the faith of well-intentioned scholars.

But whatever at times may be the difficulties of the task, conscientious, intelligent and tenacious endeavour to bring together and harmonize the conclusions reached by the two disciplines is a fundamental duty both of the exegete and of the theologian. The attitude adopted by modernist exegetes, whose pose was to proclaim loudly with a show of authority what they regarded as their historical conclusions, at the same time treating with scorn the agreement or disagreement of these conclusions with dogma, is not a Catholic attitude. It is the same God of Truth at work in the elaboration and true formulation of Christian dogma, who has spoken through the centuries in holy Scripture. Of course the ease with which religious instruction can be conveyed can certainly never be the determining factor in the objective search after truth. God has never been easy to understand. It is not for him to lower the loftiness of his message to the level of the weakness and narrowness of the ideas, inclinations and tastes of man in this or that century of his history. It is for man, humbly, with all his faith, intelligence and devotion to seek to understand ever more perfectly the God who speaks through his Scripture and his Church. The existence in every period of difficulties that cannot be resolved until a later age is a normal thing—but when that happens the essential factor in our act of faith will always be to trust in a God 'greater than our minds and hearts'.

A third condition for the soundness of the biblical movement— and it is only a complement of the first and second conditions—is trust in the Church, in the instructions of the Church, and in the general movement of thought and faith in the Church. Here again, it is for us to strive to rise to the loftiness of God's plan, and not narrow our concept of all that is the 'mystical Body' of Christ. The Church, of course, is primarily the pope and the bishops, who perpetuate for us the authority and living activity of St Peter and the apostles united with Peter in their loyalty to the message of Christ. The Church is also the whole body of priests and faithful, religious and layfolk, seeking to live for God through Christ; they too, in their own way, can give expression to the movements of the Holy Ghost in the souls of those in the Church. From among them, too, God may choose the interpreters through whom he will speak to his Church, through a Francis of Assisi, who guided medieval devotion to a very real attachment to Christ's humanity which was of particular significance at that time, or through a Margaret Mary Alacoque, who contributed so powerfully, through the devotion to the Sacred Heart, to the final elimination from the Body of the Church of Jansenist mistrust and fear of God's work, thus strengthening truth and love within it.

The Church's past is all part of the Church, including that struggle to see the faith clearly which marked the first three centuries and led to the formulation for all time of the dogma of the Holy Trinity, and including, too, the teaching of the Fathers, doctors and writers anterior to the seventh century, who studied Scripture, lived it with all their Christian souls, and passed on to us for ever the whole essence of religion and mysticism, even if their historical exegesis did not foresee and could not have foreseen the particular historical and philological interpretations required by modern progress. The anti-modernist reaction was mistaken when it confused the religious essence of patristic interpretation, noble and right-minded as it was, with its explanation of mere historical matters.

Our trust in the visible Church—which will always distinguish our exegesis from Protestant exegesis—is based on a conviction taught by faith that Christ is still present in his Church, and through her and with her is continuing his great work for the salvation and sanctification of mankind. We are all aware that, in putting into operation his plan of redemption, God laid on the men of his Church a terrifying responsibility for decision and action: we are aware, too, that the Church, like every human institution, has to seek hesitantly, humbly, patiently for the right and effective ways of forwarding the rule of God here on earth. God never promised to ratify and sanction all the decisions of those to whom he has given responsibility in his Church. We should therefore never be surprised at the mistakes, blunders and narrowness by individual Churchmen, just as we are not surprised by mistakes, blunders and narrowness on the part of any civil and military authority. How often we have to admit the multitude of our own mistakes, blunders and narrowness! It is part of our human condition. God's work can be carried on properly only through profound humility, anxious effort and earnest prayer, by the leaders on the one hand and the faithful on the other.

But what is for ever guaranteed by Christ's promise is that ultimately, even after hesitation and momentary ups and downs, the barque of the Church alone will bring each of her children to the haven of salvation, and will sail through the centuries towards the last port, the Kingdom of God in its plentitude, *usque in mensuram aetatis plenitudinis Christi* (Ephes. 4, 13). What is essential and fundamental for us Catholic theologians or exegetes is that as a visible society, under the invisible guidance of Christ, the Church alone is authorized to bring the teaching message of Christ to its true end as foreseen and willed by God. Only in the Church, in unity with the Church, can either theological or exegetical science enjoy intellectual security and a guarantee of reaching the whole truth.

PART II

Inspiration and Catholic Exegesis

INTRODUCTION

THE ESSENTIAL principle underlying the Catholic idea of holy Scripture is well known to everybody. Holy Scripture is both divine and human, it is the Word of God in human language; it is completely divine and completely human, not in the form of two linked and parallel activities, but in one single activity which is exercised entirely by man as free instrumental cause, and exercised entirely by God as principal cause.

Hence two essential duties are incumbent on the Catholic exegete, and they are inseparable and mutually inclusive:

(a) On the one hand, and before all else, he must consider and study inspired Scripture from the first page to the last, in each one of its individual teachings as well as in the complete synthesis of its statements of fact and doctrines, as the word of God, as a message from God to the human race.

In Scripture God wishes above all to communicate to us that supreme divine plan, which St Paul again and again calls the 'mystery', the 'mystery of God' (Ephes. 1. 9: 3. 4, 9: Col. 1. 26, 27; 2. 2: 4. 3 etc.), that decree of his will, so long hidden in God and finally revealed, whereby he desires to bring men to salvation in and through Jesus Christ. The divine work in this world has as its centre the Incarnation of the Word of God and it is in and through Christ that God wills to unify, raise up and give peace to the whole universe. Scripture was written throughout the course of centuries, within the limits of successive and varied civilizations and literary forms and, apparently, as events determined; yet it reveals nonetheless the unique and overall plan of a God who is above history and is its master.

This central higher truth is entirely supernatural. It springs from a divine revelation; it is doctrinal since it teaches us what God's

plan for us is, and moral, because it makes increasingly clear in the
course of the centuries, what virtues are required of men in view of
the divine plan: the sense of sin, humility, trust, the spirit of prayer,
the expectation of salvation, etc. True, these lessons will be presented
in the Old Testament under rudimentary and progressive forms
whose meaning will be made clear by the goal which determines
their course, Jesus Christ in the New Testament. Then the full light
of the complete and definitive revelation shines forth. Yet it is given,
we must note, to be constantly interpreted under the guidance of the
Church until the world comes to an end.

God, who speaks in the message of Scripture taken as a whole,
speaks also in each event, in each writer inspired by him. He alone
could raise up one after the other the prophets of the Old Testament
so that each of them in his turn might improve on the work of his
predecessor by adding new aspects of the moral monotheism taught
to the men of Israel as they made their way towards Christ. He alone
knows the limits of the revelation received and put into words by
Paul, of the revelation granted to John and James. He alone could
will in advance that one should complete the other in the interests
of his complete revelation in the Church.

The divine message, in so far as it is expressed in Scripture, is
only the last stage, the last carrying into effect of a divine activity
which is far wider and more complex.[1] Before Scriptural inspiration
properly so called, there was revelation, there was the divine action
taking place in the great events of the history of salvation, and these
events were willed and organized according to God's eternal plan,
from the call to Abraham down to Calvary, the resurrection of
Christ and the coming of the Spirit. The nineteenth century exegetes
and theologians made a mistake in method when they too often
considered scriptural inspiration as an isolated, separate phenomenon, as though the inspired author was outside time and space,
alone with God communicating his message to him. In fact, he
seems ordinarily to be the interpreter, the witness, the man who
writes the definitive account of an antecedent or, on occasion, a

---

[1]Considerable light has been thrown on this point of view by Fr P. Benoît, O.P.
in several recent articles: *La Prophétie, Somme Théologique de St Thomas*, Revue des
Jeunes edition, 1947; *Initiation biblique*, third edition, 1954, chapter I on inspiration; *RB*, 1955, pp. 258-64. See also K. Rahner, S.J., 'Über die Schriftinspiration',
in *Zeitschrift für katholische Theologie*, 1956, pp. 137-68 and the pamphlet of the same
title, Fribourg, 1958.

contemporary *revelation* which was a word or an act of God and constitutes the essence of the message.

Even in the first series of inspired books, the five books of the
Pentateuch, 'the Law', as it was called by the children of Israel,
the idea of inspiration—as it gradually came to light—was considered as a consequence, an extension of the idea of revelation.
The 'Law' was believed by Israel to be divine because it had been
given by God to Moses, it had come from God, it was a revelation
from God. In its written form it was taken by them all to be the
expression of God's revelation, and sharing in the transcendent
character of revelation. The second series of inspired books 'the
prophets' (Nebiim), were looked upon in the same way. The
prophet in Israel is essentially the man who communicates to men a
message, a command, a revelation from God. The writing down
of his prophecies, which moreover was usually attributed to the
prophet himself, would therefore share in the transcendental
character of God's message to his human interpreter.

Even when we are dealing with those who were simply Israel's
historians, those who narrated the great epic of Yahweh's wonderful
leadership of his people, the manifestation of the divine plan revealing itself in history and interpreted by the people of Israel,
logically preceded scriptural inspiration. Israel's historians only
repeat what Israel as a whole has experienced and has lived out in
its own history. Here again, the historians are 'witnesses'.

With the New Testament, it becomes all the more necessary not
to separate 'revelation' and 'inspiration' in our exegetical studies.
They must be kept closely united if we are to reach a full understanding of the divine message. 'In old days, God spoke to our
fathers in many ways and by many means, through the prophets;
now at last in these times he has spoken to us through the Son,
whom he has appointed to inherit all things, and through whom
he created the world' (Heb. 1. 1-2). Christ was the supreme source
of revelation not only in his oral teaching but also and especially
in all that he was and did, in his whole being as Son of God which
was gradually manifested to his chosen witnesses, in the inmost
characteristics of his human soul which attracted vast numbers of
men and have been the subject of the meditation of Christians for
the past twenty centuries, in his passion and death which revealed
the mystery of Redemption, in his glorious resurrection which is

the cause and the guarantee of our own. God reveals not only in word, but also, and often more clearly, in deed. The facts of Christ's death and resurrection are fundamental revelations of what Christianity is and these revelations were given to men before they were interpreted in theological terms by St Paul and St John, and before the first groups of Christians at Jerusalem gained an increasingly deeper insight into their meaning. This revelation, which is Christ's whole message was faithfully preserved in the infant Church and shaped its religious life through the activity of the Spirit in close union with the apostles. The inspired evangelist is the witness of and puts into words Christ's message, given to the world in this way. If we look on the inspired writer as a 'witness' giving utterance to God's word as it was lived by the Church, as he too lived it in union with his fellow Christians, then his own personal freedom, his own personal characteristics as a writer, clearly shown in his narrative, are easily explained. Obviously the charismatic activity of the Spirit in the infant Church, was *a fortiori* at work in the man who put the faith of this Church into verbal form. Yet he is not alone with God who speaks through him. He is also the Church's witness.

In this book I do not intend to study the psychological aspect of the phenomenon of scriptural inspiration. The various data of the problem are well known. On the one hand the Church teaches—and during the past sixty-five years she has told us many times through her supreme Magisterium—that holy Scripture is God's message, a message God has efficaciously willed in the form in which it is presented to us in Scripture. And this is true of every individual passage of the inspired writings as well as of Scripture as a whole. On the other hand, an objective study of these inspired writings clearly reveals the personal, human characteristics of each writer, his imagination, his sensibility, his mode of thought, etc., which are obvious in all their spontaneity on every page he has written. How then are we to reconcile the efficacy of the divine action which must ensure that all God wills should be written is in fact written, with the liberty of the human writer which seems to be constantly and fully in evidence? Theologians have perhaps made the task more difficult by considering the human writer as isolated, as separate from the environment in which he has been placed by God. Are we to believe that the divine activity only came into operation at the final moment when the divine message was committed to writing? Is not this act of committing it to writing the last result of a more extensive divine activity at work through time, through the various spontaneous and free manifestations of human nature, and continually at work until the final outward expression of God's teaching? How then are we to classify and clarify the precise part played by human causes in this temporal progress of the divine message? What matters is not that the exegete should determine the way in which divine and human liberty are reconciled—this is God's eternal mystery—but rather that he should keep his eye constantly on the two aspects of the problem: the transcendent depth and complexity of God's action here below which finally through various stages produces the inspired writings as the authentic expression of God's message, as 'God's word', and, on the other hand, the completely human character of this message, which is a genuine 'human word' expressing in human fashion, and in the context of a certain environment and epoch, the truth of God.

This supernatural intervention of God in the history of the human race, leading as it does to 'God's message' transmitted in Scripture, has an essentially religious and moral character. It is centred on the Incarnation of the Word of God; it is our salvation through Christ which God reveals to us through his holy Scripture. It is the history of the preparation for salvation in the past which he recounts to us in the Old Testament. To look to Scripture for 'scientific insights' providentially prepared by God for the benefit of human progress in the secular field[2], for 'intellectual enlightenment' which would miraculously place the ancient writers on the same technical level as the most recent historical critics,[3] is to condemn oneself in advance to a misunderstanding of the meaning of God's message. It is to invent valueless objections and non-existent problems. God asks us to bring to all our attempts at interpreting the divine plan, which is brought to fulfilment in history, that deep sense of 'mystery' which is the spontaneous expression of an attitude based on faith. God is greater than the human mind. Faith in the transcendent nature of God's message

[2] I have in mind the numerous Catholic works at the end of the nineteenth century dealing with the scientific significance of the first chapter of Genesis (Concordism).

[3] I have in mind the celebrated discussions at the beginning of the twentieth century on the literary form of the historical passages in Genesis.

in Scripture can alone raise us above the narrow limits of a false human logic, so that we may gradually discover what God has willed to tell us throughout the centuries and how he has done so. No exegesis would be equal to this task unless, from century to century, it were constantly enlightened and sustained by the religious, dogmatic and moral progress of the Church of Christ.

In short, we come to Scripture as to 'God's message' with a profound faith in the transcendence of the message and in the transcendence of the way the message is conveyed, which may differ greatly from what we might expect. We must ask Scripture itself to reveal to us how God has spoken, in much the same way—analogically speaking and *mutatis mutandis*—as we approach the discovery of nature, allowing her to reveal herself to us as she really is.

(b) Our faith tells us that God has established our salvation on the Incarnation. He has willed to speak to men and to save them through the Word of God made man, and he has willed that his holy Scripture, from the first page to the last, should be both divine and human, the word of God in human language. Therefore the second essential duty of the Christian exegete, if he wishes to know what God tells us through man his interpreter, is to seek to understand in as concrete a way as possible the language of the man who speaks to us in the name of God. He must therefore be aware of all the modes of human speech, of this particular mode of human speech, with its precise conditions of vocabulary, environment and period. Hence the need for the long researches of philological and historical exegesis. This task, indispensable to the interpretation of Scripture, was explained with remarkable clarity in Pius XII's Encyclical *Divino afflante Spiritu*.

So it is essential to consider the personal work of the particular writer as a whole, to grasp the fundamental purpose of his book, which determines the literary form he has chosen of his own free will and settles to what extent mention of detail is to be treated as assertion of fact. Nothing in scriptural exegesis is so disastrous as the false psychology which cuts up and isolates texts and erects them, each and all, into apodictic aphorisms or into articles of a Code, with no reference whatsoever to the general context of the work or to the cultural environment of the author. The inspired writer, the interpreter of the divine message, can only have in mind the communication of this message which is essentially religious and moral. It is not history for history's sake in the modern critical manner which interests the historian of the Exodus or of the Judges, but history in so far as it manifests the divine blessing on the chosen people, and fulfils God's mysterious plan in Israel's favour. This in no way lessens the solid value of scriptural inerrancy which applies to the whole Bible, but it does prevent us from imposing on Scripture external demands which run counter to its very nature. Always the essential thought of the inspired writer in the general composition of his book must guide us in our interpretation of each of its details. The inspired book is a human work and must first be judged according to the normal laws of human psychology, if we are to understand, as it should be understood, the message from God who is speaking to us through this man. It is in the perfectly human character of the book that God's transcendence shines forth, and this is in keeping with the logic itself of the religion of the Incarnation.

The exegete must do more than this, especially when he is dealing with a doctrinal writer, with an Old Testament prophet or a New Testament apostle,[4] with St Paul or St John. He must gradually reconstruct, as far as it is now possible to do so, the theological synthesis of the inspired author's thought, both conscious and subconscious, implicit and explicit, so that he may pierce through to the soul of God's interpreter. God acts in the deepest realm of the soul and it is there that he inspires and impresses his revelations. It is by attempting to communicate with the sacred writer's personal religious ideal that we shall succeed in passing below the surface of the actual text and in discovering the deep currents on which it is borne.[5] But it is essential to understand the man exactly as he is, with his qualities as well as his defects, in his fully developed thought as well as in that part of it where he is still groping for light, in his formal and conscious teaching and also in doctrine that is lived and experienced rather than conceptually expressed. This is certainly the ideal of historical research always to be aimed at but

[4]Pius XII makes this very clear in the same encyclical (above pp. 164-5), where he refers to Benedict XV's encyclical *Spiritus Paraclitus* (*EB.*, second edition, No. 448, p. 142; *NRT*, 1920, p. 614). We must try to understand in the inspired authors 'propriam uniuscuiusque indolem et veluti singulares notas ac lineamenta, praesertim prophetarum et apostoli Pauli . . .'.

[5]This idea is further developed in chapter X: 'Critical exegesis and theological interpretation'.

never fully realized. It is an ideal of psychological and religious insight and impossible for anyone who does not make every attempt to attune his own soul to the soul of the man he is studying. It is an effort towards theological understanding which, for us Catholics, has the advantage that it is enlightened and sustained by a permanent control, the synthesis of the essentials of Christian doctrine in the whole body of Catholic dogma. This duty to provide a religious and theological interpretation is one of the essential directives given in the encyclical *Divino afflante Spiritu*.[6]

The Catholic exegete must go still further. Sacred Scripture is not a mere assortment of isolated and independent works; the inspired writings form a complete closely-knit *whole*, from the call of Abraham down to the end of the apostolic age. But if Christianity is entirely centred round one fact, one event, Jesus Christ's coming into the world at a given moment in the evolution of the human race, the writings, the facts, the men who prepare the way for him and who follow him down the course of the centuries, can and should be studied as a whole, according to their relationship with him. True, the supreme and definitive religious judgment on this whole, as we shall shortly maintain, is beyond the competence of the historian and can only be within the province of faith. Yet, in their visible aspect, these earthly events—and even the life of Jesus—are subject to the discoveries and the judgments of the historian. One of the tasks of exegesis whose duty it is to understand the men whom God inspired and led, is also to seek to understand them according to their place and their part in the history of the people of Israel and of the infant Church, to aim to grasp and to synthesize the whole economic, social, cultural, political and religious evolution of the chosen group within the context of the general history of mankind. But all this must be done from one point of view alone, namely, of understanding more clearly God's plan in the human race, the divine work in history. It is not for nothing, nor without an overriding purpose, that God has shown us in these facts the rise of a people from barbarism towards the light of Christ, from sin towards the ideal of the Beatitudes.

This effort to understand from within and to enter the mental

---

[6] *Exegetica explanatio ad rationem potissimum theologicam spectet* (cf. above our commentary on pp. 178-179 and 157-159). I have developed the point in my article 'A la lumière de l'encyclique *Divino afflante Spiritu*' in the book *L'Ancien Testament et les chrétiens*, Paris, 1951, pp. 89-111, especially on pp. 95-99.

world of the patriarchal period, of the national and religious vicissitudes of the epic of David, of the growth and development of the idea of God and of the Covenant in the prophets of Israel from Amos to Malachias, of the fundamental currents of Old Testament religion which are 'answering God's call', and 'obedience', of the interior renewal in the exiles at Babylon under the influence of Ezechiel and of Deutero-Isaias (ch. 40 *et seq.*), and so on down to the end of the apostolic epoch, all this effort, I say, towards a literal, objective and realistic interpretation of the biblical environment, does not estrange us from the divine sense of Scripture.[7] It makes it possible for us to gain a better insight into this divine sense in all its depths.[8] In passing, we may express the conviction that this *humanistic* study of a people guided by God, of souls whom God has inspired, is worthy of its proper place in the formation of the Christian adult, at least on an equal footing with the humanistic study of the Greek and Roman mind in their pagan environment.

But while the historian examines and deepens his knowledge of the religious value of these positive aspects in the work of the men whom God inspired, he is struck by other and negative aspects, by the strange scientific, philosophical and even religious limitations of these writers, by the odd character of many things in their work, which seem to derive from folklore, legends and popular fables. He is struck too by the low moral tone obvious in certain events or circumstances, and in certain customs. The secular historian is not surprised at these characteristics. In ancient literature and history he has frequently come across these naïve historical ideas, these peculiarities of primitive folklore, these callous attitudes of primitive barbarism. But Christian exegesis as well as popular Christian feeling has been disconcerted and worried by these characteristics since the beginning. It has often allowed itself to be so preoccupied with them that it has neglected or forgotten the positive and constructive aspect of inspired Scripture and its religious glories, and devoted most of its time and labour to discussing these special problems. How are these characteristics to be reconciled with the

[7] There is no solid foundation for Paul Claudel's witticism 'the meagre breasts of the literal sense' (*Introduction au livre de Ruth*, p. 47).

[8] Cf. for more developed applications of this aspect of exegesis, my two articles in *NRT* 'La crise de l'Ancien Testament', 1929, pp. 818-39, and 'Per Jesum Christum Filium tuum' 1933, pp. 866-83.

truth of God's word, with the inerrancy of Scripture, unceasingly asserted, and rightly so, by the Church? On the other hand, if God has willed that the history of his work on earth should be described analysed and justified by men of every age, in human language and according to the human concepts prevalent at each stage of the development of this work here below, if he has willed that divine history on earth, sacred history, should be at the same time a profoundly human work, is it for us to fix *a priori* the rules of God's transactions on earth, or to decide what he should or should not do?

Holy Scripture is God's word and it is man's word. These two aspects cannot be separated, and God has willed that this should be so. It would be a grave error to dissociate, in the inspired work, the part played by the human agent and that played by the divine Inspirer. God has willed the human aspect of his message, exactly as it was, with its imperfections and defects and, in the Old Testament, the lower yet constantly enlarging state of religious ideas together with the barbarities of the period and the environment that are reflected in them, just as he has willed the poverty of the Christmas manger and the hard wood of the cross.

In this second part of my book,[9] I wish to consider more closely, both in themselves and their mutual relationship, these two essential aspects of Sacred Scripture. For such a study to be complete, it would develop into a whole treatise *De Scriptura Sacra*. In this vast field, I have chosen three questions which seem to me the most appropriate in the present state of biblical research and exegesis. In my opinion, they have the advantage of highlighting certain principles of biblical hermeneutics which, during the last century of research, have proved to be increasingly necessary. These three questions will be treated in the three chapters of Part II of this book:

(1) Chapter VIII: Sacred Scripture as man's word: the human aspects of the inspired works.

(2) Chapter IX: Sacred Scripture as God's word. In what respect

[9]Part II resumes and reshapes three review articles published during the past few years: 1. 'L'Écriture Sainte, parole de Dieu, parole d'homme', in *NRT* June and July, 1956, pp. 561-92 and 705-28; 2. 'Les limites de la preuve d'Écriture Sainte en théologie', in *NRT* December 1949, pp. 1009-29; 3. 'Exégèse critique et interprétation théologique', in *RSR*, 1951-2, Mélanges Jules Lebreton, vol. I, pp. 237-52.

and in what way does the divine message transcend the understanding and the intentions of the human author?

(3) Chapter X: Critical exegesis and theological interpretation.
The contributions and the limitations of the proof from Scripture in
theology.

Chapter VIII

HOLY SCRIPTURE AS THE WORD OF MEN
THE HUMAN TRAITS IN THE INSPIRED WORK

I HAVE described holy Scripture as *the words of men* and in so doing enumerated the chief tasks facing the exegete who, with the help of all the human means of interpretation, wishes to understand the man whom God has inspired. To expound and unravel practically and in the concrete all these different tasks would be tantamount to writing a treatise on the methods of biblical exegesis, and this is obviously not the purpose of this chapter. In a strictly objective manner, and using examples from Scripture itself, I wish merely to discover in the inspired writings those human traits mentioned above, which at first sight might seem rather difficult to reconcile with the principles of scriptural inerrancy.

The account will be quite simple. I shall give series of examples chosen from Scripture and arranged in ascending order, beginning with the simplest, easiest and most commonly accepted instances and ending with those that are the most complex, the most difficult and in some cases, the most keenly debated. In this way an attempt will be made to gain a better understanding of the profoundly human character of holy Scripture. Perhaps these examples will reveal the complex nature of the concept of scriptural inerrancy and help to rule out over-simplified interpretations which raise needless and unwarranted difficulties against Christian faith or theology.

Our path will be clear if we remember a truth that is deduced from dogma: God, who has revealed himself to us through the Incarnation, through the Word made man, gives us, in accordance with the same principle, his divine word expressed in his holy Scripture by men in a human way. All this is perfectly logical since Christianity is essentially theandric. Only God can show us in the inspired writings how far he has willed to go in this direction.

1. *Sacred Scripture can exhibit the various shades of meaning and the varying strength of human affirmation.*

The inspired writer may write *currente calamo* and progressively clarify his thought from one sentence to another: Paul, I Cor. 1. 14. 16: *neminem baptizavi . . . nisi Crispum*, and then he remembers that he has baptized others besides *Crispus: baptizavi autem et Stephanae domum.*

The inspired writer may use arguments suited to his period and environment so as to convince his contemporaries and because he himself is accustomed to argue in this way. He does not intend to attribute to his reasoning a value greater than that attributed to it by the men of his time. Certain of St Paul's arguments seem somewhat 'rabbinical'. Even if Paul's genius goes beyond the literary style he uses, it is nonetheless true that we must take this style into account if we are to appreciate the precise weight of these arguments.

The inspired author may use hyperbole in the Oriental manner. The Oriental likes to describe celestial phenomena as accompanying great events on earth; the sun grows pale, the moon ceases to give her light. Certain inspired prophetic descriptions should be interpreted as Oriental in this respect and understood as such when translated into our own languages. Hence we shall be careful to provide an Eastern and not a Western exegesis in the case of certain details in our Lord's eschatological utterances or in the Apocalypse.

The inspired text does not necessarily indicate the best or the ideal solution of a problem, even when it praises a given solution. The 'wisdom' of Ecclesiasticus is sometimes of a very high order, but for the most part it represents a practical wisdom, a combination of commonsense and shrewdness, but very inferior to the Christian ideal of the New Testament. The author intended to do no more. His intention determines the scope of his assertions.

The inspired author may express not a judgement but a hope which therefore is not to be taken as an assertion. The apostles admit that they have no indication from our Lord which would enable them to give a date for the Parousia. They therefore teach that they have not the right to declare that it is imminent. In fact, however, they hope it will take place very soon and this hope and this expectation are obvious in their letters, for instance in those of St Paul. But a wish is not the expression of a judgement.[1]

The inspired writer is often led to speak in terms of certain concrete situations existing during his lifetime. His solution is then conditioned by this situation. It is not always easy in such cases to distinguish in his decision between what is temporary and motivated by the circumstances of the period and what is definitive and valid for all time. The interpretation of 1 Cor. 7. 36-8 is disputed, but if, as many Catholic exegetes have thought, the father (or guardian) in charge of his daughter (or his ward) is in fact meant, then St Paul's words presuppose the situation in the ancient world. The father had full authority to decide his daughter's

---

[1]This seems to me the best interpretation, historically speaking, of the various eschatological passages in the New Testament Epistles and I believe it is fully in agreement with the decree of the Biblical Commission of 18 June 1915 (*DZ* 2179-81).

future, he could refuse to give her in marriage or else marry her to any man he judged suitable. It is clear that, in this case, Paul is speaking from within this situation, nor does he envisage any other or any better arrangement. Hence it is the superiority over marriage of virginity consecrated to God which he wishes to teach us here as definitive and not the power of the father to decide what his daughter's vocation should be. In the case (1 Cor. 11. 2-16) of the veil to be worn by women at Christian assemblies, it is obvious that the precise regulation concerning what should be worn is, as such, only temporary. What remains permanent is the rule that decency and respect are due to the church of God. But the whole discussion, combined with 1 Cor. 14. 34-6 and 1 Tim. 2. 11-15, presupposes in Paul a certain attitude of mind towards the position of women in conjugal, civil and ecclesiastical society, and it is not at all easy to separate the principle presented and taught by Paul as definitive, from its concrete and contingent applications. And there are grave issues at stake here, such as the greater or lesser degree of women's participation in the functions of Christian worship, their eligibility for certain grades of holy Orders, etc. The individual exegete is aware here of the limits of his own power to interpret. The Church alone is competent to judge in such matters.

During the course of the centuries, many false interpretations in this particular sphere have been put forward in all good faith. At the beginning of the present century, for instance, in a book entitled *Le féminisme condamné par des principes de théologie et de philosophie*, a Catholic priest, in other respects a well-deserving man, attempted to find in Scripture, especially in the Old Testament, a condemnation of every kind of feminism. He failed to realize that, in those days, women held an inferior position in Semitic society, and that it is this concrete situation which determines and limits the scope of certain inspired texts.[2] Similarly, many passages in the Old Testament on the treatment of servants and slaves (for example, Ecclus. 33) can only be correctly understood if they are set in the concrete situation of the time which explains them and defines their exact meaning.

Many passages in Scripture thus presuppose a concrete and temporary situation (which no longer exists) in terms of which an authoritative solution was given by the prophet, apostle or inspired writer. The individual exegete often feels he is incompetent to separate the definitive from the temporary and the contingent. These cases are among those which most stress the need for a Church to be the constant interpreter of Scripture throughout the ages.

2. *Sacred Scripture, like human language in general, only asserts, according to sound logic, the judgment it makes and not the concepts it uses to form these judgments. (Veritas est in judicio, non in simplici apprehensione).* Scientific ideas current in those days, but which have now been abandoned, may enter into the formulation of teaching which

[2]The writer went so far as to say (p. 78), 'In the Old Testament, the Holy Spirit shows us so clearly the inferior status of women that the Church has been more than justified in forbidding the reading of the Bible in the vernacular. If members of the opposite sex knew all that the Spirit of truth has to say in a general way about their defects, they might well doubt the divine origin of our holy Scriptures.'

alone the inspired writer wishes to assert. It is, moreover, of little consequence whether he did or did not believe in the ideas current in his time, for they are not what he is claiming to assert.

For example, the inspired author teaches the fact that all things were created by God, and he manifests the magnificence of creation to his contemporaries by using the current scientific terms and ideas (which he himself shares). He describes the earth as motionless and fixed in position by God (Eccl. 1. 4, Ps. 92. 2; 103. 5); the sun as moving round the earth (Josue 10. 12-13; Eccl. 1. 5-6; Ps. 18. 6-7); the moon as larger than the stars (Gen. 1. 16); the firmament as a solid platform extending above us and containing reservoirs for water; the valve is opened and the rain falls (Gen. 1. 6: 7. 11; 8. 2; Ps. 148. 4). What he wishes to assert and to teach is God's creative activity and not these scientific concepts.

The inspired authors introduce into their poetic books legendary characters from the folklore of their time to serve as a context for their statements and as a means of expression. There are instances in Job 3. 8: Leviathan; in Isaias. 34. 14: Idumea is considered to be inhabited by centaurs, satyrs, liliths. In the language of the time, this means that Idumea, once it is devastated, will become a desert, since this is the only place in which centaurs, satyrs and liliths live.

The apostles quote the sacred books under the names of the writers who were then considered to be their authors. All the psalms are quoted as David's, the sapiential books as Solomon's, the Pentateuch as composed by Moses, etc. We are not entitled to conclude from this that this attribution is taught to us by the Holy Spirit. When St Jude in his epistle (vv. 14-15) quotes the apocryphal book of Henoch as though Henoch were its author, his intention is to condemn the heretics of his time, by using this passage, not to teach us that the book is itself authentic.

3. *Sacred Scripture may admit the various methods of writing used in human documents*, provided that these methods do not distort the truth. For the sake of brevity I confine myself to a few examples taken from the Synoptic Gospels:

St Matthew's Gospel often relates in an apparently chronological order events which in fact are arranged in accordance with an ideological and catechetical plan. His formula 'At that time,' used to link one episode to another, is therefore only a literary device. Luke inserts a series of documents in the framework of the journey of Jesus from Galilee to Jerusalem (Luke 9. 51-ch. 18). This is a purely didactic framework with no intention of providing an exact chronology.

Matthew often joins to one speech made by Jesus and quoted in a given set of circumstances, other words of the Master spoken at other times but dealing with the same subject. This is simply a literary device (for example, the sermon on the mount, chs. 5 to 7; the speech to the apostles ch. 10; the speech dealing with the end of the world, ch. 24).

Matthew sometimes clarifies the conclusion of one of the speeches of Jesus by transposing from one speech to another a genuine formula of the Master's which provides an appropriate conclusion to this other speech (for instance, 'Many are called but few are chosen').

In the interests of brevity Matthew at times gives an account of an incident stripped of all its concrete details and related in only a general kind of way. It has even been suggested that certain plurals then used are intended merely to generalize. It may be permissible to identify our Lord's appearance to the holy women (plural) in Matthew with the appearance to Mary Magdalene in St John.

In a single Gospel (St Mark or St Luke) a sentence of the Master is frequently reported twice under a slightly different form. These 'doublets' do not necessarily mean that the sentence was spoken on two occasions, it may well have been used only once but reported twice because different sources or traditions were consulted.

4. *Explicit or implicit quotations or, to use more up-to-date terminology, the way sources are used and reproduced.*

We cannot expect the inspired historians to reach, let alone improve upon, the insight and exactitude of modern source criticism. History, as we know, works from sources, from documents. Even today it does not always succeed in deciding whether certain events did in fact take place and sometimes is content to indicate the oldest document which relates the event without coming to any firm conclusion as to the genuineness or otherwise of the event. Some great historical works are principally collections of documents (for instance, the *Acta Sanctorum* of the Bollandists) grouped and critcized according to rigorous methods.

Ancient history was very far from adopting these critical rules in its discussion of documents. It often contented itself with listing its documents and, where there was disagreement among them, 'reconciling' them in an over-simplified and elementary fashion. The modern historian who wants to reconstruct ancient secular history with the help of early historians tries to identify the documents used by these historians and, if he succeeds in finding them, to work directly from them as his own sources.

The question then is: is it legitimate to apply this procedure of identification and assessment of documents in the case of an inspired writer? Is it legitimate to apply to his sources, to his documents, critical methods whose purpose is to sort out the elements of truth in them, or should we begin by admitting that the documents inserted or used in an inspired book are necessarily and absolutely accurate because the writer who makes use of them is inspired?

First of all let us look at explicit quotations.

Certain of the Old Testament historical books (Esdras, Nehemias, Machabees) offer explicit documentary quotations (for example, Esdras 4. 11-16; 18-22; 7. 12-26; Nehemias 6. 6-8; 1 Mach. 8. 23-32; 10. 25-45; 12. 5-23; 13. 35-40; 14. 27-49 etc.), letters sent by or to kings or chieftains, the text of treaties etc. Independent critics admit that certain of these documents are genuine in the strict sense and are reproduced literally, while others are ancient 'summaries', current in Israel, and others again reconstructions made several centuries after the event and sometimes with insufficient foundation, etc. Is this critical treatment of the documents automatically forbidden to Catholic exegetes because of scriptural inerrancy? I do not think so. Except for the hypothesis of a spurious document intentionally forged by the inspired writer to suit his own purposes, various theories may legitimately be suggested by a Catholic if these are based on solid historical reasons—the hypothesis of a summary, of a reconstruction attempted in all good faith, etc. The principle of inerrancy does not force us to admit that history written by an inspired author has been miraculously raised above the historical methods of these ancient epochs to the same level as that of rigorous modern criticism.

The question of implicit quotations is of far wider application.

It is here that the whole question of sources can and must be raised. In most cases it is from written documents that the inspired writer has taken his precise information on the chronology of the kings of Israel and Juda, his long lists of names of families, his genealogical tables, etc. Although it is often difficult to draw a strict line between the problem of implicit quotation which concerns us here and that of literary forms which will be studied in the next section, yet in the interests of clarity, it is useful to keep the two points of view separate.[3] We shall therefore group the various phenomena of Scripture that are preferably included in the category of implicit quotations.

Preliminary observation. A decree of the Biblical Commission(1905: *DZ.*, 1979) gave a ruling on this matter. It specifies and defines in the first place the somewhat restricted concept of implicit quotation current at that date: 'a quotation for which the inspired author does not assume responsibility'; *Agitur de citatione tacita vel implicita documenti ab auctore non inspirato conscripti, cuius asserta omnia auctor inspiratus minime approbare aut sua facere intendit, quaeque ideo ab errore immunia haberi non possunt.* The Biblical Commission lays down the two conditions required if the Catholic exegete is to have legitimate

---

[3]On the problem of implicit quotations as it presented itself at the beginning of the century, see F. Prat, *La Bible et l'histoire*, Paris, 1904. See also A. Durand, 'Critique biblique,' in *Dictionnaire d'Apologétique* (Alès), vol. 1, 1911, col. 760-829 especially c. 802; A. Lemonnyer, 'Citations implicites' (Théorie des) in *Supplément au Dictionnaire de la Bible*, vol. 2, 1934, col. 51-5.

recourse to implicit quotations so defined: *ut solidis argumentis probetur:* 1. *Hagiographum alterius dicta vel documenta revera citare et* 2. *eadem nec probare nec sua facere, ita ut iure censeatur non proprio nomine loqui.* The Biblical Commission therefore regards it as legitimate in theory to have recourse, under certain conditions, to the hypothesis of implicit quotations. The first condition—'it must be shown that a document has been used'—is simple and quite natural, arising from the requirements of history itself. The second is more complex 'it must be proved that the inspired author does not give his approbation to the document, nor treat it as though it were his own, if we are to have any right to conclude that he is not speaking in his own name'. There is room here for a more or less broad interpretation. We face the whole problem of the 'historical' conscience of the ancient historian. Did an ancient historian genuinely and positively intend to guarantee the truth of every detail of a document which, as he realized in a vague way at least, he had not been able to submit to close criticism? Did he positively lay claim to the critical accuracy of our modern historians when they are laying bare the contents of a document? If so, was he asserting his intention to be critically accurate? The whole problem lies in the prudent application of the principle, and allowance must be made for the intentions of the inspired writer in the light and in the context of his environment and his times. This is an important question; it may open the door wide to admit all sorts of 'implied quotations'. It is understandable that the Church has shown prudence in her directives about the use of this criterion.

Here we shall confine ourselves to a few examples where the recourse to the theory of 'implied quotations' now seems almost necessary in the opinion of most Catholic exegetes.

(*a*) *Etymological explanations* are frequent in the Bible where derivations for the names of places and persons are given. They normally have a very markedly popular character.

We know that in all countries the common people very often invent as an afterthought etymological explanations for the name of a given place or given tribe on the basis of quite arbitrary associations of ideas or words. Is it legitimate to admit that here too the sacred writer is content to hand down to us the popular derivations customary in his environment or should we be obliged to believe that, by virtue of inspiration, these derivations are the true linguistic explanations of the words in question, and should therefore be accepted by present-day scholars?

It is now generally recognized that the inspired writer is only reporting these attempted etymologies as he found them in the folklore of his country. The literary form he adopts, which is that of popular history, clearly shows that he has no intention of offering us scientific derivations of the modern kind, but popular derivations in the style of his own times.

Here are a few examples taken from ten chapters of Genesis, 16 to 26:—16. 13 (Atta el Röi); 16. 14 (Lachai Röi); 17. 17; 18. 12-15; 21. 6 which give three derivations of the name Isaac (these clearly show by their differences that the writer intended to give a simple report and to make no attempt at criticism); 19. 22 (Segor); 21. 31 (Bersabee); 22. 14 (Yahweh Yireh); 25. 25 (Jacob); 25. 30-1 (Edom); 26. 20 (Eseq); 26. 21 (Sitna); 26. 22 (Rechoboth); 26. 33 (Schibea).

(b) Genealogical tables, the chronology of the kings, lists of officials, etc.

We find, for instance, in the books of Kings, Paralipomena, Esdras and Nehemias, a number of such lists. There are those of the successive kings of Israel with the length of each reign, synchronisms, lists of David's and Solomon's officials, heroes during David's reign, etc. It is probable that these are based on documents found in archives. Does the inspired author intend to guarantee all their details or only to assure us that they were documents found in archives more or less contemporary or close to the events, documents which he judges to be of use to him in the writing of history and in substance true, although he has had no means of checking them or subjecting them to critical analysis? It will therefore be incumbent upon the modern historian to study the value of these documents and their proximity to the events. He must then determine their historical value. It is for him to reconcile —with the aid of Assyrian chronology for instance—certain dates at variance with one another in the chronology of the kings of Israel and Juda and in their synchronization.

(c) Collated documents reporting the same fact twice.

The theory of various 'documents', as applied to Genesis and to the other books of the Pentateuch, distinguishes in the Pentateuch, as is well known, between the documents to which have been given the names Jahvist (J), Elohist (E), Deuteronomical (D) and the Priestly Code (P). In this way, it has been possible to discover in the Pentateuch, a certain number of doublets—two accounts of the same events, but derived from different sources. There are divergencies in these accounts, since the two traditions are themselves divergent, but they have been combined in a single text by the inspired writer. Here are classic examples from Genesis:

There are two accounts of the Creation; P—1-2. 4ᵃ; J—2. 4ᵇ—25. These two accounts have been placed side by side in spite of their divergencies. As against the well known order of the six days in the first we have the order in the second, according to which man was created first (2. 7), after man the plants (2. 9; cf. v. 4), then the animals (2. 19) and finally woman (2. 21). Moreover the second account is much more anthropomorphic than the first.

There are two accounts of the Flood (chapters 6-7) combined into one. When they are separated, they show considerable divergencies. In J, Noe is to take seven pairs of each species of clean animals (to serve as food) and two pairs of those that are unclean (to preserve the species). In P, Noe is to take only two pairs of both the clean and the unclean animals (for according to P man did not yet eat meat). In J, the deluge lasts for forty days and Noe then opens the window to release the birds (8. 6) and fourteen days later, he leaves the ark. In P, the period between the beginning of the Flood to the exit from the ark lasts for more than a year (7. 11 and 8. 14).

Some have maintained that two accounts of Joseph sold by his brother can be identified (J and E; 37. 12-36). In one, Joseph is sold directly by his brethren to Ismaelite merchants at Juda's suggestion and taken by them into Egypt. In the other, he is thrown into a well at the suggestion of Ruben who counts on being able to free him afterwards. He is then taken out of the well by Madianites who are passing that way—unbeknown to Ruben and the other brothers (hence Ruben's despairing grief) and taken by them into Egypt.

Hence the classic hypothesis: these varying accounts are different versions of the same event, related in different circles in Israel. They were written down and have been combined not as we should do today, by a method of comparison and critical choice between the various versions, but quite simply by compilation. Instead of choosing between them, the inspired author (or one of his predecessors) combines these accounts. But by the very fact of this juxtaposition, he warns us in practice that he does not intend to decide between the two versions or to suggest they have equal value. His aim is merely to lose nothing of the treasures of Israel's tradition. This naïve method of writing history has nothing in it that contradicts inspiration.

If this hypothesis is accepted, the Catholic exegete is able to tackle the problem of the sources of the Pentateuch. If it is not, he cannot even formulate the problem. Both attitudes existed and were debated at the beginning of the present century in Catholic circles, but the broader attitude has become common since the encyclical *Divino afflante Spiritu*.

5. *Holy Scripture contains different literary forms* to be interpreted according to the norms of the period in which these books appeared and not according to *a priori* norms drawn up in our own times.

Various literary forms have always been recognized in the Bible. There are lyrical songs religious in character, funeral elegies, wedding songs, parables, fables with a moral, prophetic books with their various shades of meaning (symbolic gestures, refrains, riddles) sapiential books, and even love songs in the Canticle of Canticles. None of these offers any difficulty. The real problem arises when we have to deal with the various historical forms.

In the first place, there may be fictional historical forms whose sole aim, in the mind of the inspired writer, is to supply moral or didactic teaching and not to provide an account of real events in the past. In modern literature there are didactic or philosophical works written in the form of historical tales or dialogues (this is simply a form of literary presentation: examples are J. de Maistre's *Soirées de Saint-Petersbourg* and Taine's *Vie et opinions de F. T. Graindorge*). There are historical novels which only preserve the context of history and not its facts (for example, those of Sir Walter Scott), edifying biographies which do not aim to offer a complete picture of the hero but only what is calculated to do good, while the rest is left out on purpose. Similarly, in inspired literature there may be various literary forms. And just as today the author would be the first to protest if we took to be accurate history what he has planned as a historical novel, or as real events episodes he has imagined as fictional examples with a didactic purpose, so, too, the inspired author desires to be interpreted according to his intentions and not otherwise. It is of little consequence that because of ignorance of ancient literary forms Catholic exegetes in the past failed to understand a book in accordance with its true literary form. Provided faith and morals were none the worse for this, provided also that, even when thus understood, the inspired work preserved for the Church its function as a book 'for the furtherance of Christian doctrine and life', divine Providence was not obliged to prevent these accidental errors in interpretation. It is therefore possible today to discover that a book, interpreted in the past as strictly historical, was in reality a kind of moral fable, intended to inculcate an edifying lesson, not to state historical facts, or no more than an imaginary tale situated in the past, but not a historical narrative.

Finally, we may find in the inspired literature as in all literature down the centuries, historical forms in which there are varying degrees and shades of meaning in the historical statements as such. Historical statements are not on the same level or of the same kind in the Song of Roland as in the works of de la Gorce or Thureau-Dangin. Can similar differences of degree and form be observed between the various historical books of the Old Testament? This question was keenly discussed among Catholic exegetes at the end of the nineteenth and at the beginning of the twentieth centuries.

(*a*) Some of these exegetes would admit no gradations at all in inspired historical writing. They were even inclined to extend the range of historical form to everything which, to however small an extent, seemed to come under this category, and in any case, to all that had hitherto been regarded by exegetes as strictly historical. For each of these books they postulated the minute accuracy of our twentieth century historians. It followed that inspiration was held to have so transformed the historical writing of the fifteenth, tenth or fifth century B.C., that it offered, as far as strict accuracy is concerned, the same characteristics and advantages as contemporary historical writing. (b) Other exegetes rightly attempted to distinguish the various shades of meaning in the historical forms in use among the ancient Israelites and to look for these shades of meaning in the inspired writings, since the latter would have to be interpreted according to the literary form current at their time.[4]

Catholic exegetes were overjoyed to find the principle of 'literary forms' in holy Scripture clearly established and formally approved in the encyclical *Divino afflante Spiritu*.[5]

Concrete examples. Obviously I cannot set out here a general classification of the various historical 'forms' in the Old and New Testaments. Such a huge task can only be undertaken in large volumes bearing the titles 'Introduction to the Old Testament' and 'Introduction to the New Testament'.[6] I shall confine myself to pointing out a few examples of these special and unusual cases which raise or have raised in its most acute form the problem of scriptural inerrancy.[7]

[4]It is easy to gain a knowledge of these controversies by glancing through the *RB* from 1895 to 1907 with its considerable number of articles by Fr Lagrange; cf. also his book *La méthode historique*, (1903). See *Études* during the same period: F. Prat, 'Les historiens inspirés et leurs sources' (20 February 1901); 'Progrès et tradition en exégèse' (5 November and 5 December 1902); A. Durand, 'État présent des études bibliques en France' (20 November 1901 and 5 February 1902) and his articles 'Critique biblique, Exégèse, Inspiration, Inerrance', in *Dict. Apol. de la Foi cath.*; etc. Cf. for the opposite, strictly conservative view: Fr Méchineau, *L'idée du livre inspiré*, Brussels, 1907 (and various articles in *Études*, from 1897 to 1907); Fr Fonck, *Der Kampf um die Wahrheit der Heiligen Schrift seit 25 Jahren*, Innsbruck, 1905, etc.

[5]*Divino afflante Spiritu*, 11. 3, *Peculiaria munera interpretum nostris temporibus*, third subdivision: *Monumentum generis litterarii*, praesertim in historia; cf. *EB*, 2nd edn, Nos. 558-60; *NRT*, 1946, pp. 709-10 and the commentary on the Encyclical, above pp. 165-70.

[6]It is common knowledge that one of the important tasks of fundamental theology is to bring fully to light the historical value of our Gospel narratives, to show that they are the expression of a solid tradition coming from the apostles as witnesses of the events described.

[7]The reader may profitably consult: J. Schildenberger, *Vom Geheimnis des*

(a) Books which though apparently historical in form, seem in fact to be didactic writings, philosophical and religious discussions or theses.

Does the Book of Job relate a genuine dialogue between Job and his friends or is this dialogue more probably a philosophical and religious essay on the problem of evil, composed by the author under the form of a dialogue? This second hypothesis seems to be adopted today by the majority of exegetes, whether higher critics or Catholics, and it is far and away the more convincing. The existence of Job, the story of his trials and of his fidelity in the midst of affliction, may have been genuine facts and well known in Israel, although we cannot be certain of this. On this historical or traditional foundation, the inspired author wrote a didactic dialogue with a view to casting some light on the problem of evil.

For the past fifty years a number of Catholic exegetes have been wondering whether Tobias and Jonas may not also be essentially didactic works rather than history properly so called. If so, their authors would have intended to teach their contemporaries an important moral or religious lesson by means of a fictional account remarkably evocative and instructive in character and set in the context of ancient history.

In support of this view, it has been pointed out that, in the case of Tobias,[8] there are grave historical difficulties in several details of the story, that there are certain connections with the Assyrian work 'The Wisdom of Ahikar', that the style is clearly moralizing and didactic and, finally, that the sequence of events is artificial, contrived and out of the ordinary. Even though there may be a historical nucleus in the tale, the poetic licence used by the author is manifest. His fundamental intention, the teaching he wishes to offer us, is essentially moral—unshakeable fidelity to God in time of trial, confidence in his Providence, the extolling of prayer and works of mercy, the appreciation of family life. All these are traits which, together with the delicacy and charm of the writing, make this work one of the pearls of Israel's literature.

Catholic exegesis is increasingly inclined to adopt a similar interpretation in the case of Jonas, as is pointed out very clearly by Fr Feuillet, professor at the Institut Catholique in Paris, in the Jerusalem Bible, *The Book of Jonas*, 1951, Introduction, pp. 10-15. The arguments he there adduces, like those of other exegetes, lead him to conclude that the book is intended as 'a piece of didactic fiction'. The dogmatic purpose of the inspired author, who was keenly aware of the needs of his time, is to inculcate an important lesson in religious universalism (Yahweh's mercy is shown

Gotteswortes. Einführung in das Verständnis der hlg. Schrift, Heidelberg, 1950; and in *Initiation biblique*, third edition, 1954, ch. 6, 'Les Genres littéraires,' by A. Robert and A. Tricot, pp. 280-356; A. Robert and A. Feuillet, *Introduction à la Bible*, vol. 1, pp. 66-8; 123-39. Cf. also the older work: F. Von Hummelauer, *Exegetisches zur Inspirationsfrage mit besonderer Rücksicht auf das alte Testament*, Fribourg, 1904, see also *A Catholic Commentary on Holy Scripture*, 32a ff.

[8]Among the most recent are A. Clamer, *La Sainte Bible* de Letouzey, vol. IV, 1949, pp. 387-411; R. Pautrel in *La Bible de Jérusalem, Le livre de Tobie*, 1951, Introduction; A. Robert in *l'Initiation biblique*, 3rd edn, 1954, pp. 135-138. A. Miller, O.S.B. in *Die Heilige Schrift des Alten Testaments*, IV, 3. *Das Buch Tobias*, 1940, pp. 3-10, concludes that there is no overwhelming reason for rejecting a historical basis for the essential parts of the narrative, but that the book of Tobias is not historical in the strict sense of the word.

even towards Ninive, the capital of pagan Assyria) as a prelude to Christian universalism. The line of thought he thus traces, following as it does the second part of Isaias and the Songs of the Suffering Servant, foretells the universal call of the Gospel message.

(*b*) *Historical books of an edifying character with a precise and limited religious purpose in which there is deliberate omission of past events which would scandalize or surprise the writer's contemporaries,* and which sometimes recount past events with anachronisms and in the context of the institutions of the period in which the author himself lived.

These characteristics are found in Chronicles (Paralipomena). The author is principally interested in the history of worship, of the temple and of the Levites. He lived in a period (probably the third century B.C.) at which the Pentateuch was complete and, as the 'Law of Yahweh', was considered authoritative, and he sees the events of the past in the light of this body of legislation. He often omits from his history of God's people and of the kings of Juda anything which might scandalize his contemporaries, anything which goes counter to the 'Law of Yahweh'. Sometimes, like some authors of edifying biographies in our own day or like medieval artists who painted the Stations of the Cross, he describes past events in the context of the customs and institutions of his own time. From certain points of view, his work is that of a theologian or a canonist, assessing the facts of past history in the light of the religious and liturgical ideals of his own period. The exegete will have to bear this literary form in mind if he is to provide an accurate interpretation of his material.[9]

(*c*) *The Midrash as a means of edification, the Haggadah.*

In the last days of Judaism, we meet a special literary form, the Midrash, very frequently to be found in the Talmud. The Midrash originated in oral commentaries on the Old Testament, the text of which was interpreted either by a legal commentary (Halakah) or by a commentary whose aim was to edify and which took many different forms. It was known as Haggadah. This Haggadic Mid-

[9]It is obviously impossible to determine in a few sentences the 'literary form' of a work of this type. From our present point of view, we wish merely to note a few of its characteristics so as to acquire a better understanding in accordance with the recommendations of the Encyclical *Divino afflante Spiritu*, of the literary forms used in those distant times (*quaenam dicendi formae antiquis illis temporibus adhibitae sint:* see above, pp. 168-9). These summary indications may be completed with the help of A. Lods, *Histoire de la littérature hébraique et juive*, 1950, pp. 634-43. This posthumous Protestant work, which represents the radical point of view, needs considerable correction. On the other hand, there are the studies of recent Catholic writers: A. Clamer, 'Paralipomènes', Introduction, in the *La Sainte Bible* (Letouzey edition, IV, pp. 13-20); H. Cazelles, 'Le Livre des Chroniques', Introduction, in the *Jerusalem Bible*, 1954, pp. 10-17; and A. Robert's observations in *Initiation biblique*, third edition, 1954, pp. 130-33, 308-9.

rash took every sort of form; it often developed into a kind of homiletic commentary on the sacred text, a collection of moralizing maxims, sometimes of curious stories, and all this was intended to edify the community and to give it a greater attachment to its sacred books. The norm was its 'value for edification' much more than its 'historical truth'. This Haggadah, which is frequent in the Talmud, is sometimes very pleasing and evocative, sometimes dull, and occasionally rather ridiculous. The occasion for it is often a biblical text, but as the form developed, the Haggadah might also be quite self-contained. Its aim was to encourage piety, love of the law, and the virtues. It often became a list of marvels full of extraordinary or even fantastic events.

Are there inspired Haggadoth in holy Scripture? Did God use this literary form to train the people of Israel for its high mission?

The question has been asked in connection with some of the books of the Bible. To answer it a delicate sense of shades of meaning is required and an understanding of what the 'truth' of holy Scripture involves.

The book of Judith is perhaps a story written in this form and provides a free treatment of a traditional historic episode intended to underline the final and necessary triumph of Yahweh's cause. In the article by A. Condamin, S.J. 'Judith' (in Fr d'Alès's *Dict. Apologétique*), in the commentary by Fr A. Miller, O.S.B. ('Judith' in the *Bonn Bible*, 1940, p. 4 ff.) and in Fr Barucq's introduction to 'Judith' in the *Jerusalem Bible*, pp. 12-15), may be found the reasons that prompt a number of Catholic exegetes to attribute to the inspired author of this book a very free use of his sources in the construction of his narrative, as well as the difficulties (*fere insolubiles*) which, according to Fr Höpfl, O.S.B., prevent us from considering the book as 'history' in the strict sense of the term.

Esther also seems to have been intended by the author to approximate to the literary form of the Haggadah. In his commentary (Bonn, 1941,) Fr Schildenberger, O.S.B., gives (pp. 23-33) reasons proving that the work is *eine freigestelte Erzählung eines geschichtlichen Kerns*—i.e., a narrative which develops freely round a historical nucleus. Fr Barucq, O.C., in his commentary on 'Esther' (pp. 76-7) lists the details in the story 'which are difficult to place in the history of the reign of Xerxes' and on pp. 77-8 the methods 'which belong to the art of the story-teller rather than to that of the historian.'

We do not claim to solve such complex problems in these few lines. We merely wish to show that the hypothesis of an 'inspired Haggadah' here and there (that is, an existing literary form used, under the inspiration of the Holy Spirit, for nobler ends), should not be necessarily excluded *a priori* by Catholic exegesis. Cf. the encyclical *Divino afflante Spiritu* (cf. *EB*, 2nd Edn, N. 558, and above, pp. 168-9).

(d) Popular traditions as a literary form.

Every nation writes the history of ancient times with the help of ancestral traditions, accounts that are partly historical, partly poetical, which in their passage from one generation to another, gradually simplify the facts, group them around some more outstanding personality, and artificially link stories which are independent of one another. And so, little by little, composite, picturesque and graphic stories are built up in which it is sometimes difficult to distinguish between the historical foundation and the work of popular imagination.

Can we say that since this literary form existed in Israel, as among all peoples, God willed to make it contribute to the realization of his plans for his own people and so willed to establish it through inspiration as part of Israel's sacred writings? If so, then he must have accepted this literary form just as it was with its own particular historical value. Yet, by means of this literary form, he made his people understand, with the passage of time, that they were truly God's chosen people. He made them aware of their religious task, of their duty towards Yahweh, of their messianic hopes. God therefore spoke to these men through men like themselves using the only literary form then possible. Although at this lower level, the sacred book belongs to the same category as other human books, it yet remains unique because in this unsophisticated form it tells us the unique story of this world, the history of God's actions and it does so under the impulse of God himself.

Further, this literary form determines the scope of the inspired author's assertions. It is as though he said: 'I am handing on to you these old Israelite narratives as they took shape in the course of centuries, and with the free development proper to stories of this kind. Although I cannot guarantee all the details, I can guarantee the substantial historical truth of the essential facts and especially the great lessons which emerge from them, such as God's special Providence towards his people Israel, the preparations for the coming of the Messias, the men who prefigured him in human history as "types" of the Messias. This, and nothing more, is what I wish to assert as true.'

This problem was clearly defined in 1902 by Fr Lagrange in his famous lectures at the Toulouse Institut Catholique (4-11 November). They were published shortly after in book form with the title *La méthode historique, surtout dans l'exégèse de l'Ancien Testament* (English trans. by E. Meyers, *Historical Criticism and the Old Testament,* 1906). Here he gave concrete shape to the theory of literary forms in the writing of history which he had already put forward in 1896 (*RB.* V, 1896, pp. 505-18). After keen controversy between Catholics (especially from 1902 to 1907) and after the decree of the Biblical Commission, dated the 23 June 1905 (*DZ*, 1908; *EB,* 161), which did not yet accept as a general thesis the principle of literary forms in the writing of history, but accepted it in certain clearly defined concrete cases, after the encyclical *Spiritus Paraclitus* of Benedict XV (1920), which accepted more explicitly the actual principle of literary forms in the writing of history whilst condemning its excessive use (*DZ*, 2188; *EB,* 461-2), and after the persistent work of Catholic exegetes leading to an increasingly clear assumption of the principle of literary forms as strictly essential to the true interpretation of many stories in the books of the Pentateuch: after all these preliminaries, the long section on literary forms in the encyclical *Divino afflante Spiritu* came as the consummation and justification of fifty years of effort in the field of research and in the attempt to reach an increasingly accurate assessment. This slow yet sure progress towards a precise formulation, ruling out all rash and fanciful solutions, is of vital interest.

It is easy to discover significant concrete examples of this literary form in many of the Pentateuch narratives, for instance in the story of the patriarchs (Gen. chapters 11-50), and to throw into relief their character as collective, popular accounts, as ancestral traditions. In fact it was the study of these accounts which gave rise to the earliest applications of *Formgeschichte* (with H. Gunkel). There is no need to point out that work of this kind is done in very different ways by the various exegetes and that it is often hard to find the sure path, equally removed from an exaggerated and sceptical type of criticism and from a naïve confidence in the strictly historical accuracy of the documents. We need not dwell on these examples here; what is important for our purpose is to draw attention to the literary form provided by popular traditions. We should, moreover, note that recent archæological studies (cf. those of W. F. Albright) have more than once led to the recognition of the valuable truths and the accurate information contained in these popular traditions.

Of course the four sub-sections above do not exhaust the varieties of literary forms in the writing of history. Yet I hope that, with the aid of the four aspects just mentioned, I have enabled the reader to acquire an adequate grasp of the extent and complexity of this problem from the point of view of scriptural inerrancy.

6. *Holy Scripture may and does include pseudepigrapha* and this without prejudice to inspiration, provided however, that the pseudepigraphic procedure is not a dishonest trick to deceive the community of the faithful.

It is essential to distinguish between the pseudepigraphic procedure and the traditional attribution of a given document to a given inspired author. In the latter case it is not inspiration which is in question but the value of ecclesiastical tradition. Inspiration is not involved in the problem of discovering whether Moses is the author of the Pentateuch or St Paul of the Epistle to the Hebrews, since these two documents do not themselves claim that their author was Moses or St Paul. Inspiration is only involved when the document itself states that it was written by a given author or directly expresses the views and ideas of this or that person.

This may occur in two ways which are at opposite poles, and between them it is possible to imagine others:

(a) By means of a literary method existing in Jewish as in all literatures. The Greek Book of Wisdom and Ecclesiastes may be put forward as the work of Solomon, as expressing Solomon's ideas on true wisdom (cf., for instance, Wisdom 7: 9. 7-18), or as expressing the views of Solomon, so well endowed with this world's goods, on the vanity of these same goods (cf. Eccles. 1. 12-18; 2. 1-19). This is a literary fiction which did not deceive the writer's contemporaries and does not deceive experienced readers any more than we ourselves are deceived today by novels written in the first person, as though the actual life of the writer were involved. There is no conflict whatever between such a purely literary fiction and inspiration or inerrancy.

(b) At the opposite end of the scale, it is possible to conceive that there is a deliberate intention to deceive by using the name of a person of the first rank in order to gain credit on his authority for doctrines it is desired to propagate in Israel or in the Christian Church. This method was used by a large number of writers of apocryphal gospels and by various Gnostic authors during the second century. An intention of this kind cannot be reconciled with the principle of scriptual inerrancy.

Between these two extremes there are intermediary forms and on some of these it is not always easy to pronounce judgement as to their compatibility with inspiration. To take some examples: there are grave difficulties over the authenticity of the second Epistle of St Peter. The letter is part of the canon of inspired Scripture.

If Peter did not write it, it must be the work of an author who clearly wanted the letter written by him to be considered as St Peter's (cf. 1. 1, 18; 3. 1) and the advice he gives to be accepted also on the authority of Peter. Fr Chaine in his commentary on the *II^a Petri* (1939) suggests as a solution to the problem that the author, who may have been a disciple of Peter, had a position of authority in the Church or else had been delegated by some such authority. Hence he was aware that he was transmitting apostolic teaching and expressed it in the way which would make it most effective. 'This is a case of pseudonymity, but pseudonymity justified by a mission or a situation which, given the literary customs of the time, allowed an author to write in this way' (*Ép. cath.*, Introd., p. 31). This particular problem of the *II^a Petri* continues to be discussed among Catholic exegetes.

A problem of the same type arises in the Old Testament in the case of Daniel. According to many critics, the book must have been written in the second century before Christ, at the time of the Machabees, whereas the supposed author Daniel lived in the Persian period. The second century author recounts in the form of prophecies events which in fact took place from the sixth to the second centuries. He relied on these to gain a more ready acceptance for his own prophecies concerning future events. Together with this more radical interpretation, there are a large number of others of various shades which we cannot study here. From the point of view of inspiration, it is difficult to understand how the Holy Spirit could inspire an author to describe past events while claiming that they were prophecies of those to come, and this for the purpose of ensuring that his own prophecies would be believed because, apparently, 'former' prophecies backdated in this way, had come true. Would he not be 'inspired to deceive his readers'? It is therefore understandable that this problem, which is of grave importance as regards principles, is very much to the forefront among Catholic exegetes, and that no solution has so far gained the support of them all.

The most recent Catholic exegetes who expressly give the period of the Machabees as the date of composition meet the difficulty we have pointed out by insisting on certain essential aspects of the question; for example, the *apocalyptic* nature of Daniel. In this context the only thing that matters is the prophecy of the messianic era to come; this is the fundamental purpose of the inspired author's teaching. Hence the interpretation in prophetic form of past events is only intended as a religious explanation of former facts in their relation to the divine plan as a whole (cf., for instance, J. de Menasce, O.P., 1954, in the introduction to his translation of Daniel, pp. 12-17 in the *Jerusalem Bible*: A. Brunet, S.J., in *Sciences ecclésiastiques*, Montreal, October 1955, pp. 253-55. Cf. also the observations of J. Steinmann, *Daniel*, 1950, in the 'Témoins de Dieu' series, pp. 38-9 and pp. 170-80 and by H. Gazelles, *Daniel*, in the encyclopedia *Catholicisme*, III, pp. 447-54). A more extensive examination of these solutions belongs to a specific course in Old Testament exegesis. From the point of view of inspiration, our task has been simply to draw attention to the problem as it presents itself to exegetes who are believers.

7. From the point of view of inspiration and inerrancy, there is the particularly grave problem *of moral difficulties raised by certain narratives and judgements in the Old Testament*.

In reading the Old Testament the Christian, trained according to the ideals of Christ, is bound to be shocked and disconcerted by various collections of facts and judgements that seem to him impossible to reconcile with the religious and moral sense of Christianity. This problem can be raised by offering a few examples classified under headings, and I shall attempt to provide a general solution at the end.

(a) *Examples of lack of sincerity*, which provoke no blame from the narrator and seem even to give him pleasure. For instance, Abraham's subterfuge in pretending that Sara was his sister, with the prospect of seeing her carried off to the harem of the foreign king, and all this to ward off a danger threatening him personally (Gen. 12. 10-21; 20. 1-18); Jacob's subterfuge to deprive Esau of his rights as eldest son (Gen. 25. 29-34) to obtain by fraud, at Rebecca's instigation, the blessing of Isaac his blind father, a blessing destined for Esau (Gen. 27. 1-40); and finally the trick he used to increase his wages when he was in Laban's service (Gen. 30. 25-43). Then there are the subterfuges that the Israelites used, on orders from Yahweh on the eve of their departure from Egypt, to obtain from the Egyptians the loan of valuable objects which they were to take away with them (Exod. 3. 22; 12. 35-6). Jahel is praised as 'blessed among women' (Judges 5. 24) for promising hospitality to Sisara and then in spite of this, treacherously killing him while he was asleep (Judges 4. 17-22). Now it should be pointed out at once, before at a later stage offering explanations that go more deeply into the problem, that fundamentally these things are all due to the national mentality of the period. We are dealing with tricks whose purpose is to deceive one of the nation's enemies or to ensure the superiority of the Israelites over neighbouring nations (Israel as descending from Jacob is superior to Edom as descending from Esau). To the Israelites of those days, this type of behaviour seemed to be tactics of war, and in their view, the tactics of a 'good war' (whether a 'shooting' or a 'cold' war).

(b) In the light of Christianity, *instances of cruelty* and, according to the documents, cruelty on occasion ordered by Yahweh, seem to us today to be a very serious difficulty.

There is no point in insisting on the cruel methods of warfare at the time, on the massacres and the pillage which followed victory in Israel as well as in all the nations of the period. This was everywhere the custom of the times. The Bible confines itself to reporting the facts as they took place, teaching us in this way at what a low human level God chose the people he willed to unite to himself by a covenant and to prepare so that one day it might give birth to our Saviour.

But we must pause to consider the part attributed to Yahweh himself in the Bible, first in regard to the methods of warfare, in particular the custom of *Herem*, a curse or an interdict announced in the name and by order of Yahweh on an enemy and, once the victory was won, implemented by the massacre of every man, woman and child, by setting fire to the town, etc.; then we have to consider the behaviour of the prophets of Yahweh or Yahweh's chosen ones towards the enemies of Israel and of Yahweh, towards unjust Israelites themselves, towards the prophets of Baal, etc.

The *Herem*. Here are a few particularly significant instances: Josue's campaign of conquest in the land of Canaan is represented throughout the Book of Josue as waged under the sign of the interdict, of the *herem*, commanded by Yahweh. At Jericho, all the inhabitants, without exception, are massacred, the town is burned down, destruction is total and final (Josue 6. 17, 21, 24, 26). In the minds of the actors in the drama and of its narrator the whole pattern seems to be that of holocaust in which Jericho is offered to Yahweh in sacrifice, and it is forbidden to men to derive even the slightest advantage from it under pain of a very grave sin against God. Achan took part of the booty for himself and so was stoned with his sons and daughters and all of them, together with all their possessions, were burned (Josue 7). The same interdict is laid, sometimes with certain reservations, on the town of Haï (Josue 8. 22, 24-6, 28-9), on Maceda (10. 28), Lebna (10. 30-1), Lachis (10. 32), Heglon (10. 35), Hebron (10. 37), Dabir (10. 39-40), and on Asor (11. 10-15). In 11. 20 we read by way of conclusion: 'For it was the intention of the Lord that their hearts should be hardened, and they should fight against Israel, and fall, and should not deserve any clemency, and should be destroyed as the Lord had commanded Moses.' Here we have the carrying out of the command given by Yahweh concerning the cities of Canaan (Deut. 20. 16-18) where the reason for it is stated: 'Lest they teach you to do all the abominations which they have done to their gods: and you should sin against the Lord your God.' Cf. also the regulations in Deut. 7. 1-7.

Still later, we find the same type of 'interdict' (1 Kings 15) practised by Saul on the Amalecites by order of the prophet Samuel. As a punishment for having taken some ewes and oxen, Saul saw his dynasty deprived of the royal succession, and Samuel himself cut Agag to pieces 'before the Lord' and so fulfilled the *Herem*. And other examples could be quoted.

A thorough discussion of these facts would have to begin with the problems of the literary form of these narrative passages in Josue. Everything in fact goes to prove (and in particular the light thrown on the question by Judges and other subsequent books) that the radical and systematic destruction of the Canaanites must have been far less complete than the accounts in Josue would lead us to believe. We learn that Canaanite centres continued to exist on Palestinian soil until a much later date. We note the profound influence of the Canaanites, their rites and their religious ideas on the Israelite people. There seems to be in Josue a simplified systematized literary form, which probably corresponds only very imperfectly with the real facts of Israel's occupation of Canaan. Further, the general command to apply the interdict attributed to Yahweh in Deut. 7. 1-7, is reported in a book which, as an increasing number of exegetes agree, was composed several centuries after the conquest of Canaan. But these questions, very important though they are from the historical and exegetical standpoint and so requiring attention to be drawn to them here, do not alter the fact that the inspired author lays the responsibility for the interdict on Yahweh himself. And this is the problem from the point of view of inspiration and the moral value of the Old Testament.

A second observation also of great importance, but which again does not get to the root of the problem, is the following: both the cruel character of the interdict and the massacres (which amount to the same thing) as well as the fact that they are attributed to the orders of the nation's god, are found among many other ancient peoples.

King Mesa of Moab (ninth century B.C.) boasts in his famous inscription (line 11-12) that he has captured the city of Ataroth 'killed all the people in the city, a sight pleasing to Kamosh' (the god of Moab); (line 16) that he has killed all the inhabitants of

Nebo, 7,000 in number, men, women etc., because he had dedicated the city to Kamosh. A still more horrible form of cruelty is found among the Assyrian kings. The inscriptions commemorating their victories are full of descriptions of atrocities committed against conquered peoples, their leaders and their populations. The war during which these atrocities occurred was, so the same inscriptions tell us, waged at the instigation of the Assyrian gods, and under their protection and leadership. Nowhere is there any sign of regret for these atrocities from the religious standpoint. The kings detail these atrocities in the same spirit of serenity and confidence in their gods as they manifest when they speak of their victories and the divine protection. Non-Semitic peoples, the Indo-European Persians for instance in the inscriptions of Darius, reveal a similar notion of war, a war of atrocities which arouses no remorse in the victors as they stand before their gods. They seem convinced that the gods approve of these atrocities and that it is they who have led their people to victory. Among these various peoples, the king considers himself the viceroy of the god, and his representative. The king's victory is the victory of the god; the ferocity of his repressive measures is the execution of the justice of the god who has been gravely offended by the resistance of the enemy who is now conquered.[10] The same convictions are present in Israel. The nation is in the hands of Yahweh and is led by Yahweh; the people and the writers who give expression to the people's thoughts, attribute to Yahweh the initiative in the nation's collective acts. In a number of cases, it is a type of 'literary form' to attribute such acts to Yahweh.

A third observation comes nearer to the heart of the matter. The religious idea which inspired the interdict was, in principle, a just one. Israel's duty to remain faithful to Yahweh and to his covenant demanded that the nation should abstain from all idolatrous worship, that the people should avoid all danger of religious contamination. The measures taken to achieve this were, (in keeping with the customs of the time) *human interpretations* of Yahweh's will and of the divine words which established the pact of alliance between Yahweh and Israel. From the standpoint of history we cannot understand the cruelty of Israel's wars and the national belief in the part

[10]A good account of these historical facts and of their assessment from the point of view of history will be found in H. Stieglecker's articles, 'Härte und Grausamkeit im Alten Testament' (*Theologisch-praktische Quartalschrift*, 1950, pp. 9-30 and 105-28; 1951, pp. 103-118 and 210-25).

played by Yahweh in such sanguinary acts of repression unless we view these acts and these convictions in the context of the ideas then prevalent, and at the moral and religious level at which God found the people he had chosen.

Answers along these lines must however be completed by a higher principle, namely, the progressive character of the revelation God gave to Israel; to this I return below. It is only too obvious that there is an immense gap between the spirit of the Book of Josue, viewed in the environment of its time, and the doctrine of universal and boundless love taught by Christ and made manifest at its culmination in the sacrifice of Calvary.[11]

The behaviour of the prophets or of Yahweh's elect towards the prophets of Baal, towards the enemies of Yahweh and Israel, towards unjust Israelites, etc.

The most impressive examples are found in the violent struggle of Elias and, after him Eliseus, against the anti-religious fanaticism of Achab and Jezabel. After the discomfiture of the prophets of Baal and the miraculous descent of the fire from heaven which consumed the holocaust prepared for Yahweh, Elias had the 450 prophets of Baal put to death at the hands of the people (3 Kings 18. 40). When Ochozias sent messengers to capture Elias, on two occasions by order of Elias fifty men and their leader were struck down by fire from heaven and so died (4 Kings 1. 9-12). Later, when Jehu had seized power, he invited the prophets and worshippers of Baal who had formerly been under Achab's and Jezabel's protection, to come to what he falsely said was to be a sacrifice to Baal in his own temple. When they had gathered there, with no means of defence, he had every one of them massacred by his soldiers (4 Kings 10. 18-28).

Before attempting at the end of this section to provide a more fundamental answer to the problem, I must point out here and now, in connection with this struggle between Elias, Eliseus and Achab's dynasty, that the issue in Northern Israel between the religions of Yahweh and Baal was of the utmost gravity. The Baal in question was the god of the Sidonians and Jezabel who came from Sidon

[11]It should be noted that in Israel itself this cruel *Herem* later became expulsion from the community: cf. Esdras 10. 8. The same formula was to be used by the Church-*Anathema sit*-in the sense of expulsion from the Church and the loss of all share in the Church's spiritual benefits, yet in the hope, expressed in a similar case by St Paul (1 Cor. 5. 5) that, as a result of this punishment, the soul of the culprit might 'be saved in the day of our Lord Jesus Christ'.

encouraged his worship. This proud and wilful queen (3 Kings
18. 4; 19. 2; 21. 4-16; 4 Kings 9. 30-1) used every possible means to
suppress the religion of Yahweh, had his altars overthrown and a
large number of the prophets of Yahweh put to death (3 Kings
18. 4; 19. 10, 14) and engaged in a struggle to the death with Elias
(3 Kings 19. 2), the intrepid defender of Yahweh's religion. In this
struggle, waged with equal fanatacism on both sides, the cruel death
of the prophets of Baal seemed to their contemporaries a just return
for the murder of the prophets of Yahweh by Jezabel. The observations we have already made on the *Herem* are also applicable here.
It must be added that the story of Elias which taken as a whole has
features of great beauty (cf. chapters 17 and 19), is obviously in the
category of the popular tradition and has the simplifications and
the slightly fabulous setting of this historical form together with all
the vehemence of popular feeling at any time of extreme and
decisive crisis. We should note above all that the spirit which
inspired these acts of violence was expressly rejected by our Lord
in Luke 9. 54. The apostles had suggested, in terms that recall in
fact the passage in 4 Kings 1. 9-12, that they should command fire
to come down from heaven on the Samaritans who refused to
welcome Jesus. They were severely reprimanded by the Master.
The Vulgate together with a certain number of Greek manuscripts,
here adds: *Nescitis cuius spiritus estis. Filius hominis non venit animas
perdere sed salvare.*

King Jehu, anointed king by order of Eliseus, in opposition to
Achab's dynasty (4 Kings 9. 1-13), is shown to have perpetrated
abominable acts of cruelty in his seizure of power. He had seventy
of Achab's sons massacred (4 Kings 10. 1-10) and boasted that in so
doing he had fulfilled the prophecies of Elias and proved 'that there
hath not fallen to the ground any of the words of the Lord, which the
Lord spoke concerning the house of Achab' (4 Kings 10. 10). He
killed the forty-two sons of Ochozias king of Juda (4 Kings 10. 11-14)
and all the remaining members of the house of Achab (4 Kings 10.
17): 'And he slew all . . . to a man, according to the word of the
Lord, which he spoke by Elias' (4 Kings 10. 30) and on that account
he was praised by Yahweh: 'because thou hast diligently executed
that which was right and pleasing in my eyes, and hast done to
the house of Achab according to all that was in my heart: thy
children shall sit upon the throne of Israel to the fourth generation.'

It is easy to notice how far Jehu's ambition and his desire to make sure of permanent possession of power form the fundamental reasons for these acts, and not zeal for the purity of Yahweh's worship. Moreover the Bible (4 Kings 10. 29, 31) openly blames him for having left standing the golden calves set up by Jeroboam at Bethel and Dan. But what interests the inspired writer is that the prophecies of Elias have been fulfilled. He concludes that since Jehu's dynasty had maintained itself for four generations, the cause of this favour must have been the securing of Yahweh's final triumph over the Baal of Jezabel and the carrying out of the divine judgement on the dynasty which had almost separated Israel for ever from its God. Later, by order of Yahweh himself, the prophet Osee (1. 4-5) stigmatizes the massacres committed by Jehu: 'And the Lord said to him: . . . for yet a little while, and I will visit the blood of Jezrahel upon the house of Jehu, and I will cause to cease the kingdom of the house of Israel.' Finally, the antithesis of this conduct and the doctrine of Christ is manifest throughout the Gospels (for example in Matt. 5. 21-4, 38-48).

(c) *Feelings of vengeance and curses against one's enemies* find expression in a certain number of events in the Old Testament, in various psalms, in passages of Jeremias, etc.

The principle of the blood feud was deeply entrenched in the Semitic soul. It arose in great part from the need to ensure one's own defence and the defence of one's family, clan, tribe, etc., in the absence of any supreme authority. The more violent the revenge, the more obvious was a man's valour and strength. Cain was to be avenged seven times (Gen. 4. 15) Lamech boasts that he had avenged seventy-seven times the wrong he had suffered (Gen. 4. 24). The formula 'an eye for an eye and a tooth for a tooth' so clearly condemned by our Lord (Matt. 5. 38) as finally overriden by the progress of divine revelation had, in its time, been no more than a regulation intended to control the right to revenge; repression was not to be disproportionate to the wrong suffered. The spirit of revenge appears in particularly shocking form in several Bible stories, for instance, in the revenge of the Gabaonites on the descendants of Saul (2 Kings 21) following on an oracle from the Lord (21. 1) and approved by David; and again in David's request to his son Solomon that, after his death, he should execute Semei who had formerly insulted him and whom he had promised by oath to pardon during his lifetime (3 Kings 2. 8-9).

It is clear that this 'spirit of revenge' is one of the characteristics of the Old Testament against which our Lord reacted with the utmost vigour. To the threat of a sevenfold revenge for Cain (Gen. 4. 15), to the sevenfold revenge of psalm 78. 12, to Lamech's seventy-sevenfold revenge (Gen. 4. 24) he clearly opposes in Matt. 18. 21-2, the duty to pardon not only seven times as Peter suggests, but seventy times seven. And, together with other passages, Matt. 5. 21-6, 38-42, 43-8 is, under three different aspects, a great lesson in the love of our enemies, diametrically opposed to this spirit of revenge.

The comminatory psalms calling down the vengeance of Yahweh upon the enemies of the nation or the personal enemies of the psalmist, are often singularly disconcerting and disturbing to the priest as he says his breviary.[12]

I need not dwell here on the psalms in which the psalmist asks for the defeat of the enemies of his country, a necessary consequence of the victory of Israel, but I shall confine myself to a few examples characterized more particularly by the spirit of revenge, especially personal revenge: 57. 7-11 ('The just shall rejoice when he shall see the revenge; he shall wash his hands in the blood of the sinner'; 77. 24 (the same image and, in addition; 'the tongues of thy dogs be red with the same'); 78. 23-9 (with very violent curses such as: 'Add iniquity upon their iniquity; and let them not come into thy justice.'); 108. 6-19 (a series of curses against a personal enemy, his wife, his children, etc.); 136. 7-9 with the appalling 'Blessed he that shall take and dash thy little ones against the rock'); see also Jeremias 18. 21-3, against those who have plotted against the prophet.

The difficulty is certainly diminished if we draw attention to the fact that there often underlies these prayers for punitive action on God's part a very acute sense of God's justice, which renders to every man according to his works. This is very forcibly expressed in the terrible psalm 108. 6-19, quoted above. The man whom the

---

[12]See the list of these psalms in an article by M. Van Imschoot, in the *Coll. Gand.*, 1940, pp. 89-93 together with various very useful remarks about them. The author divides these psalms into two groups: those which ask God to cause suffering to Israel's enemies: ps. 78. 6, 12; 82. 10. 19; 128. 5-8; to the enemies of the psalmist: ps. 5. 11; 6. 11; 7. 10, 16; 9. 12; 27. 4; 30. 19; 34. 4-6; 39. 15; 53. 7; 57. 7-11; 68. ps. 23-9; 108. 6-19; 138. 19; 139. 9-12; 140. 10; 142. 12. Cf. also H. Junker, 'Das theologische Problem der Fluchpsalmen,' Trier, *Pastor bonus*, 51, 5-6, p. 71 seq.

psalmist curses 'remembered not to show mercy', he 'loved cursing, and it shall come unto him'; 'May it (cursing) be unto him like a garment which covereth him', etc. In the then still incomplete state of the progressive divine revelation granted to Israel, heaven hardly occurred to the psalmist as the means whereby Yahweh's true justice might be made manifest. It seemed to them that divine justice should be exercised in the punishment of evil men here on earth. The genuine solution can only come from two essential points in Jesus's revelation. It is in the light of eternity on the one hand, and of God as the God of love and mercy and wanting us to be like him, on the other (Luke 6. 36; 1 John 3. 11, 14. 16-19, 23; 4. 7-11), that Christ definitively corrects the inadequacies of the Old Testament. To these points I shall return later.

(d) The Old Testament's defective sexual morality

Polygamy was for long considered as authorized, in keeping with the customs found among the surrounding Semitic peoples. Abraham had two wives, Sara and Agar: Jacob had two wives, Lia and Rachel, and Jacob also had children by Bala and Zelpha, Lia's servants. Esau had two wives (Gen. 26. 34); David had several wives. The scandalous harem of Solomon (3 Kings 11. 1-13), in which there was a large number of women of various nationalities, resulted in the introduction into the land of Yahweh of his wives' foreign cults. Polygamy, however, became increasingly uncommon and, by the time of Jesus, monogamy had become the general rule though it was not considered as strictly obligatory.

Divorce was expressly authorized (Deut. 24. 1-4), provided certain conditions in the interests of the repudiated wife were observed. It is well known that the reason justifying a legitimate divorce, as laid down in Deut. 24. 1, was very strongly disputed at the time of Jesus by the rival schools of Hillel and Schammai. In the history of moral practice among the Israelites, the actual passage in Deuteronomy had acted as a means of controlling the caprice of the husband and hence was of advantage to the wife. Our Lord plainly declared that this former practice would no longer be permitted and that marriage was indissoluble (Matt. 5. 31-2 and 19. 3-9).

Other examples of sexual licence appear in the Old Testament. Their existence is noted and in fact authorized by the texts which actually limit and regulate them. Examples are: the liberties taken by victorious troops with women captured in war and treated as booty (the liberties in question are brought under regulation in the interests of these women by Deut. 21. 10-14); the fact that in practice the marriage and the family of slaves were looked upon with contempt, called forth regulations in the interests of the salve in Exod. 21. 2-6, etc.

As a contrast to these defects, it must however be noted that in the Old Testament there are many passages of great beauty dealing with the marriage union and the family spirit, from the earliest text in Gen. 2. 2 ('bone of my bones, and flesh of my flesh') which proclaims the close union of man and woman, down to the symbolism of the marriage union as representing the love of Yahweh for Israel, dating from the book of Osee. Finally, mention must be made of the delicate refinement of the book of Tobias.[13]

These four kinds of moral difficulties raised by the Old Testament are only instanced here as specific examples. Other aspects requiring cautious handling and giving rise to objections might also have been envisaged. But these four groups seem sufficient to stress the gravity and complexity of the problem. How is it to be solved?

The fundamental principle of a solution seems to lie in a clear understanding of the *progressive character* of Old Testament revelation taken to its ultimate logical conclusions. God freely chose for himself a given people in its own concrete social and ethnic environment and whose moral and religious level was no higher than that of the surrounding peoples. The directives he was to give them would have to be adapted to the ancestral customs of this people, to its understanding and to its spontaneous moral reactions. It is not surprising that the beginnings are obviously very humble and that the movement towards a higher level is very slow, as is any collective change in a whole nation. The divine work in Israel is essentially the moral and religious education of the nation towards an increasingly inward and an increasingly profound moral monotheism, towards an increasingly higher concept of the nature of the covenant between Yahweh and his people, a concept that could one day develop into that of the Church as the mystical body of the incarnate Word. This education was slow and difficult. It had to be realized not in

<hr>

[13]Cf. A. Gelin, 'Le mariage d'après l'Ancien Testament, Rayons et Ombres' in *Lumière et Vie*, June 1952, pp. 7-20. This is an excellent piece of popularization for pastoral purposes.

some ideal race of men, not in stained-glass window saints, but in a very real race of men as sin had made them and continued to shape them, a race swept along by its passions and often in revolt against the voice of the Lord.

It would be a great mistake to imagine that each of Yahweh's commands in the Old Testament was given in a definitive way and at the definitive moral level of the New Testament. Our Lord himself laid down a principle of the greatest importance for our present purpose, when he said in Matt. 19. 8: 'Because Moses by reason of the hardness of your heart permitted you to put away your wives.' He therefore teaches us that in the Old Testament there were laws which were represented at the time—and rightly—as coming through Moses from God, as having divine authority and yet which were conditioned by the hardness of men's hearts. There is then in certain laws belonging to the moral Code of the Old Testament an adaptation permitted by God in view of human weakness. The progressive character of Old Testament revelation as a stage on the way to a higher level, is still more clearly emphasized in Matt. 5. 21-48 where Jesus takes the moral formulas of the Old Testament one by one: 'Thou shalt not kill . . . Thou shalt not commit adultery . . . whosoever shall put away his wife . . . an eye for an eye and a tooth for a tooth' and shows how inadequate they are for salvation and how they need either additional teaching or a downright alteration of the former doctrine, even though they had been promulgated in the name of Yahweh. The proposition that there was an adaptation and an act of condescension on God's part in view of the lower moral level of the chosen people is by no means a new one invented in the twentieth century. Fr Pinard de la Boullaye[14] in a very thought-provoking article published in *RSR* IX, 1919, pp. 197-221, pointed out that applications of this argument of a divine act of condescension (*sunkatabasis*) are found in the earliest ecclesiastical writers, the Fathers of the Church: St Justin, Tertullian, Clement of Alexandria, Origen, St Athanasius, St Cyril of Alexandria, St John Chrysostom, St Gregory Nazianzen, etc. In the moral and religious education of the Jewish people we find the same process at work as in the soul of a sinner when the grace which is leading him to the point

[14]His article was planned from the point of view of the history of religions with the title: 'Les infiltrations païennes dans l'Ancienne Loi d'après les Pères de l'Église' and with the sub-title: 'La Thèse de la Condescendance'.

of conversion exercises a moral and religious attraction. God gives him grace but at the level of his moral mediocrity, at the level of his passions, while calling him to something better and then to something better still, until he comes to the fullness of the light.

We can obtain a clear view of the education of the people of Israel through progressive revelation by insisting on its two essential characteristics: God's loving call, and man's response faithfully adhered to. A. Gelin in an excellent popular article; 'Morale et Ancien Testament' (in the review *Catéchistes*, No. 15, third quarter 1953, pp. 133-7)[15] gives an excellent account of this idea (p. 135):

> This education operated in a unique moral climate, the climate of the Covenant, God's offer of love and his call to fidelity. 'Biblical man' unlike 'Greek man' does not work out his own personal integration and his own social stability, he hears a call from on high. God speaks (Hebr. 1. 1) and his word is both a revelation of himself and a moral statement. The religion of Sinai implies the moral Law, and the essence of the biblical message is moral monotheism. God expects an answer and hence human life become a drama. Men either consent to 'know' God (the word is essential), or else frustrate God's action by a concrete attitude of refusal.

Thus it is possible to understand that fidelity to moral monotheism, fidelity to Yahweh the one only God, is for Israel the primordial obligation, the essential mission. To abandon Yahweh for the Baals, for strange gods, is the capital crime; to prevent the worship of Yahweh from contamination by the Canaanite cults is the chief preoccupation of the leaders of the people. If then the divine command to be faithful to Yahweh above all else finds concrete expression and realization in the context of ancestral customs, in methods of waging war that contradict the Christian ideal with their executions and punishments revolting to us so, it is men's 'hardness

---

[15]The author refers the reader to his own book: *Problèmes d'Ancien Testament*: Paris-Lyon, Vitte, 1952, 110. p., third section: 'Morale et Ancien Testament', pp. 71-92. Cf. by the same author: *Les Idées maîtresses de l'Ancien Testament*, Lectio divina, 2, Paris, Éditions du Cerf, 1948, 88 p. Cf. also the article: 'De inferioritate morali Veteris Testamenti,' by H. Kruse, S.J., in *Verbum Domini*, vol. 2, 1950, pp. 77-88.

of heart' at that epoch which subjected the divine command to such limitations. An order fundamentally divine has been applied and interpreted by men. We may openly condemn today the way in which God's orders were carried out in those days, while understanding and recognizing Yahweh's overall guidance of the people of Israel towards moral monotheism. We shall not then be astonished to find that, at a later period of Israel's history, a prophet like Osee condemns the acts of Yahvist zeal committed by Jehu with all the cruelty characteristic of a usurping general. Once again, the Old Testament revelation was a progressive one which will reach its final term in Christ.

As I have already said in connection with the comminatory psalms, it is only in the light of certain essential truths on which religion was based by Christ (truths which were partially elaborated during the last centuries of the Old Testament): an eternity beyond this world, the constant expectation of which dominates the whole moral teaching of Jesus; the love of God, our Father, for us each and all, made manifest in the Incarnation and the Redemption; the duty of mutual love among men, modelled upon, and sharing in the gratuitous love of God for us: it is in the light of these truths finally revealed that the problems incompletely stated in the Old Testament find their resolution: the problem of the divine punishment of human acts, which we have no longer to envisage as necessarily taking place on earth; the duty of charity applying to all men without exception, enemies as well as friends, Gentiles and Samaritans as well as Jews (cf. the plain teaching of the parable of the Good Samaritan, the enemy of Israel, proposed to the Jews by Jesus as a model of charity; cf. also the whole doctrine of St Paul on the equality of Jews and pagans in relation to the call to faith); the duty of fundamental sincerity ('Let your speech be yea, yea: no, no . . .', Matt. 5. 37), in imitation of God's sincerity (cf. St Paul, 2 Cor. 1. 17-20). The duties regarding marriage and chastity are founded on and defined by Christ's revelation. The abolition of divorce, for instance, and the holiness of marriage are made clear by the converging lessons of Matt. 5. 31-2; 19. 3-6; 1 Cor. 7. 10-11; Eph. 5. 22-3.

The great moral lesson to be drawn from the Old Testament would appear to be founded above all on the principle of this progressive education of the people of Israel by God, who had chosen them for his own. From the moral point of view, the Old Testament teaches us that there was a slow movement towards better things from century to century; it teaches the idea of one only God, the source of the moral life, and this idea grows deeper and deeper from the revelation on Sinai and through the prophets, preparing men increasingly to acquire that sense of God's Fatherhood which was to become an experienced reality with the coming of the Son; the idea of the Covenant, maintained in spite of Israel's unfaithfulness and so showing the gratuitous nature of God's love, destined too to reach its consummation in the doctrines of grace and redemption; the formation and progress of the idea of the Reign of Yahweh and of the Messias as bringing this Reign into being.[16]

This effort to come to a better understanding of the evolution of Israel's ideas, the growth of her messianic hope and God's plan as realized in the Old Testament, the effort also to replace the old minute analyses of the moral difficulties by these broad views, all this seems to us to mark a great progress in the study of the Old Testament.[17]

It is time to bring this chapter to an end. We may sum it up as follows—God speaks to us through men. He has willed that the difficult stages of the people of Israel's slow progress towards that Israel of God into which it was destined to be absorbed should be shown to us in all their stark reality. The Christian religion is, in the first place, a fact, an *event*. This event can only be perfectly understood against the background of its historical preparatior. throughout the centuries. Christ, the centre of the divine plan of salvation, entered history from the moment Abraham made his act of faith, Abraham who had so little understanding of the meaning and the scope of Yahweh's blessing promised to him and his descendants. The men of Israel were taken by God in their native barbarism, they answered his call at the level of their habits, customs and their psychology, and these were still often of a gross nature. Yet, obedient and believing in their own rough way, the men of Israel were to move towards the climate of Christianity. God willed that this progress from the shadows to the light, from a world of

---

[16]Cf. 'La crise de l'Ancien Testament', in *NRT*, 1929, pp. 181-39, third part: 'Ce que doit être l'enseignement Catholique de l'Ancien Testament' and in the book: *L'Ancien Testament et les Chrétiens*: 'A la lumière de l'encyclique *Divino afflante Spiritu*', pp. 99-105.

[17]Cf. the books mentioned above: Catholic, p. 191-5; Protestant, pp. 121-2.

egoism to Christian charity, should be manifested in all its human truth. If we look at this movement in its final outcome, which is Christ, the divine work will be revealed to us as growing more luminous century by century within the field of human actions with all their weaknesses. This preparation for Christ throughout history helps us to understand the Christ who has come. For centuries, God was drawing nearer to men, through his revelations, through the activity of his human envoys, through the flow of events, through facts which were types of things to come, until the day when his incarnate Word, the living Word of the Godhead, came to our earth to give meaning to all that was past, all that is present, and all that is to come.

Chapter IX

HOLY SCRIPTURE, THE WORD OF GOD

In what respect and in what way does the divine message transcend the understanding and the intention of the human author?

The Fundamental Principle

As was stated from the outset, the fundamental principle governing the part played by God in holy Scripture is the realization and the revelation of the mystery of God. God works through the facts of Scripture and tells us in Scripture his own divine plan for the Kingdom of God, for the raising of man to the supernatural order and for his eternal salvation through the Incarnation of the Word, the centre of the whole divine economy—the preparation of this plan in Israel in the Old Testament, its realization at a given point of time through Jesus Christ, and its reception in a new Israel, the Church, Christ's mystical Body.

God as the master of history, as the master of all human psychology, while respecting man's freedom, makes events and the religious and literary powers of men serve to establish and to reveal his plan. God alone can see this plan as a whole, he alone can comprehend the interdependence of its various parts and understand to the full all their moral and religious value in terms of the mentality of the men of each century. Our act of faith in the truth of Scripture is above all an act of faith in this divine unity of Scripture, in God's control of the events and the words of Scripture in the interests of an overall plan whose centre is Jesus Christ and whose consummation is the ultimate share that men will receive in the eternal love of the Son for the Father in the Spirit.

The inspired authors most certainly were granted a great share in the understanding of this mystery. God has a supreme respect for the mind which transmits and the minds which are to receive his messages. But is this understanding complete and adequate? What exactly did Abraham understand when God told him how great his posterity was to be? What did Isaias understand when he prophesied the transcendence of Emmanuel, or Micheas when he caught a glimpse of salvation from Bethlehem? And if the prophets were unable to penetrate the full meaning of their own message, how much less must they have been able to have a complete view of the place and scope of their individual message in the totality of the whole divine plan, in the doctrinal synthesis foreseen by God!

If God willed that the Old Testament should be a kind of progressive ascent towards the fullness of the light, we draw near to the divine understanding (which alone is fully objective) of the Scriptures when we try to discover this progressive movement without falling into any hasty form of concordism but with complete exegetic and theological honesty and insight. If God willed that the Old Testament should announce, predict and in some measure prefigure the New, we are entitled, with the inspired authors of the New Testament, to find in the Old Testament anticipations, symbols, 'types' of Christian realities. If God willed that the whole of Scripture, the New and the Old Testaments, should accompany the human race in its intellectual progress until the end of time and should be relevant and alive in every era from generation to generation, we should expect that the Christian message itself, while remaining fundamentally one and the same, will constantly adapt itself to developing thought and developing civilization, will ceaselessly explain itself in such a way that it remains in perfect communion with living humanity and so links it ever more closely to the living God.

If we are to interpret Scripture in this way and in the fullness of its divine value, it is not enough to be first class historians or literary critics; we must enter into a close religious communion with the divine spirit of Scripture. All Scripture must be read in the same spirit in which it was written, that is, under the active impulse of the Holy Spirit. This communion must be individual and emerge from a deep Christian awareness and from a personal dedication in answer to God's call. It must be a communion within the fellowship of the Church through faith in the vision of the divine message which the Church possesses. It is in union with the Holy Spirit, the same Spirit which enlightens and guides the Church, it is in union with the Church enlightened and guided by the Holy Spirit, that every Catholic reads holy Scripture. And the nearer he is to Christ in the Church through his whole supernatural life, through his enlightened faith and his effort towards holiness, the better is he able to perceive the profound religious riches of Scripture. Of course this does not dispense anyone from keeping in touch with current progress in the human, literal interpretation of the inspired writings. A twentieth century adult does not testify to the glory of the plenitude of divine inspiration if he reads Scripture with the mind of a medieval child. Yet it would be worse still if he read it without that spirit of faith in the transcendence of the mystery of God which, in every era, is the essential principle underlying a Christian reading of the Bible.

Two applications of this fundamental principle

I shall now attempt to clarify this fundamental principle by discussing two traditional theses which apply it and indicate its full scope. The first of these is shared by the majority of believing Christian exegetes, Protestants and Orthodox not in communion with Rome, as well as Catholics. The second in its absolute form is characteristic of the Catholic Faith. Yet it seems, even though only partially and unconsciously, to be still active in some aspects in the method used by several contemporary non-Catholic exegetes.

First Thesis. The unity of the divine plan presented to us in Scripture

If holy Scripture in its entirety is centred on the fundamental fact of our faith, the Incarnation of the Word of God; if this 'mystery', foreseen by God from all eternity and prepared from the first beginnings of the human race, is the essential object of Scripture in the unity and continuity of its realization in history, then the highest point of Christian exegesis is that at which we understand as a whole, as far as this is possible, the unity, internal cohesion and profoundly religious value of this divine 'mystery' in its successive stages throughout the passage of time: its preparation in the Old Testament; its historical realization in the person and the works of Jesus as narrated in our Gospels; the development of its religious, dogmatic and moral significance in the New Testament and, in these same books of the New Testament, the foreseeing of the forward movement of Christianity's future in Christ until the end of time, until the consummation in heaven of the Kingdom of God. But only God knows the full details of this divine plan as a whole. Only he fully perceives the interdependence of its parts from the beginning to the final goal. He alone foresees its effective development from age to age until the end. This unity of the divine plan manifested in Scripture has at every epoch been beyond the understanding of the narrators of and the actors in this divine historical drama. Holy Scripture, since it is the Word of God, has never been limited by what the inspired writers, used by God to utter it, have consciously perceived and been aware of within it. At its highest point, it rises above their thoughts and their will as God's interpreters.

Hence this is tantamount to saying that a purely human though literal exegesis may and does actually discover in our time, at the present stage of the realization of God's plan, a large number of partial aspects of this divine plan, yet it will only reach the final synthesis through and in faith. This 'total biblical theology' which is the supreme goal of exegesis is fully revealed only to the believer.[1]

An exegetical task of this kind is immense and all-embracing. In the present chapter I intend to treat briefly its characteristic aspects in connection with one specific point: the way in which the Old Testament prepares for the New and, as a corollary, the close union of the two Covenants in the unity of the divine plan.

Second thesis (essentially Catholic). For Catholics holy Scripture is not self-sufficient. It is entrusted to a society, the Church, which is the continuation of Christ himself and throughout the centuries lives by his thought and his teaching. In her Christ's doctrine, thus 'lived', unfolds its meaning and adapts itself to the development of the Church's life and thought, since the Church herself is involved in the general progress of mankind.

Scripture is certainly an essential factor in the life of this Church and a sacred, indestructible norm in her thought and her action. But, according to Catholics, Christ the Church's founder intended that Scripture should be given to us within the structure of the Church's life. It is to be ever more intensively 'lived' by the Church, ever more deeply probed by the mind of the Church as her inner life progresses towards the full stature of Christ. Through her inner

---

[1] I refer again at this point to the books mentioned on pp. 191-6 and 121-2 which emphasize the extent to which this way of looking at Scripture is now understood and developed by many Catholic and Protestant exegetes.

life under the influence of the Holy Spirit, in the light of her dogma which develops and deepens in the minds of Christians, the Church is led to a better understanding of Scripture and, through her efforts to form a synthesis of the various texts of Scripture in relation to the present state of her dogma and her devotion, to the discovery of deeper, richer, more luminously Christian interpretations.

This concept of the part played by the Church is not a theory that has come into existence recently, it is clearly active from the beginnings of Christianity. Whoever studies, on the basis of the scriptural texts of the New Testament, the progressive formulation of our most ancient dogmas during the first Councils—the dogma of the Trinity, the Christological dogmas—is forced to note that no private exegete, reasoning according to a purely human logic, could arrive by strict deduction at all our most ancient dogmatic formulas by using scriptural texts alone. He may show that these formulas are perfectly in harmony with these texts in their literal sense and that Christian life under the direction of these formulas continues to be the same, and gives an increasingly deeper understanding of Christian life in earlier times as it was directed by these scriptural texts. But he will be obliged to note that certain of these formulas and the scriptural texts fully correspond only through and in the Christian life of the Church. The experience of those early centuries continues to be the same in the many succeeding generations of Christians.

We must not be afraid to deduce, from the fact that in the history of Christianity our faith had been formulated in this way, the following essential principle: God, who alone sees the ultimate connection between the doctrinal passages scattered throughout Scripture, gives to his Church, enlightened by the continual presence of the Spirit, the privilege of progressively gaining a deeper insight into the dogmatic synthesis he intended and willed from the beginning, and this as a result of the moral endeavours of the saints, the religious needs of the mass of the faithful, the scientific work of the exegetes, theologians and doctors, and the directives of the Magisterium. Once more, this dogmatic synthesis must be perfectly at one with the faith of the early Church, with the scriptural texts that reveal that faith and with the Christian message which was complete in its essentials at the end of the apostolic era. But we cannot deny the part played by the Church, if we are to make any objective study of the real evolution of our faith. It is clear that this part played by the Church is something far wider and deeper than her function as the controller of the interpretation of Scripture, as the eventual and final judge of that meaning of its texts which is binding on our faith, for this function is only one part of the Church's total rôle.

It must not be objected that I am mixing up and unduly confusing two different aspects of Catholic theological life, namely scriptural exegesis properly so called and the development of dogma. I am not confusing them, I am stating that they are closely related to each other. As thinking believers, we cannot justify from a theological standpoint the genuine, authentic development of dogma by comparison with the sometimes still rudimentary and, in a sense, still incomplete character of some of our scriptural texts, unless we admit that these texts, lived in the Christian life of the Church, and clarified by the whole of Catholic dogma as it has developed, have revealed to the Church guided by the Spirit, a richer, deeper, more complete meaning than that which can be logically deduced from the actual words by a strict critical exegesis. It is this more complete meaning which has been rightly called the plenary sense of Scripture.

I. *Interpretation of the Old Testament in the Light of the New*

The first Thesis applied

By his whole attitude and his explicit teaching Christ told us that he came to perfect the morality of the Old Testament which was one of preparation (Matt. 5). He told us on many occasion that, from the beginning, all the expectation of all the prophets and of the people of the Old Testament was directed towards him, and that in him all the ancient promises were fulfilled.

St Paul has explicitly clarified the historical meaning of the Old Testament. The centre of gravity of the history of Israel was the promise made to Abraham (and renewed to the other patriarchs), and the object of this promise was Jesus the Christ (this theme is frequent in his great epistles: Galatians, Romans, etc.); it was by his faith in Christ that Abraham was justified (St Paul continually makes this assertion). By the promise, Christ was from the beginning with the children of Israel, playing his part in all the events of their history, accompanying them in their journey as the miraculous rock of the Jewish legend: 'and the rock was Christ' (1 Cor. 10. 4). The Jews were those who had hoped in Christ before his coming (Ephes. 1. 12). Through the severe discipline of the Law and its observances, they were kept on the path that led to Christ, just as the child is led to school by the slave, the *paedagogos* (Gal. 3. 24). Their life was transformed by the gift from on high, the promise of the Messias, and their whole history was directed towards its accomplishment.

The people of Israel prepared the way for the Church, the Israel of God. In the divine plan, the Church was to be the heir to the faith of the patriarchs, the religion of the prophets, the sacrifices of the priests, the generosity of the 'poor' of Israel; or rather, the Church was the perfection, the consummation of what had been a long and intricate preparation. Israel had been the shadow in the past of the Church which is the divine reality manifest in this world.

Slowly down the ages, from Abraham to Moses, from Moses to David, from David to the exile, from the exile to Christ, the Jewish soul gradually made ready for the Christian soul, the Jewish people made ready for the Church, the mystical body of Christ. God had chosen this people, not through any merit on its part, 'thy father was an Amorrhite, and thy mother a Cethite, and when thou wast born . . . thou wast cast out upon the face of the earth' (Ezech. 16. 5); and he formed in this people, by his revelations, his graces and his punishments also, a 'remnant', living by the thought of the prophets and destined one day to become the Israel of God.

A few examples of this interpretation of the Old Testament in the light of the New [2]

(a) *The development of the exalted idea of God in Israel.* To begin with Moses, we see Yahweh presented at that time under aspects which were destined increasingly to free Israel from every false and narrow concept of its God. Freely and by an act of grace, Yahweh chose Israel. This God of the little nation of Israel gradually appears to his people as he who, far from being the peculiar property of the nation he protected, as were the Semitic gods, would manifest his power

[2]The two examples which follow are a summary of the more detailed accounts in my two articles, 'La crise de l'Ancien Testament' in *NRT* 1929, pp. 818-39. and 'Per Jesum Christum Filium tuum', ibid, 1933, pp. 866-83.

over the other nations and over nature and reveal himself as the
master of all natural forces. This God whom it was forbidden to
represent by images or symbols, appears more and more clearly as a
being superior by nature to everything visible and tangible, and so
even the simplest souls will realize something of God's spirituality
and transcendence. This God does not seem concerned primarily
with worship and sacrifices but with obedience to his moral precepts,
to the Decalogue. Thus there grew up in Israel that moral monotheism which was unique in the ancient world.

The prophets were never to cease raising the soul of Israel to an
increasingly profound understanding of the divine attributes. Amos
drew attention to his justice. Osee to his tender but jealous love,
Isaias to his grandeur and transcendence. Jeremias taught the
Israelites a more inward religion, Ezechiel called their attention to
the demands of God's holiness, deutero-Isaias, in the period of the
exile, enlarged the universal scope of Yahweh's religion and the
place of suffering in the service of God. The Psalms, Israel's book
of prayer, taught Israel increasingly to be constantly searching for
God, and to have that confidence in him, which is the soul of true
religion.

In the course of her journey through the centuries, Israel received
from God these exquisite texts which are of eternal value and were
to be repeated by our Lord: 'Though shalt love the Lord thy God,
with thy whole heart, and with thy whole soul, and with thy whole
strength' (Deut. 6. 5) and 'Be ye holy, because I the Lord your God
am holy' (Lev. 19. 2).

Of course any historian can find historical evidence of this increasingly clear progress of Israel in moral monotheism and will
reach this conclusion on the basis of the literal sense alone of the
scriptural texts. But where he will only see an interesting historical
fact which clearly created a climate favourable to the birth of
Christianity, the exegete who is also a believer will discover, in the
light of the New Testament, a plan willed by God and God's positive
intervention through the agency of Moses and the prophets in the
history of Israel.

(b) *The Covenant between God and Israel leading to the Church, Christ's
mystical body.* Christ linked the society he founded to the society or
people of Israel whose history is seen as a preparation for Christianity,

introducing gradually into the Israelite community the religious attitudes which were to find in the religion of Christ their fulfilment and their consummation.

Jesus understood his work as a supreme fulfilment of Israel's expectation ('I am not come to destroy but to fulfil', Matt. 5. 17); he chose twelve apostles who 'shall sit on twelve thrones, judging the twelve tribes of Israel' (Matt. 19. 28). St Paul considers the Christians as the true sons of Abraham (Gal. 3. 29; 4. 31) and the Christian community as the Israel of God (Gal. 6. 16). One point must be emphasized: Paul expressly taught that the whole outlook of the Old Testament was centred not on the Law but on the *promise*, God's free and gratuitous choice of Abraham's posterity.

Now this covenant manifested increasingly clearly in the course of the ages the fundamental characteristics of the choice God was to make of his Church. There is a gratuitous covenant on God's part, a divine gift (hence the way is prepared for the Christian doctrine of grace); a covenant whose final goal will only become fully clear during the last centuries before Christ.

The ultimate goal of this covenant was the establishment of the reign of Yahweh over the world (in the early days Christianity was preached as the coming of the Kingdom); the covenant was characterized by the promise of an astonishing posterity for Abraham (a posterity whose meaning would only be revealed in its final outcome, in Jesus Christ). The covenant, which God always kept, was constantly violated by acts of infidelity on Israel's part and so implanted in men's souls an acute sense of sin (and this sense of sin is the foundation of the Christian doctrine of Redemption). The idea of the covenant became spiritualized as a result of the nation's misfortunes, at least in the noblest souls of Israel, and these were to constitute the 'remnant' announced by the prophets (and this 'remnant' was to become the nucleus of the Christian Church). The covenant in the last centuries before Christ was destined, as men realized, to be fulfilled in the future, in the prospect of 'better times', and this prospect, which became increasingly eschatological in character, was directed towards the end of time (and so Christian thought would be helped to turn easily towards the world of the future, towards eternity). In this evolution of the idea of the Covenant, ideas that are even specifically Christian are seen to come temporarily to the surface of Israel's consciousness at certain periods:

the idea of redemptive suffering in the second part of Isaias, the idea of universalism in the same book and in Jonas.

Here again a strict historical exegesis, divorced from faith, can note these essential characteristics of Israel's religion. It can observe these ideological links between Israel's religion and that of Christ; but only intellectual understanding based on belief in the divine and human value of the Incarnation will permit us to see in these characteristics of the religion of Israel a gradual ascent towards a higher truth and so, *pro modulo nostro*, to grasp the true meaning of Israel's evolution in the mind of God.

(c) *The expectation of the Messias in Israel.* We cannot attempt to sketch here, even in its main outlines, the complex and intricate history of the messianic hope in Israel. Such a subject requires a whole volume. Every exegete is aware of the manifold problems regarding dating and interpretation which this branch of study presents and the numerous points that remain obscure. It is certain however that, if the evolution of the messianic hope still remains difficult to follow from period to period, the fact of this hope, such as it was on the eve of Christ's coming, cannot be contested. For the precise purposes of this chapter what is important is to emphasize how this messianic hope was always closely united to and incorporated in the events and the persons of Israel's history. It is because David was the national sovereign *par excellence* (in whom the whole ideal of the nation's mind was fulfilled) that the Messias to come was thought of as a son of David. It was with David in mind, a native of Bethlehem, that the prophet Micheas saw salvation emerging from a birth at Bethlehem. It was on account of the great rôle of the prophets in Israel that the prophecy of Deuteronomy promising Israel a line of prophets for as long as her history should last (Deut. 18. 15 seq.) was interpreted as referring to him whom Israel awaited as the prophet *par excellence*, the Messias. And so the examples continue. The need for this 'saviour' was experienced in times of national disaster and his characteristics were determined on the basis of the concrete realities of the nation's life. In a word, we are not to imagine the messianic expectation and its expression in our inspired texts as heavenly phenomena appearing from on high from beyond space and time. It is through a more intimate understanding of Israel's history with all its vicissitudes, its trials and its revivals, that we shall reach a better understanding of the messianic hope. Here, too, faith penetrating to the total meaning of the Incarnation must be linked with a very accurate historical interpretation if we are to have a true appreciation of Israel's messianic hope.

(d) *The Old Testament development of the terms in which Christian dogma was to be expressed.* Jesus was born into the Jewish environment at a given moment in history. It is from the thought processes of this environment that he himself chose the terms in which to express his own mission, his own doctrine, and by choosing them, conferred on them a definitive Christian value. He declared that it was he who would establish the reign of God on earth and, although he gave a unique height and depth to this idea, he maintained intact the foundations it had acquired in Israel in the course of the centuries. He gradually led his disciples to recognize that he was the 'Christ', the 'Messias' of Israel's expectation (the confession of Peter: Mark 8. 29; Matt. 16. 16) and, though he infinitely enlarged the scope of the word by the implicit inclusion of the attributes of his own personality, he preserved its ancient and fundamental meaning of 'anointing' by God.

He presented his teaching in the religious terms common in Israel: 'justification' in the sight of God; the antithesis of 'the just' and 'the sinners'; the 'poor' are blessed, (and the word 'poor', *ébiônim* had a more complex meaning in Israel than among us today) and a host of other expressions which are being carefully studied in our times,[3] as they evolved from the earliest period down to that of Jesus and on his lips acquired a deeper meaning in the Christian synthesis while remaining in line with the past. It is in the context of the ancient commandments—$\dot{\epsilon}\nu\tau o\lambda a\acute{\iota}$—(the greatest of the commandments (Matt. 22. 37); the duty to keep the commandments of the Decalogue (Matt. 19. 17) seq.); the second commandment like unto the first (Matt. 21. 39); that he inculcates the obligations of the new Law. But he extends to all men without exception the precept of brotherly charity (parable of the good Samaritan, which excludes all racial distinctions: Luke 10. 29-37) and admits no limits to the duty to forgive (Matt. 18. 21-2). He returns to the

---

[3]We have especially in mind the *Theologisches Wörterbuch zum Neuen Testament* begun by G. Kittel (already mentioned) from which so many terms could be listed here as examples.

ancient Decalogue but gives it a far deeper significance (Matt. 5. 21. seq.).

For his hearers Christ's preaching was vibrant with the religious past of the Old Testament. They found in it many a familiar image—God the shepherd of Israel (Jesus, the good shepherd); Israel, Yahweh's vineyard ('I am the vine, you are the branches'), etc.; literary devices their piety cherished (parables; Semitic metres) etc. But this past looks towards new and hitherto unheard-of prospects ('Never did man speak like this man', John 7. 46).

What was true of Christ during his life on earth was equally true after his death. For his disciples and for the first Christian converts from Judaism, the cross of Christ became intelligible because it stood out against the background of the sacrifices of the Old Law (cf. among other texts the Epistle to the Hebrews) and because it appeared interpreted beforehand by Isaias, chapters 52, 53 (cf. for example, Acts 8. 32-5). In this way, they were ready to understand and to express its redemptive value. When the early Church desired to express to herself and to tell others all that Christ was, as he had revealed himself to her, it was in the texts of the Old Testament devoted to the Wisdom of Yahweh that she first found a vocabulary most suited to her purpose.[4]

These few examples—chosen from many—are sufficient to give us an understanding of this remote preparation for the Christian revelation through the vocabulary of the Old Testament. Any historian can take note of this fact without departing from the literal exegesis of the texts. It seems natural enough to him that Jesus and his disciples should draw upon their times and their religious environment. The Jewish contemporaries of Jesus were happy to rely on the whole of their religious past in order to understand him. But for us Christians, the point of view is the exact opposite: it is in the light of Christ that the meaning of the Old Testament as a whole becomes clear, it is through and in Christ that we reach a better understanding of all that prepared the way for him.

---

[4]Cf. J. Lebreton, *Les origines du dogme de la Trinité*, Book 2, ch. 1 paragraph 3: 'La Sagesse'.

(e) Facts, events, persons and formulas in the Old Testament: symbols and types that prefigure and prophesy the facts, the events, the persons and the truths of the New Testament.

As we have seen, the Old Testament, in the total evolution of its history, and above all through the evolution of its religious thought, forms a progressive ascent (in spite of temporary recessions, checks and deviations) towards Christ and Christianity. Through its prophets (often obscurely and in an involved kind of way) it announces Christ and Christianity. These aspects of the Old Testament are clearly manifest to anyone who studies them; he need not set aside the literal meaning of the inspired texts, but he acquires a deeper understanding of this literal meaning.

Can we go further and discover in certain particular facts and in certain persons in the Old Testament a prophetic meaning, a foretaste of the realities of the New Testament? Can we even discover occasionally in certain formulas of the Old Testament an almost prophetic capacity for expressing realities belonging to the New? If so, this would be a (limited) extension of prophecy properly so-called, but with this difference that it would be not a conscious and willed prophecy on the part of the human author, but intended and uttered by God alone as the principal author of Scripture.

Now we find that from the first days of Christianity, from the times of Jesus, his apostles and evangelists, the Old Testament was looked on in this light. Christ saw in Elias a type of John the Baptist and he considered that the Jewish expectation concerning Elias's literal return had been fulfilled in John the Baptist (Matt. 11. 14; 17. 12-3). When Christ instituted the Eucharist, he did so in terms which recalled, in relation to his own blood of the New Testament, the blood of the Old Covenant with which Moses sprinkled the people (Exod. 24. 8) as a former 'type' of the New Covenant.

St Paul (Rom. 5. 14) pointed to Adam as the type of the Christ to come (τύπος τοῦ μέλλοντος) and, in the celebrated passage in Rome. 5. 12-19, emphasized that this comparison was possible because both Adam and Christ were the sources of things to come, were initial causes; on the other hand, St Paul underlines the essential differences that separated them (vv. 15-9). This word τύπος is the root of the expression 'typological sense' which we tend to prefer nowadays to the other terms (spiritual sense, allegorical sense, etc.). St Paul uses the same word again (1 Cor. 10. 1-11) when he compares the Israelites at the time of the Exodus with certain Christians at Corinth and their apparent tendencies. All these Israelites 'in Moses were baptized, in the cloud and in the sea' (the crossing of the Red Sea), all 'did eat of the same spiritual food' (the miraculous manna) and 'all drank the same spiritual drink' (the water from the miraculous rock), like these Corinthian Christians who had been baptized and had received the Eucharist; and yet what happened to the Israelites might happen also to them: 'but with the most of them God was not well pleased'. Paul further stressed this parallel by seeing in the 'miraculous rock' a presence (in some sense) of Christ in the midst of the Israelites in the desert: 'and the rock was Christ'. He concluded with these words: 'Now these things were done in a figure of us': ταῦτα δὲ τύποι ἡμῶν ἐγενήθησαν (v. 6), and further on (v. 11): 'Now all these things happened to them in figure; and they are written for our correction, upon whom the ends of the world are come': εἰς οὓς τὰ τέλη τῶν αἰώνων κατήντηκεν. This seems to suggest that it is the privilege of Christians who are people 'upon whom the ends of the world are come', to be able to be prefigured in this way. In Gal. 4. 21-9, he makes a very detailed parallel between Sara and Agar, as pre-figuring respectively the Jerusalem from on high, the mother of Christians, and the earthly Jerusalem, the mother of the Jews. He uses this expression: 'Which things are said by an allegory': ἅτινά ἐστιν ἀλληγορούμενα, (4. 24). But from this point of view, what is of far greater importance is the constant insistence in St Paul's letters (for instance, Gal. 3. 7-9, 14, 16-8, 29; Rom. 4. 1-5, 9-13, 16-25, etc.) upon Abraham as the father of all believers and justified by his faith: 'Now it is not written only for him, that it was reputed to him unto justice, but also for us, to whom it shall be reputed, if we believe . . .' (Rom. 4. 23-4). Cf. other examples: Rom. 9. 6-13; 11. 4-5 (Christians form the 'remnant' chosen by grace and pre-figured in the 7,000 men saved in 3 Kings 19. 18), etc.

The evangelist St Matthew offers a fair number of cases of typo-logical application, for instance, Matt. 3. 1: the desert through which the Israelites returned from exile (Matt. 1-3) to their native land so long desired, is seen as the symbol of the desert in which John the Baptist announced that the Kingdom of God had begun. The preaching of Jonas, which Jesus treated as a symbol of his own

(Luke 11. 29-30), is given the exact sense in Matt. 12. 39-41 of a figurative prophecy of the resurrection of Jesus. Matthew likes to form his own sentences with words from the Old Testament used formerly in similar situations; for instance, the angel's words to Joseph in Egypt telling him to return to his own country, are an exact reproduction of those used in Exod. 4. 19 instructing Moses to go back to Egypt. Cf. also Matt. 2. 15 and Osee 11. 1; Matt. 2. 19 and Jer. 31. 15; Matt. 26. 31 and Zach. 13. 7 (it should be added that these cases are often closer to 'accommodation' than to the typological sense).

The first Epistle of St Peter compares salvation through Christian baptism with the rescuing of the eight persons saved from the Flood in Noe's ark (3. 20-1) and expressly says: 'Whereunto baptism being of the like form, now saveth you also'.

The Epistle to the Hebrews contains a good deal of typology, especially in its comparison between the supreme priesthood of Christ and the priesthood of Melchisedech (6. 20-7. 28), and in the antithesis of the sacrifice of Christ, the sovereign priest, by which he entered once and for all into the heavenly Holy of Holies, and the annual sacrifice of the Old Covenant by the High Priest in Israel (8. 1-10. 18).

On the strength of similar examples and under various other influences (Philo, for example, and the secular exegesis of Alexandria), Christian exegesis in the early centuries acquired in certain circles, in particular among the Christians of Alexandria, a very pronounced and often excessive allegorical character. It is not part of our task here to give an account of the various movements that make up the history of exegesis. On the chief and best representative of allegorical exegesis, Origen, the recent books of Fr Daniélou and Fr de Lubac[5] may be consulted with profit.

St Thomas introduced a distinction[6] that has become universally accepted, between the words of the inspired author which establish the literal sense, and the things signified by these words, which establish the spiritual sense (which we now prefer to call the typological sense, since the literal sense is often eminently spiritual). *Ipsae res significatae per voces etiam significant aliquid . . . Significatio qua*

[5] J. Daniélou, *Origène*, Paris, La Table Ronde, 1948 and H. de Lubac, *Histoire et esprit. L'intelligence de l'Écriture d'après Origène*, Paris, Aubier, 1950.
[6] *Summ. Theol.* Pars I, Quaest. I. art. 10; Quodlibet 7, quaest. 6.

voces significant res, pertinet ad . . . sensum litteralem. Illa vero significatio qua res significatae per voces iterum res alias significant dicitur sensus spiritualis, qui super litteralem fundatur et eum supponit. It is then easy to see that the literal meaning expressed by the phrase as the inspired author thought it, must be consciously grasped by him, while the typological sense which is expressed by the things to which he refers depends on God alone who alone creates and disposes according to his own plan the things, the events and the persons in this world. Yet it must be added that this 'type' must be studied as the sacred author presents it with the characteristics he high-lights and which normally provided the foundation for the typological interpretation.

The typological sense of Scripture (and this is true also of its plenary sense) has aroused keen interest among Catholic exegetes— as well as among a certain number of Protestants—during the past twenty years, and has given rise to a fairly copious literature (both books and articles).[7] The subject has even given rise to polemics between two opposing tendencies in modern minds; there was, for example, the fairly strong opposition (*Dieu vivant*, No. 14, 1949, pp. 75-94) of Paul Claudel, Louis Massignon and Fr Jean Daniélou, against an article by Fr Steinmann (*La Vie intellectuelle*, March 1949). This is not the place to write the history of these controversies.

[7]A very complete account of the numerous studies devoted to the various senses of Scripture may be found in Canon J. Coppens book *Les Harmonies des deux Testaments. Essai sur les divers sens des Écritures et sur L'Unité de la Révélation*, Cahier VI of the *NRT*, Tournai, Casterman, 1949. We may mention in addition to the works listed on pp. 191-5 and the two books by J. Daniélou and H. de Lubac just indicated above, the following recent articles: J. Gribomont, 'Le lien des deux Testaments selon la théologie de Saint Thomas,' in *Eph. théol. Lov.*, 1946, pp. 70-89 'Sens plénier, sens typique et sens littéral,' ibid., 1949, pp. 577-84; H. de Lubac, S.J., ' "Typologie" et Allégorisme', in *RSR* 1947, pp. 180-227; 'Sens spirituel' ibid., 1949, pp. 542-76; C. Spicq, O.P., 'Bulletin de théol. bibl.,' in *Rev. Sc. phil et théol.*, 1948, pp. 85-94; ibid., 78-81, remarks by Fr Dubarle; J. Daniélou, S.J., 'Les divers sens de l'Écriture dans la tradition chrétienne primitive,' in *Eph. théol. Lov.*, 1948, pp. 119-26; L. Cerfaux, 'Simples reflexions à propos de l' exégèse apostolique,' in *Eph. théol. Lov.*, 1949, pp. 565-76; A. Miller, Zur Typologie des Alten Testamentes,' in *Antonianum*, 1950, pp. 425-34; W. J. Burghardt, 'On early Christian Exegesis', in *Theological Studies*, 1950, pp. 78-116; A. Fernandez, 'Nota referente a los sentidos de la S. Scriptura,' in *Biblica*, 1954, pp. 72-9 (on the articles by J. Coppens, J. Daniélou, J. Gribomont); I. de la Potterie, 'Le sens de la parole de Dieu,' in *Lumen Vitae*, 1955, pp. 15-30; A few other studies devoted exclusively to the plenary sense will be mentioned later.

Protestant studies on this subject (cf. pp. 121-2): A. M. Hunter, *The Unity of the New Testament*, Philadelphia and London, 1944; *Interpreting the New Testament 1900-50*, London, 1951; C. H. Dodd, *According to the Scriptures*, London, 1952; H. H. Rowley, *The Unity of the Bible*, London, 1953; S. Amsler. 'Prophétie et typologie,' in *Rev. de théol. et phil.*, 1953, pp. 139-48.

The principles and the scriptural examples brought forward above make it possible for us to arrive at the following conclusions:

I. Typological (or spiritual) exegesis, to be found in Christian thought from the earliest times and constantly continuing with various alternatives down to our own time, is to be considered legitimate and justified from the supernatural standpoint both theologically and historically, and spiritually fruitful.

II. This typological exegesis has found its surest, deepest expression in those inspired texts of the New Testament which are the foundation of dogmatic or theological conclusions of immense importance: Christ the second Adam; Abraham the father of all believers; the Christian Church as Israel according to the Spirit by contrast with Israel according to the flesh, etc.

III. In so far as it proceeds on the analogy of these fundamental examples and of others to be found in the Fathers or the liturgy, and which have become part of the treasury of Christian devotion: for instance the traditional 'types' of the sacrifice of Calvary—the sacrifice of Isaac, the trials of Jeremias, Isaias's Suffering Servant, etc.; the traditional symbols for Mary—the new Eve, the Ark of the Covenant, etc., in so far then, as it proceeds on these lines, typological exegesis will prove uplifting and enriching for Christian souls, and will avoid degenerating into mere human virtuosity and ingenuity, brilliant rather than solid or constructive.

IV. Typological exegesis will prove justified to the extent that it fits naturally into the general evolution of Israel's history and thought as they move towards Christ and Christianity, as I have shown in the previous pages. In his fine book *La lecture chrétienne de la Bible* (quoted above), Fr Charlier has underlined the following principle governing typological interpretation: 'the typological value of an Old Testament fact is only certain if on the plane of historical evolution and by internal continuity it is linked with the fulfilment in Christianity of the prototype we read into it' (p. 325).

Our Christian understanding of the Old Testament will be all the more accurate and a greater inspiration to our devotion in proportion as it refuses to attach itself to isolated and incidental superficial resemblances, and remains ever attentive to the overall movement of Israel's gradual progress towards Christ. Any priest, as he recites the Psalms in his breviary, knows that God loved Israel, for her own sake doubtless, but still more as preparing the way for the Church of Christ. He knows that the kings of David's line are called blessed in the Psalms for their own sakes no doubt, but still more because they were signs and figures of the supreme Anointed One, Jesus the Christ. In a sense then, in his present-day devotion, *a fortiori* he can think of Christ in the passages where the king is exalted, of the Church as the community of the faithful in the passages where Israel is praised, and so on. If God's plan is essentially centred on the mystery of the Incarnation, we enter into it when we pray in this way.

Explanatory note. In principle I have vindicated typological exegesis of the Old Testament in the light of the New. May I go further and admit a typological exegesis of the New Testament (and so by implication of the Old Testament) in the light of the consummation of God's kingdom in the blessedness of heaven? Such an exegesis would be in line with the fundamental logic of Christian typology. If God's reign is merely in a state of preparation in this world and is only fully realized in its consummation in heaven, if the Church militant only reaches its full stature in the Church triumphant, if grace is essentially an *initium gloriae* (a beginning of glory), if faith prepares us for vision, and so forth, must we not conclude that religious realities in this world, as they prepare the way for the ultimate realities of heaven, must be capable of prefiguring and proclaiming their future accomplishment, and so of directing souls towards them?[8]

II.   *Sacred Scripture in the Light of Dogma as a living reality in the Church*

The second Thesis applied.

(*a*) God alone can contemplate from the beginning the total synthesis of Christian doctrine, essentially communicated in the apostolic era and growing more explicit and more highly developed until the end of time in Christ's Church. God alone can contemplate

---

[8]Contemporary exegetes increasingly tend to admit the possibility of an eschatological-typological exegesis of the New Testament, although it was more rarely practised by the Fathers and offers fewer traditional or universally accepted examples. Cf. J. Coppens, *op. cit.*, pp. 89-90; R. E. Brown, *The Sensus Plenior of Sacred Scripture*, Baltimore, 1955, p. 19.

from the beginning and in terms of this synthesis, the ultimate connection between the doctrinal texts scattered throughout Scripture.
So that the full Christian doctrine and the continual light of Scripture might always be present, indefectible and unerring at every
period, God has willed to found a Church composed of pastors and
of the faithful, which lives ever more intimately Christ's own life
throughout the centuries and discovers ever more clearly this same
Christ in inspired Scripture. Scripture has been given to us as
something that must be lived, penetrated, interpreted in and by the
Church of Christ and in the light of this same Church's doctrinal,
moral and mystical progress. The part the Church is called upon
to play is by no means limited to guidance and control of scriptural
interpretation by the Magisterium. It is brought into action also
in the collective Christian thought, in the common religious life of
the Church's children, both pastors and faithful, under the influence
of the Spirit. It is not just a matter of projecting artificially into the
scriptural formulas a conceptual explanation that has been acquired
after five, ten or twenty centuries of Christian faith. It is rather to
draw the logical consequences of the dogma which teaches that
Christ infallibly guides his Church by discovering in the light of
doctrine already explicit or in the process of becoming so, what
announced and prepared it in the inspired texts. This is what has
been rightly called the plenary sense of Scripture, that is, in accordance with the definition which has been admirably formulated by
several writers over the past twenty years, that deeper sense, willed
by God, obscurely glimpsed, grasped implicitly but not explicitly
elucidated by the human author, which becomes explicit through
the instrumentality of the whole of revelation as it is lived at any
given moment in the Church and so clarifies more completely the
inspired texts in the eyes of the believer.[9]

[9] R. E. Brown, *The Sensus plenior of Sacred Scripture*, 1955, Baltimore, p. 92, offers
the following definition which he believes can be deduced from previous attempts:
'The *sensus plenior* is that additional, deeper meaning, intended by God but not
clearly intended by the human author, which is seen to exist in the words of a
biblical text (or group of texts, or even a whole book) when they are studied in the
light of further revelation or development in the understanding of revelation.'
The author gives (pp. 89-92) and in an appendix (pp. 151-3), a choice of definitions
put forward during the past twenty years by Catholic exegetes. On this plenary
sense, in addition to this very useful synthesis of R. E. Brown's and the various
studies on the senses of Scripture quoted on p. 262, note 7, an interesting article
by G. Courtade may be read, 'Les Écritures ont-elles un sens plénier?' in *RSR*,
1950, pp. 481-99 (against the plenary sense) and the reply by J. Coppens, in *Eph.
théol. Lov.*, 1951, pp. 148-50.

An attempt must now be made to clarify these principles by applying them.

1. Christ, the God-Man, involved in the concrete environment of his time and in the mentality of the period, clearly spoke in language perfectly suited to his hearers, corresponding to their religious formation and their noblest aspirations which he had shared since his childhood. But transcending his environment and his time by his superior knowledge as Man-God, he alone was able to create a theandric language contemporary with every epoch.

In this world,[10] a man, even if he is a genius, is rarely fully master of his own thought, whose fundamental principles may remain below the level of his consciousness. He is never master of the future of his teaching, for the latter escapes his control as soon as it is formulated. Does he even know what history will have done a century later with his most cherished ideas? Since Jesus is God-Man, he is complete master of his teaching both in the realm of its inherent values and in that of its active power over men. As men's Creator and able to penetrate to the most secret places of human nature, he knows the power over our life and thought possessed by the least idea, the least emotion introduced by him into the souls of his disciples. As master of the future, he knows under what form— thought, action, rite, prayer or precept—he should communicate a given truth to men so that, progressing in accordance with man's nature, it may develop without ceasing to be itself, and become more explicit without losing its identity. Jesus does not leave his doctrine to the hazards of history which would inevitably do away with or deform certain parts of it. He does not deliver it over to the whims of individual interpretation which, even when forced to acknowledge the weight of evidence, still keeps its privilege of turning the blind eye. Jesus

[10]I quote at this point a page from the chapter 'Exégèse catholique, exégèse protestante' pp. 284-5) in my book *Sous les yeux de l' incroyant*, 2nd edn, Brussels, 1946. This chapter aimed to emphasize the temporal and, at the same time, supra-temporal aspect of Christ's teaching and the need of its constant interpretation in and by the Church. Two examples of scriptural interpretation (the founding of the Church and the institution of the holy Eucharist) showed the essential part played by this method of exegesis in Catholicism (in opposition to liberal Protestantism).

knows that a Church, his Bride, is the continuation of himself, and that she understands him by word or action. He knows his Church in advance both in the state in which she now is and in the process of her evolution, and in her he will continue to live until the end of time. This is why the revelation Jesus left to his Church, a revelation in the strictest sense complete and perfect, was not to be and could not be perfected in any human fashion, as would be the case with a philosophical doctrine passed on to his disciples by some thinker, but in a far deeper, far more living fashion, at once divine and human. The thinker is in fact only one point in history and he is doomed to disappear. Jesus commands the future and himself controls the destiny of the words he has entrusted to it.

He alone is able to cast into the soil of humanity a doctrine so perfectly adapted to man's psychology and human evolution, that it will grow, develop with mankind without ceasing to be itself, and this is because he alone knows the secret of life, he alone can see the tree in its seed. Such a type of teaching is doubtless unprecedented, unique, but is not Christianity the only divine religion, and is not the soul of Christ unique in history?

All Catholic theologians agree, I think, as to this plenary sense of Christ's words in the Gospel. But several may object that in the Gospel we are dealing with the words of Christ, Man-God and supreme source of revelation, and not with the words of inspired apostles. The plenary sense of the supreme word of revelation is not absolutely identical with the plenary sense of inspired writing as such. Agreed. But this transcendent and unique case is fundamentally the essential principle underlying all the other examples of the plenary sense, and gives the reason for and throws its light on them all.

2. I now pass from Christ's teaching in the Gospels to the teaching of the apostles in their Epistles. I said at the beginning that all exegetes have an essential duty to aim at understanding as intimately and as deeply as possible each of the inspired writers (Paul, John, etc.) not only from the standpoint of human psychology, but above all in line with the whole living and lived synthesis of their

religious and theological ideas. This study must be as objective as possible, strictly faithful to the texts and during this primary work of literal interpretation must scrupulously avoid any unconscious introduction of our present thought as twentieth century Christians into that of Paul.

But this effort at strictly literal interpretation will sometimes note in Paul's thought ideas that are adumbrated but left incomplete, tendencies which do not yet reach their full development, various aspects of his thought which are not yet completely reconciled, and so this attempt at a strictly literal interpretation of the man himself must be continued by an effort—through the analogy of faith and the flowering of Paul's thought in the Church—to reach the thought of God speaking through Paul. The living synthesis of Paul's thought, which is the final aim of Pauline exegesis, is not for us Christian interpreters merely the thought of a man, as in the case of the thought of a philosopher or a secular moralist; it is the expression of God's thought, it is a message from God. It can only be fully understood in its deepest and ultimate sense by God. True it is, in Paul, something personal, something intimately lived, closely incorporated into the aspirations and experiences of the man. Yet at the same time it is, and much more profoundly, God's possession and he alone knows the secret of the most central truths of his revelation.

Paul therefore in his own thought is transcended by a greater than himself, by the very Master of all thought who has only expressed himself completely in the human thought of Christ. Of course the sincere exegete may nowhere put in a 'finishing touch', so as to make Paul say what the Church says today, but he must be able to note Paul's 'unfinished work', Paul's 'limitations' and in this he is guided by the more complete answers offered by the Church as a result of the progressive explicit definition of divine revelation.

In any case, Paul's 'unfinished' work is not merely something negative. 'Unfinished' implies 'beginning', and how often, in a short section of a sentence, in the logical convergence of two lines of thought, the exegete will acknowledge how astonishingly up-to-date St Paul can be!

God who has made man, like society, capable of evolution and progress, wills that divine truth which is always substantially identical with itself, should grow in the minds and hearts of men and be constantly adapted to the forward movement of man's life on earth.

Hence in the present-day dogmatic synthesis which has issued from the inspired writing of the Epistles of Paul, there will be explicitations, developments which existed only in germ, only virtually in the considered thought of St Paul and appeared there under a quite different aspect, in spite of the fundamental identity between them. All this was part of God's original plan, for he is the one and only Master of time and its epochs, of past, present and future.

The Church alone is kept in being by God as 'magistra veritatis', mistress of truth, it is in her alone that the Christian synthesis is fashioned as God wills, in her alone that we can find it and live it more and more perfectly as the centuries go by. This is why the fundamental interpretation of holy Scripture by the Church is not merely a matter of correcting the individual errors of the exegetes, of simply remedying the 'obscurities' of Scripture; it is essentially deduced from the very nature of holy Scripture as God has conceived it; Scripture has been given to us, destined to be continually interpreted by the Church.[11]

How often as he considers more closely the conclusions drawn by the Church from the texts of St Paul in our Catholic dogma, the exegete notes that, on the one hand, these conclusions make explicit and complete what only appears in outline in St Paul and, on the other, that they are perfectly homogeneous with St Paul's

[11]In this way, so it seems to us, we can reconcile the strictly critical task of the exegete, historian and philologist, as he studies St Paul in the context of the ideas of his times and of his literary and religious personality, and the supremely contemporary task of the theologian as he contemplates dogma as it is today and attempts to penetrate it in all its depth and in all its value as truth and life, either in the light of all it preserves and uplifts in the field of nature and human reason (arguments drawn from rational principles and from the sense of what is befitting), or in the light of its history through tradition down to the thought of the apostles and the thought of Christ from which it originates (arguments from tradition and from Scripture). The two tasks of the exegete and the theologian, if the right methods are followed, must be kept separate while they are engaged in technical research, until such times as the limit of present possibilities has been reached in both cases. And neither must lose sight of the other, each must shed light on the other, on the strength of his own principles; it must be realized at the outset that each complements the other by virtue of the very principles of our faith. God's thought transcends that of his inspired interpreters.
These tasks are complementary and interlinked. This means that critical, historical and philological exegesis play an irreplaceable part in the formation of the great synthesis of Catholic dogma. As the source of revelation (*fons revelationis*), Scripture must be interpreted faithfully and with the greatest reverence. The most recent Encyclicals have shown how strict the method must be and have plainly rejected pseudo-spiritual interpretations attempting to work in defiance of the literal sense. And this also means that in addition to strictly historical exegesis, there is the life of the Church, the progress of the Church's thought or, to be more precise, the gradual explicit formulation of Christ's thought in the Church.

thought and carefully follow all its trends. A given contribution to Christian thought from Paul's pen in a given text only acquires its genuine value for Christian life as a whole in the precise terms the Church uses to complete it and to make it explicit. And surely this is precisely what is meant by the plenary sense?[12]

3. In the divine plan, the theological synthesis of each inspired New Testament author's thought is only part of a greater doctrinal synthesis, whose centre God alone knows and whose manifold ramifications he alone can see. Paul's thought has to take its place beside that of John, Peter and James, so that all their thoughts may together constitute the Christian synthesis. An exegete interpreting secular authors is never allowed to elucidate, to clarify or to make explicit the thought of one writer by using the thought of another of the same or a previous period, unless he is able to discover and prove by historical facts that one influenced the other or that there was at least some common influence exercised by their environment upon both. But if, on the contrary, we are dealing with inspired writers who are witnesses to the climate of thought in the infant Church—and on the Christian hypothesis this climate of thought is guided by God towards his total divine synthesis just as they themselves also are—the Catholic exegete will have to take into account this divine factor in his interpretation. This will certainly not give him the right as an exegete to read rash concordances into the writings of different inspired authors, but it will often help him in cases where the thought of Paul, John or Luke seems to come to a halt, to gain a better insight, in the light of the total revelation as it grows increasingly explicit, into the radical agreement between the various individual inspired thoughts. It will help him to discern more clearly the general direction of each particular movement of thought towards the doctrinal synthesis in its present stage of development, it will help him to a better understanding and a better vindication, before the demands of his conscience as a historian, of the progress of dogma as it has evolved in the Church, on the basis of the convergence of various inspired writings whose implications

[12]In addition to the plenary sense, mention must also be made at this point of what used to be called the 'consequent' sense, that is, the deduction of a further truth from some scriptural teaching used as a major premiss, with the help of a *rational* principle used as the minor premiss. This is not a scriptural sense in the strict meaning of the word, but it does play a part in the formation of the Christian theological synthesis.

have been 'lived' in Christian thought. Here again, this whole process is only seen to be coherent and intelligible in the light of the
concept of the plenary sense of certain inspired texts.

4. It seems logical to extend still further the fundamental
principles in this field by considering, in its entirety, the Church's
task. The doctrinal synthesis of the mystery of Christ, founded as it is
upon primitive tradition and Sacred Scripture, becomes explicit
throughout the centuries in the Church. The Church's understanding of divine revelation is called upon to grow ever deeper 'unto
the measure of the age of the fullness of Christ' (Ephes. 4. 13). At
each stage in this development, the thought of the inspired writers
shows itself rich in new inferences and applications which were not
explicitly stated in previous centuries, but which now are seen to
be in line with this thought. If the exegete, using the correct method,
always adheres to his duty to note as precisely as is humanly possible
the degree to which the conscious teaching of the inspired writers
was explicit, in the light of the information provided by the environment and the period in which these writers lived, then he
should also be able, as a theologian, to recognize and bring to light
the homogeneous nature, the fundamental continuity clearly existing between the doctrinal synthesis of the first century and the
Catholic synthesis of the twentieth. At this point, the great Christian
criteria are relevant: the analogy of faith, the rôle of tradition, the
interpretation of the Magisterium. What is relevant above all is that
fundamental sense, which the exegete must preserve, of the divine
thought adapting to each era our understanding of the mystery of
Christ in and through the Church. The divine thought causes the
understanding of Jesus Christ[13] to grow increasingly explicit
throughout the centuries in our Christian minds guided by the
Magisterium.

In the great edifice whose builder is God, in the temple whose
corner-stone is Christ (Ephes. 3. 20-2), each of the apostles had his

[13]The Church does not claim that she possesses a special charismatic gift in the
field of philology or history. What she does in fact claim is that she alone is fully
fitted by God's power to understand and to give increasingly better expression,
in the process of time and in the light of the Spirit, to the mystery of God as
realized both in the past and in the present in Jesus Christ, as written in the
Scriptures. It is to the extent that Christians—pastors, doctors, exegetes or the
ordinary faithful—are closely united to the Church, to her spirit and her life, that
they will be fitted to understand the essence of the scriptural message.

part and God himself determined his place in the building as a whole. The foundations, laid by each one independently of the others, met and joined at the precise spots foreseen by the divine Architect. Each man's style of architecture is predestined to harmonize with that of the others in the interests of the beauty of the whole. The Temple is faithfully built on the foundations that have been laid, under the guidance of the same Spirit who inspired the apostles and the prophets and who enlightens God's Church until the end of time.

CHAPTER X

CRITICAL EXEGESIS AND THEOLOGICAL INTERPRETATION

(Contributions and limits of the proof from Holy Scripture in theology)

DURING PERIODS like our own, when Catholic theology is feeling its way, searching for precise formulas in the face of difficult problems such as those of original sin, the *raison d'être* of the bloody sacrifice of the Cross, the place of human values in the supernatural concept of life, etc., we often turn, quite legitimately, to holy Scripture and require it to provide a firm answer to these questions, to put forward a formula founded on the infallible Word of God. The same has been true when a dogma needed to be defined: the Immaculate Conception, the infallibility of the Pope, the Assumption of the Blessed Virgin.

It is quite obvious that we have first to examine 'God's word' in the Old Testament. But it seems to me that there is often a mistake in method, a wrong attitude in the way the question is put. From one point of view, too much is asked from holy Scripture, and from another too little. I shall attempt in this chapter to show that this is so. Since I have been teaching New Testament exegesis I have often been struck by the theological limits to the part played by the individual exegete apart from the judgment of the Church. We may rightly be astonished at the confidence and speed with which certain exegetes or theologians of earlier times used to pick out this or that theological truth as formally taught by the inspired writer. At this point, I wish to emphasize the complex nature of the doctrinal proof from holy Scripture and suggest, by means of a few examples taken mostly from St Paul, what the individual exegete, engaged in an objective study of the sacred texts, can deduce with greater or less certainty, and what the Church alone, going beyond all the work of philology and history, yet in conformity with the latter's findings, can deduce and propose to our faith.

This is a vast question and full of delicate shades of meaning. I intend to envisage it successively under three aspects that are more or less complementary and will determine the three sections of this study. In the first section, I shall state the problem generally and attempt to explain in what sense too much is asked of Scripture and in what sense too little. In the second section, on the basis of the classic concept of 'scriptural statement,' or 'scriptural teaching', I shall try to bring to light the very wide margin that may exist between 'scriptural statement' interpreted historically and philologically by the individual exegete, and the same assertion as understood and sanctioned dogmatically by the Church. In the third section, I shall aim to clarify these findings by a few concrete examples taken from the theology of St Paul, from his style of thought, from the manner in which he gave expression to his doctrine. It will then remain to end this study by presenting a few conclusions to which it gives rise.

PART I

The problem can be stated by choosing three examples of major Catholic doctrines in which holy Scripture is invited to say all it has to say, to contribute all it has to contribute. Note that in each case we encounter the same difficulty. A question arises as a result of aspects of truth which have been recently brought to light or have been more or less hinted at by present-day knowledge, or have quite simply arisen from our mentality as men of this modern age. In the past, this question was framed in very different terms in relation to a very different doctrinal background. And so we come to the point at which we ask the exegete to transpose two backgrounds of thought across twenty centuries, to interpret not what the inspired author *said* but what *he would have said*, had he lived today.

First example: the problem of original sin

We possess a very ancient narrative (Gen. 2-3) which is part of Israel's traditions. Whatever the date of its composition—and it is very uncertain—we can no longer think today, in the light of what we know about man's history upon this earth, that this narrative was transmitted over a period of hundreds of thousands of years by human memory. Therefore, God brought it about that, at a given time, this narrative came to the surface in the literature of Israel (its human origins, its historical antecedents are of slight importance), in order to transmit to mankind from God the revelation of a fact of religious importance which was to determine the life of mankind for ever. The revelation is told in popular language and is interwoven with anthropomorphisms (God does not in fact walk in a garden in the cool of the evening), with symbolical passages (the symbolism of God modelling clay to make a human body and breathing into it). No type of philology will ever be able to distinguish here definitively and with certainty between the religious thought and the context in which it is presented, for the simple reason that, in my opinion, they were not clearly separated and formed an undifferentiated whole in the human thought of the inspired author. Later, the actual progress of revelation in Israel clarified and interpreted certain elements in the narrative, such as the significance of the serpent symbol. Finally, God enlightened the mind of St Paul on a particular day when the apostle was writing to the Romans (5. 12), so that he interpreted this primitive narrative once again in the light of the fact of Christ, the new Adam. Paul, using the method so frequent in his Epistles, wanted to see in Adam and in Adam's sin the exact antithesis of Christ and Christ's grace. Yet it was not primarily the misery caused by Adam nor Adam as an individual which at that moment was the centre of his attention. His aim was to exalt the work of Christ by contrast with Adam. The individual exegete may do his utmost to progress as far as possible in the subtle interpretation of Paul's thought, he may identify the presuppositions Paul inherited from Judaism, and the new light brought to bear by the life of Christ, but when he deals with points Paul could not even have imagined (for instance, the present scientific position in regard to monogenism and polygenism), he will soon see, I think, that the exegete may begin the argument and even carry it up to a certain point, but that the complete interpretation of the definitive religious truth belongs to the Church alone. We shall explain shortly why this is so.

Second example: redemption through the bloody sacrifice of the Cross

When Paul, with his Semitic and Jewish mentality, contemplated after his conversion the crucified Christ (before his conversion the crucifixion had directly challenged all his ideas concerning the Messias), he saw this bloody sacrifice standing out quite naturally against the background of all the blood-sacrifices of Israel. For him expiation by the shedding of blood raised no problem, it corresponded quite naturally to his habits of thought.

The same does not hold true of ourselves. It is precisely what Paul felt there was no need to explain or to justify that in our day needs explanation and justification. We know the great efforts that are being made by contemporary theology to gain a deeper insight into the profound meaning of the blood-sacrifice of Christ. There is no need to remind the reader of all the theories, beginning with the most harsh and legalistic, which have left their traces in the sermons of Bossuet. These systems accentuated the punitive justice of God demanding a punishment proportionate to the sin and inflicting it on the innocent Christ, who acts as a substitute for sinners and bears in their stead all the weight of the divine anger. More recent theories accentuate the fact that Christ of his own free will made reparation for us, offering to the Father the act of total love by renouncing all created things that stand in opposition to God, so that this act of love and obedience, performed by the Head of the whole race, a man like ourselves and in solidarity with mankind, might establish in this world the definitive order, the total reparation for the order that had been violated.

We agree that a more careful exegesis of St Paul's writings can and should help us to make a choice between these systems. But in view of the gulf between the outlook and presuppositions of the past and the present, it is easy to understand how the fact that Christian thought does develop sets a barrier between the exegesis of the past and religious thought today. The total thought of the Church throughout the centuries, and not historical and philological exegesis alone, will make a definitive choice possible.

Third example: the problem of human values in the Christian concept of life

Is a Christian humanism excluded by St Paul's thought? Does his concept of life radically oppose that esteem for human values that is so extolled today? Here again it would surely be a mistake to search among Paul's formulas for an indisputable answer to a question that is now asked in very different terms from any he could have imagined at a time when Christianity had only just been born and when it was hoped that Christ's second coming was imminent. Certainly, Paul's thought never begins with man, not even with man rising up to God; it begins always with God, and God coming down to meet man. Paul could never have considered our concept of Christian humanism, which takes man for its point of departure. But if we are willing to travel with him for a long time and not to fasten on to certain of his formulas, we shall find, I believe, all the principles of a profoundly human Christianity in his writings. We shall note what a broad view he has of the expansion of Christianity in the context of human institutions, of the way in which Christ not only 'redeems' them, 'frees them from sin' and 'restores them to order' but also and above all, supernaturalizes them.[1]

These problems, I believe, are offered to the individual exegete in such a way that, in one sense too much is asked and expected of him, and in another, too little.

Too much is asked when we want Scripture alone to decide in every case and to decide by means of texts considered as juridical definitions, statute-book decisions, to be interpreted in absolute and definitive formulas. We fail to restore these texts to the context of the living thought of the inspired New Testament writer. What then is the significance of these texts in the inspired writer's mind? They are efforts to express, as well as may be, with words already in use, with old formulas inherited from the Old Testament, the new revelation given to mankind in Christ or to the Apostle in particular. To tell of Christ and the entirely new character of his message, he has at his disposal only concepts and words traditional among the Jews, and he has taken them just as they are in his environment, in the education he has received. They are the starting-point of his thought. Yet this new reality, communicated by God, is infinitely richer than the traditional concepts and words. But it has to be understood and expressed with these concepts and these words as the starting-point. It is surely clear, therefore, that if we wish to know what the inspired author is stating as the truth, we must above all put ourselves in line with this effort of his thought, we must attempt to find the formulation which is being sought at least as

---

[1] I have recently discussed this question in an article 'Les "valeurs humaines" dans le théologie de Saint Paul' *Studia Biblica et Orientalia*, Rome, 1959, vol. II, pp. 232-46.

much as the formula which is complete, we must guess what is suggested at least as much as discover what is said. The true greatness of holy Scripture is not that it is something final; that which is final is the Church growing into the fullness of Christ. The true greatness of holy Scripture is that it is a starting-point, a foundation, a source, but a continual starting-point, an immovable foundation, an indefectible source with which the Church must always remain in contact.

It is in this sense, so it seems to me, that too little is asked of holy Scripture, less in fact than it can provide. The ideal of theological work in this field is that one should make one's own, that one should 'live' the movement of the mind, the effort of thought and expression of the inspired writers; one should set out with them from the Old Testament and climb with them towards the new reality which Christ is; one should adopt the direction of their thought if one is to succeed in continuing along this path with the Church. It is important always to be aware of this living character of sacred Scripture, of this forward movement which it expresses and asks should be continued.

This is precisely what the Church, the community of Christian souls united to its pastors, is ceaselessly doing. The movement of thought inculcated by Paul joins, in the doctrinal life of the Church, the movements of thought inculcated by John, Peter, etc., and the Church continues these movements as she harmonizes and unifies them. It is in the synthesis of the various trends of her inspired thought, 'lived' by the Church in accordance with her vital growth in Christ, that she leads us to an increasingly rich theological formulation, one that is increasingly precise, while at the same time she has possessed from the beginning, in essence, the fullness of her doctrine. In the construction of the mystical body of Christ, Paul, Peter, John are only particular sections of the vast building they are destined to form, that unity whose total plan is in the hands of God alone; and he brings it into effect only in and through his Church.

PART II

We can attempt to clarify these ideas by linking them with the classic formula which is the conclusion of every treatise *De Scriptura Sacra:*

Quidquid docetur a scriptore sacro docetur a Spiritu Sancto ('whatever is taught by the sacred writer is taught by the Holy Spirit').

Since, under the present dispensation which is wholly dominated by the idea of the Incarnation, God's inspired word is offered to us as a divine and human utterance, a message from God thought out and expressed in human terms, it is by interpreting, by understanding perfectly the words and thought of a man, of the inspired writer, that we are informed of what God wishes to say to us and does say to us in a way that is fully adapted to our nature. This is well brought out in the classic formula 'All that is taught by the sacred writer is taught by the Holy Spirit'.

But what does the inspired writer teach us? There is no need to return to the numerous examples adduced and interpreted in Chapter VIII, the conclusion is obvious: the truth God communicates to us in his Scripture does not emerge in the same way from each of these various sacred writings. The psychological background and the style of their statement were very different in the case of the Yahvist narrator of the history of the patriarchs in Genesis, and the courtier of 1 and 2 Kings writing his Memoirs of David. Yet it has to be admitted that these two writers were not in complete control of the literary form on which they depended and would not have been able to assess the precise scope of their assertion as we attempt to do today in regard to their testimony.

The problem was seen to be still more complex when the moral teaching of the Old Testament was in question. The formula 'an eye for an eye, a tooth for a tooth' which Jesus entirely rejected in the Sermon on the Mount, had been, in the Old Testament, 'an inspired word, the Word of God', but only as signifying something 'better' by comparison with a previous state of barbarism, only as destined to check the excesses of Semitic blood feuds. The authorization of divorce had been an inspired word, a Word of God, but only, as Jesus said (Matt. 19. 8; Mark 10. 5) by way of allowance for the hardness of the human heart at that particular stage of the evolution of civilization: *ad duritiam cordis vestri* ('by reason of the hardness of your heart'). This shows the extreme complexity of doctrinal assertion in holy Scripture and the grave error we should fall into were we to treat all its assertions as being at the same religious level merely because they are all 'God's words'.

But are these degrees of assertion perhaps absent in the New

19

Testament since here we have 'God's word' in its definitive absolute form with no qualifications whatsoever? Yet here too the problem most certainly exists. Here too we must distinguish between what is contingent and what is definitive in a New Testament assertion. And this is an aspect of scriptural interpretation that is too frequently neglected.

Very many cases could be quoted but I shall confine myself to three examples from St Paul's teaching.

1. *The distinction between an absolute and definitive moral or religious stipulation and the concrete, temporary circumstances of its application.*

Is it always so easy to determine by the help of philology and history alone whether a given moral or disciplinary regulation laid down by St Paul is conceived by him, and willed by God, as a definitive moral or ecclesiastical rule binding for as long as the Christian Church shall last, or whether in the concrete it has been conditioned by the social and cultural situation at the time it was issued and to which early Christianity had to adapt itself? If the latter is the case, then the rule is to be interpreted as only provisional; as applying only to the first Christians in given, local Churches. I have already instanced (pp. 215-16) the position of women in conjugal, civil and ecclesiastical society as St Paul saw it. True, any well-informed exegete will easily be able to discern certain cases in which Paul's essential moral teaching is obviously independent of the social circumstances in which it was presented; the latter were no more than a temporary and contingent context in which the teaching was to be applied. But when Paul (1 Cor. 11. 2-16; 14. 34-46; 1 Tim. 2. 11-5) insists on excluding women from all active share in the direct acts of public worship, even if, as a historian, I observe that in this connection Paul is influenced by his background of Semitic thought and ancestral Jewish tradition, am I entitled to conclude as an individual exegete, that today, when the social background of antiquity is no longer the same, there is no longer any reason for this exclusion and that women ought to be admitted to the priesthood and the episcopate in the Christian Church? It is obvious that the individual exegete is incompetent to decide. God who is master of the epochs of human history may in fact have chosen the tradition and customs of one period to fix in the structure of his Church some elements which he wishes to be definitive. He alone can tell me whether this is so. Such examples clearly reveal the need for a Church as interpreter of Scripture. Of course, exegesis, on the basis of various scriptural texts in St Paul and elsewhere, can begin the argument and carry it on for some distance, as it would be easy to demonstrate. But the Church alone reaches and authoritatively sanctions the definitive interpretation.

2. *The influence of personal psychology, character, hopes and ways of action on the expression of doctrine*

The personality of St Paul, as everybody knows, was extremely rich and deep. His remarkable intellectual vigour, enlightened and guided by God, stimulated by an intense need to think out his faith, made him the first theologian of the Church. The immense range of his mind, his profound knowledge of his environment and his time, his practical understanding of the vast possibilities offered to the spread of the Christian faith by the organization of the Roman Empire, his iron will steeped in the love of Christ, made him the leading apostle of Christianity. It was his ambition—and he realized it—to establish Christ wherever Rome had established herself. The intensity of his interior life, of that loving union with Jesus Christ which began at Damascus, his astounding gift for coining the exact phrase in which to express in vivid fashion his own religious experience, made him a master of Christian mysticism. God had chosen and prepared his instrument. One of the joys of the exegete is the discovery everywhere in Paul's works of the signs of the riches of his soul.

This effort to acquire a psychological understanding of St Paul's letters has sometimes forced the modern exegete to modify the interpretation of Pauline texts and to read in them a different sense from that accepted by his predecessors in this field. Here are two cases which will make this point clear.

In the first place, we may take Paul's hope in the imminent second coming of Christ. An objective study of numerous convergent passages in the New Testament is increasingly bringing contemporary exegesis to recognize that in early Christianity, among the faithful as a whole as well as among the apostles themselves, there existed a keen hope that Jesus would soon return as the judge of the world and the founder of the final Kingdom. The inspired apostles nowhere asserted as part of their apostolic message that this event would certainly take place in the near future, but they clearly hoped that it would (cf. above p. 215). This hope is obviously apparent in St Paul's first letter: 1 Thess. 4. 15-7, and subsequently in several other passages: 1 Cor. 7. 26-31; 15. 51-2; 2 Cor. 5. 1-10; Rom. 13. 11-2.

It is therefore clear that, for him, the problem of the resurrection of the body, which he hoped was to take place at a more or less early date, did not arise in the same terms as it does today after an interval of nineteen centuries. The problem of the intermediate state between death and resurrection did not then demand the immediate solution, which seemed so necessary to the Catholic Church in the fourteenth century when she defined through Benedict XII in 1336 (after the hesitations of his predecessor John XXII) that the souls of the elect enjoy the beatific vision as soon as they return to God and do not have to wait until the resurrection of the body.[2]

This prospect of an imminent Parousia also influenced Paul in his emphatic exhortation to virginity (1 Cor. 7. 26: 'for the present necessity'; 29: 'the time is short'; 31: 'the fashion of this world passeth away'). He hastens, however, to affirm in the same passage the abolute and definitive value of virginity before God independently of time and period (32-5).

It was from the same point of view that Paul advised the Christians of his time to remain in the social status in which they found themselves, even, in the event, to remain slaves. This advice also had in mind the essential interests of security for apostolic propaganda (1 Cor. 7. 20-4). Nevertheless, here as always, Paul's essential line of thought is predominant. Only one thing is of any account in this world and that is to prepare ourselves for the Kingdom of God, to get ready for it in our moral and religious lives. Nothing else has any ultimate value.

The expectation of the Parousia in the near future was also in part responsible for Paul's prophecy of the conversion of Israel after that of the Gentiles and as a reaction to the stimulus of the latter. He thinks of it in terms of the situation of his times, of a conversion of Israel which he hopes is imminent, which has perhaps—

[2]This same problem has been frequently brought forward and discussed during the present century by Protestant writers on the basis of holy Scripture alone. This has been done quite recently by O. Cullmann, *Immortalité de l'âme ou Résurrection des morts? Le témoignage du Nouveau Testament*, Paris-Neuchâtel, 1956.

who knows? (Rom. 11. 15)—been predestined in the divine plan to give the signal for the Parousia. Naturally any theological exegesis of the prophetic character of this passage will be inadequate unless it takes full account, in the details of its interpretation, of this outlook and hope in Paul.

The other example I wish to bring forward is the influence on Paul's moral and religious teaching of the very exact view he had taken from the beginning, and frequently exhibited, of the conditions that were absolutely essential if Christianity was to effect a successful and peaceful penetration of the Roman world. He wanted at all cost to prevent Christianity from appearing as a subversive or disturbing force threatening the structure of Roman society or the security of the Roman State. This, in addition to the hope of an imminent Parousia, was a further motive for insisting that new Christian converts from paganism should preserve the social status and the standards of life they possessed before their conversion. Any exegete attempting to deduce from Paul's writings general rules concerning the social and economic doctrines of Christianity in connection with the advancement of the working classes, without taking into account the motive of expediency regarding the apostolic mission in his teaching, would falsify the apostle's thought. Paul's clear insistence on perfect loyalty to Rome (for example, in Rom. 13. 1-7) is also partly explained by this preoccupation with the apostolate. This certainly does not nullify the principle emphasized in these passages of the Christians' obligation to submit to the established power, but it does make it possible for us not to exaggerate the importance of these and other similar texts in an overall theological study of the rights of the State and the duties of citizens.

Briefly then, any text, even an inspired text, if it is to be understood, must be set in the context of the mind and heart of the man who is speaking to us. To understand it in any other way, to treat it as an article in a Code, a sentence that has come down from heaven from beyond space and time, is to court certain failure in the attempt to see precisely what God wants to tell us through this man.

3. *The influence of literary devices and of the literary psychology of the inspired author on the scope of his assertions*
We all know what a great influence the literary temperament of

an author has on the manner in which he puts forward his assertions. An 'oratorical assertion' by a great preacher, gathering together and simplifying a whole complex of ideas, is not the same
thing as a rigorous formula scientifically elaborated by a great
theologian. There is a considerable margin between a lyrical out-
burst and a didactic thesis.

But it is sometimes forgotten that the epistles of St Paul, full
though they are of profound theology, occasionally have the
characteristics of the oratorical form and also, at times, of the
lyrical. The scope of his assertions may in such cases be considerably
modified.

At this point, we shall only take one instance, one literary device
he frequently uses and which is very characteristic of his style of
thought, namely antithesis, and we shall choose two examples of it
from among a great many.

The first, in 2 Thessalonians (2. 3-12), is the antithesis between
Christ and his adversary the 'man of sin', 'the son of perdition'. In
this diptych of opposites, inspired in great part by the Old Testament, Paul delighted to contrast as completely as possible Christ
and his adversary of the last days. Each of these two will be
'revealed' (ἀποκαλυφθήσεται), each will have his Parousia
(παρουσία), each will perform signs and wonders, will have at his
command an 'ἐνέργεια', one for good, the other for evil. Finally,
each is presented as a determined 'individual.' Suarez concluded
that the 'individual character of Antichrist' was 'of faith' (*res
certissima et de fide*). The majority of theologians today show much
more reserve in their interpretation and consider that in the Church
of God the opinion that Antichrist will be a collectivity or even an
institution, can be quite freely held. The interpretation of this
'antithetic assertion' of St Paul does not seem so simple today as it
did in the days of Suarez.

Everyone is familiar with another antithesis, the famous contrast
between Adam and Christ (Rom. 5. 12 seq.), the classic foundation
of the whole theological thesis on original sin. There is no need to
repeat the exegesis of this fundamental passage, which has had such
a profound influence on moral and religious ideas. I wish merely to
draw attention to its literary psychology. As I have already said,
Paul is primarily interested here not in the misery caused by Adam,
but in Christ, and in glorifying the grace of Christ. And so that the

greatness of Christ's gift may be thrown into relief, the exact antithesis must be described, the complete contrast with the harm done by Adam. At first sight, one would think that it was in attempting to reach a full understanding of the reality of Christ that Paul, by way of contrast, came to understand the reality of Adam. On the other hand, it seems impossible to fail to note the painful effort and the hard work the development of this idea obviously involved for Paul. He is seeking to clarify his thought by means of a process of reasoning which, it must be admitted, remains imperfect and incomplete from a certain point of view.[3] The formula he uses grows increasingly precise until finally in v. 19, it has become fully elaborated: 'For as by the disobedience of one man, many were made sinners: so also by the obedience of one, many shall be made just.' If there were not, beyond this text as it stands, twenty centuries of research and definitive decisions by the Church, if I remained an isolated exegete using only my private judgment, and without the Church's guidance, I might instinctively be tempted to conclude that when St Paul stumbled upon this vigorous antithesis (and that he did stumble upon it, is proved by the anacoluthon in v. 12), he could never have suspected the formidable inferences Christian thought would deduce from this oratorical amplification. He would never have been able to imagine that the question of 'monogenism versus polygenism' would be connected with this text and depend upon its interpretation.

Of course, I am quite aware that I am only putting forward an objection calculated to cast greater light on the problem, the equivalent, that is, of St Thomas's *videtur quod non*, and I am not unaware of the partial and also the well-established answers that can be offered. But what I wish to emphasize is the margin that exists between Paul's thought as it may be understood in its historical context by the individual exegete, and the immense doctrinal inferences that have been deduced gradually over a period of twenty centuries from this thought. No doubt there is a homogeneity and a continuity between St Paul's thought and Catholic dogma, and

[3]Any theology student will, for instance, raise the objection that the sins committed between the time of Adam and that of Moses, were, by virtue of Paul's own principles regarding the pagan conscience, understood as sins and therefore deserving of punishment, and might even have been deserving of death. And this would not imply any injustice on God's part. This objection is based on our ideas concerning the relations between obligations and sanctions, but St Paul has not chosen to argue from this point of view in the passage under consideration.

the Church has not arbitrarily added to the message handed down by Paul something foreign to its nature. Yet it is nevertheless true that this example clearly indicates the essential part played by the Church in the interpretation of Scripture and in particular of the doctrine in question. The Catholic exegete, who is fully conscious of the precise limits of his own conclusions, soon sees that the Church's light enables him to recognize more clearly the action of God in the human gropings of Paul's thought and style. The thesis of the inspiration of Scripture necessarily requires the corresponding thesis of the Church's authentic interpretation.

To sum up: I began with the universally accepted and apparently simple formula, 'What is taught by holy Scripture is taught by the Holy Spirit'; and I have been studying this formula only in relation to the essential purpose of holy Scripture, that is, doctrinal assertion in the field of religion and morals. My whole effort has been directed to emphasizing the extreme complexity of this idea of doctrinal assertion and the very difficult task it imposes on the individual exegete. His difficulty is not to discover, as perfectly as possible and with all the shades of meaning that can be identified, what the sacred writer, what St Paul thought. This is his normal professional task as a philologist and historian. He may have made more or less a success of it, according to the state of his documents and his own powers as an exegete. No, his real difficulty is to pass from ascertainment of facts to a value-judgment, to an authoritative statement, to pass from Paul's psychology and convictions which find expression in this text, to the authority of God telling me through Paul that a given doctrine is of faith and must be a definitive norm for my thought and my life.

PART III

In this third section I wish to make more concrete, to 'factualize' the observations made, by showing how they are applied to certain particularly thought-provoking points in St Paul's theology.

St Paul's strong personality has set an indelible stamp upon his message. In his writings, more than in those of any other inspired writer, each text demands for its full understanding to be set in the whole synthesis of his doctrine. In his writings more than in those of any other man, there are evident that effort of thought and that tension in style which show that his aim was to reach and to express as well as possible truths which are beyond human understanding. His efforts often lead to those admirable lapidary phrases which abide in the memory of every Christian. Yet sometimes also, because of the very greatness of the revelation this thought has to grasp and combine into a whole, it remains in various ways still incomplete. It opened the way and pointed out the paths to be followed after its own day by Christian theology. The point ultimately reached at this later date throws light on the original intuitions of the apostle chosen by God to point out the way. His thought did not always succeed in grasping and indicating the point of reconciliation between two truths which it asserted. And it is often at such points where Paul's reconciliation is not complete, that heresies have crept in. St Paul's epistles, it must be admitted, had been the innocent occasion of a great number of heresies in the Church of God: Lutheranism, Calvinism, Baianism, Jansenism.[4] Yet, I believe, one of the joys of the Pauline exegete is to be able to note how sound a judgement the Church showed at those times when there was thus a danger of heresy, and so remained faithful to the thought of St Paul as a whole. Special arguments, commentaries on texts, may often have been poor enough during these times of discussion, yet the ultimate decision has been very sound and very accurate because the Church took a total view of the Pauline message, for the excellent reason that she was engaged in 'living' it to the full.

If we are to have an accurate appreciation of Paul's message, we must begin with what is seen to be the deepest, most intimate, most spontaneous reality in his soul as a disciple and apostle of Christ. We must start from what shines through every page of his letters and controls the greater part of his ideas as well as his emotions. Whoever studies the Pauline letters closely will soon

[4]It may be asked why God did not cause Paul to speak in such a way that all possibility of those weaknesses and heresies, which have done so much harm to God's Church, would have been avoided. In my opinion the question no longer arises as soon as we understand on the one hand the tremendous place God wishes to leave to human freedom in the building up of his kingdom in this world—it is we poor men with the clumsy hands of ignorant workers whom God has made the builders of his Church; and on the other hand, the rôle of guide, necessary and inevitable in the nature of things, which God has willed to give to his Church. We only have the fullness of light—and we cannot judge properly without it—in the great Church of God. God wants us to grow accustomed to 'seeing' in union with her.

discover—in company with the majority of exegetes ancient and modern[5]—that Christocentricity is the key to Paul's thought and

[5]Although with different shades of meaning, the exegetes of the past fifty years both Catholic and Protestant, agree in placing the centre of, or at least recognize as an essential point in, St Paul's theology, the idea of 'Christ, Saviour of men', of 'Christ freely given to men for their salvation'. For H. J. Holtzmann (liberal Protestant; *Lehrbuch der neutestamentlichen Theologie*, 1st edn, 1897, 2nd edn, 1911, Tübingen, II, p. 256) 'Paul's doctrine simply expresses the way in which the apostle objectivized the fundamental experience of his life'. The victory over death of the risen Christ, manifested to the apostle in the vision of Damascus, made him understand the great principle 'through death to life': death to all the past of Judaism and of the human race, to the Law, to the flesh, to death itself: life as a new creature with the risen Christ. G. B. Stevens (Anglican, *The Theology of the New Testament*, Edinburgh, 1901, p. 330 seq.) believes he has found the reasons for the evolution of Pauline thought in the contrast between two experiences, on the one hand, the pre-Christian experience of the Apostle, a lived experience of the moral inadequacy of the Law (Rom. 7), and on the other hand, the revelation of Christ at Damascus which, by setting him personally free, provided Paul with the central point of his moral and religious life. According to P. Feine (a Protestant with conservative views: *Theologie des neuen Testaments*, 1st edn, 1909, 3rd edn, Leipzig, 1919, pp. 196-8), the principle which makes it possible to understand Pauline theology should be sought in the doctrine of salvation through Christ. It is the revelation and the saving action of God through Christ at a given moment in history which forms the centre of the whole of Paul's thought and apostolate. This central point, present from the beginning and which never subsequently varied, justifies and explains at every moment the new doctrinal aspects of Paul's thought. Fr Prat, S.J., in the second volume of his *Théologie de saint Paul*, (1st edn, 1909, 6th edn, Paris, 1923, II. p. 22 seq.), attempts to determine 'what is most personal and most characteristic in St Paul's theology', to 'identify the true centre of Pauline doctrine' which, in his opinion, is primarily a 'soteriology', and he puts forward this very valuable and thought-provoking formula: 'Christ as Saviour making every believer a partner in his death and his life.' E. Lohmeyer (a Protestant exegete: *Grundlagen paulinischer Theologie*, Tübingen, 1929) systematizes Paul's theology by means of two essential concepts, the concept of 'divine revelation' with a resultant 'faith' in the believer, and the concept of the holy community 'living by this faith, the Church'. But he makes the full discovery of the essential aspects of St Paul's Christocentricity when he gives a detailed explanation in the second part of his work (pp. 62-156) of what 'faith in Christ' means in Paul's religion and doctrine. R. Bultmann (Protestant: *Theologie des Neuen Testaments*, Tübingen, 1948, pp. 186-348) starts from the idea that Paul's theology does not speculate on God's essence, but is a study of the relations between God and man (Bultmann's formula is '*die paulinische Theologie ist zugleich Anthropologie*'), that the purpose of his christology is not to define Christ but simply to show how and why Christ has brought us salvation (his formula is 'die paulinische Christologie ist zugleich Soteriologie': the Pauline Christology is at the same time a soteriology); thus he comes to the conclusion that the best way to understand and summarize Paul's doctrine is to begin with man. The whole of St Paul's theology is condensed under two headings: I. Man before the revelation of faith (pp. 186-266); II. Man under the dispensation of faith (pp. 266-348). The central place occupied by faith in Christ is obvious in this system. Fr P. J. Bonsirven, S.J., (*L'Évangile de Paul*, Paris, 1948, p. 34 seq.,) shows that we must not ask the Apostle for a systematic theological method aiming to unify theses by deducing them from higher principles and by linking them in strict order'; Paul is 'a mystical genius expressing his own experience'. In the formation of Paul's doctrine, Fr Bonsirven attaches very great important to the vision at Damascus. He represents 'the first intuition which came at Damascus,' as a 'divine light (2 Cor. 4. 6) illuminating the whole horizon, revealing the whole of Christian economy, showing Jesus Christ as the universal

that it is from this starting-point that his theology is to be understood as it unfolds and systematizes itself in the closest relation with the personal life of the apostle and with the historical facts as far as we know them. From the moment of Paul's conversion, the revelation of Jesus Christ established itself at the centre of the soul of this Jewish convert. Christ revealed himself to Paul, gave himself to Paul, and Paul gave himself wholly and entirely to Christ. It is a wonderful experience to find how all the thought of Paul before his conversion took on a new consistency, a higher value once it was linked with Christ and discovered its foundation in him.

Christ revealed himself to Paul in the totality of his earthly existence, his life, his death on the cross and his resurrection. He revealed himself in his place in Jewish history as Israel's Messias. He revealed himself in his relation with God the Father, for he is the Son of God. Paul is not a philosopher constructing a doctrine based on his own ideas. He had submitted to the concrete fact of the coming of Christ into this world.

For Paul, this revelation of the gift of Christ or, more accurately, this personal application to Paul of the gift of Christ came to him in a sharply defined form. It was a gratuitous grace suddenly received at Damascus with no merit on his part for he was an enemy and a persecutor.

Paul always remembered with deep emotion this religious experience at Damascus: 'But when it pleased him, who separated me from my mother's womb, and called me by his grace, to reveal his Son in me': ἀποκαλύψαι τὸν υἱὸν αὐτοῦ ἐν ἐμοὶ (Gal. 1. 16). In this text he made perfectly clear both his sense of the absolute gratuitousness of the divine call (who separated me from my mother's womb) and also (to reveal his Son in me, ἐν ἐμοὶ) the personal intimate relation, the total hold of Christ upon him, which began at Damascus, and the active presence of Christ in Paul, the action by which Christ raised up Paul to higher things. This presence comes spontaneously to his lips in more than a hundred passages: *in Christo*. ἐν Χριστῷ, or διὰ Χριστοῦ.

But it was not long before Paul's personal religious experience

mediator, and God therefore living and active within him'. The whole book thus stems from this idea of 'Christ the Mediator', the intuition Paul received from divine revelation, and emphasizes the close link, in Paul's mind enlightened by God, between his central intuition and the other convictions expressed in his epistles.

was seen by him as just one particular case of the state of all human beings without exception. For them all, as for himself, the coming of Christ, the gift of Christ is a work begun by God alone, a work that is wholly gratuitous. How often the Apostle delights to contemplate this divine economy, this mystery of the will of God, hidden in him for centuries and which consists in the recapitulation of all things in Christ (Ephes. I. 10; 3. 9)! God gave Christ to the world at the moment he had willed to do so, as he willed and because he willed. For all men as for Paul himself, the gift of Christ is the gift of a permanent presence, of a direct action of Christ within each soul and in the Church. Each man is 'in Christ'; each Church, each community is 'in Christ'.

These two ideas, of grace and of the wealth of meaning in the expression 'in Christ', were not implanted in Paul by the vision at Damascus alone; he received them also from the infant Church.[6] The twofold principle of a religion of grace, on the one hand, and of Christ as the centre of all things, on the other, was 'lived' out in the Church from her earliest origins. From the moment of the resurrection, she was conscious of this life of Christ in the Church, of Christ present among his people and leading them back to the Father by his life-giving action upon them. We can never sufficiently emphasize what faith in the resurrection of Christ meant in the realm of dogma for the first Christians. In the same way the religion of God's gift of Christ, of the gratuitous love of God in Christ, of the guidance of the Spirit who is a gift from on high, all this body of religious truth linked to the idea of grace and made manifest by the gift of Christ, was 'lived' at the deepest level by the infant community of the Church. God gave himself, God gives and will give himself. His people thank him, pray to him and wait for him.

Paul lived and thought out the most remote consequences of these essential truths in the religion of grace and of Christ as centre of all things. In this intellectual process his mentality as a Jewish convert, a former Pharisee, a child of the Diaspora, the various circumstances of his life as well as the systematic opposition he met from the Jews and the demands made by his apostolate to the Gentiles, all played their part. The fact that the historian can identify such human causes does not mean that St Paul's witness is thereby less divine,

[6]A combined study of the teaching of the Gospels, of the opening section of the Acts and of the other Epistles in the New Testament, would make this clear.

or loses anything of its divine value. God speaks to us through the whole personality of Paul.

This central point of Pauline theology once established, we must now study three points in his doctrine which, I consider, will be of assistance in throwing light on the intensive and vigorous theological effort of thought which is so characteristic of the apostle. It is a highly personal characteristic and it was a driving force in his life rather than a systematization pushed to its furthest logical consequences. As examples we shall take three aspects of his doctrine of Redemption, Paul's concept of (1) the divine initiative in the work of our salvation; (2) the divine plan of salvation; (3) man's answer in the act of faith.

They can be studied briefly and from one point of view alone, that of the close relation between Paul's psychology as a convert Jew and Christian truth, and this with the intention of identifying what we may call the 'incomplete' and the 'complete' elements in St Paul's thought as he endeavours to put the revealed doctrine into words. My purpose is to demonstrate this characteristic *effort* in thought and style, often enough providing a mere beginning or suggestion demanding to be further developed. And this is an effort which it is important to recognize in St Paul's writing as well as, in a general way, in those of several inspired authors.

I propose to study these three points in accordance with a method applicable to many in Pauline doctrine: Paul's thought before his conversion, that is, the complex of Jewish ideas which conditioned his mentality; Paul's thought after his conversion, after the revelation of Jesus Christ.

In this examination of the Pauline doctrine, it is impossible for the interpreter to distinguish from the historical point of view between what is due to revelation and what is due to Paul's thought as he reflected on revelation. As an exegete, he can only verify the result of God's action and man's closely united.

(1) *The divine initiative in the work of our salvation*

Paul before his conversion. The exalted idea of God was the great victory of the Old Testament. Like every first-century Jew, Paul had a profound sense of God's supreme power, of his absolute liberty, of the divine initiative in all things. Like other Jews he was not given to making any distinction between the 'permissive' and the 'absolute' will of God. The Old Testament had accustomed him to look on God as the conscious and deliberate cause not only of the good fortune but also of the misfortunes of Israel. If Palestine was invaded by an enemy army, it was because Yahweh, as the prophets had often declared, had gone to these enemies and had aroused in their hearts the desire to invade Israel, so that they might execute upon Israel the punishments decreed by God. If Pharaoh refused to allow the Hebrews to leave Egypt, it was because Yahweh had hardened Pharaoh's heart so that his glory might be all the better revealed in Israel's deliverance. Yahweh is even represented on occasion as sending an evil spirit into the soul of king Saul, a 'spirit of error' into the mind of the false prophets.

Paul after his conversion. How well Paul had been prepared by his Jewish sense of God's free initiatives, to understand the complete gratuity of the economy of grace! 'Or who has first given to him, and recompense shall be made him?' (Rom. 11. 35). Paul, the persecutor received Christ gratuitously by the free act of God, and this was one particular case in the immense economy of God's pure gifts and of his gratuitous favour: 'So then it is not of him that willeth nor of him that runneth, but of God that sheweth mercy' (Rom. 9. 16). The priority given by the Jews to the initiatives of God now appeared in concrete form in the great divine initiative, the centre of all the rest: revelation and the bringing to pass in time of the 'mystery' hidden in God from all eternity, the mystery of his plan to recapitulate and centralize all things in Christ, God's only Son. And, we must immediately add, an initiative of love preceding the sacrifice of redemption. God had no need of an act of satisfaction to be offered to him in order that he might turn again towards us, his anger at length appeased. It was he (2 Cor. 18) who, of his own free will, reconciled us to himself through Christ, it was he whose love was first made manifest to us sinners. 'But God commandeth his charity towards us; because when as yet we were sinners, according to the time, Christ died for us' (Rom. 5. 8). No system of redemption could claim to be genuinely Pauline if it failed to place love above justice.

But the same sense of the all-powerful divine initiative which Paul owed to his Semitic mentality, prepared him much less effectively to turn his attention to the problem of the reconciliation of grace with freedom, and this is a problem of which an apostle with a Greek education would have been automatically aware. This explains why he never established any link between the two truths of grace and freedom, both of which he held. This is why we find frankly one-sided statements such as the famous Chapter 9 of Romans (on the vessels of wrath which God is free to create), and which, when read by a rigid and intransigent Western logician, were one day to give birth to Calvinism. A deeper Pauline synthesis, and one less dependent on details, has made it possible for the Church to pass beyond and to reject the narrow and one-sided logic of Calvin.

(2) *The divine plan for our salvation*

Paul before his conversion. Like every Jew, Paul had a strong sense of Israel's election, of God's plan for Israel. This loving plan for Israel had two landmarks for traditional Jewish thought, in the shape of two essential historical events.

On the one hand, there was the promise made to Abraham and, according to tradition, renewed in each of the three generations of patriarchs. It had developed over the centuries and had become the great Messianic promise. In spite of ups and downs, in spite of an ebb and flow throughout the ages before Christ, the hope in the Messianic promise was clearly and solidly established in Jewish hearts on the eve of Christ's coming. It exhibited dissimilar, even contradictory, aspects but it was deep and strong.

On the other hand, the second event which showed God's great love for Israel was the giving of the Law to Moses on Mount Sinai. Israel had the unique privilege of knowing God's will and so of being in a position to please him, but this Law was accompanied by blessings on those who kept it and curses on those who violated it.

This economy was twofold; there was the economy of the promise and the economy of the Law. Between these two aspects of the will of divine Providence for the nation, Israel never seems to have noticed any contradiction. Promise and law seemed to Israel one homogeneous whole in which God's holy will and the goodwill of the nation were destined to harmonize.

Paul after his conversion. In the soul of Paul the convert Jew, a profound change in his appreciation of religious values took place under the influence of divine revelation. The two aspects of Jewish thought just recalled seemed to him two essentially different concepts of religion itself. On the one hand, there is the religion which is a pure gift of God, a free, gratuitous communication by God of his own justice, his own sanctity, and on the other, the religion which is no more than a contract: human justice, good works accomplished by man's natural powers and rewarded by the good-will of God. The first concept is the only true one. It is the economy of grace, of the gratuitous gift of sanctity; God's own justice becomes ours in Jesus Christ 'who from God is made unto us wisdom, and justice, and sanctification and redemption' (1 Cor. 1. 30). Regenerated and receiving a new birth in Christ, we are made immediately holy by the very holiness of Christ. All that is now needed, and it is sufficient, is that this new creation within us should subdue to itself the whole of our human nature and that the life 'I live now in the flesh, I live in the faith of the Son of God' (Gal. 2. 20). The second concept is now outmoded. It is the economy of the Law, of the self-interested contract, of man's complacency as he faces God. There is now no longer any human complacency, nor any possibility of human pride, since everything is a gratuitous gift and the greatest glory of God consists in men receiving as much as possible from the goodness of God.

The Church has 'lived' this doctrine from the beginning and all Christian holiness is its admirable expression. But though the doctrine is there from the start in Paul's epistles, yet as a 'lived' doctrine, only after many centuries and alas! many heresies, was it finally stated in the Church as a doctrine in speculative form, in rationally formulated theses.

And, it must be recognized, this was due to the partial incompleteness of Paul's doctrinal statements. I shall enumerate a few of these very rapidly. In Paul's own lifetime, the vehemence of his attacks on the Law gave rise to accusations against him of amoralism, of fundamental opposition to every form of Law ('some affirm that we say, let us do evil, that there may come good'—Rom. 3. 8) and St James in his epistle (2. 14 seq.) judged it necessary to put the matter in its right perspective. What efforts have been necessary in face of Pelagianism, Semi-pelagianism, Lutheranism, Baianism, Jansenism, until the concepts of 'supernatural' works (and St Paul never used this adjective) and 'natural' works were finally evolved and so full justice could be done to Paul's teaching. Paul always held fast to two statements which he set side by side although at first sight they appear contradictory: 'Man is saved by faith and not by works' and 'Every man will be judged according to his works'. He does not seem to have sought explicitly a resolution of this apparent contradiction. Yet the profound logic of his thought has led Catholic exegesis to our classic solution of supernatural works originating in our faith, works of Christ in us, gifts of Christ extending even to our own assent to them ('O God, who crownest thy gifts').

The justice and holiness of Christ which become ours, are they 'imputed' or 'communicated, shared'? Catholic exegetes and theologians very rightly show that Paul's *total* thought always presupposes an inner transformation in man, who has become a new creature and henceforth lives by the Spirit and is worthy to be called 'holy', in and through Christ. But as opposed to these two solutions, an exegesis that is too slavishly bound to the Jewish concept of justification as it was before Christ, together with too narrow an interpretation of such isolated texts from St Paul as Rom. 4. 3-5, 7-8, etc. (under the influence of the personal crisis in the soul of Martin Luther), have led millions of men to the Lutheran concept of the *fides fiducialis* and of imputed justice, man remaining intrinsically sinful, etc., and so have torn them away from Catholic unity.

Another striking feature in Paul's writing is the contrast between the different manner in which these two aspects of our redemption are taught. On the one hand what we now call our elevation to the supernatural order, and on the other, our deliverance from sin, from the domination of the flesh and of death. The first aspect is continually recognized implicitly and everywhere presupposed in the concepts of 'new birth', participation in 'God's justice', 'life in and according to the Spirit'. We may say that it is the main concept and yet it is nowhere explicitly formulated and developed as the second aspect is constantly throughout the Epistles.

Nevertheless the true thought of St Paul, the thought which was implicit in the logic of his whole doctrine, emerged clearly in the Church's interpretation. The remarkable thing about this evolution in the interpretation of St Paul through the centuries, is the perfect balance, and, after perhaps several hesitations of some leaders, the serene certainty of the Church's final decisions. How often we are reminded of von Hügel's image: 'The Roman Catholic Church is like a great ship seeking her direction; first she rolls this way, then she rolls that, till she finds her equilibrium; and then how wise are her judgements! How magnificent her decisions!' (*Letters to a Niece*, London, 1928, Introduction, p. xxxvi).

(3) *Faith, man's answer to God's gift*

St Paul before his conversion. As a Jew, Paul had learned to honour the supreme homage of man to God represented by the faith of the Old Testament: man was no longer to rely upon human powers but on God alone. 'In Isaias, to believe is to accept God's guidance, to obey, and for the rest, to leave all in the hands of God without counting upon one's own strength or ability.' The finest formulation of the faith of the Old Testament is perhaps that of the Psalm (19. 8): 'Some trust in chariots, and some in horses: but we will call upon the name of the Lord our God.' This element of confidence present in Jewish faith is certainly not absent from the Pauline faith.

St Paul after his conversion. Faith in God now becomes more precisely defined. God has given himself in Christ and faith in God now takes the concrete form of faith in Christ.

The element of trust, of abandonment of all human support, of all human title in order to lean upon God alone and upon Christ is maintained as an essential theme in Paul's doctrine. We are familiar with the famous Chapter 4 of Romans, containing the formula Luther was to make his own: 'But to him that . . . believeth in him that justifieth the ungodly, his faith is reputed to justice . . .' (Rom. 4. 5). The formula is accurate, but it only expresses one aspect of Paul's thought and will only be completed and more sharply defined elsewhere, by the logic of his whole doctrine. The formula tells us that the Christian does not trust in his own power, his own wisdom, his own natural justice. Henceforth, only one single power, one single wisdom, one single justice count for him, and they come gratuitously from on high as a pure gift from God, as a share in the very justice of God through Jesus Christ. And yet certain expressions of this doctrine remain partially obscure, incomplete. Luther gave a very unfortunate interpretation to this 'unfinished' doctrine. For us Catholics—and the logic of Paul's thought most certainly requires this conclusion—this justice is not juridically 'imputed' to man, it is communicated to him and becomes his own. Christ is given to us, he is in us. The slightest shade of meaning in Paul's thought misunderstood and you have heresy.

To this element of trust, of total abandonment, two others are added and incorporated. They are classic, well-known elements of faith according to St Paul: firstly, the share of the intellect submitting entirely to Christ's truth (*assensus intellectualis*). It is clear that for Paul the Christian must believe intellectually that Jesus is Lord, that he redeemed us by his death on the cross, that he rose again and that his resurrection is the source and guarantee of our own, that he is seated at the right hand of the Father, that he will come again to judge the living and the dead, and so forth. Secondly, there is the share of the will, offering all its devotion to Jesus Christ, renouncing itself and living only by him: 'for me to live is Christ'; wishing that all its human life should henceforth proceed from him ('in that I now live in the flesh, I live in the faith of the Son of God'), that henceforth it should be a life controlled and inspired by faith (Christians are οἱ ἐκ πίστεως). We all know how rich in meaning is this concept of faith according to St Paul.

This enquiry could be continued at length and it would be seen with increasing clarity how personal Paul's thought is, 'lived' rather than speculative, and closely dependent on his vigorous individual personality. His statements can only be perfectly understood in the light of his thought as a whole, and his thought cannot be separated from his character and his soul.

CONCLUSIONS

FOUR CONCLUSIONS, quite naturally, emerge from all the facts so far noted. They are not new and have already been partly dealt with in the course of this book. But if they are assembled at this point, they may perhaps throw light on one another and so bring out more clearly that splendid but difficult process which is called the dogmatic proof from holy Scripture.

The first three conclusions concern the part played by the exegete or the theologian, the fourth represents an attempt to understand the part played by the Church.

First conclusion. Since, in the economy of the Incarnation under which we live, divine truth is transmitted by men, by the inspired writers, we shall arrive at the words God has spoken by understanding man and man's thought. One sometimes used to hear it said: 'I accept Scripture as "the Word of God", I do not need to know anything about the human author, what, humanly speaking, may have determined his judgment, what may have been its temporal or local context; all that is of very little importance; it is God who is speaking.' To talk like this is to lose sight of the infinite complexity of scriptural assertion. I shall not grasp it as it really is, as God wills it, as the expression of divine truth, except in the mind and heart of the inspired writer, which I must understand as perfectly as possible, in human fashion, by using historical methods and, in the divine order, by adhering as he did to the faith and to the Church.

Second conclusion. Since scriptural assertion is, by hypothesis, so complex, what is the norm which will best enable the exegete to understand, as it should be understood, the assertions of the inspired writer? There will be general agreement, I think, in accepting the following norm, commonplace enough yet often forgotten: all other things being equal, the value of a scriptural assertion is measured by the importance it has in the author's theological synthesis. It is in the synthesis of the whole thought of St Paul that I shall discover the probative force and the degree of assertion in each of the passages in his writings that are a basis of our faith. This is no doubt an ideal difficult to attain, since it presupposes that we extend our inquiry into the deepest regions of the inspired writer's religious consciousness, to the profound central point of his thought and of his interior life from which the rest quite naturally emerges. But this is an ideal we must adopt straight away as the goal towards which we strive, if we are always to remain on the line that leads to the true interpretation.

Nevertheless, there must at once be added the truth which will emerge from the two conclusions which follow: this theological synthesis of the inspired author's is built up by us also in the light of the present state of Catholic Dogma, in the light, too, of the whole Catholic synthesis. True, I shall study Paul as an historian must, with all the critical requirements of historical method, and I shall never play false with my integrity as an historian in order to achieve a conformism between history and faith. But I shall study Paul as a believer should, well knowing that he is only a witness accredited by God, an authorized guarantor of a divine truth which transcends him as it does all of us, a truth which is greater than he, a truth which God alone will be able to tell us in the beatific vision and which men, even the greatest among them, can only stammer out. And this leads directly to the third conclusion.

Third conclusion. Divine revelation infinitely transcends its inspired interpreters. These, chosen by God from among the Jews of the first century of our era, struggle, on the basis of concepts and words inherited from the Old Testament, to express as well as they can, with God's help, the revelation which they have received. Scriptural assertions therefore are seen, as has been said often enough, as a kind of starting-point, a source, an essential, immutable foundation, to which we must always be returning, rather than a final outcome, a final term. For this term is the full growth of Christ in the Church. We should misunderstand the meaning of the New Testament if we lost sight of this aspect of effort towards the perfect expression of a new truth, this aspect of a movement of thought towards a summit which will be more clearly formulated in days to come. It is this movement of thought, this effort to reach the total synthesis which the Church must continue from century to century, and every Christian in the Church must play his part. True, the whole of revelation was given to us in the apostolic age, but, in terms of the divine system of pedagogy, it was to become explicit, to be formulated and synthesized in and by the Church.

Fourth conclusion. Above and beyond all the work of the exegetes and the theologians, there is then the work of the Church. The Church, through the thought and life of her pastors, her doctors, her saints, her theologians and all her faithful, lives and thinks holy Scripture as a whole. In her, Paul's thought joins that of Peter and John and together they are subordinated to the thought of Christ. These thoughts react on one another, cast light on one another. And this is as it should be since the same infallible Spirit inspired them all.

But there is more than this; the Church, so closely linked to the past through her Scripture and her tradition, is perpetually obliged to re-think her dogma, to re-read her holy Scripture in terms of the present. And it is at this point that a principle of primary importance makes its appearance; it must be thoroughly understood and all exaggeration and minimization avoided. New Testament Scripture is never for the Church the book of a past that has gone and which can only be reached through history. It remains a book of the present, which grows clearer in the light of the doctrinal acquisitions of the passing centuries. In a certain sense—which must be properly understood however, if we are to avoid mere caprice—in a certain sense the New Testament has as it were a twofold context: first the context of the period of its publication, then the context (homogeneous of course with that of its origins) of each era until the end of time. Through this higher charism of the Church, dogmatic conclusions are drawn from the inspired texts, from Pauline texts, conclusions which the exegete could not prove were explicitly in the consciousness of the inspired author, in the consciousness of Paul. But what he does indeed see, with the Church, is that these conclusions are necessary today so that, in the Catholic synthesis as it now is, the authentic Pauline message may be given its full place, its full significance. Thus the Pauline message is interpreted not only by the natural context of his own time, but by the context of thought today.[1]

It is this great work which the Church accomplishes from century to century, in spite of, and often because of, the errors and heresies of men. When, in the twentieth century, we look at the whole of this work done by the Church, a profound feeling of admiration is bound increasingly to be awakened in us, at the superior understanding the Church has and has always had of the inspired writers, and at the way she has guided the Christian spirit throughout the centuries in fidelity to their message. I am not speaking now of the individual exegesis of given passages by the Fathers of the Church, which would provide a fairly large crop of errors in interpretation and of obvious misconceptions. I am speaking of the quiet, sure and infallible bearing of the Church at the time when texts that have been wrongly understood by heretics threatened to lead her towards disaster. The clash of discussion between orthodox and heretical exegetes may have been rather disappointing at the time. But over and above the theologians and the exegetes who all do their best with the limited resources of each epoch, there has stood the Church which by the power of the Holy Spirit sees clearly and gives sure guidance.

Increasingly the experience of Christian life confirms this dogmatic truth: the holy Scriptures which are to accompany mankind throughout the centuries, are not self-sufficient. They can only be understood as God wishes them to be, if they are constantly interpreted by the Church.

[1]Therefore any idea of an extrinsic and arbitrary intervention by the Church must be clearly set aside. We are dealing with a deeper interpretation which is closely linked to the synthesis of inspired thought, of Pauline thought, and rethinks it in terms of the whole progress of Christian doctrine. Between historical, rigorously scientific exegesis and ecclesiastical exegesis, any cleavage would be illegitimate and contrary to the very principles of the Church. The Church needs the work of its exegetes, historians and philologists. She cannot do without their exertions or ignore their conclusions. She perfects their work, but in completing it, she fully accepts it. The Church which came into existence at a given moment in history as a result of the Incarnation, must always maintain, and has never failed to maintain a close link with history.

INDEXES

GENERAL INDEX

INDEX OF NAMES AND PLACES